Australia's American Constitution and the Dismissal

Australia's American Constitution and the Dismissal

How English Legal Science Marred the Founders' Vision

David Long

LEXINGTON BOOKS
Lanham • Boulder • New York • London

Published by Lexington Books
An imprint of The Rowman & Littlefield Publishing Group, Inc.
4501 Forbes Boulevard, Suite 200, Lanham, Maryland 20706
www.rowman.com

6 Tinworth Street, London SE11 5AL, United Kingdom

British Library Cataloguing in Publication Information Available

Library of Congress Cataloging-in-Publication Data

Names: Long, David (Lawyer), author.
Title: Australia's American Constitution and the dismissal : how English legal science marred the founders' vision / David Long.
Description: Lanham : Lexington Books, [2021] | Basd on author's thesis (doctoral - Griffith University, 2019) issued under title: The Australian constitution, originalism and the dismissal. | Includes bibliographical references and index. | Summary: "David Long traces the cause of the 1975 Australian constitutional crisis to the influence of English legal positivism which was adopted by the High Court in 1920 when it abolished the federal scheme and therewith the sovereign States going against the fundamental premise of a constitution"— Provided by publisher.
Identifiers: LCCN 2021002325 (print) | LCCN 2021002326 (ebook) | ISBN 9781793641953 (cloth) | ISBN 9781793641960 (epub)
Subjects: LCSH: Constitutional history—Australia—20th century. | Constitutional law—Australia—American influences.
Classification: LCC KU1760 .L66 2021 (print) | LCC KU1760 (ebook) | DDC 342.94—dc23
LC record available at https://lccn.loc.gov/2021002325
LC ebook record available at https://lccn.loc.gov/2021002326

To my wife, Jennifer,
and my children
Simon, Jessica, and Caitlin.

Contents

Preface

The idea of natural right as a principle of political wisdom has almost lost its original meaning in the world of modern politics, even though it still exists veiled behind every attempted justification of political or legal activities. While the United States is the only regime expressly dedicated to the principles of natural right, the legacy of that nation's founding found fertile soil on the Australian continent in the 1890s when the people of the separate Australian colonies sought the independence of their union from a more benign Britain than the one defeated by America in 1776. The Constitution of the United States that was ratified in 1788 was framed by that country's founding fathers in recognition of the principles that all men are created equal with certain unalienable rights and that governments derive their just powers from the consent of the governed. Those principles had already found eloquent expression in the American Declaration of Independence.

While the natural rights expressed in the Declaration are the endowment of all men, their embodiment in a federal republic was only possible by the prudent deliberations of American statesmen at a convention in Philadelphia concerning the best way for them to live together. Natural right in that sense is the reservation of specific individual liberties from law, and hence from the duties of political life, yet they ultimately depended for their force on the deliberations in Philadelphia concerning the best way for the American people to live together. Aristotle explains in the first book of his *Politics* that the polis is formed as a result of a natural impulse in man;[1] man is naturally at home in society. In his discussion of natural right in the *Nicomachean Ethics*, however, he says first that, "Of the political sort of justice, one kind is natural and another is conventional."[2] He then shows with a single example how something that exists according to nature can be improved upon by human action.[3] This is Aristotle's account of natural right and it bears out his description of the prudent man: "We say that people are in fact prudent about something whenever they calculate well with a view to some serious end in matters of which there is no art."[4] As it became apparent that the diversity of the American states and weak Articles of Federation could not provide for the safety and happiness of the American people, it was only naturally right that a remedy would be sought in the convention.

Guided by their own sense of what was just and those principles expressed in the Declaration of Independence, the deliberations of the men who convened in Philadelphia with James Madison to frame a more perfect union for the American people represent a more complete expression of what is naturally right later augmented by the prudent inclusion of the Bill of Rights.

It is also important to note that while the personal liberties expressed in the Bill of Rights are often viewed as the American people's natural rights, they were not originally part of the Constitution. In *The Federalist*, Alexander Hamilton argued against the idea of a Bill of Rights, since "the proposed Constitution, if adopted, will be the Bill of Rights of the Union."[5] In other words, the participation of an equal people in a republican regime where government powers were limited provided sufficient protection of citizens' liberties.

It was the lesson of the United States that moved the Australian colonial representatives to gather in convention in 1891 in their first attempt to frame a federal constitution and unite the peoples of the self-governing Australian colonies. While the idea of a Bill of Rights played no part in the deliberations of that convention, the Victorian colonial delegate Alfred Deakin called for a federal constitution that could not be altered without the consent of the people of the various states, thus pointing to the democratic principle that underpinned those deliberations. His expression of that principle was unique in the British Commonwealth, where constitutional change was effected either by an agreed change in the conventions of responsible government, by legislation, or by both. When the current Australian Constitution was framed at a Convention of elected delegates in 1897–1898, the people's consent to any change in the Constitution found itself more forcefully expressed in section 128, where alterations could only be made with the consent of the people given both federally and in a majority of states. By fixing the meaning of the Constitution to the deliberations of the Convention and with its ratification by the Australian people, the founders of the Australian Constitution, like their American counterparts, sought what was naturally right or just for the Australian people while acting prudently to secure the results of their deliberations from alterations that less prudent men might be tempted to impose casually. The implications of that section are of profound jurisprudential importance, as this book reveals.

Legal positivism is opposed to and denies the truth that a constitutional plan or scheme can be naturally right or just for a people of particular social habits. As a science, legal positivism must deny the power of unaided human reason to discover the foundational principles of just government and that arrangement of its powers which will secure the happiness of a people. For that reason, the scientific theory of legal positivism, the validity of which rests on mere assertion, implicitly denies the truth that a democratic nation must hold in the justice of its founding and the nation's future if it is to long survive. Confidence in the justice of its cause is the bond holding a nation together that renders force unnecessary.

The Australian and American Founders reckoned for the future without knowing how an abstract English theory—legal positivism—could so affect the human mind as to mar the vision of what was thought to be by nature right and just.

NOTES

1. Aristotle, *Politics*, 1253a30.
2. Aristotle, *Nicomachean Ethics*, 1134b18.
3. Aristotle, *Nicomachean Ethics*, 1134b35.
4. Aristotle, *Nicomachean Ethics*, 1140a30.
5. Alexander Hamilton, *The Federalist Papers, No. 84*, ed. Clinton Rossiter (New York: New American Library, 1961), p. 515.

Acknowledgments

This book would not have been possible without the assistance and support of many people. The articulation of the numerous issues researched and traversed has been a labor of love lasting many years. It has made many demands upon my wife Jennifer who has been a constant source of encouragement and support throughout.

I must also thank my academic colleagues at Griffith University, Dr. Kieran Tranter and Dr. Chris Butler, without whom this work would not have reached the form it has taken. Each of them in his own way brought to it an inquiring objectivity and the demand that I explain more precisely what I was arguing and why.

It would be impious not to acknowledge my first teacher and friend, the late Dr. Richard Staveley who, at that moment in a young man's life when he can choose, introduced me to the study of political philosophy—especially that of Plato and Aristotle and the lovers of wisdom who followed—an introduction that both changed my life and permitted me to see and understand the problems with which this book is really concerned. Without Dr. Staveley's early instruction, I would not have been intellectually or morally capable of the theoretical insights to which my research alerted me. However, any deficiencies in this book are wholly those of the student.

David Long

Chapter 1

The Issues

INTRODUCTION

The Australian polity has faced two serious political crises since its federation in 1901, the first in 1920 and the second in 1975. Those two events, one in relation to the Constitution's federal scheme, the other, the Constitution's responsible government, changed the intrinsic character of the Australian Constitution without the consent of the Australian people. Each crisis in its own way represented the influence of the English legal science that discarded common sense for a dogmatic methodology that fundamentally changed the way in which the Australian people had chosen prudently to live together. Those changes continue to this day. It is important to begin with a brief history of the political events of 1975, events to which this book leads. They will be examined in greater detail in the penultimate chapter. However, it is equally important that certain theoretical issues be addressed in advance. A more understanding of the contentious nature of those issues at this early juncture will make it possible for the reader through the course of this book to grasp their influence in the analysis and a better understanding of the constitutional questions associated with each crisis, why the crises arose, and how the constitutional questions must be answered.

THE DISMISSAL

On November 11, 1975, the Commonwealth of Australia was rent by a major political crisis when the Australian Governor-General, Sir John Kerr, dismissed the nation's prime minister, Edward Gough Whitlam, and appointed the leader of the opposition, Malcolm Fraser, as a caretaker prime minister in his place. The Governor-General's actions precipitated a wave of public dissent accompanied at times by some personal violence. Such were the passions that were set free from customary restraint by Kerr's actions. What excited the passions of Whitlam's supporters to such an extent was the fact that Whitlam and his government had the confidence of a majority of the members of the nation's House of Representatives and the confidence of the popularly elected chamber was the traditional criterion under the conventions of responsible government for the appointment of a prime minister. The Governor-General's action in dismissing a prime minister, who had the confidence of the House, was unprecedented in the Australian nation's short history and was viewed by Whitlam's supporters as the theft of their government's electoral victory in the previous year, and therefore as a breach of the conventions of responsible government. Those conventions, which had originated in the Westminster Parliament in London, had been observed in the self-governing British colonies on the Australian continent. They held that a prime minister would continue in office while they commanded the support of a majority of the popularly elected members of the relevant chamber. The supporters' opinion that the dismissal was the result of malfeasance was sustained by the fact that the Whitlam government had been forced to an early election in 1974 by an opposition-controlled Senate using the same tactics it would use in 1975.

The Australian Parliament in 1975 consisted of two Houses divided politically. Edward Gough Whitlam was commissioned as prime minister to form a government in December 1972 when he led the Australian Labor Party (ALP) to its first electoral victory in the House of Representatives over the Liberal and Country Party coalition (the Coalition) since 1946. However, the ALP did not win control of the Senate, which remained under the control of senators loyal to the Coalition. While the constitutional term for an Australian government is a maximum of three years,[1] Whitlam was forced to call a general election for the whole Parliament in April 1974 when the "Coalition and its allies-of-the-moment in the Senate voted to defer action on supply Bills."[2] This considered strategy of the Coalition took advantage of the situation of a government struggling to control an inflation rate that increased from historically low rates of approximately 2.5–3.5 percent per annum to 6 percent in 1972, 9 percent in 1974, and 15 percent in 1975, mostly under the effects of large increases in international crude oil prices,[3] while also attempting to implement the kinds of social programs it had been unable to carry out since 1949. The ALP was electorally successful in the House of Representatives in the 1974 election and Whitlam was again commissioned to form a government. The Coalition remained in opposition in the House under a new leader of the opposition, Malcolm Fraser. In the Senate, however, the Coalition and its allies were numerically equal to the ALP. When the ALP lost two senators during 1975 and the number of Coalition-supporting senators increased by two, the Coalition obtained control of the Senate.[4] Public opinion of the Whitlam government fell during 1975 when two ministers were forced to resign for misleading the Parliament.

The events of 1975 that concluded with the dismissal of Whitlam as prime minister can be stated briefly, but as will be seen, the Coalition parties' control of the Senate made a repeat of their 1974 strategy possible. In August 1975, the government's annual supply Bills to finance its budget were introduced into the House of Representatives. The Commonwealth Constitution requires governments to obtain appropriations for the ordinary annual services of government—that is, supply—on an annual basis. The two appropriation Bills, Nos 1 and 2, were passed by the House of Representatives on October 8, 1975. The two Bills were introduced into the Senate and given a first reading on October 14, 1975. When the second reading of Bill No. 2 was moved the same day, the Senate voted to defer consideration and resolved that the Bill would be passed if the prime minister were to call an election. The second reading of Bill No. 1 was moved on October 16, 1975, but consideration of that Bill was also deferred, with the Senate resolving not to consider the Bills until the government submitted itself to the judgment of the people. After being reintroduced to the House of Representatives on October 22 and read and passed a first, second, and third time, the Bills were reintroduced into the Senate and were again deferred subject to the said resolution. With temporary supply granted earlier by the Parliament expected to run out by the end of November, the two Bills were introduced into the Senate on three separate occasions, the last on November 5, 1975, and on each occasion consideration of the Bills was deferred by the opposition-controlled Senate, which passed a resolution making the passage of the supply Bills through the Senate conditional upon the government calling a general election and submitting itself to the judgment of the people.[5] The Senate's resolutions were in identical terms and stated that "this Bill be not further proceeded with until the Government agrees to submit itself to the judgment of the people, the Senate being of the opinion that the Prime Minister and his Government no longer have the trust and confidence of the Australian people."[6]

Despite the Senate's action and its resolution, Whitlam refused to call an election. On November 10, 1975, fearful that temporary supply would run out before the disagreement between the Houses was resolved, Governor-General Sir John Kerr[7] sought the advice[8] of the Chief Justice of the High Court,[9] Sir Garfield Barwick, asking whether the Governor-General could legally withdraw a prime minister's commission and commission a caretaker government, which could then obtain supply.[10] On the morning of November 11, Barwick tendered a brief advice of less than two pages in writing to the Governor-General, which concluded that, without supply, Prime Minister Whitlam must either resign or call an election: "If, being unable to secure supply, he refuses to take either course, Your Excellency has constitutional authority to withdraw his Commission as Prime Minister." Later that day, Kerr withdrew Whitlam's commission[11] and that of his government, and appointed the then leader of the opposition, Malcolm Fraser as a "caretaker" prime minister. After the appointment of Fraser, the Senate passed the supply Bills into law and Kerr[12] accepted Fraser's advice to dissolve both Houses of Parliament and call a general election. It was the first time in the life of the Commonwealth that a government with the confidence of the House of Representatives had been dismissed by the Governor-General. It was also the first time that a Senate had denied supply to such a government. In the election that followed the dismissal, Fraser received an overwhelming victory in both the House of Representatives and the Senate and was appointed prime minister by Kerr.

Under the Westminster conventions of responsible government, a government denied supply by the popularly elected House of Commons was obliged to either resign or call an election.[13] By the end of the nineteenth century, it was a commonly held opinion and one expressed during the Australian Constitutional Convention of 1897–1898 (the Convention) that the power of the House of Lords to either amend or reject supply had been abandoned to the House of Commons. Under the Commonwealth Constitution, however, the Senate's power to refuse supply was undeniable, given that, subject to express reservations, the Senate was said to have the same legislative power as the House of Representatives.[14] If the Senate's power to reject supply is accepted, the question that arises is whether the existence of the Senate's power to refuse supply changes the conventions of responsible government by imposing an obligation on a government to resign if supply is refused or even threatened by the Senate. This question remains moot even though both Kerr and Barwick argued that the government became responsible to both chambers, and therefore was obliged either to resign or call an election if the Senate chose to deny supply, whether through outright rejection or by deferral. As will be shown, the Founders did not support the view of either Kerr or Barwick. Even when viewed in light of the Senate's power, the conventions remained unchanged.

CONSENT OF THE GOVERNED

The influence of the American Constitution and the arguments of that founding in the *Federalist Papers* on the federal scheme of the Australian Constitution have been recognized by Australian legal scholars and the judiciary since federation in 1901. That recognition, however, has generally been limited to an acknowledgment that the Constitution is federal and its division of powers resembled that of the United States: federalism being one element of the Constitution's scheme. Indeed, the early Court described the *Federalist Papers* as a textbook.[15] What has never been recognized, however, has been the existence of links between the Commonwealth Constitution and the political science on which the US Constitution was based and to which it was dedicated. That knowledge is critical to the scheme of the US Constitution, for it shows that the text was a prudent construct built on principles grounded in the nature of man.[16] While the Australian Founders did not express those principles in the manner laid out in the American founding documents, the records of the 1897 Convention debates show clearly that the delegates were intent on incorporating them where that was possible. Thus, while there was no uniform or universal adult franchise in the colonies, the delegates took care to place no impediment in the Constitution to a future franchise that reflected the principle of male and female equality. At the commencement of the 1897 Constitutional Convention, the delegate Bernhard Wise thought the proposed Constitution would give effect to a "true democratic Federation."[17]

As democracy implies the equality of the citizens, the logical corollary of that equality, as Harry V. Jaffa explained,[18] is an obligation to obtain the consent of the governed before a Constitution becomes binding.[19] That principle was evident in the colonial governments' process for the selection of delegates to the Convention and the ratification of the draft Bill after completion and its adoption has been attributed to the forethought of Dr. John Quick. In contrast to the 1891 Convention,[20] the 1897 Convention, both in its organization and its purpose, was controlled by an Australasian *Federation Enabling Act* (FEA), enacted in similar terms by each participating self-governing colony that became an original state in 1901.[21] In the New South Wales version of the FEA, section 11 provided for the election of ten delegates by every person qualified and entitled to vote in New South Wales. By section 32 of the FEA (NSW), after the conclusion of the Convention, the draft Bill for the Constitution was to be submitted to the electors of the colony for their acceptance or rejection. Similarly worded provisions were included in each of the other four colonial FEAs.[22] When the five colonial referenda of 1898 in respect of the draft Constitutions were inconclusive, further FEAs were enacted in 1899 by six colonies—the sixth being Queensland—and the colonial people approved a slightly amended Constitution.[23] This emphatic demand for the colonial people's consent to authorize their delegates, to ratify the draft Constitution, and to approve any amendment was unique among British colonial constitutions. Section 128 of the ratified Constitution requires any proposed alteration to obtain the people's consent both federally and in a majority of states and is further evidence of the Australian Founders' respect for the principle of the consent of the governed. Only the US Constitution at that time had embraced the principle of consent of the governed, a principle traceable to the Declaration of Independence.[24] Its source, ultimately, can be found in the political science of the English philosopher John Locke's *Second Treatise of Government*,[25] where he argued from the contract nature of society that the people enjoyed a right to alter or abolish a government that breached the people's trust.[26] This, too, was expressed in the *Declaration of Independence*. As Jaffa pointed out, however, the right of revolution abates when regular elections are able to change government peacefully. In 1776, the American people were forced to exercise this right against the government of King George III. By the time the Australian colonies desired their independence, the United Kingdom had voluntarily reformed its constitution and transferred power from the monarch and House of Lords to a democratically represented House of Commons that offered no opposition to the Australian colonists.

By seeking the consent of the peoples of the colonies for the federal Constitution, the Australian Founders had adopted the same principle as that relied on for the US Constitution and explained by James Madison in *Federalist 49*:

> As the people are the only legitimate fountain of power, and it is from them that the constitutional charter, under which the several branches of government hold their power, is derived, it seems strictly consonant to the republican theory, to recur to the same original authority, not only whenever it may be necessary to enlarge, diminish, or new-model the powers of the government.[27]

While *Federalist 49* was not referred to during the Australian Constitutional Convention, its influence is clear in the statement by the South Australian delegate, Sir John Downer, in relation to the proposed provision for amending the Constitution:

> no fundamental change should be made in this Constitution without Parliament and the people saying it shall be done, or without Parliament passing an amending law, and the people do not say the amendment shall not be made. It is a power of veto, inserted for greater safety, and to prevent Parliament altering a Constitution which concerns the people, without the consent of the people, whom Parliament may not represent in its action in the matter.[28]

In this way, the Australian people approved their new Constitution while reserving their right in section 128 to prevent any future changes without the twofold consent of the majority. After ratification of the Constitution had occurred, the draft was enacted by the Westminster Parliament giving what was believed to be legal efficacy to the people's expression. This action, however, was based on the mistaken belief that the Westminster Parliament was the sovereign authority over the Australian colonies. As will be shown, the incorporation of the principle of the consent of the governed in section 128 of the Constitution asserts a different principle, one inconsistent with Westminster sovereignty over the Commonwealth of Australia. Other than some few amendments since federation, the only Constitution consented to has been the one ratified by the people in 1899. It was argued that the sovereignty of the Westminster Parliament rendered the Commonwealth Constitution subject to the Imperial legal authority of the Privy Council, despite the fact that the Constitution placed decisions regarding the interpretation of the Constitution in the original jurisdiction of the High Court.[29] This argument will also be shown to be false.

The effect of the incorporation of the "consent of the governed" as the founding principle of both the Constitution and its alteration was to assert both the people's sovereignty over the document and the meaning of the Constitution to be that to which the people gave their consent. The effect[30] of incorporating this principle into the Constitution is to place a construing court seeking the meaning of the Constitution under a moral obligation to discover the meaning consented to. That meaning has been described as the original intention and more recently the original public meaning.[31] Only a brief consideration of these terms is necessary to show the congruence of these two phrases. The difficulty that arises with "original public meaning" is that, without greater detail, it is perfectly consistent with an interpretation that is the literal meaning of the text as understood by the ratifiers[32]—literalism by another name—unless consideration is given to the constitutional scheme or theory advanced by the Founders in justification for the text.

Australian jurisprudence since 1920 has assumed that, as the Constitution is a piece of Imperial legislation, its interpretation will be a literal interpretation of the meaning of the text in 1901, the time of federation. When the original public meaning is approached from the point of view of the consent of the governed, it poses the important question: to what meaning did the people give their consent? The answer to that question lies in a consideration of both the source and nature of the opinions of the consenting people at the time of ratification.

A brief reflection is sufficient to show that neither the Australian nor American people undertook an in-depth, linguistic, grammatical, and syntactical examination of the words, sentences, and clauses of their draft Constitution, including all their connotations and denotations. The Australian Convention debates, on the other hand, were extensively reported by colonial newspapers and journals, and these were written to inform the public of the arguments for and against aspects of the scheme being considered by the Convention. Further, as occurred in the United States, prior to the colonial referenda leading members of the Convention addressed public meetings throughout Australia in order to educate the people about the political scheme and its relationship to the Constitution. If the public debates prior to 1897 are included, the education of the public to understand the scheme of the Constitution won the public's support and the Constitution's ratification. This fact is equally true of the American people and their Constitution. It is implicitly proved by the origin of *The Federalist Papers* as an explanation of the political scheme or theory of the Republic. Supreme Court Chief Justice John Marshall alluded to the political dimension of the American Constitution in *Gibbons v Ogden*,[33] where he cautions against an interpretation that relies on a theory *not* found in the Constitution. That theory or scheme of the Constitution is the bridge between the text and the way of life under the scheme of the Constitution. That scheme is the substance of the political arrangement captured in outline in the form of the Constitution. When the question is asked, "To what did the Australian and American people consent?", the only logical answer is *the scheme as represented by the text*. Their knowledge of the relevant scheme, however, was obtained from their respective Founders—the meaning the delegates originally intended. The American people sourced their knowledge from the speeches and essays of their founding fathers, which included *The Federalist Papers*, contemporaneous notes of the 1787 Philadelphia Convention, and the Declaration of Independence.[34] The Australian people's opinions about their Constitution's scheme, the original public meaning of the text, are found in the Founders' opinions recorded in the 1897–1898 Convention debates.[35]

In both the United States and the Australia, since the ratifying public's original public meaning was derived from their respective Founders' explanation of the political scheme that the text supported, an equivalence between the original public meaning and the Founders' originally intended meaning can reasonably be inferred.

Arguments for and against original intention (of various meanings) as the object of constitutional construction have been evident in both jurisdictions for a considerable time, although its prominence in US jurisprudence appears to have arisen as a reaction by Justice Antonin Scalia to progressive decisions of the Supreme Court in relation to the Bill of Rights. It is worth reminding ourselves that, in the early nineteenth century, Chief Justice John Marshall sought to interpret the Constitution consistently with the founding fathers' original theory of the Constitution—he was, after all, one of them. The same can be said of the early judgments of the Australian High Court.

ORIGINAL INTENT IN AUSTRALIA

The debate in Australia about the efficacy of an interpretative jurisprudence that seeks the meaning of the Constitution as originally intended by the

Founders has been neither as vigorous or as extensive as that in the United States. As the leaders of the Australian debate have been Greg Craven, Jeffrey Goldsworthy, and Haig Patapan, their contributions to the scholarship on original intention will be reviewed. In the second part of this section, a similar task will be undertaken in relation to the leading opinions on the topic of original intent in the United States. The US debate is much broader than it is in Australia, not only because of the existence of a constitutional Bill of Rights, but also because it involves a school of thought that is far more critical of the influence of legal positivism.

The Australian debate about what the Founders intended was triggered largely by the 1988 High Court decision in *Cole v Whitfield*,[36] when the court turned to the Constitutional Conventions of the 1890s to discover how the Founders had understood specific words in section 92 of the Constitution. That jurisprudential step appeared to be unprecedented given the High Court's rejection of that source thirteen years earlier.[37] The first High Court had, during argument in 1904, refused the parties leave to consult the Convention debates in the case of *Sydney Municipal Council v Commonwealth*,[38] although the reported argument[39] suggests that only O'Connor J was absolutely opposed. In his 1991 analysis of the effect of *Cole v Whitfield*, where it was said that the High Court had substituted the Founders' motive for the text, Peter Connolly asked, "What was so wrong about the first High Court view"[40] of the federal limits on Commonwealth powers? His rhetorical question, "One asks oneself where all this leaves the *Engineers' case*?",[41] which implies its inconsistency with the Convention debates, will be addressed in chapter 4.

What Connolly refers to as the "object" of the Founders,[42] I have, throughout this essay, variously referred to as the Founders' "original intention" or "original intent," the Constitution's "originally intended meaning," or the "Founders" intentions and understandings. In their respective contexts, these descriptions all allude to the same idea: that of the meaning or theory of the Constitution, its federal scheme and responsible government, which were ratified by the people at colonial referenda and which can be attributed to the Founders. While the Convention's debates are now often consulted by the High Court, the court has not adopted the Founders' federal theory of the Constitution, a theory that follows the federal scheme of the US Constitution as described by the American jurist Joseph Story.[43] The main reason for this failure has been the Court's adoption of the legal positivist interpretative jurisprudence of literalism in 1920 after the majority's reasons in the *Engineers' case*.[44]

If the most obvious evidence of the influence of legal positivism in the interpretations of a Constitution is a jurist's resort to a literal construction which is usually announced as an intention to discover the plain or natural meaning of the text, the jurist is not prevented by his science from considering the text in light of other considerations. The natural meaning of the words can be interpreted in the light of the Constitution's overall structure and a section can be further illuminated by a semantic analysis of its connotations and denotations. This process allows a class of meanings to be identified from which the jurist can, with a value judgment, choose a relevant meaning. What legal positivism does not permit is the ascertainment of the political scheme that the Founders intended by the Constitution's text, from any source other than the text, including statements by the framers. The relaxation of that rule in the 1988 case of *Cole v Whitfield*[45] permitted recourse to the Constitutional Convention debates only "for the purpose of identifying the contemporary meaning of language used, the subject to which that language was directed and the nature and objectives of the movement towards federation,"[46] but not the political scheme of the text; the Court preserving its positivist credentials by when it refused to consider "the scope and effect . . . which the founding fathers *subjectively* intended the section to have,"[47] that is, the Founders' intended purpose.

In his essay,[48] Greg Craven adopts a series of hypothetical reservations regarding an originalist interpretative methodology, which seem to preclude him from identifying a single theory of originalism. As a result, he omits to relate the essential features of the theory of the Constitution,[49] particularly the federal frame that is supported by the text. He asserts that originalism is difficult to define satisfactorily, describing the kernel of the theory as "a mystical incantation 'fidelity to the framers'"[50] and, in its purer forms, as the sacred and supreme duty of the judiciary "to ascertain the intentions of those who wrote that document, and to give effect faithfully to those intentions."[51] He renames this pure form as overriding originalism, "the notion that the wishes of the Founders are paramount that lies at the heart of original intent."[52] Craven does not descend to particularize either their intentions or wishes; rather, he adopts a similar analytic plan to some US scholars, who suggest different hypothetical meanings for the Constitution depending on who is consulted but without showing why they might not actually all coincide in a single meaning. Craven suggests that when a judge is satisfied "that the words in question do not truly reflect the intentions of the Framers, then that judge will be duty-bound to give effect to the intention over the words."[53] This assertion is actually a denial of original intent and an apology for progressivism, a course he urges expressly on the Court when it identifies "necessary constitutional reform."[54] He identifies the two strands of High Court jurisprudence—literalism, which since the *Engineers' case* is "the mode" of interpretation;[55] and "progressivism"[56]—and correctly concludes that neither could be reconciled easily with original intent jurisprudence.[57]

One of the most active contributors to the debate on original intent in Australia is Jeffrey Goldsworthy, who has drawn on many of the terms used in this essay in a single scholarly article.[58] By locating the Constitution's "original meanings in 1900,"[59] it is unclear whether he is seeking the Founders' meaning or the meaning of the Constitution as an Imperial Act.[60] He declares, as a principle, that the meaning of a statute, unless amended, is its "original intended meaning,"[61] but that it cannot be rigidly interpreted and applied in accordance with the Founders' intentions without reference to contemporary values. He terms this moderate originalism, which he defines as original intended meaning moderated "by five ways":[62] judicial construction, stare decisis, elastic constitutional terms, irrelevance of Founders' application intentions, and purposive interpretation over literalism.[63] As he cites no limit to any of these five factors, his moderate originalism will actually become progressivism. He says that law-makers have two intentions: their "enactment" intentions and their "application" intentions.[64] His search for an original "meaning" led him to identify three different meanings: the "sentence"[65] or literal meaning; an "utterance" meaning, "determined by contextual as well as textual factors"[66] explaining the author's meaning and known to the audience; and the "speaker's intended meaning."[67] The meaning of a legal text, "such as the Constitution, is its utterance meaning rather than its speaker's meaning."[68] When Goldsworthy asks about the original meanings of constitutional provisions in 1900, "the extent to which those original meanings are determined by the intentions of the people responsible for creating it,"[69] one begins to see the source of his confusion. He shares a textualist approach in common with the US jurist Antonin Scalia or even Mitchell Berman, where the text is subject to social change. Goldsworthy downgrades the significance of section 128 of the Constitution when he says "moderate originalism is consistent with constitutional law changing without any formal constitutional amendment"[70] as a result of his "five ways." He therefore denies the need for any greater interpretative flexibility, since "alterations of substance should first be approved by the people."[71] His solution appears as a moral imperative: "Section 128 *should not* be evaded by lawyers and judges disguising substantive constitutional change as interpretation."[72]

In *Politics of Interpretation*,[73] Haig Patapan implicitly identifies the interpretative methodology of Griffith CJ in *Baxter's case*[74] as originalism that looked to American precedents. "[It] took into account the political and legal context of the founding relying on the historical facts and circumstances to give meaning to the text."[75] Patapan says that implicit in this methodology "was a political vision of a co-sovereign federalism that was largely consistent with the views of the framers of the Constitution,"[76] that is, the framers' original intended meaning. After pointing out that the power of altering the Constitution rests with the people in section 128, he suggests that "the

Founders' intentions, and the intentions of the electors who have amended the Constitution, should have a paramount role in the interpretation of the Constitution."[77] He interprets the court's current acceptance of an original meaning as a development of the High Court's method of interpretation, in which "sovereignty resides in or derives from the people and therefore the Constitution is founded upon popular sovereignty"[78] and concludes that the change from the legal sovereignty of the Imperial Parliament to that of the people is radical.[79] He implicitly follows Marshall CJ, one of the founding fathers of the United States, by identifying the link between the constitution's authority and the will of the people as "an expression of Lockean liberal constitutionalism."[80]

Summary of Australian Original Intent

The essays on originalism by Craven and Goldsworthy explore a number of different aspects of the topic, as each seeks to arrive at an explanation consistent with its overall views of constitutional interpretation. As a result, each reveals a preference for a theory of originalism that leads to progressivism. Patapan's analysis of originalism, on the other hand, is an attempt to discover the theory of the Constitution from more than an examination of the text. In that regard, he has paid significant attention to what I refer to throughout this book as the federal "scheme" as part of the theory of the Constitution.

ORIGINAL INTENT IN THE UNITED STATES

When retired Australian High Court Chief Justice Anthony Mason expressed his thoughts on constitutional interpretation, he spoke of US Supreme Court Justice Antonin Scalia's emphatic support of originalism and explained that "the United States debate centres on guarantees of individual rights, whereas our problems relate to the interpretation of powers and are therefore different."[81] It is true that rights in the US Constitution are usually expressed in a way that is a limit on legislative powers in the Constitution, but it has been progressive judges who have turned their interpretative powers on particular rights, giving them a meaning that is broader than human nature from which they are derived in order to narrow the ambit of specific powers and broaden the scope of private action. In his *Commentaries on the Constitution of the United States*, Justice Joseph Story, who sat with Marshall on the Supreme Court, provides two rules of construction: "I. The first and fundamental rule in the interpretation of all instruments is, to construe them according to the sense of the terms, and the intention of the parties."[82] And

> II. In construing the Constitution of the United States, we are, in the first instance, to consider, what are its nature and objects, its scope and design, as apparent from the structure of the instrument, viewed as a whole, and also viewed in its component parts.[83]

Having explicated each of the two rules, Story turns to the judgment of Marshall CJ in *McCulloch v Maryland*,[84] where Marshall identifies that sovereign powers were reserved to the states that were "positively recognised by one of the articles in amendment of the constitution, which declares, that 'the powers not delegated to the United States by the constitution, nor prohibited by it to the states, are *reserved to the states* respectively, or to the people.'"[85]

In his recitation of the Tenth Amendment, Marshall identifies the sovereign powers of the separate sovereign federal and state entities. While Marshall advances the plain meaning rule of construction in *Gibbons v Ogden*,[86] he also acknowledges the existence of a particular theory in the Constitution, rejecting a construction advanced "in support of some theory not found in the Constitution."[87] Marshall's statement is the key to understanding the meaning of originalism for both the US and Australian Constitutions.

The threshold question confronting an American jurist, therefore, is whether the rights referred to in the Constitution have no rational meaning other than the ipse dixit of the positive law of the Constitution or whether they are inferences from facts identifiable as human nature. If the former, then the court's interpretation of the meaning and extent of a constitutional right is nothing more than the expression of the subjective preferences of particular judges; if the latter, however, then the rights are implications from observable facts of human nature and a court's interpretation of a right or indeed of offending legislation would need to properly reflect the purpose the right sought to secure, and to be guided by what was objectively known about that end by the authors of the Constitution and the source of the Founders' understanding of that right. Because the US Constitution articulates the natural rights expressed in the Declaration of Independence, a construction that ignores or is inconsistent with implications from those moral principles will misrepresent the Constitution.

Retired Chief Justice Mason did not sufficiently examine Scalia's originalism. He preferred to accept what is a token reference to an original meaning without further inquiry. As a result, he did not identify Scalia's legal positivism and the effect of that on the interpretation of limitations to legislative powers. The distorting effect of legal positivism on Scalia's argument became clear when Scalia sought to link his theory of democracy and majority rule to the Constitution. Having expressed the opinion that democratic theory is nothing more than majority rule, he concluded that if the people want something, the state ought not to deny it to them: "The whole theory of democracy . . . is that the majority rules; that is the whole theory of it. You protect minorities only because the majority determines, that there are certain minority positions that deserve protection."[88]

In other words, it is only the positive law approved by the majority that guarantees the minority any rights, which means only that what the majority gives, the majority can take from the minority, even while enjoying the benefit of that right. The majority cannot err. As there is no reason or principle to qualify the rightness of the majority's decision, a judge will find no constitutional objection to a majority who deny rights to others: who demand abortion on demand,[89] the enslavement of a race of people,[90] or the confiscation of the property of the wealthy.[91]

Thomas Jefferson, the author of the Declaration, asserted that for the will of the majority to prevail, it must be reasonable since the minority enjoy the same rights as those enjoyed by the majority. The principal author of the Constitution, James Madison, concurred with Jefferson when he argued that the majority may only do what the whole society could do unanimously.

Whatever be the hypothesis of the origin of the *lex majoris partis*, it is evident that it operates as a plenary substitute of the will of the majority of the society for the will of the whole society, and that the sovereignty of the society as vested in and exercisable by the majority, may do anything that could rightfully be done by the unanimous concurrence of the members.[92]

Jaffa accepts Madison's unqualified hypothesis and the requirement of prior unanimous consent when he characterizes Madison's argument as, "Majority rule can arise only among those who have previously reached such an agreement to honor and respect each other's natural rights."[93] However, while unanimous consent to the origin of the society is the necessary condition for the operation of majority rule, participation in the process of ratification implies that the participating parties have unanimously agreed to be bound by the decision of the majority or to leave. Those who remain, remain bound. Madison alludes to this when he qualifies the "hypothesis of the origin of the *lex majoris partis*."

Judge Robert Bork is reputed to have been nominated to the Supreme Court on the basis of the assumption that he was an originalist. This opinion was accurate if it was based on an article Bork wrote in 1968 where he describes how judicial review in the Constitution safeguards the rights of minorities: "We continue to believe there are some things no majority should be allowed to do to us, no matter how democratically it may decide to do them."[94] However, as Jaffa explains, his views regarding the natural rights theory of the Constitution were not dissimilar to those of Justice Scalia. Evidence of this Jaffa finds in the extract from Justice Iredell's opinion in the case of *Calder v Bull* cited by Bork as evidence of the uselessness of natural rights:

> The ideas of natural Justice are regulated by no fixed standard; the best and the purest men have differed upon the subject; and all that the court could properly say, in such an event, would be that the legislature (possessed of an equal right of opinion) had passed an act which, in the opinion of the judges, was inconsistent with the abstract principles of natural Justice.[95]

American scholarly literature on "original intent," like the Australian literature, has been distracted by attempts to identify the effects of different hypothetical connotations of that phrase without attempting to analyze their validity. In 2013, Keith Whittington provided a survey of the state of originalism, which he defines as the "discoverable public meaning of the Constitution at the time of its initial adoption."[96] While he states that originalism fixes the meaning of the text historically as a guide for the courts, he does not believe it, stating that "uncertainty and indeterminacy are inherent in the originalist approach to constitutional interpretation."[97] He does not attempt to understand the text in light of the principles of the scheme that the Constitution supports. In other words, in Whittington's understanding, one can be classified as an originalist provided one simply interprets or expands on the meanings, connotations, and denotations of the words of the Constitution as they were known at the time of the founding.

In his article "Originalism is Bunk,"[98] Mitchell Berman takes a similar approach to analyzing originalism to that of Greg Craven and Jeffrey Goldsworthy, albeit with greater dissection of detail. He begins by suggesting that originalists have "shifted their allegiance from original intent to original public meaning,"[99] which reflected the originalists' recognition that "it was by virtue of ratification that the Constitution became law"[100] and which pushed many "away from framers in favor of ratifiers."[101] This therefore corrects his original definition of originalism's core claim as "the theory that judges 'should be guided by' the Constitution's original meaning (or the framers' intent, or the like)."[102]

Berman states his purpose as evaluating "the truth of originalism as a thesis concerning how the US Constitution ought to be interpreted."[103] As part of that evaluation, though, he dissects originalist jurisprudence into different "dimensions," namely, the *target* of the interpretation (object), the *weight* that the target plays in the interpretative theory (strength), the *character* of the reasons supporting the strength of the target (status), and the particular *interpreter* who is obligated to follow originalist interpretation (subject).[104] Each of these dimensions is further distinguished according to other criteria: whether the object is the framers' intention, the ratifiers' understandings, or the original public meaning; the strength of the originalist target, whether strong, moderate, or weak; the status or character of the reasons, whether hard or soft; and whether the subject (the contemporary interpreter) is judicial, a public official, or a citizen.[105] He shows the distraction of this type of analysis when he admits that "we are still just scratching the surface of potential diversity."[106]

While Berman uses three discrimina that identify the source of meaning (the object), the framers' intentions, the ratifiers' understandings, or the original public meaning, he also argues that, as the result of ratification was that the Constitution became law, the originalists moved away from the Founders' original intentions to the ratifiers' understandings, as the latter were closer to their original public meaning.[107] He declares that "theorists who maintain that interpreters 'have no choice but to respect the original meaning of [the Constitution's] text' are hard originalists."[108] He rejects hard originalism, describing it as not merely false but also pernicious because of its tendency "to bolster the popular fable that constitutional adjudication can be practised in something close to an objective and mechanical fashion"[109] that, if taken literally, negates the whole purpose of any originalism. As the only alternative to an objective construction is a subjective one, Berman's criticism of "hard originalism" is subjective.

Berman's notion of originalism is actually textualism—a legal positivist construction of a text. This is clear when he relates approvingly that Justice Scalia "would temper originalism with some deference to social changes other than judicial precedent,"[110] legal positivism in league with progressivism. He cites Scalia's opinion in *Grutter v Bollinger*[111] that the Constitution proscribes government discrimination on the basis of race but ridicules Justice Thomas who, in the same case, had referred to Justice Harlan's famous declaration that "[our] Constitution is color-blind"[112] by invoking a literal construction to point out that the Constitution does not say this anywhere. "Not only does the constitutional text say no such thing . . . but the best evidence of the original intentions is that the framers did not intend to constitutionalize a principle of strict colorblindness."[113] To those who think originalism supplies the one, true interpretive method, Berman objects: "That such assertions are obnoxious would be more easily forgiven were they not, in addition, false."[114] Berman traces the interest in originalism to a speech by Justice Scalia in 1986,[115] which traversed some of the difficulties he detects in an originalist methodology, including the attribution of a collective intention to a report by a large number of people. In relation to a Congressional report, Scalia questioned whether "a majority of them even *read* the committee report."[116] While he characterized his originalism as "what was the most *plausible meaning* of the words of the Constitution to the society that adopted it,"[117] he thought the issue for "original intent" was not whether "intent" should govern, but "whether *original* intent should govern as opposed to some manner of interpretation that permits application of the provision to evolve over time."[118] Scalia commences his article "Originalism: The Lesser Evil"[119] by recounting the wide range of material that Chief Justice Taft consulted in *Myers v United States*[120] in order to determine "the text of the Constitution and its overall structure."[121] He thought this "a prime example of what, in current scholarly discourse, is known as the 'originalist' approach to constitutional interpretation."[122] However, Scalia rejects Taft's originalism. Taft's "reputation as one of the greatest Chief Justices rests not primarily upon his opinions but upon his organisational and administrative skills."[123] Of the *Myers* decision, Scalia says, "What attracts my attention about the *Myers* opinion is not its substance but its process"[124] and he repeats with approval the legal positivist opinion of Chief Justice Hughes, who overturned the *Myers* decision: "The Constitution is what the judges say it is."[125] A similar comment was made by Isaac Isaacs during the Australian Constitutional Convention.[126] Scalia prefers originalism because it provides consistency and predictability,[127] not because it is correct.[128] George Anastaplo, in a lengthy criticism, described Scalia's jurisprudence as legal positivism, which he shared with "the dominant scholarly opinion."[129]

Strict originalism, according to Paul Brest,[130] construes words and phrases very narrowly and precisely, with the aim of construction being "to ascertain and give effect to the intent of its framers and the people who adopted it."[131] Strict originalism has been rejected in the United States in favor of a form of moderate originalism, which Brest defines as follows: "The text of the Constitution is authoritative, but many of its provisions are treated as inherently open textured."[132] Brest's moderate originalism appears to be the inspiration for Jeffrey Goldsworthy's own moderate originalism.[133] Brest identifies Marshall CJ's insistence on the plain meaning rule as "a canon of interpretation paradigmatic of textualism."[134] Marshall had said that the rule required a consideration, if necessary, of both the spirit of the Constitution and its letter, the former being "collected *Chiefly* from its words."[135] Brest agrees with that implicit limit on the plain meaning rule when he relates that, in *McCulloch v Maryland*, Marshall decided against Maryland's tax on the National Bank exclusively on the basis of the federal structure—something that is not expressly stated in the Constitution's text.[136] Brest does not consider that either the text or originalism are authoritative, and proposes an alternative that he calls "adjudication."[137] He disposes of the Declaration of Independence, which rests political sovereignty on the consent of the governed as inadequate, since those currently present did not consent and those who did "are dead and gone."[138] This argument, however, is merely semantic. There is no practical way of obtaining the consent of people as they reach their majority other than by implication from their compliance with the Constitution which protects their right to reject or amend it without demanding their express consent first. Further, Brest is silent on the likelihood that American citizens, by virtue of a civic education that shows the superiority of republican government over other regimes, daily give informed consent by participating in the political life of the nation. In the absence of principle, Brest proposes that constitutional adjudication "should enforce those . . . values which are fundamental to our society."[139] Brest agrees that his objection is vague but asserts that two fundamental values are "the integrity of majoritarian processes and the rights of minorities"[140] and concludes that nonoriginalism, rather than strict or moderate originalism, will better achieve them. Brest has introduced two contradictory values into his analysis—majoritarianism and the rights of minorities—but is silent about the natural rights that could reconcile them.

Lewis Lehrman turns to *Ogden v Saunders*,[141] where Marshall states that he found the meaning of the Constitution in the writings of the wise and learned men who wrote the treatises on the laws of nature whose writings were known to the Founders.[142] Lehrman states that "Marshall plainly affirms that the meaning of the Constitution is to be found in its incorporation of the natural law into the positive law."[143] As this is the case, Lehrman concludes that a "judge cannot know in such a case what the positive law of the Constitution is unless he knows what the natural law is."[144] Lehrman relies on the judgments of Marshall CJ, in *Marbury v Madison*[145] and *Ogden v Saunders*[146] in order to show that the Chief Justice relied on documents other than the Constitution, rather than only the plain meanings of the words, in order to demonstrate the principles on which the Constitution rested.

Summary of United States Original Intent

The jurisprudence of Patapan and Lehrman has much in common. Their support for an original intent jurisprudence has permitted them to correctly identify the schemes of their respective Constitutions without the distorted image given to the text by legal positivism. A construction that seeks the Founders' original intention stands in direct opposition to a legal positivist construction methodology. Legal positivism first manifests in constitutional construction as a concern to interpret the text in isolation from the political scheme or any qualitative context that the text sustains. The distinction between facts and values which is the principal assumption of all positivist theory has been described as originating in a statement by the English philosopher, David Hume, to the effect that it is impossible to derive the Ought from the Is and that moral distinctions cannot be derived from reason.[147]

LEGAL POSITIVISM

Legal Text and Political Context

A methodology that has been common to the interpretation of both the Australian and US Constitutions for at least a century and that can be linked directly to the dismissal has been the English judicial theory of legal positivism. Since it is often represented as a science, and hence something theoretically superior to common sense, it is important that its claim to veracity be examined. Legal positivist constructions of the Commonwealth Constitution by Justices of the High Court of Australia were introduced initially by precedents from Privy Council decisions that asserted a rule of literal construction of laws, distinguishing the legal text of a Constitution from the political scheme or objects intended by the Founders. While these judgments prefaced their remarks as constituting a rule for the interpretation of Imperial laws,[148] the source of the distinction between the text and the political scheme is to be found in the legal positivist theory of the English legal scholar Albert Venn Dicey, who specifically excluded parliamentary speeches from an interpretation of Imperial legislation.[149]

Dicey's literalist rule for interpreting a Constitution is similar to the common law rule stated by Willes J in *Millar v Taylor*.[150] That rule, which suggests literal interpretations, excluded the parliamentary history of changes to a Bill from the interpretation of ordinary legislation, there being no written Constitutions at that time. However, while Dicey claimed that "the English Bench have *always* refused, in principle at least, to interpret an Act of Parliament otherwise than by reference to the words of the enactment,"[151] John Magyar explains that, after stating the common law rule, Willes J and the other three Justices on the panel ignored it and consulted the parliamentary records in relation to the effect of the legislation on the prior law.[152] Although *Millar v Taylor* was thereafter cited by scholars as the source of an exclusionary rule and hence, literalism, Magyar reports that the rule was not observed even in the nineteenth century; in 1887, Lord Fitzgerald in *Caird v Sime* gave the "first clear judicial statement indicating that [*Millar v Taylor*] stood for the exclusionary rule . . . [then] proceeded to make arguments based on Hansard,"[153] which defeats the purpose of literal constructions. Despite his practice of citing cases where they are authoritative for a legal proposition, Dicey does not cite *Millar v Taylor* in his textbook or any other authority for his exclusionary rule. He explains the rule in the section entitled *Parliamentary sovereignty and the Rule of Law* to distinguish it from the common law rule. Dicey's literalism, while of the same effect as the common law rule, is based on Austin's positivist premise of parliamentary sovereignty being expressed by legislation, not by expressions of subjective appreciation or approbation in parliamentary debates. *Millar v Taylor* was not cited as an authority for literal interpretations in any of the relevant Privy Council cases.

Dicey accepted John Austin's distinction of legal sovereignty from political sovereignty but disputed Austin's concept of the paramountcy of the will of the electorate:

> The judges know nothing about any will of the people except in so far as that will is expressed by an Act of Parliament, and would never suffer the validity of a statute to be questioned on the ground of its having been passed or being kept alive in opposition to the wishes of the electors.[154]

Expressed differently, judges have no regard for the electors' concerns for the injustice of a law. Dicey defined sovereignty under the British Constitution as being of two types: that of the Parliament, which he called legal; and that of the electorate, which he called political.[155] Having defined Parliament as consisting of the monarch and the two houses, Dicey concluded:

> The principle of Parliamentary sovereignty means neither more nor less than this, namely, that Parliament thus defined has, under the English constitution, the right to make or unmake any law whatever; and, further, that no person or body is recognised by the law of England as having a *right to override or set aside the legislation of Parliament.*[156]

He differentiated between the appearance of the English Constitution as a "mere collection of practices or customs"[157] and its legal form, which showed it "based on the law of the land."[158] According to Dicey, British courts are only moved by legislation that is the will of the Parliament and legally sovereign, but "will take no notice of the will of the electors," the political sovereign.[159] Dicey admitted that the distinction was drawn from John Austin's[160] positive definition of sovereignty:

> It should, however, be carefully noted that the term "sovereignty," as long as it is accurately employed in the sense in which Austin sometimes uses it, is a merely legal conception, and means simply the power of law-making unrestricted by any legal limit.[161]

John Austin defined his study of jurisprudence as a study of the aggregate of laws and rules established by political superiors.[162] Political superiors are those exercising supreme government; government becomes nothing more than an exercise of force: "But, taken with the meaning wherein I here understand it, the term superiority signifies *might*: the power of affecting others with evil or pain, and of *forcing* them, through fear of that evil, to fashion their conduct to one's wishes."[163] Austin reveals that his science of jurisprudence does not determine the moral or political quality of a law or distinguish between a tyranny, a democratic republic, or a constitutional monarchy. It purports to be a Newtonian science of the might or forces that move people to act or cease acting. He termed these the positive laws, and distinguished them from the question of whether a law is just or unjust:

> For (as I have already remarked) Justice is often synonymous with general utility, although it properly signifies conformity to a given law. . . . The existence of a law is one thing: its merits or demerits are another thing. Whether a law be, is one inquiry: whether it ought to be, or whether it agree with a given or assumed test, is another and a distinct inquiry.[164]

The judgment that how a law or an action "ought to be" should be left as a matter of "another and distinct enquiry" is a value judgment. As the subjective character of value judgments is a matter of individual subjective taste, they are not capable of any objective investigation or distinct inquiry. Neither David Hume nor Austin was aware of the effect of the fact/value distinction on value judgments that they continued to make, for they nowhere acknowledge that the characterization of human choices as feelings makes them subjective. However, if Justice is a feeling, then only the person feeling something can know it. It cannot be known objectively for no one else can feel your feelings. What Austin and his followers have overlooked is that, being based on an evaluation, every human choice—including juristic ones—is subjective. Once the positivist distinction between facts and values is accepted and only facts are capable of scientific proof, any determination by human reason is ultimately subjective. Every juristic decision, the appropriateness of a particular rule of construction, the characterization of a political scheme of a Constitution, its meaning or interpretation, the relevance of evidence, are, according to the theory of legal positivism,[165] value judgments and thus subjective.

Since every choice, every decision, involves an evaluation, all choice is subjective. This conclusion was recognized by the German sociologist Georg Simmel, who in 1892 published *Einleitung in die Moralwissenschaft* (*What is Called Normative Science*).[166] He explained that once you attribute objectivity to only scientific knowledge and subjectivity to evaluation, then anything that requires "evaluation" is reducible to a subjective feeling which is not objectively knowable: "Science itself does not establish or prove norms, but merely explains norms and their correlations. For science always raises only causal, not teleological questions."[167] By concluding that "value is nothing objective . . . but arises only in the subjective process of preferring."[168] Simmel had joined Nietzsche's conclusion that values are subjective to the view that science was objective. It was Nietzsche, about whom Simmel is reported to have written a book, who first identified the logical conclusion of the positivist distinction of scientific knowledge as objective and evaluations as subjective and hence, the subjectivity of all knowledge, when he said: "The learned judge correctly that people of all ages have believed they know what is good and evil, praise- and blameworthy. But it is a prejudice of the learned that we now know better than any other age."[169] If that comment is viewed in light of his earlier statement about reason: "But logical evaluations are not the deepest or most fundamental to which our audacious mistrust can descend: faith in reason, with which the validity of these judgments must stand or fall, is, as faith, a moral phenomenon,"[170] all human knowledge rests on a value judgment and hence is subjective.

The effect of the fact/value distinction in legal positivism is that the jurist's construction or interpretation of a Constitution, including a consideration of the best or the most just or most *appropriate* or *relevant* methodology or precedent, at any step where there are choices to be made, is therefore subjective.

Dicey's legal positivist theory relates principally to the British Parliament and the British Constitution. His definition of parliamentary sovereignty appears to be independent of a normative dimension: legislation would be a *validly* enacted British law if it deprived the electorate of its legal right to vote and hence of Dicey's political sovereign. As Dicey's definition of sovereignty is deduced from the British Constitution, it is not applicable to all Constitutions. The British Constitution consists of a combination of legislation and parliamentary conventions or practices.[171] The former can be changed by the Parliament and the latter can be ignored.[172] Dicey uses the word *sovereignty* in the sense defined by Austin and then adopts that definition as its *legal* sense. Dicey refers to the concept of the "political sovereign," which he defines as the citizen body with the constitutional means of regularly influencing the country.[173] Yet according to his theory, while they may influence the country, the courts will take no notice of this power.[174] He qualifies power as "political," but limits its meaning to the voting public—even though the political is far more numerous in Britain, but the House of Lords is unaffected by that sovereign.

Because it purports to be a positive science of law, Dicey's legal positivism concerns itself only with interpreting the legal text or legal aspect[175] of legislation, while ignoring the political context of that law. When Dicey speaks of the political sovereign as the will of the people or the wishes of the electors, however, he has already *assumed* that the legal sovereign, the Parliament, is democratic and therefore an important influence on the meaning of the laws. It is that complete political scheme that is excluded by Dicey's theory of construction, even while assuming it. A legal positivist construction or interpretation of a Constitution will consider the legal text isolated from the political scheme or theory, even though that political scheme conditions the law. That political context was what Marshall referred to as the theory of the Constitution. When Richard Staveley wrote on the topic of the Governor-General's reasons for dismissing the Whitlam government, he described judicial positivism as

> that mode of juridical construction whereby the jurist seeks to isolate himself from politically partisan interpretation of positive laws by confining himself to explicating the meaning of the language used in the laws without attempting to evaluate any reasonableness of intent or purpose in the law.[176]

Staveley's description of judicial positivism links its theoretical orientation to the underlying assumption common to all positivism: the subjectivity of value judgments, which are assumed to be incompatible with the scientific perspective. Dicey's jurisprudence of which legal positivism was an interpretative assumption rejected any objective consideration of the political scheme of the British Constitution that would determine its overriding character. Dicey's theory of sovereignty was premised on the fact that, in the British Constitution, the Westminster Parliament, having the power to enact legislation and a system of courts to enforce adherence, was by his definition sovereign. There was no supreme law, no legally objective standard in the form of a written Constitution, against which an exercise of the Westminster Parliament's legislative power could be held to be invalid or ultra vires by a court of competent jurisdiction.

That, however, is not the case with the Commonwealth Constitution. As has been demonstrated already, the Australian Founders rested the Constitution on the consent of the governed and any alteration of it must obtain their consent. As with the US Constitution, the Commonwealth Constitution is the supreme law of the land. Legislation enacted by the Commonwealth Parliament was intended to be tested against that supreme law by the High Court and to be invalidated or limited if in excess of its jurisdiction.[177] Unlike the United Kingdom, the Commonwealth Constitution vests the power of amendment of the Constitution—the Diceyan indicia of the *legal sovereign*—and hence the authority with which the Parliament must comply, in the hands of the people—or, in Dicey's words, in the hands of the *political sovereign*. As the legal sovereign of the Commonwealth Constitution is vested in the Australian people and the Imperial Parliament does not possess the power to amend the Constitution, the Imperial Parliament is not sovereign with respect to Australia. The corollary of the coincidence of the legal and political sovereign in the Australian people is that it is not theoretically possible to separate the legal from the political, as they are like the concave and convex surfaces of a sphere.

Anne Twomey argues that the Commonwealth remained subject to Imperial Parliamentary sovereignty after federation, despite section 128 of the Constitution,[178] by virtue of the principle of paramount force: "After federation, the Commonwealth and the States were still bound by British laws of paramount force."[179] She asserts that Australia became truly independent of Britain by the passage of the *Australia Acts*[180] in 1986, one by each of the Australian Parliament and the Imperial Parliament. Her argument is that Imperial legislation of paramount force abandoned its sovereignty; this implies that an Act of Imperial paramount force can so surrender its Imperial paramount force that it cannot thereafter assert its paramount force by amending its law. This argument, however, means only that the Imperial Parliament acquiesced in the face of Australian paramount force. If sovereignty is as Dicey described it, a more logical argument would acknowledge that an unequivocal act of sovereignty by a particular people, as exercised peacefully by the Australian people or belligerently by the United States in 1776,[181] in which the Imperial Parliament acquiesces, would sever Imperial sovereignty. It is trite law that the Imperial Parliament can always amend its own laws unless, politically, it has surrendered sovereignty. That is the case with the Australian and US Constitutions.

Twomey implicitly acknowledges the force of this argument and the importance of the political to understanding the legal when she says of the British abandonment after the 1930 Imperial Conference that both its power of disallowance of reserved Bills and its refusal of consent: "they were stripped away, simply by the change of convention concerning who advised the Sovereign in relation to the exercise of these powers."[182] Westminster had acquiesced in, or deferred to, the independence expressed by the Constitution, as shown by it never having sought to legislate an amendment.

Brendan Lim also relied on Dicey's explanation of British sovereignty when he said that Griffith's reference to the framing of the Constitution by a "Representative" Convention "said nothing, of course, about the legality of the Constitution."[183] Lim's argument implies that Dicey's view of British sovereignty is an exclusive definition that rejects a claim of sovereignty or binding law arising by compact. The example of the people of nine American states in 1787–1788 who, through ratification, agreed to make their Constitution the supreme law as an expression of their sovereignty comes immediately to mind. Lim's argument implies that the Constitution of the United States was not a valid law because it was never enacted by the Westminster Parliament. His argument is inconsistent, however, with the historical fact that was documented by Thomas Erskine May citing William Blackstone, that the source of the separate Houses of the British Parliament, and with it the British Constitution, arose from a compact otherwise called the Great Charter, or Magna Carta: "The main constitution of Parliament, as it now stands, says Blackstone, was marked out so long ago as the seventeenth year of King John, A.D. 1215, in the great charter granted by that prince."[184]

Blackstone describes the Magna Carta as "a mere interior *treaty* between the king and his natural born subjects,"[185] that is, an agreement or compact. William Gummow distinguishes his opinion from that of both Twomey and Lim by implicitly attributing sovereignty to the Australian people, reciting the Preamble and section 128 as indicia of that purpose, which were present from the beginning.[186]

Dicey's views of constitutional law[187] were cited thirteen times during the Convention.[188] On the other hand, the work of Professor James Bryce was far more influential in relation to the US Constitution and was cited more than fifty times.[189] While it is often acknowledged that Australia's Constitution initially drew its federal form from that of the United States, it is not generally recognized that the Australian delegates sourced the original intent of the American Founders from documents such as the *Federalist Papers*[190] and the *Commentaries on the Constitution of the United States*[191] by Justice Joseph Story, as well as the analysis in *The American Commonwealth*[192] by James Bryce.

The scheme of the Commonwealth Constitution—federalism on the one hand and the conventions of responsible government on the other—determined the way the Australian people agreed to live together. By examining that order of living together, this book will show how it was changed without their consent. The question concerning the right order by which the people of the several Australian colonies would live together was answered over three sessions at the Constitutional Convention, held at Adelaide, Sydney, and Melbourne, respectively, in 1897 and the first quarter of 1898. It resulted in a Constitution that combined a federal scheme with responsible government. At every relevant stage, the consent of the people was sought: first in the election of delegates from four of the five colonies that attended the Convention, then in the legal requirement of each colony that the draft Constitution be consented to by each of the peoples of the colonies at referenda.[193]

Conclusion—Legal Text

If legal positivism is only concerned with the text of a positive law, and the qualitative aspect of that positive law represents a certain political character that is dependent on that positive law, then a construction of that positive law without regard to that political consideration will change the political character of the law and hence, how the people will live together. Where the law is a Constitution embodying specific, political characteristics such as federalism or responsible government, a legal positivist construction—that is, a literal construction of the text—may purport to be made in isolation from those political characteristics, but will change the political scheme of the Constitution. This can occur deliberately through design, through ignorance of the political scheme or by accident. However, unless a judge has a care of the political scheme in mind when construing a constitutional provision, changes to that scheme are unavoidable. Ultimately, the question must be asked: Did the people consent to that change? The contrast between a construction that sought the Founders' original intention and a legal positivist construction is apparent in the decisions of the early court,[194] both before and after the appointment of Isaac Isaacs in 1906.

KELSEN'S NORMATIVE ORDER

Hans Kelsen's theory of legal positivism continued the changes made by Georg Simmel to Auguste Comte's positivism, building on the distinction between facts and values and Comte's subjectivity to develop a pure theory of normative law.[195] This brief critique will focus on the fundamental assumptions of his theory and the contradictions that his assumption of the validity of the fact/value distinction cause. In the Preface to his book on the pure theory of law, Kelsen claims that "one of the most difficult tasks of a general theory of law is that of determining the specific reality of its subject and of showing the difference which exists between legal and natural reality"[196] for individual behavior may or may not conform with the order, the existence of which is the reality in question: "The legal order determines what the conduct of men *ought* to be. It is a system of norms, a normative order."[197] Kelsen asserts that "the pure theory of law eliminates the dualism of law and Justice and dualism of objective and subjective law."[198] One could be excused for thinking that Kelsen would provide an objective analysis of just laws. However, if by "normative order" you imagine Hans Kelsen's theory of legal positivism as postulating the best legal order for human flourishing, you would be mistaken. Kelsen's "normative" is a word without value even though his use of the word "normative" is the basis for his claim to have eliminated a purported dualism between objective and subjective law. While his theory of legal positivism has confirmed jurists in both Australia and the United States in their belief in the fact/value distinction, it has had little appreciable effect on judicial decision-making that was not already possible under the theories of Austin and Dicey. Kelsen's theory has gained the most traction inside the academies as a law-centered philosophy where it has seeded newer theories of the same genre, a genre that calls law "normative" according to a definition.[199] Despite his claim to have eliminated the dualism, Kelsen accepts the positivist assumption that distinguishes scientifically proven facts from subjective values:

> As used in these investigations, the concept of law has no moral connotation whatsoever. . . . The problem of law, as a scientific problem, is the problem of

> social technique, not a problem of morals. The statement "A certain social order has the character of law, is a legal order" does not imply the moral judgment that this order is good or just.[200]

The argument behind the positivist assumption that excludes "moral judgment" from the science of law lies in the Enlightenment's elevation of mathematics and natural science over human reason's deliberative power for considering the best means for securing his natural ends, that is, natural right. Thomas Hobbes describes reason as mathematical, as nothing more than addition and subtraction: "where these have no place, there reason has nothing at all to do,"[201] a conclusion that seemed validated by Isaac Newton's physics. When Hobbes explains that those who dislike monarchy call it tyranny, his analysis foreshadows positivism's rejection of the need to make any moral judgment about the regime. It therefore anticipates a possible predictive science of human behavior. Kelsen says of a science of law that "a science has to describe its object as it actually is, not to prescribe how it should be or should not be from the point of view of some specific value judgments."[202] His assertion of the descriptive character of his study ignores the fact that, as it will not be mathematical, it will not be scientific and accurate like Newton's physics; rather, it will only be his own opinion of the law and, like any opinion, subject to rational, but not scientific, evaluation. Even at this early point of his argument, it is possible to see the disjuncture between Kelsen's opinion of what law is and the opinion of the citizen who sees the law as just or unjust. He asserts that a scientific description of law is a comprehensive statement of what law is because its Justice or injustice, its goodness or badness do not exist as facts. Kelsen's theory, however, is not scientific but merely his own opinion from which he personally has excluded a consideration of its Justice or injustice, that is, how law actually "is." In essence, he repeats Hobbes's argument that there is no distinction between tyranny and monarchy.[203] In 1941, Kelsen had said of natural law:

> But none of the numerous natural law theories has so far succeeded in defining the content of this just order in a way even approaching the exactness and objectivity with which natural science can determine the content of the physical laws of nature, or jurisprudence the content of any given positive legal order.[204]

Kelsen's dismissal of natural law due to its inexactness when compared with natural science is not evidence of the subjectivity of values, but his preferment of a jurisprudence that determines the "content of any given positive legal order" is evidence of his own worthless value judgment. It is therefore evident that his jurisprudence is based on a value judgment. Kelsen's comparison of natural law with natural science repeats the theoretical comparison of man with matter made by Hobbes, which found no difference between them. As a result, Kelsen looks for a theoretical science of morality when only a practical science is possible—one that is mostly true, where choices are dependent on varying circumstances in the context of natural right imperfectly understood, where the different conditions of happiness of different peoples are also evidence of better and worse understandings of what is by nature right.

Kelsen's self-contradiction is implicit in the passage from the 1925 German edition of *Das Algemeine Staatslehre*,[205] which he omits from the 1949 English translation, an omission first noted by Strauss in *Natural Right and History*.[206] The literally translated passage reads:

> [It] is completely absurd the contention that there was no law in despotism, but caprice of despots rule. . . . After all, even the despotic governed state represents some order of human behaviour. . . . This order is just the legal system. To deny her the character of the right is only a natural law naivety or overstatement. . . . What is interpreted as arbitrariness is only the legal possibility of the autocrat to take any decision in himself, to unconditionally determine the activity of the subordinate organs, and *to abolish or amend norms* once set with general or only special validity. Such a state is a legal state, even if it is considered disadvantageous. But he also has his good sides. The not so rare call for dictatorship in the modern constitutional state shows this quite clearly.[207]

Kelsen asserts that the law is a norm, a rule expressing the fact that somebody ought to act in a certain way.[208] Thus, the despotic state can abolish or amend laws (norms) at will to legalize any action ex post facto. Kelsen says of law:

> The rule of law says: If A is, B ought to be. The rule of law is a norm. The rule of law is a norm . . . the meaning of the connection between two elements established by the rule of law is the ought.[209]

His definition of the rule of law, therefore, anticipates a command that one ought to murder certain innocents. As this makes the law a norm, Kelsen's theory states that a person ought to so act. Given the brutal and barbaric actions of Hitler's Nazi regime during World War II, the deleted passage above, which expressly rejects natural right as an effective criterion of injustice and invokes the subjectivity of values, actually acquits the Nazi government of any injustice in the murder of five million people. As all values are subjective, criticism of Hitler's values—which are no better or worse than Roosevelt's or Churchill's—is also subjective.

The question that his definition of the rule of law immediately raises is: What does he mean by the "ought"? Kelsen's answer to this question is sophistic: he defines law by saying law is normative, because obedience to law is what one *ought* to do. He asserts this regardless of the character of the regime that enacts that law. According to Kelsen's theory in 1925, one *ought* to obey a law that demands murder of innocents. And that explains why he had to delete the above passage from the English translation in 1949. What one ought to do is neither moral nor immoral; it is normative according to his definition. He asserts that people ought to obey the law to avoid punishment for disobedience, but that is to misstate the nature of a normative or moral act, for it is not undertaken for its own sake. The motive to obedience is not deliberate choice and moral character but rather fear. Further, if law is normative on its face, to be obeyed because it ought to be obeyed whether through fear or some other reason, Kelsen is proposing a science of the "ought" not the "is." When Kelsen defines law as determining how men *ought* to be and refers to it as *normative*, he implies the existence of deliberate choice. As his *ought* consists of both the *ought to* and the *ought not*, deliberate choice determines which alternative in light of the any particular circumstances; in other words, obedience, his normative, depends on a value judgment, a subjective preference, according to his theory. It was Aristotle who explained that choice implies the existence of a standard: "all knowledge and every choice have some *good* as the object of their longing."[210] Kelsen avoids the necessity of a standard by relying on the command theory and defines two kinds of value, one objective and one subjective:

> The value predicates involved in judgments to the effect that certain behavior is lawful or unlawful will here be designated as "values of law," while those involved in judgments to the effect that a legal order is just or unjust will be called "values of Justice." Statements asserting values of law are objective, statements asserting values of Justice are subjective judgments of value.[211]

While he attributes objectivity to "values of law," his objective value, illegality or unlawfulness, is a statement of fact. What Kelsen does not seem to realize, however, is that he has defined the "value of law" with respect to a purpose or *telos*, which he claims is objective, for his *telos* of law is obedience. Obedience, his value judgment for the purpose of law by which he describes law as normative, is the particular end that the particular law seeks; the particular end is sought for what the legislator thinks is the good of society. Kelsen's choice of obedience as the purpose of law is a Kelsen value judgment. Therefore, his "value of law" is not objective but instead is his value judgment and thus his subjective preference. He unwittingly makes the same error when he attempts to use the analogy of food in order to explain the meaning of Justice:

> When we judge a legal order or a legal institution as just or unjust, we intend to say something more than when we call a dish of food good or bad, meaning to say that we find or do not find it pleasing to the palate. The statement that a legal institution, e.g. slavery or private property, is just or unjust does not mean that somebody has an interest in this institution or its opposite. Its significance is that the institution in question corresponds or does not correspond to a norm whose validity is presumed by the person making the statement. But this norm is not a norm of positive law. Nevertheless, a judgment of Justice claims to state an objective value.[212]

But don't we mean more about Justice than we do about food, as Kelsen asserts? Kelsen's explanation of the subjective nature of value judgments and judgments of Justice exemplifies his problem with subjectivity. He describes food as good or bad, meaning only that it is pleasing, which is a subjective feeling.[213] But on what basis does he distinguish food from nonfood? The purpose or *telos* of food, its natural purpose and hence its goodness, is its nutritious and life-sustaining quality, which it has regardless of its taste. In contrast, something is bad if it is poisonous even if it has a pleasing taste (e.g., the taste of almonds). Kelsen argues that food is only pleasing and good because of a norm. But poison, which can also be pleasing, must therefore be good by that same norm even though it is not life supporting. When Kelsen's example of food is applied to law, the defect in his argument is clear. The identification of something as food requires a judgment of its benefit in accordance with the natural purpose or *telos* of food, so that it can be distinguished from poison; the purpose of food being life supporting and that of poison its opposite. While *taste* is subjective, food's life-sustaining quality is objective and good when compared with poison, which is bad. The application of this metaphor to law clarifies what is absent from Kelsen's positivist argument. A good law, like good food—for example, the proscription against murder—is life supporting and hence good for society. Good laws therefore sustain a nation and the happiness of its people in accordance with the natural end or *telos* of man, the political animal. Bad law, on the other hand, is poisonous. The institutions of government are the work of man, but they aim at some good and the laws are not neutral as to that good.

Conclusion—Kelsen

A legal positivist construction methodology, by precluding any consideration of any theoretical aspect of a Constitution other than its text or form, will be blind to any alteration of its underlying theory or substance to something consistent with the new meaning of the text. Nor will it be concerned to inquire about the nature of the good that the new Constitution seeks. Kelsen was obliged to omit a passage when translating his book into English because by denying the existence of natural right, it implied there was no difference between a law promoting murder and one promoting peace. The passage Kelsen was omitting from his English translation suggested that there was no substance to criticisms of the Holocaust. Unfortunately, his analogy with food and taste suggested there was no difference between food and poison. By omitting that passage, Kelsen's theory collapsed under the inherent inconsistency of a distinction between facts and values.

Kelsen's confused arguments in support of his theory of normative law have not refuted the need for natural right, within the framework of which questions concerning a just or good order of human society can be determined. His description of law as normative, as the "ought," uses the word as a noun, the name of a something to be done under penalty. The defect in his argument is clearest when he is not able to define food in a way that precludes poison. In ordinary speech, "ought" is a verb that indicates the correctness of human deliberations directed toward how man should act in order to live well rather than basely. As such, it also applies to the result of deliberations about the form and content of a Constitution that represents the best or most just way of people living together. Legal positivism is inconsistent with any consideration of the meaning of a Constitution that purports to provide for such a way.

CHAPTER SUMMARIES

The arguments detailed above are incorporated, where relevant, into the arguments addressed in each of the subsequent chapters and, where necessary, enlarged further.

Chapter 2 provides the detail of the Founders' original meaning of the Constitution, the meaning that was later ratified by the people. It will examine the Constitutional Convention debates of 1897–1898 that drafted a Bill for the Commonwealth Constitution that combined a federal distribution of the powers, which assumed the separate sovereignties of the Commonwealth and the states with a form of responsible government after the Westminster parliamentary conventions. In meeting these requirements, the Convention was obliged by the colonial establishing legislation to draft a federal Bill embodying responsible government under the Crown. It will show that the federal element of the Constitution relied upon the distribution of powers in the US Constitution with the people represented proportionately in the House of Representatives and the states represented equally in the Senate. The chapter shows that the Victorian delegate, Isaac Isaacs opposed a US-derived federal scheme and sought support for a unitary Constitution similar to either the

Canadian or British Constitutions, in which the states would have few powers and little role in the government of the Commonwealth. Chapter 2 also examines the Convention debates to establish how the Founders originally intended the conventions of responsible government to operate and to identify whether any variations of those conventions were adopted.

Chapter 3 examines decisions of the early High Court to demonstrate that it gave effect to the original intention of the Founders at the Convention. It argues that there is an implicit principle in the Constitution that obliges the court to construe the document in order to reveal that original intention. The decisions of the early court that articulate the twin doctrines of mutual prohibition (or immunity of instrumentalities) and states' reserved powers are examined to show that the court construed the Constitution's text in light of the political scheme intended by the Founders. It argues that the judgments of the early court recognized both expressly and implicitly the separate sovereignties of the Commonwealth and the states, and shows that the twin doctrines of mutual prohibition and the states' reserved powers were necessary implications from the Constitution and were derived from the US Constitution. This chapter shows that the early court's construction included, inter alia, reference to materials recognized through both public notoriety[214] and common knowledge[215] to infer that the Constitution's federal character and its distribution of powers were based on the US Constitution and that it expressly rejected a unitary Constitution.[216] It shows that Isaac Isaacs, both as Counsel for the State of Victoria and after his appointment to the High Court in 1906, cited Privy Council decisions that advanced legal positivist authorities for a literal construction of the Constitution's text as mandatory.

Chapter 4 examines the majority judgment in the *Engineers' case* that was authored by Justice Isaacs[217] for the High Court. It will argue that he construed the Constitution in order to replace the Constitution's federal scheme with one that approximated the unitary form for which he had argued at the Constitutional Convention. To achieve this, he asserted the preeminent nature of the Commonwealth Constitution as a piece of Imperial legislation, insisting on a legal positivist construction of the text, the authority for which was Privy Council decisions that espoused Dicey's positivist distinction between the legal text and the political context for interpreting Imperial legislation. Isaacs rejected any consideration of implications from the text on the basis of his judicial fiat[218] in order to prevent the doctrines which arose from the political scheme explicated by the early court from being raised. In order to forestall any appeal to the source of those doctrines, he also rejected US Supreme Court decisions as authoritative for the Commonwealth Constitution.[219] The chapter shows that Isaacs's conclusion, which purported to abolish the states' reserve powers doctrine, was not the result of a coherent argument but rather of incoherent logic and a mere assertion. Chapter 4 also demonstrates that his rejection of the doctrine of immunities enunciated by the early court was based on an intentional misstatement of the facts in an analogous case of *D'Emden v Pedder*.[220] Based upon its analysis of the *Engineers' case*, this chapter shows that Isaacs's use of the legal positivist distinction between the legal text and the political scheme allowed him to replace the Constitution's federal scheme with a unitary scheme similar to the one he sought at the Convention.

Chapter 5 looks at Isaacs's legal positivist legacy in the decisions of Sir Owen Dixon (Justice from 1929 to 1952 and Chief Justice from 1952 to 1964) and Sir Garfield Barwick (Chief Justice from 1964 to 1981) to show how Isaacs's judgment in the *Engineers' case* became the authority for future High Court legal positivist jurisprudence. That jurisprudence relied principally on a literalist methodology that distinguished between the legal text of the Constitution and its political scheme. The chapter shows that Dixon's attempt to modify some aspects of Isaacs's judgment by reestablishing the authority of US Supreme Court decisions[221] was largely unsuccessful, given his own legal positivist methodology. While Barwick's judgments purported to follow Dixon's methodology, an examination of his judgments shows how he further entrenched Isaacs's literalism and the separation of the legal from the political scheme.

Chapter 6 examines the written arguments of Australian Governor-General Sir John Kerr and High Court Chief Justice Sir Garfield Barwick, and demonstrates that the Governor-General does not possess a power, either prerogative or constitutional (statutory), with which to withdraw the commission of a government that has the confidence of the House of Representatives. In respect of the arguments advanced by the Governor-General, the chapter shows that Kerr ignored the means and purposes by which the conventions of responsible government were incorporated by the Founders into the Constitution. It examines Kerr's assertion that his power was a personal discretion, a Royal prerogative with which to dismiss the government. It shows that he adopts a literal construction of the Constitution and relied on the supporting arguments of legal positivist jurists that have no relevance to the political scheme of the Commonwealth Constitution.

The chapter then examines the arguments that Sir Garfield Barwick advanced in his book *Sir John Did His Duty*,[222] which asserted that the Governor-General in 1975 held "constitutional authority" to withdraw a prime minister's commission, even one with the confidence of the House of Representatives. It shows that his argument refutes Kerr's claim to a prerogative power, characterizing it instead as statutory, that is, as a constitutional power[223] that can be exercised without antecedent ministerial advice. The chapter will argue that Barwick's literal construction of the Constitution is undertaken without regard to the historical practice of responsible government in Australia, as intended by the Founders. It will also show that his argument was inconsistent with the Constitution, the practice of responsible government at federation and the legal opinion by the Leader of the Constitutional Convention. The examination of their arguments will suggest that both Kerr and Barwick imported a condition precedent from outside of both the Constitution and Australian in relation to the exercise of the Governor-General's purported powers.

Chapter 7 concludes the book with a reflection on the effects of the two constitutional crises faced by Australia and a brief statement on judicial review. It examines the claim that the Governor-General's dismissal of the government in 1975 was in accordance with the right of the people to abolish or alter a government that fails to secure their health and happiness.

NOTES

1. Commonwealth of Australia Constitution, s. 28.

2. Bach, Stanley, *Platypus and Parliament: The Australian Senate in Theory and Practice* (Department of the Senate, Canberra, 2003) The Crisis of 1974–1975.

3. OPEC crude oil prices rose from US$1.82 a barrel in 1972 to US$10.43 in 1975.

4. Bach, Stanley, *Platypus and Parliament: The Australian Senate in Theory and Practice* (Department of the Senate, Canberra, 2003) The Crisis of 1974–1975.

5. Commonwealth of Australia, Parliamentary Debates, House of Representatives, 8 October 1975, pp. 1221–43.

6. Commonwealth of Australia, Parliamentary Debates, Senate Official Hansard, 16 October 1975, pp. 963–4. As a general principle, a government responsible to the democratic chamber will resign, either when it loses a vote of no confidence (Sir Garfield Barwick, *Sir John Did His Duty* (Griffin Press, 1983) pp. 41–2) in that chamber or if it is unable to secure the passing of its supply Bills. However, as the resignation of the government is a matter of convention, and according to Barwick conventions are not justiciable, they are not legally obligatory. Barwick's view will be tested later in the book.

7. Immediately prior to his appointment as Governor-General, John Kerr had been Chief Justice of the New South Wales Court of Appeal. Before his appointment as Chief Justice of the High Court, Sir Garfield Barwick had been the Attorney-General in the government of Prime Minister Robert Menzies and a leading and successful barrister in private practice.

8. The report that Sir John Kerr had sought the advice of Sir Anthony Mason, then a Justice of the High Court, was first published in Jenny Hocking, *Gough Whitlam: His Time* (Melbourne University Press, 2012). Sir Anthony released a statement, published in the *Canberra Times* on 27 August 2012, regarding his discussion with Sir John. Of significance for this book was his endorsement of Barwick's

advisory letter to the Governor-General: "I said that the Chief Justice had shown me the letter and I had replied, 'It's OK.'"

9. The High Court of Australia was created by Chapter III of the Commonwealth Constitution to have a similar jurisdiction to that of the US Supreme Court. It has an original jurisdiction and a final appellate jurisdiction for all matters, state and federal, subject to special leave. Section 74 invests the Court with the power of judicial review in relation to the limits inter se of the constitutional powers of the Commonwealth and the states. The development of the Court at the Constitutional Convention is not relevant to this book.

10. The history of the parliamentary dispute, the circumstances of Barwick's participation in it, and the terms of his advice were published in his short volume *Sir John Did His Duty* (Serendip Publications, 1983) (hereinafter, *Sir John's Duty*, when cited within the body of this book).

11. While Kerr's action technically was a withdrawal of the prime minister's commission, it is generally referred to as the dismissal.

12. As this book includes references to the writings of jurists who have spoken ex-curial at certain times and curial at others, the inclusion of an honorific to distinguish the one and the exclusion of the honorific to reflect the other caused sections of the work to lack that clarity of style which a reliance on the context alone could have provided. Accordingly, after an initial identification of the person by his or her honorific, I have usually (but not always) chosen to dispense with the inclusion of the honorific to which the writer was entitled and have relied on context to permit the reader to correctly identify the character of the source.

13. In the days before the rigidity of the political party system, a prime minister's resignation allowed another to attempt to secure the support of a majority of the House of Commons. If successful, the monarch would appoint him as the new prime minister.

14. Commonwealth of Australia Constitution, s 53.

15. *Sydney Municipal Council v Commonwealth* (1904) 1 CLR 208 at 213 per O'Connor J.

16. These are expressed in the Declaration of Independence.

17. Official Record of the Debates of the Australasian Federal Convention, Adelaide (1897) 144 (Bernhard Wise).

18. Harry V. Jaffa, *A New Birth of Freedom; Abraham Lincoln and the Coming of the Civil War* (Rowman & Littlefield, 2000) p. 112.

19. This principle, the consent of the governed, was first expressed by the English philosopher, John Locke when he said: "Men being, as has been said, by nature, all free, equal, and independent, no one can be put out of this estate, and subjected to the political power of another, without his own consent": John Locke, *Two Treatises of Civil Government* (Cambridge University Press, 1960) pp. 374 §.95.

20. See John Quick and Robert Garran, *The Annotated Constitution of the Australian Commonwealth* (Angus & Robertson, 1901) pp. 122–3.

21. Western Australia appointed its delegates from its Parliament. Queensland did not participate in the Convention but ratified the draft Bill in 1899 in order to become an original state.

22. FEA(VIC) ss. 11 & 33, respectively; FEA(SA) ss. 10 and 33, respectively; FEA(TAS) ss. 12 and 33, respectively. Pursuant to the FEA(WA) ss. 17 and 28, provided, respectively, for the Western Australian delegates to be elected by members of both Houses of that Parliament sitting and voting together and for the ratification of the draft Bill after it was approved by the Parliament.

23. The FEA (NSW) 1895, s 35 authorized a decision by 50,000 votes to affirm the draft Bill. The FEA (NSW) 1897 s 2 amended that number to 80,000. The Queensland Parliament enacted the *Australasian Federation Enabling Act (Qld) 1899*, which authorized the holding of a referendum.

24. Martin Diamond, W.M. Fisk, H. Garfinkel, *The Democratic Republic* (Rand McNally, 1966) p. 43. See also *McCulloch v Maryland* 4 Wheat 316; 17 US Rep 159 (1819) 404–5 per Marshall CJ: "The Government of the Union . . . is, emphatically and truly, a Government of the people. In form and in substance, it emanates from them. Its powers are granted by them, and are to be exercised directly on them, and for their benefit." See also *Marbury v Madison*, 5 U.S. (1 Cranch) 137 176 (1803).

25. John Locke, *Two Treatises of Civil Government* (Cambridge University Press, 1960) p. 374 §95.

26. While Locke initially argues from the premise of the compact nature of society for the protection of property to the right of revolution (p. 460 §222), he later argues that the right of revolution is analogous to the right of an individual to defend himself against violence to his person or property (p. 465 §228). The right of self-defense whether of an individual or of the people does not require the premise of an original state of nature for its justification, since it assumes for each case that the execution of the law is ineffective, or that the law is unjust. The right of self-defense, therefore, is consistent with natural right.

27. A. Hamilton, J. Madison and J. Jay, *The Federalist Papers*, ed. Clinton Rossiter (New American Library, 1961) pp. 313–34.

28. Official Record of the Debates of the Australasian Federal Convention, Melbourne (1898), 727 (Sir John Downer).

29. Commonwealth of Australia Constitution Chapter III, section 74.

30. It has been suggested by some that "consent of the governed" would not be a principle binding on later generations who have not consented. This argument overlooks one fundamental aspect of the Constitution: as an expression of the legal sovereignty of the Australian people, the Constitution is, therefore, the supreme law that they alone can change.

31. Mitchell Berman considered this a shift of allegiance rather than an incremental refinement of meaning: Mitchell N. Berman, "Originalism is Bunk" (2009) 84(1) *New York University Law Review* 1, 4.

32. This seems to be Mitchell Berman's meaning: Mitchell N. Berman, "Originalism is Bunk" (2009) 84(1) *New York University Law Review* 1, 6. Paul Brest, "The Misconceived Quest for the Original Understanding" (1980) 60 *Boston University Law Review* 204.

33. *Gibbons v. Ogden* 22 U.S. (9 Wheat.) 1, 188 (1824).

34. Harry V. Jaffa conducts a debate with Judge Robert Bork (a 1987 Supreme Court nominee) and Bork's supporters over the need to "recognise the principles of

the Declaration of Independence as the principles of the Constitution." Harry V. Jaffa, *Storm over the Constitution* (Lexington Books, 1999) p. 3.

35. The assumption that the Commonwealth Constitution was Imperial legislation led to the adoption of the interpretative rule that a construing court will not resort to the parliamentary debates in order to understand a law. The High Court of Australia adopted this rule, preventing access to the Constitutional Convention debates in aid of understanding sections of the Constitution.

36. *Cole v Whitfield* (1988) 165 CLR 360.

37. *Attorney-General (Cth); Ex rel McKinlay v Commonwealth* (1975) 135 CLR 1 at 17; but see Re Webster (1975) 132 CLR 270 at 279.

38. *Sydney Municipal Council v Commonwealth* (1904) 1 CLR 208.

39. Ibid., 213–4.

40. P.D. Connolly, "*Cole v Whitfield*—The Repeal of Section 92 of the Constitution" (1991) 16(2) *University of Queensland Law Journal* 290, 292. Connolly J. was a long-serving member of the Queensland Supreme Court.

41. Ibid.

42. Ibid.

43. Joseph Story, *Commentaries on the Constitution of the United States* (Hilliard Gray & Co, 1833). Story's *Commentaries* has been cited by the High Court in only three judgments since federation, all in the past decade: see *Momcilovic v R* (2011) 245 CLR 1 at 131; *Cunningham & Ors v Commonwealth of Australia & Anor* (2016) 259 CLR 536 at 579; *Jones & Anor v Treasury Wine Estates Limited* (2016) HCATrans 242. *The Federalist*, on the other hand, has been cited in High Court judgments forty times since federation, the first by Dixon J in *Victorian Stevedoring & General Contracting Company Pty Ltd v Dignan Informant* (1931) 46 CLR 73 at 90.

44. *Amalgamated Society of Engineers v Adelaide Steamship Co Ltd* (1920) 28 CLR 129. Griffith CJ had earlier implicitly dismissed that type of construction as being "Negatived by the Preamble to the Act itself": (*Baxter v Commissioners of Taxation (NSW)* (1907) 4 CLR 1087 at 1110).

45. *Cole v Whitfield* (1988) 166 CLR 360.

46. *Cole v Whitfield* (1988) 166 CLR 360 at 385.

47. *Cole v Whitfield* (1988) 166 CLR 360 at 385; emphasis added.

48. Greg Craven, "Original Intent and the Australian Constitution—Coming Soon to a Court Near You" (1990) 1 *Public Law Review* 166.

49. See Marshall CJ, who rejects a meaning "in support of some theory not to be found in the Constitution": *Gibbons v Ogden*, 22 U.S. 9 Wheat. 1, 188 (1824).

50. Greg Craven, "Original Intent and Australian Constitution—Coming Soon to a Court Near You" (1990) 1 *Public Law Review* 166, 167.

51. Ibid.

52. Ibid.

53. Ibid.

54. Ibid., 170; emphasis added. He does not explain why the exclusion of the monarch from the Constitution would be a reform or why a constitutional monarchy where sovereignty rests with the people would not be a republic.

55. Ibid., 173; emphasis in original.

56. Ibid., 174.

57. Ibid., 175.

58. Jeffrey Goldsworthy, "Interpreting the Constitution in Its Second Century" (2000) 24(3) *Melbourne University Law Review* 677 at 677, 678, 679, 680, 682, 683, 686, 688, 696.

59. Jeffrey Goldsworthy, "Originalism in Constitutional Interpretation" (1997) 25(1) *Federal Law Review* 1.

60. *Amalgamated Society of Engineers v Adelaide Steamship Co Ltd* (1920) 28 CLR 129 at 142.

61. Jeffrey Goldsworthy, "Originalism in Constitutional Interpretation" (1997) 25(1) *Federal Law Review* 1, 12.

62. Jeffrey Goldsworthy, "Interpreting the Constitution in Its Second Century" (2000) 24(3) *Melbourne University Law Review* 677, 678.

63. Jeffrey Goldsworthy, "Originalism in Constitutional Interpretation" (1997) 25(1) *Federal Law Review* 1, 50.

64. Ibid., 30.

65. Jeffrey Goldsworthy, "Constitutional Implications and Freedom of Political Speech: A Reply to Stephen Donaghue" (1997) 23(2) *Monash University Law Review* 362.

66. Ibid.

67. Ibid.

68. Ibid.

69. Jeffrey Goldsworthy, "Originalism In Constitutional Interpretation" (1997) 25(1) *Federal Law Review* 1.

70. Ibid., 50.

71. Ibid., 50.

72. Jeffrey Goldsworthy, "Interpreting the Constitution in Its Second Century" (2000) 24(3) *Melbourne University Law Review* 677, 684; emphasis added.

73. Haig Patapan, "Politics of Interpretation" (2000) 22(2) *Sydney Law Review* 247.

74. *Baxter v Commissioners of Taxation (NSW)* (1907) 4 CLR 1087 at 1093.

75. Haig Patapan, "Politics of Interpretation" (2000) 22(2) *Sydney Law Review* 247, 248.

76. Ibid.

77. Ibid., 247, 266.

78. Haig Patapan, "Politics of Interpretation" (2000) 22(2) *Sydney Law Review* 247, 270.

79. Ibid.

80. Ibid.

81. Sir Anthony Mason, "Constitutional Interpretation: Some Thoughts" (1998) 20(1) *Adelaide Law Review* 49.

82. Joseph Story, *Commentaries on the Constitution of the United States Vol. 1* (Hilliard Gray & Co, 1833) p. 383.

83. Ibid., 387.

84. *McCulloch v Maryland*, 17 U.S. 4 Wheat. 316 (1819). *McCulloch's case* raised two important questions: the right of the State of Maryland to impose a tax upon the Bank of the United States incorporated under federal law and the right to incorporate the Bank when no express power existed in the Constitution. Marshall held that the power to incorporate while not express was a means of carrying other powers into effect, a power implied by the "necessary and proper" clause in the Constitution (US Constitution, Article 1, Section 8). The equivalent section in the Australian Constitution is section 51(xxxix).

85. Joseph Story, *Commentaries on the Constitution of the United States Vol. 1* (Hilliard Gray & Co, 1833) p. 401; emphasis added. The applicability of the emphasized words to section 107 of the Commonwealth Constitution was denied by the majority of the High Court in the *Engineers' case*. It is that denial of that element of the form that is explicit in the Constitution, which indicates that the plain meaning rule must itself be recovered by a resort to the original intention of the Founders by a consideration of the 1897–1898 Constitutional Convention debates.

86. *Gibbons v Ogden* 22 U.S. 9 Wheat. 1 188 (1824).

87. Ibid.

88. Justice Antonin Scalia, *Rome Address*, Origins, CNS Documentary Service, Vol. 26, No. 6 (27 June 1996)

89. Justice Antonin Scalia in his Rome Address in 1996 was quite prepared to accede to this demand: "If the people, for example, want abortion the state should permit abortion."

90. Harry V. Jaffa, *Storm Over the Constitution* (Lexington Books, 1999) p. 115.

91. Aristotle, *Politics*, 1381a15–18.

92. Gaillard Hunt (ed), *The Papers of James Madison* (G.P. Putnam's Sons, 1910) p. 570.

93. Harry V. Jaffa, *Storm over the Constitution* (Lexington Books, 1999) p. 118.

94. Ibid., 128–9.

95. *Calder v Bull* 3 U.S. (1Dall) 386, 398–9.

96. Keith E. Whittington, "Originalism: A Critical Introduction" (2013) 82(2) *Fordham Law Review* 375, 377.

97. Ibid., 403.

98. Mitchell N. Berman, "Originalism is Bunk" (2009) 84(1) *New York University Law Review* 1.

99. Ibid. Lawrence Solum's textualism is apparent when he explores different methodologies for identifying the original intent from the text of the Constitution without regard to the scheme of the Constitution. He avoids qualitative (value) judgments as subjective (Lawrence B. Solum, "Original Methodology" (2017) 84(1) *University of Chicago Law Review* 269, 284), unaware that a choice of methodology is itself a value judgment that would render the result of the analysis subjective. Nor is he aware that the recognition of a value judgment is not a scientific truth, but must be, therefore, a value judgment.

100. Mitchell N. Berman, "Originalism is Bunk" (2009) 84(1) *New York University Law Review* 1, 9.

101. Ibid.

102. Ibid., 5.
103. Ibid., 9.
104. Ibid., 15.
105. Ibid., 15.
106. Ibid.
107. Ibid., 9.
108. Ibid., 6.
109. Ibid., 8.
110. Ibid., 35.
111. *Grutter v Bollinger*, 539 U.S. 306, 346–49 (2003).
112. Mitchell N. Berman, "Originalism is Bunk" (2009) 84(1) *New York University Law Review* 1, 92.
113. Ibid.
114. Ibid., 96.
115. Ibid., 9.
116. Antonin Scalia, "Address," in Edwin Meese (ed), *Original Meaning Jurisprudence: A Sourcebook* (U.S. Department of Justice, 1987) p. 102; emphasis added.
117. Ibid.; emphasis added.
118. Ibid., 103.
119. Antonin Scalia, "Originalism: The Lesser Evil" (1989) 57 *Cincinnati Law Review* 849.
120. *Myers v United States* 272 US 52 (1926).
121. Antonin Scalia, "Originalism: The Lesser Evil" (1989) 57 *Cincinnati Law Review* 849, 852.
122. Ibid., 851.
123. Ibid., 850.
124. Ibid., 851.
125. Ibid.
126. Official Record of the Debates of the Australasian Federal Convention, Melbourne (1898) 283 (Isaac Isaacs).
127. Antonin Scalia, "Originalism: The Lesser Evil" (1989) 57 *Cincinnati Law Review* 849, 855. Compare: "The attempt to deduce any consistent rule from them has not only failed, but has disclosed an increasing entanglement and uncertainty, and a conflict." *Amalgamated Society of Engineers v Adelaide Steamship Co Ltd* (1920) 28 CLR 129 at 142.
128. Antonin Scalia, "Originalism: The Lesser Evil" (1989) 57 *Cincinnati Law Review* 849, 855.
129. George Anastaplo, "In re Antonin Scalia" (1999) 28(1) *Perspectives on Political Science*, 22.
130. Paul Brest, "The Misconceived Quest for the Original Understanding" (1980) 60 *Boston University Law Review* 204, 204–5.
131. Ibid.
132. Ibid., 205.
133. Jeffrey Goldsworthy, "Originalism in Constitutional Interpretation" (1997) 25(1) *Federal Law Review* 1, 19.

134. Paul Brest, "The Misconceived Quest for the Original Understanding" (1980) 60 *Boston University Law Review* 204, 206.

135. Ibid.; emphasis added.

136. Ibid., 217.

137. Ibid., 224.

138. Ibid., 225. He invalidates his argument when he admits that they validate by participation or acquiescence, as with any legal proceedings.

139. Ibid., 227.

140. Ibid. The electoral college system of the US Constitution contradicts Brest's view that majoritarianism is a US value. It was intended to prevent a tyranny of the majority, by which "value" the natural rights of the minority could be imperiled.

141. *Ogden v Saunders*, 25 U.S. (12 Wheat.) 213, 353–54 (1827). Brest has therefore misunderstood Marshall's plain meaning rule.

142. Lewis E. Lehrman, "On Jaffa, Lincoln, Marshall and Original Intent," in H.V. Jaffa (ed), *Original Intent & The Framers of the Constitution* (Regnery, 1994) p. 7.

143. Ibid. See *Ogden v Saunders*, 25 U.S. (12 Wheat.) 213, 345 (1827). Further, it must be noted that Marshall's comment was directed at the Constitution in its totality, not just the Bill of Rights. His comment that "we must suppose that the framers" appears to have been the source of Griffith CJ's statement in *Baxter v Commissioners of Taxation (NSW)* (1907) 4 CLR 1087 at 1106: "The framers of a Constitution at the end of the nineteenth century may be supposed to have known."

144. Lewis E. Lehrman, "On Jaffa, Lincoln, Marshall and Original Intent," in H.V. Jaffa (ed), *Original Intent & The Framers of the Constitution* (Regnery, 1994) pp. 6–7.

145. Ibid.

146. *Ogden v Saunders*, 25 U.S. (12 Wheat.) 213, 213 (1827).

147. David Hume, *A Treatise of Human Nature Vol. 2* (JM Dent & Sons, 1966) pp. 177–8. It must be noted, however, that like his predecessor Thomas Hobbes, Hume had abandoned the idea that there is a natural end or *telos* of man, which would provide a natural standard against which to judge the morality of human actions.

148. *Vacher & Sons Ltd v London Society of Compositors* (1913) AC 107 at 119.

149. A.V. Dicey, *Introduction to the Study of the Law of the Constitution*, 3rd ed. (Macmillan, 1889) p. 332. The theory of legal positivism underwent many changes during the twentieth century in the works of jurists such as Hans Kelsen, H. L. A. Hart, and Joseph Raz, to name three. Their influence, while prominent in academe, however, is unrecognizable in Australian High Court decisions while the principal distinctions of Austin and Dicey are still evident. They will, therefore, constitute the single focus of this book. I include a short review of Kelsen's principal work for it shows his own realization of the unavoidable effect of defining values as subjective on his theory and ascribing "normative" to law.

150. *Millar v Taylor* (1769) 4 Burr 2303 at 2332 per Willes J.

151. A.V. Dicey, *Introduction to the Study of the Law of the Constitution*, 3rd ed. (Macmillan, 1889) p. 332; emphasis added.

152. John Magyar, "*Millar v Taylor* as a Precedent for Statutory Interpretation" (2018) 47(3) *Common Law World Review*, 217, 218; Willes J considered the passage

of the original bill through the Parliament including the Journals of the House of Commons; at 219, in the same case, Justice Yates held the "idea of the Legislature, is plainly discoverable from the debate." The Lord Chancellor also.

153. John Magyar, "*Millar v Taylor* as a Precedent for Statutory Interpretation" (2018) 47(3) *Common Law World Review* 217, 219–20.

154. A.V. Dicey, *Introduction to the Study of the Law of the Constitution*, 3rd ed. (Macmillan, 1889) p. 70.

155. Ibid., 67–9. Dicey is less convinced of its worth in his Introduction to the 8th edition, where he refers to it as a possible distinction: "The new convention, which all but compels a Ministry defeated at a general election to resign office, is, on the face of it, an acknowledgment that the electorate constitutes politically the true sovereign power." A.V. Dicey, *Introduction to the Study of the Law of the Constitution*, 8th ed. (Liberty Classics, 1915) p. lxvii. Dicey's conclusion that "the Commonwealth of Australia itself is, as regards the Crown and the Imperial Parliament, nothing but a large self-governing colony" (p. 393) is indicative of the distortion that his definition of sovereignty caused.

156. A.V. Dicey, *Introduction to the Study of the Law of the Constitution*, 3rd ed. (Macmillan, 1889) p. 38; emphasis added. This passage implicitly distinguishes sovereignty for the Constitution from Dicey's sovereignty.

157. Ibid., 393.

158. Ibid.

159. Ibid., 70.

160. As a Professor of Jurisprudence, Austin presented his lectures at the University of London. They were first published in 1832 as *The Province of Jurisprudence Determined*, representing a Benthamite positive science of jurisprudence. The term "positivism" as a methodology of the social sciences was the work of Auguste Comte, who coined the word "sociology" to describe his new science of "social physics," that is, of man in society: Auguste Comte, *The Positive Philosophy*, trans. Harriet Martineau (Calvin Blanchard, 1856) p. 258.

161. A.V. Dicey, *Introduction to the Study of the Law of the Constitution*, 3rd ed. (Macmillan, 1889) p. 69. This positivist definition of sovereignty assumes power rather than any notion of right as the criterion for authority and thus repeats Thomas Hobbes's assertion that the Leviathan, the state, is sovereign. It is to that extent inconsistent with the principle on which the US and Australian Constitutions were founded: that government derives *only* "its just powers from the consent of the governed."

162. John Austin, *The Province of Jurisprudence Determined* (John Murray, 1861) p. 2.

163. Ibid., 15; emphasis added.

164. Ibid., 233. The influence of the theory of utilitarianism, the greatest good for the greatest number, is also detectable in this statement.

165. Adrienne Stone, "Judicial Reasoning," in Cheryl Saunders and Adrienne Stone (eds), *The Oxford Handbook of The Australian Constitution* (Oxford University Press, 2018) p. 474: "Consistently with the *Engineers*" approach, the High Court has developed principles of "characterization" that favor broad interpretations of

Commonwealth power; that . . . focus on the legal and practical operation of the law rather than its purpose; and disregard the justice or wisdom of the law.'

166. Georg Simmel, *Einleitung in die Moralwissenschaft* (Verlag von Wilhelm Hertz, 1892).

167. Simmel is cited and translated in Leo Strauss, *Leo Strauss on Political Philosophy*, Catherine H. Zuckert ed. (University of Chicago Press, 2018) p. 55. The passage referred to occurs in Georg Simmel, *Einleitung in die Moralwissenschaft* (Verlag von Wilhelm Hertz, 1892) p. 321: "Was man normative Wissenschaft nennt, ist thatsächlich nur Wissenschaft von Normativen. Sie selbst normirt nichts, sondern sie erklärt nur Normen und ihre Zusammenhange, denn Wissenschaft fragt stets nur kausal, nicht teleologisch." The translation was confirmed by Marcel Noest, assistant director, Institute of Modern Languages, University of Queensland.

168. Leo Strauss, "Leo Strauss on Political Philosophy," in Catherine H. Zuckert (ed), *The Leo Strauss Transcript Series* (University of Chicago Press. Kindle Edition) p. 56. Strauss omits certain words from his quotation. The passage referred to occurs in *Einleitung in die Moralwissenschaft* (Verlag von Wilhelm Hertz, 1892) p. 232: "Sie vergessen dabei, dass Werth überhaupt nichts Objektives ist, dass weder Gold noch Silber, weder Nahrung noch Kleidung an und für sich Werth besitzen, sondern denselben erst im subjektiven Prozess ihrer Schätzung erhalten." The translation was confirmed by Dr. Marcel Noest, assistant director, Institute of Modern Languages, University of Queensland.

169. Friedrich Nietzsche, *Daybreak*, eds. Maudemarie Clark and Brian Leiter, trans. R.J. Hollingdale (Cambridge University Press, 1997) p. 9 §4.

170. Ibid., 4 §4.

171. A.V. Dicey, *Introduction to the Study of the Law of the Constitution*, 3rd ed. (Macmillan, 1889) p. 344. Dicey refers to these as "practices, which, though commonly observed, are not laws in any true sense of that word at all" and for that reason are not acts upon which the court will rule. This, however, is a circular argument, for he began with a definition of sovereignty that excluded such conventions rather than a definition of law that sought to reconcile legislation and conventions.

172. The abuse of a parliamentary convention can be seen in the contrast between William IV in 1832, who was prepared to accept the advice of his prime minister to create sufficient Peers to pass the Reform Act of that year, and the refusal of Edward VII in 1909 to accept the advice of his prime minister to create sufficient Peers to ensure the passage of supply through the House of Lords.

173. A.V. Dicey, *Introduction to the Study of the Law of the Constitution*, 3rd ed. (Macmillan, 1889) p. 353.

174. Ibid., 70. In other words, Dicey's theory is relative to his definition of sovereignty. One need only to consider his view of sovereignty as defined to see it that it is inconsistent, for example, with the Declaration of Independence of the peoples of the US colonies who, as British subjects, declared their independence from the United Kingdom and demonstrated their supreme sovereignty by the establishment of the Republic.

175. Ibid., 314. Isaac Isaacs uses this phrase in *Deakin v Webb* (1904) 1 CLR 585 at 597, submitting that "all the High Court can look at . . . is its legal aspect."

176. R.W. Staveley, "The Conventions of the Constitution: Kerr's Folly" (1976) 11(1) *Politics* 16.

177. See *Attorney-General (Cth) v Colonial Sugar Refining Company Limited* (1913) 17 CLR 644 at 651–2 per Viscount Haldane. Unfortunately, through a process of injudicial decisions, the High Court has all but abjured that jurisdiction.

178. Ann Twomey, "Independence," in Cheryl Saunders and Adrienne Stone (eds), *The Oxford Handbook of The Australian Constitution* (Oxford University Press, 2018) p. 105. A possible inference from Twomey's "paramount force" is that the Imperial Parliament might at any time have enacted an amendment. Twomey's argument is only hypothetical. Her example of the reservation of laws for Royal assent (Constitution, s 58) as an exercise of British sovereignty over domestic governance misrepresents the intention of the provision by construing it literally, rather than by reference to its originally intended meaning. A more complete discussion of the purpose of the reservation power (and a rebuttal of Twomey's construction) is given by Griffith CJ in *Baxter v Commissioners of Taxation (NSW)* (1907) 4 CLR 1087 at 1130–1.

179. Ann Twomey, "Independence," in Cheryl Saunders and Adrienne Stone (eds), *The Oxford Handbook of The Australian Constitution* (Oxford University Press, 2018) p. 105.

180. Ibid., 117.

181. American War of Independence, 1776.

182. Ann Twomey, "Independence," in Cheryl Saunders and Adrienne Stone (eds), *The Oxford Handbook of The Australian Constitution* (Oxford University Press, 2018) p. 106.

183. Brendan Lim, "Legitimacy," in Cheryl Saunders and Adrienne Stone (eds), *The Oxford Handbook of The Australian Constitution* (Oxford University Press, 2018) p. 325.

184. Thomas Erskine May, *A Treatise upon the Law, Privileges, Proceedings and Usage of Parliament* (Charles Knight, 1844) p. 16.

185. Sir William Blackstone, *Commentary on the Laws of England Vol. 1* (Clarendon Press, 1765) p. 252.

186. William Gummow, "Common Law," in Cheryl Saunders and Adrienne Stone (eds), *The Oxford Handbook of the Australian Constitution* (Oxford University Press, 2018) pp. 192–236.

187. A.V. Dicey, *Introduction to the Study of the Law of the Constitution*, 3rd ed. (Macmillan, 1889).

188. Official Record of the Debates of the Australasian Federal Convention, Adelaide (1897) 307, 910, 911(2), 912, 913(2), 952; Official Record of the Debates of the Australasian Federal Convention, Sydney 312, 313; Official Record of the Debates of the Australasian Federal Convention, Melbourne 1686, 1727, 1728.

189. Official Record of the Debates of the Australasian Federal Convention, Adelaide: 30, 98, 100(2), 102, 135(2), 158, 176, 209(4), 243(3), 244, 288, 289, 293, 296, 325, 536, 537, 538, 582, 646, 665, 704(2), 963, 965, 1015; Official Record of the Debates of the Australasian Federal Convention, Sydney: 56, 287(2), 288, 536(5), 584, 588, 637, 663; Official Record of the Debates of the Australasian Federal Convention, Melbourne: 344, 684, 685, 720, 1703(2),1704(2).

190. A. Hamilton, J. Madison and J. Jay, *The Federalist Papers*, ed. Clinton Rossiter (New American Library, 1961). The essays of the individual authors were referred to thirty times during the Convention. See also chapter 2 of this book.

191. J. Story, *Commentaries on the Constitution of the United States* (Hilliard Gray & Co, 1833). Justice Story's work was referred to fifteen times during the Convention. See also chapter 2 of this book.

192. J. Bryce, *The American Commonwealth*, 3rd ed. (Macmillan, 1895). Professor Bryce, a lawyer, was referred to fifty-four times during the Convention.

193. *Federation Enabling Act* (NSW), s 32. Each of the participating colonies, except Queensland, enacted a version of the *Federation Enabling Act* in which the relevant terms were identical, although Western Australian delegates were absent. For the purposes of my essay, reference will be made only to the *Federation Enabling Act* (NSW). Western Australia enabled a referendum to be held in 1900 by passing Act No. LV of 1900 which authorized its people to decide whether to accept or reject the draft Bill that had already been accepted by the other five colonies. While the people of the Queensland colony did not participate in the Constitutional Convention, the Parliament enacted the *Australasian Federation Enabling Act (Qld)* in 1899 and participated in a referendum held that year, when the other colonies held their second referendum.

194. The phrase "early court" is used to refer to the first three appointments to the High Court of Australia, the Chief Justice Sir Samuel Griffith, Sir Edmund Barton, and Richard O'Connor, which were made in 1903. The phrase "early court" also refers to decisions of the High Court when the original appointments of Griffith CJ, Barton, and O'Connor JJ comprised a majority on the Bench. Isaac Isaacs and Henry Higgins were appointed to the bench in 1906; Justice Richard O'Connor died in 1912.

195. Hans Kelsen, *The General Theory of Law and the State*, trans. Anders Wedberg (Oxford University Press, 1949).

196. Ibid., xiv.

197. Ibid.; emphasis added.

198. Ibid., xvi.

199. Among those cultivars, I include those scholars who accept both the fact/value distinction of all positivism and Kelsen's argument that the law is "normative" before enunciating their own further refinements. A defining issue in these theories is whether they have correctly characterized law as normative while maintaining the assumption of command under penalty.

200. Hans Kelsen, *The General Theory of Law and the State*, trans. Anders Wedberg (Oxford University Press, 1949) p. 5.

201. Thomas Hobbes, *Leviathan* (Cambridge University Press, 1946) p. 25.

202. Hans Kelsen, *The General Theory of Law and the State*, trans. Anders Wedberg (Oxford University Press, 1949) p. xiv.

203. Thomas Hobbes, *Leviathan* (Cambridge University Press, 1946) p. 121. It is worth noting that, four pages earlier, Hobbes states what will become Newton's first law of motion.

204. Hans Kelsen, "The Pure Theory of Law and Analytical Jurisprudence" (1941) 55 *Harvard Law Review* 47.

205. Hans Kelsen, *The General Theory of Law and the State*, trans. Anders Wedberg (Oxford University Press, 1949).

206. Leo Strauss, *Natural Right and History* (University of Chicago Press, 1953) p. 4, n 2:

> "Vollends sinnlos ist die Behauptung, dass in der Despotie keine Rechtsordnung bestehe, sondern Willkür des Despoten herrsche . . . stellt doch auch der despotisch regierte Staat irgendeine Ordnung menschlichen Verhaltens dar . . . Diese Ordnung ist eben die Rechtsordnung. Ihr den Charakter des Rechts abzusprechen, ist nur eine naturrechtliche Naivität oder Überhebung . . . Was als Willkür gedeutet wird, ist nur die rechtliche Möglichkeit des Autokraten, jede Entscheidung an sich zu ziehen, die Tätigkeit der untergeordneten Organe bedingungslos zu bestimmen und einmal gesetzte Normen jederzeit mit allgemeiner oder nur besonderer Geltung aufzuheben oder abzuändern. Ein solcher Zustand ist ein Rechtszustand, auch wenn er als nachteilig empfunden wird. Doch hat er auch seine guten Seiten. Der im modernen Rechtsstaat gar nicht seltene Ruf nach Diktatur zeigt dies ganz deutlich" (Hans Kelsen, *Algemeine Staatslehre*, [Berlin, 1925], pp. 335–6).

207. Emphasis added. Dr. Marcel Noest, assistant director, Institute of Modern Languages, University of Queensland, Australia provided a literal translation of the German original into English.

208. Hans Kelsen, *The General Theory of Law and the State*, trans. Anders Wedberg (Oxford University Press, 1949) p. 36.

209. Ibid., 46.

210. Aristotle, *Nicomachean Ethics*, trans. R.C. Bartlett & S.D. Collins (University of Chicago Press, 2011) p. 1095a 14–5.

211. Hans Kelsen, *The General Theory of Law and the State*, trans. Anders Wedberg (Oxford University Press, 1949) p. 48.

212. Ibid.

213. Feelings, tastes, pain, and pleasure are truly subjective because no one else can know them as feelings the way the body of the subject does. They are, however, objectified by speech. But to know them as a feeling is to feel them.

214. *D'Emden v Pedder* (1904) 1 CLR 91 at 113.

215. *Deakin v Webb* (1904) 1 CLR 585 at 596.

216. See also *Attorney-General (Cth) v Colonial Sugar Refining Company Limited* (1913) 17 CLR 644 at 652.

217. Sir Owen Dixon, "Marshall and the Australian Constitution" (1955) 29 *Australian Law Journal* 423.

218. Dixon J rejected this aspect of Isaacs's argument in *West v Commissioner of Taxation (NSW)* (1937) 56 CLR 657 at 681.

219. *True* federalism was a term applied by Viscount Haldane to the Commonwealth Constitution, which he found was based on that of the United States: *Attorney-General (Cth) v Colonial Sugar Refining Company Limited* (1913) 17 CLR 644 at 651–2.

220. *D'Emden v Pedder* (1904) 1 CLR 91.

221. Philip Ayres, "Federalism and Sir Owen Dixon," address to Eleventh Conference of The Sir Samuel Griffith Society (Melbourne, 9–11 July 1999) p. 142.

222. G. Barwick, *Sir John Did His Duty* (Griffin Press, 1983).

223. See George Winterton, *Parliament, The Executive and the Governor General: A Constitutional Analysis* (Melbourne University Press, 1983) p. 150, where Winterton draws the same conclusion. Winterton dates the Preface of his book at June 1982 with publication occurring in 1983. Barwick's Preface is dated September 1983. It can safely be assumed that Barwick had read Winterton's work, although he does not refer to it or cite it.

Chapter 2

The Constitutional Convention, 1897–1898

INTRODUCTION

The Constitutional Convention of 1897–1898, led by Edmund Barton QC, framed a draft Bill[1] for the Constitution that combined a federal distribution of the powers that assumed the separate sovereignties of the Commonwealth and the states with responsible government after the Westminster parliamentary conventions. Regarding the federal distribution of powers approved by the Convention, it argues that the states retained legislative powers not withdrawn from them or vested exclusively in the Commonwealth. By doing so, the Convention adopted a federal model that followed the scheme of the US Constitution and maintained the separate sovereignties of the states and the Commonwealth. For responsible government, the Convention balanced a federal government's responsibility only to the House of Representatives, with a requirement for equal coordinate powers (except for laws appropriating annual supply or imposing taxation) in a second chamber in which the representation of the various states was equal.

This chapter will also show that the Victorian Attorney-General and delegate Isaac Isaacs argued for a Constitution that resembled the unitary scheme of the British or Canadian Constitutions; that he argued against the provisions that established the federal scheme of the Constitution; and that he sought to include provisions that would lessen the influence of the states on the government of the Commonwealth. To those ends, he opposed the conjunction of equal representation of the states in the Senate with that chamber's coordinate legislative powers with the House of Representatives, as found in the US Constitution. Further, he argued for the referendum as a means of resolving legislative conflict between the two Houses.

This chapter commences with a section that outlines the pathway taken to federation, first regarding the formation of the 1891 convention from which a draft constitution emerged, and then the formation of the 1897 Constitutional Convention, the elements of the federal scheme and responsible government proposed by Barton as leader of the Convention and Isaacs's responses to those proposals. It will then examine the debates that shaped particular provisions in the draft Bill concerning federalism and responsible government. These debates concerned equal state representation in the Senate, the Senate's coordinate legislative powers in relation to money Bills,[2] the reserved powers of the states, the debate relating to legislative deadlocks, and the amendment of the Constitution.

PATHWAY TO FEDERATION

The incentive to federate is reported to have been the emergence in the 1880s of French and German interests in the colonization of South Pacific islands, particularly New Guinea and the New Hebrides. "The Executive Council of Queensland, on 17th July, 1883, resolved that the Home Government should be invited to move in the direction of a federal union."[3] The first step was the adoption of a resolution proposed by Samuel Griffith by the Australian colonies in November 1883 for the establishment of a Federal Australasian Council.[4] Defense of the colonies was again an impetus toward federation when the Premier of New South Wales, Sir Henry Parkes, called for a Convention to appoint a great national Government for all Australia:

> [T]hey must appoint a Convention of leading men from all the colonies—delegates appointed by the authority of Parliament who would fully represent the opinion of the different Parliaments of the colonies. . . . This Convention would have to devise the Constitution which would be necessary for bringing into existence a Federal Government with a Federal Parliament for the conduct of national business.[5]

The Imperial government in 1885 had legislated for a Federal Council that the colonies, other than New South Wales, had requested. Parkes considered "the proposed scheme for a Federal Council, besides being unauthorized in its origin was incurably defective."[6] The mutual defense of the colonies was behind a conference of representatives of the six Australian colonies and New Zealand, which was convened in 1890 when Parkes proposed a resolution that "the best interests and the present and future prosperity of the Australian colonies will be promoted by an early union under the Crown."[7] An additional resolution called for the appointment by colonial legislatures of "delegates to a National Australasian Convention to consider and report upon an adequate scheme for a Federal Constitution,"[8] such delegates to be no more than seven. The delegates assembled in Sydney on March 2, 1891, electing Sir Henry Parkes as president and the Queensland Premier, Sir Samuel Griffith as vice-president. The convention debated a series of resolutions before the drafting of the terms of a draft Bill began. Of significance for this essay is the first of the principles forming "an enduring foundation for the structure of a federal government":

> That the powers and privileges and territorial rights of the several existing colonies shall remain intact, except in respect to such surrenders as may be agreed upon as necessary and incidental to the power and authority of the National Federal Government.
>
> . . .
>
> And, subject these and other necessary provisions, this Convention approves of the framing of a federal constitution, which shall establish:—
>
> A parliament, to consist of a senate and a house of representatives, the former consisting of an equal number of members from each province . . . the latter to be elected by districts formed on a population basis, and to possess the sole power of originating and amending all bills appropriating revenue or imposing taxation.[9]

Even at this early stage, the influence of the US Constitution on the direction of the Commonwealth Constitution is evident. Of significance for the 1897 Constitutional Convention is the fact that the Constitutional Committee for the 1891 convention included among its number Edmund Barton, Alfred Deakin, Sir Samuel Griffith, Sir John Downer, and Andrew Inglis Clark.[10] The final drafting of the Bill on behalf of the convention was undertaken by Griffith, Kingston, Barton, and Clark.[11]

Quick and Garran report that the necessity for equal representation of states in the Senate was conceded by Parkes from the outset, "subject to the definite and unequivocal condition that the House of Representatives should have the predominating voice in finance and in the control of the executive."[12] When the convention concluded, it became obvious that the draft Bill for a Constitution would not be acceptable to either the colonial Parliaments or the people.[13] It was criticized as a compromise with faults, for its federal principles, for the composition and powers of the Senate and equal representation, and for the inadequacy of its financial provisions. It was opposed by members of the Labor Party, which in 1891 had entered the New South Wales Parliament for the first time.[14] The draft 1891 Bill received perfunctory treatment in three colonies, but in the other three colonies it received no treatment at all.[15]

Despite the treatment the Bill received from antifederalists, Quick and Garran report that "the federal spirit was only just beginning to awaken. The Commonwealth Bill, though neglected by the Parliaments, had helped to educate the people."[16] The formation of an Australian Federation League in 1893 pledged "to advance the cause of Australian Federation,"[17] with seventeen branches along the Murray River valley by May confirming Edmund Barton's undertaking the previous year.[18] When Barton convened a public meeting of federalists in the Sydney Town Hall in July to form a League, an attempt by members of the Democratic Social Federation to capture the meeting failed and the League was duly formed. It is reported by Quick and Garran that the League was foremost in organizing and educating the citizens toward federation and that it formed a nucleus of federalists in Sydney and a connecting link between the country leagues, which began to spring up in numbers in the border districts of New South Wales and Victoria.[19] By the beginning of 1894, leagues had been formed in many Victorian towns, and they were also formed in South Australia by 1895. The agitation of the leagues and the education of public sentiment that they engendered prepared the colonial peoples for the 1897 Constitutional Convention, but it was the suggestion of Dr. John Quick, made at a meeting attended by members of the Australian Natives Association and members of the Australian Federation League, that seemed to bring matters to a head.

THE PLAN FOR THE CONVENTION

This section outlines the origin of the plan for a Constitutional Convention and the principles by which a Convention would be guided in preparing a draft of a Constitution. The 1897 Constitutional Convention was established after a two-day meeting of supporters of federation in 1893 unanimously adopted a resolution by Dr. John Quick that

> the Legislature of each Australasian colony should pass an Act providing for the election of representatives to attend a statutory Convention or Congress to consider and adopt a Bill to establish a Federal Constitution for Australia, and upon the adoption of such Bill or measure it be submitted by some process of referendum to the verdict of each colony.[20]

Quick then drafted an Australian Federal Congress Bill, the main features of which became the basis of the *Australasian Federation Enabling Acts* afterward passed by the Parliaments of the five participating colonies.[21] That draft Bill was prepared at a conference of the colonial Premiers in 1895.[22] It was enacted with largely similar operative terms by each of the participating colonial Parliaments, commencing with New South Wales in December 1895.[23]

The *Australasian Federation Enabling Act 1895* (NSW)[24] provided, inter alia, that the duty of the delegates was to draft a federal Constitution under the Crown;[25] that the delegates were to be elected by the voters of the colony;[26] that New South Wales would be one electorate;[27] that the Convention would adjourn while the draft Bill was considered by the colonial Parliaments;[28] that after the Convention had concluded, the draft Constitution would be submitted to the voters for their acceptance or rejection;[29] that the affirmative vote for the draft Bill in New South Wales had to be at least 50,000;[30] and if New South Wales and two other colonies accepted the Constitution, it would go to London for enactment by the Imperial Parliament.[31] These provisions were replicated in similar terms in FEAs enacted by the colonies of Victoria, South Australia, and Tasmania.[32] All the colonial FEAs provided for enactment of the draft Constitution by the Westminster Parliament, a step that generally is viewed by modern commentators[33] as the sine qua non of the Constitution's legality on the assumption that the British Parliament was sovereign for that purpose.[34]

The idea that the Imperial Parliament is the foundational source of the legality of the Commonwealth Constitution needs to be contrasted with the source of the preeminent constitutional principle of federalism in the founding documents of the US Constitution, which vest sovereignty in the people of that nation. The colonial Parliaments' insistence on the draft Constitution obtaining the consent of the people of the several colonies can be reasonably understood only if understood as an expression of the sovereignty of the people of the Australian colonies. Bernhard Wise drew attention to this fact at the very beginning of the Convention when he compared the opening words of the Convention's first resolution, "To enlarge the power of self-government of the people of Australia," with the preamble of the draft Bill of 1891, "Whereas the Australian Colonies have agreed to unite," and concluded:

> Our form not only is something more than the assertion that the union is different from a union of States, but it is a declaration that the Constitution which we are about to frame emanates from the people, and that it is for the benefit of the people as a whole that its powers and functions should be exercised.[35]

He attributed that declaration of the "seat of sovereignty under the Federal Government"[36] to the United States.[37] The Australian people as the source of sovereignty was confirmed in the colonial FEAs as well as in the express terms of section 128 of the Constitution. When the Commonwealth Constitution is viewed in that brighter light, it can be seen that its enactment by the Imperial Parliament was not an expression of Imperial sovereignty but rather an act of registration of the Constitution at Westminster of an independent, self-governing people.[38]

THE CONVENTION'S PLAN FOR THE CONSTITUTION

The Convention was held over three sessions. The first sitting commenced in Adelaide on March 22, 1897,[39] with statements of principles and the delegates' responses to that statement. It resulted in the tabling of a draft federal Bill on April 12, 1897.[40] Delegates spoke to the draft Bill and amendments were moved and voted on. When the first session adjourned on May 6, 1897,[41] a copy of the draft Bill was made available to, inter alia, each of the colonial Parliaments for their consideration and suggested changes. Proposed amendments were forwarded to the Convention for consideration at the second session held in Sydney between September 2 and 24, 1897.[42] This review extended to a third session held in Melbourne between January 20 and March 17, 1898.[43]

While all the colonial FEAs obliged the 1897 Convention to frame a federal Constitution,[44] at the commencement of the Convention Edmund Barton expressed the opinion that the people had directly appointed this Convention and the inference was that "the Convention shall originate the Constitution."[45] Rejecting the opportunity to refine and perfect the draft Bill approved by the 1891 Convention, he proposed that "resolutions defining the principles and conditions upon which and the powers and functions with which the federal authority should be constituted"[46] be drafted and voted on.

Barton was elected as leader of the Convention and the Convention resolved that he frame the resolutions for its consideration.[47] He presented an outline of the federal element of the political scheme of the Constitution. The first of his principles expressed the reserved powers doctrine, which he confirmed when he said that "the individualism of the States after Federation is of as much interest to each colony as the free exercise of national powers is essential to that aggregation of colonies which we express in the term Federation."[48] He expressed a desire for a constitution that was midway between the individuality of the states in a confederation and the absorption of the states in a unitary Constitution: "We cannot adopt any form of government the tendency of which will be, as time goes on, to turn the Constitution towards unification on the one hand, and towards a loose confederacy on the other."[49]

Barton suggests that this federal Constitution represents the middle ground between unitary and confederate constitutions. He describes the reservation of state powers as one of the "principal conditions of Federation—those matters which must be granted as guarantees of the security of the federating colonies."[50] He dismisses the notion that "a Parliament consisting of one House could be designated a Federation"[51] and confirms that it is the backbone from which federalism derives: "The first [resolution] is that the several colonies are not to be touched in any of their powers, privileges, and territories, except perhaps where a surrender is necessary to secure uniformity of law and administration in matters of general concern."[52]

The Parliament would consist of two chambers. In one, "the principle of nationhood and the power and scope of the nation . . . will be expressed in the National Assembly, or House of Representatives."[53] The other chamber, a States Assembly, was not a House of Review but instead was to "have the basic principle of Federation conserved in that Chamber which is representative of the rights of the States; that is, that each law of the Federation should have the assent of the States as well as of the federated people."[54]

The continuance of the sovereignty of the states subject to defined exceptions was guaranteed after federation because the territory of each colony was preserved "subject to the determination of the people of such colony themselves."[55] Barton warned that if the independence of the states extended too far into the areas of the national government, the federal government would tend toward a "mere loose confederation."[56] On the other hand, if only the federated people and not the states as entities were represented in the federation, there would be a gradual, day-by-day encroachment until the federation would "more nearly approach the unified or 'Unitarian' system of government."[57] He considered two Houses of the Parliament to be mandatory, as there was a legal requirement in the FEAs that the Constitution be federal and rejected the idea that government by a Parliament of one House "could be designated a Federation."[58] The federal principle, he argued, was reinforced by the equal representation of the states in the States Assembly, which would preserve the states' individuality[59] as equal sovereign entities, and hence protect their interests: "It is one consequence of the Federation that the Chamber that has in its charge the defence of State interests will also have in its hands powers in most matters co-ordinate with the other House."[60]

Barton linked the idea of responsible government to the resolution that demanded the House of Representatives would "possess the sole power of originating all Bills appropriating revenue or imposing taxation,"[61] but he rejected the idea that the Senate should have the power of amendment since responsible government required that "ultimate control of taxation and expenditure must be in the hands of the National Assembly,"[62] which alone had the authority to remove a government: "I take it under the system of responsible government there is one power, and one only, that places it in the control of the representatives to *demand the expulsion* of the Government."[63] Barton explained that the Constitution would embrace the system of responsible government consisting of a Governor-General and [their] advisers. He opposed the idea of an elected Governor-General. As the appointment of an Australian would bring an unavoidable degree of partisanship, "it will follow that by electing a man from one side, we shall be electing a man who may have a strong temptation to the thwarting of one Ministry and unfairly assisting another."[64]

ISAACS'S SCHEME

Even at this early stage of the Convention, the objection to a federal scheme by Victorian Attorney-General Isaac Isaacs was evident. When he replied to Barton's proposed scheme, he claimed to lay down a principle that would lead to a "Federation in the true sense."[65] He objected to the states' equal representation in the States Assembly, although he accepted that it was inevitable,[66] because it was copied from the US Constitution where it was a compromise and not a principle.[67] The idea behind Isaacs's opinion had been rejected by both the American Founders[68] and US Supreme Court Justice Joseph Story.[69] Isaacs asserted that the federal scheme was motivated by less populous states' unfounded fear of the more populous states,[70] implying that the states' interests were identical.[71] He described the smaller states' argument for equal representation as the demand for a shield, but maintained that, still being dissatisfied, they demanded equal powers for the Senate as a sword.[72] His principal objection, however, was that it was antidemocratic that a small state such as Tasmania, with one-eighth of the population contributing one-eighth of the revenue of New South Wales, had equal power with that state over the nation's finances.[73] He cited a Canadian authority to the effect that the United States suffered from not having a cabinet system of responsible government.[74] When he was challenged by two delegates denying that Canada was a federation, Isaacs responded: "It is a Federation upon the centralisation principle, just as the United States is a Federation on the decentralisation principle, the principle I hope we shall follow."[75] He rejected the Senate's limited coordinate powers regarding money bills, again arguing that it was based on a US compromise.[76] He also rejected both the states' equal representation in the Senate, and that House's coordinate powers because they were American in origin.[77] He called for a deadlock clause to be included in the Constitution, invoking the concept of a constitutional safety valve: "We must recognise that the people are superior to the Legislature, and that their convenience and rights must be first consulted." When the Victorian delegate, Sir William Zeal, questioned the effect of an appeal to the people, Isaacs called the people the paramount political principle.[78] While he suggests that disputes between the chambers would be resolved by appeals to the people, his attacks on the essential characteristics of the Senate, equal representation, and coordinate powers imply that the principle that he was laying down was purely democratic, with all power in the one democratically elected chamber—not dissimilar to the Westminster Parliament, as that scheme was understood at the time—in other words, unitary.[79] His assertion that responsible government means responsibility to the people[80] is incorrect as the Leader of the Convention, Edmund Barton QC pointed out. The Parliament is responsible to the people, but the government under responsible government is responsible to the popular assembly.[81]

Barton argued that the referendum was appropriate for determining a new Constitution and altering an old one, but it was not only unwieldy and expensive, it was inconsistent with ministerial responsibility and responsible government which required a government to resign or seek the people's support at an election when it lost the support of the popular assembly. Barton saw the referendum as dangerous to constitutional government since a government might evade the people and stay in office as long as it liked, even though it had been defeated at a referendum.[82]

Isaacs's assertion of the people as the paramount political principle and the one to which disagreements between the two chambers be referred is similar to Thomas Jefferson's own proposal in his *Notes on the State of Virginia*: that a constitutional convention of the people be elected if it is thought necessary by two of the three branches of government—executive, legislature, judiciary—to alter the Constitution or to correct breaches of it.[83] Barton's arguments for rejecting Isaacs's are similar in character to James Madison's response[84] that Jefferson's proposal was dangerous. Madison agreed that the people were the legitimate source of power for a republican Constitution and its alteration, but he argued that every appeal to the people undermined public confidence in the Constitution. He claimed his greatest objection to Jefferson's proposal was the destruction of the constitutional equilibrium of government that such appeals would have.[85]

Barton explained to the Convention that it was a federal constitution that was being drafted,[86] with a number of *exclusively* federal powers.[87] He identified the second chamber, or States Assembly, as the constitutional defender of state interests, "which will keep legislation within Constitutional limits"[88] by scrutinizing legislation to confine its operation to the constitutional power.[89] He warned of the danger of having either House as the sole chamber; a National Assembly would inevitably lead to unification, and even with equal representation, a States Assembly would lead to a loose confederation:[90] "a majority of citizens dominating the State interests, or the State interests dominating the national life."[91] He proposed that money bills might be amended or vetoed in detail by the States Assembly since members of the States Assembly were popularly elected as in the National Assembly.[92] He preferred responsible government to the US executive, but suggested that the government would only be responsible to the National Assembly.[93] Responsible government would need to be made compatible with the States Assembly "having much larger power in money matters"[94] than in the colonies, including veto in detail "to a certain extent."[95] In the 1891 draft Constitution, the Senate held equal powers with respect to all legislation other than money bills, which the Senate could affirm or reject but could not amend.[96] Barton argued that the clauses would be drafted to prevent a government from tacking, a legislative procedure involving "the mixing up questions of taxation together instead of keeping them in one bill, and of tacking to an Appropriation Act extraneous subject of expenditure, for instance that a bill is lost."[97]

As tacking was not allowed, he thought it not only very serious but an extremely culpable thing for supply to be rejected.[98] Isaacs objected to the states having sovereignty and asserted that "the popular House is supposed, so long as it lives, to represent the popular will."[99] Barton replied that Isaacs was wrong. By resting the two chambers on different democratic bases—that is, national and state—Barton implied that the regime was a mixture of different representations of the public interests.

The first draft of the Constitution was presented to the Convention delegates on April 12, 1897.[100] Barton moved that the Convention consider the Bill in detail as "a Committee of the whole"[101] before speaking briefly to it, explaining that the bulk of the Bill followed the 1891 Bill, and describing how the new draft differed.[102] He said of the draft Bill: "It is a Bill to carry out the different conclusions of the three committees."[103]

Only certain clauses of the draft Bill[104] are relevant to this essay, namely, the causes that relate to the federal scheme and responsible government. Regarding the federal scheme, this chapter focuses on the debates relating to equal representation in the Senate;[105] the reservation of powers to the states not exclusively vested in the Commonwealth[106] and the inconsistency of a state law with a Commonwealth law;[107] the resolution of deadlocks between the House of Representatives and the Senate; and the alteration or amendment of the Constitution. Regarding the scheme of responsible government, the chapter examines the debates that relate to clauses associated with executive power, and money bills and coordinate power.

FEDERAL FEATURES OF THE DRAFT BILL

This section examines the Convention debates as they relate to the federal elements in the Constitution: equal representation of the states in the Senate, the states' reserved powers, the deadlock resolution, and alteration of the Constitution.

Equal Representation in the Senate

As identified already, equal representation of the states in the Senate was considered by Barton to be one of the key elements of a truly federal Constitution. The delegates from the larger colonies had conceded the need for equal representation in the Senate. However, because the coordinate powers of the Senate could give the smaller states power to control a government's legislative program in the House of Representatives, equal representation was inextricably tied up with the coordinate powers regarding money bills. The Victorian premier, Sir George Turner, although opposing equal representation in theory, accepted that the delegates from the more populous states had agreed "to the proposition that [the smaller States] should be entitled to have equal representation with the more populous States."[108] Turner demanded, however, that the Senate's powers regarding money bills be in the form of the 1891 compromise, without which "Federation will be impossible."[109]

Isaacs did not believe there was a logical justification for either equal representation or the Senate's coordinate powers. He thought there was "an intensely strong and, in my opinion, overpowering political justification"[110] for equal representation, for without it would be no federation, but it "must not be accompanied by such excessive powers as will allow the smaller States to dominate the larger ones."[111] Isaacs invoked a purely democratic principle: "the will of the majority of the people *on national questions*—which is in effect the very hypothesis on which we federate—the will of the whole of the Federation collectively and proportionately, shall be done."[112]

Where there was conflict between the two Houses, he thought it necessary to ascertain the will of the majority by a referendum of the people. "I certainly strongly hold to the view that there should be some power of ascertaining in a definite and decisive way the will of the people if the two branches of the Legislature differ."[113] He advised that he intended to vote for equal representation and "endeavour to have embodied in this Constitution some provision relating to deadlocks."[114] As he saw the power of government residing in the people and a popularly elected House of Representatives, he opposed the two-to-one numerical nexus between the two chambers. Membership of the House would be in proportion to population,[115] but with twice as many representatives as senators.

The South Australian delegate, Patrick Glynn, referred to Alexander Hamilton's essay[116] in *The Federalist Papers* to justify equal representation in the Senate. While accepting that it was a compromise, Hamilton argues that it appealed to two principles of justice: where one people were incorporated into a nation, every district ought to have a proportional share in the government; where independent and sovereign states were bound together by a simple league, the parties, unequal in size, ought to share equally in the common council. Drawing from these two examples, Hamilton concludes that "it does not appear to be without some reason that in a compound republic, partaking both of the national and federal character, the government ought to be founded on a mixture of the principles of proportional and equal representation."[117]

Equal representation of the states was embodied in clause 9 of the draft Bill which, where relevant, provided that: "The senate shall be composed of six senators for each state, and each senator shall have one vote."[118] The draft Bill provided a nexus between the two chambers in clause 23 so that there would be twice as many representatives as senators. The issue of Senate representation was, therefore, again prominent in the debate when clause 23 was considered. Isaacs referred to the part of clause 23 that established that nexus "as nearly as practicable there shall be two members of the House of Representatives for every one member of the Senate."[119] He provided a number of arguments as to why a nexus should not be fixed: that the Senate would refuse to approve legislative changes to the quota which might result in Victoria's representation in the House of Representatives declining from 24 out of a total of 120 in 1897 to 13 in 1941;[120] that changes in the size of the Parliament would involve significant costs to the Commonwealth and the size of Representative constituencies would make them unwieldy;[121] that it was illogical for Senate numbers to be increased proportionately with House of Representative increases when membership of the Senate was not elected on a proportionate basis;[122] and that as there was no nexus in the US Constitution, it was not essential to federalism.[123] The relationship between the two chambers, he argued, should be for the federal Parliament to determine.

In his response, Barton described Isaacs's argument as "in its essence an elaborate argument against the proportion of two to one being maintained between the House of Representatives and the Senate."[124] He explained the nexus between the two Houses as being related to the relevant powers of each and "to give that protection by which you think the proper exercise of those powers will be really secured."[125] The nexus, he argued, would prevent a wide disparity in numbers between the two chambers, and the Senate eventually becoming only a committee of the House and losing all public support.[126] He dismissed Isaacs's statistical projections: "There can be no statistics of prediction. I for one am entitled to my independent judgment about the matter. . . . The statistician has never yet and never will occupy the position of a prophet."[127]

In its review of the draft Bill after the conclusion of the first session, the NSW Parliament took issue with clause 9, which guaranteed equal representation in the Senate and no less than six senators for each state,[128] and sought to replace it with representation proportional to population,[129] with a minimum number of three senators for any state. The Victorian delegate,

Henry Higgins, after pointing to the disparity in populations between New South Wales and Tasmania, urged a strictly democratic solution, arguing that consent of the states was necessary when entering "a league, but as soon as you are in a league the consent of the people is sufficient."[130] Josiah Symon, distinguishing the states from their people, asked Higgins: "Are the states, in [your] judgment, to be represented in the federation?"[131] When Higgins replied, "Certainly not," Symon accused him of not being a federationist at all. "My hon. friend . . . is going for a unification."[132] Higgins replied that the word was a mere phrase but did not deny its accuracy.[133]

Isaacs attacked equal representation in the US Senate by suggesting it caused that nation's civil war and could have the same effect in the Commonwealth unless the Constitution "is so framed as to give full play to the will of the people as it may be expressed at any particular time."[134] He argued that American federalism as it then stood had rejected the federalism of its Founders and cited the work of John Burgess,[135] who had written of the US Constitution: "I do not think that it need be feared that the doctrine of the sovereignty of the several states will again seriously threaten this development."[136] Isaacs argued that equal representation in the United States had been a disaster and would be counterproductive for the Commonwealth, and that neither the Victorian Assembly nor the Victorian people would accept equal representation.[137] He thought equal representation a vicious principle, "indefensible on the ground of reason and of logic . . . [and] branded with the disapprobation of history."[138] Isaacs's criticism of equal representation in the US Senate as the cause of the civil war ignores the fact that slavery preexisted that Constitution—a fact that is irrelevant to Australia. It also ignores that the fact that the Supreme Court in *Dred Scott v Sandford* had held that slaves were not human beings but property, whose ownership was protected by the Constitution[139] while Abraham Lincoln's presidency threatened that "no more slave states would be added to the Union."[140]

Despite his concerns, Isaacs declared that he supported equal representation because without it there would be no federation. He therefore appeared to support a compromise[141] while seeking constitutional provisions that either lessened states' powers or made their future abatement possible. With some minor amendments that did not affect equal representation, clause 9 was passed by the Convention, including by Isaacs.[142]

States' Reserved Powers

Reserving to the states powers not surrendered to the Commonwealth was the principle of the first resolution approved by the Convention.[143] During the initial debate, Barton had set out the importance of protecting state interests from encroachment by the federal authority:

> The State interests must be conserved, not only by safeguarding their full right to exercise all functions reserved to them, but by making the powers to be exercised by them so certain that there can be no doubt, even if the matter is referred to the Supreme Court, about the clearness of the definition.[144]

The draft Bill provided that

> all powers which at the establishment of the Commonwealth are vested in the Parliaments of the several colonies and which are not by this Constitution exclusively vested in The Parliament of the Commonwealth, or withdrawn from the Parliaments of the several States are reserved to, and shall remain vested in, the Parliaments of the States respectively.[145]

The Convention did not attempt to identify the particular powers that were reserved to the states, which were under the colonial Constitutions, full and plenary. However, as the delegates were framing a federal Constitution after that of the United States, they had only to grant specific powers to the Commonwealth and reserve every power not vested *exclusively* in the Commonwealth to the states, which could amend their Constitutions if other powers that met the constitutional requirements were needed. Geoffrey de Q Walker argues that it is a misconception to understand the doctrine of reserved powers as being based on implications from the Constitution following *McCulloch v Maryland*, rather than on the express provision.[146] This is true if a literal construction is used that ignores all implications from the separate sovereignties of the federal scheme, its historical roots in the US Constitution and the US Supreme Court authorities on the same. What Walker refers to as "the two doctrines" are found in the decision by Marshall CJ in *McCulloch v Maryland*,[147] which explicates the principles from which the limits of federal and state powers in a federal Constitution can be drawn. Walker does not refer to Story's conclusion that the Tenth Amendment was an affirmation of a necessary rule of construction of the Constitution which, as an instrument of limited and enumerated powers, "follows irresistibly, that what is not conferred, is withheld, and belongs to the state authorities, if invested by their constitutions of government respectively in them; and if not so invested, it is retained by the people, as a part of their residuary sovereignty."[148]

When Story's explanation is applied to the trade and commerce power, section 51(i), of the Commonwealth Constitution, it invites the conclusion that the Commonwealth's power to legislate for domestic trade and commerce is limited to that "among the States"[149] but subject to the Constitution. When Griffith stated in argument in *D'Emden v Pedder*[150] that "I do not think there is any material difference" between the Tenth Amendment of the US Constitution and section 107 of the Constitution,[151] he affirmed the same principle referred to by Story. While the federal character of the 1897 draft Bill followed that of the United States, the issue of primary concern to the Convention and the one in its two forms that occupied the delegates was the interaction between the Commonwealth legislative powers and those reserved to the states. The distinct sovereignty of the States was a live issue at ratification of the US Constitution. Alexander Hamilton dealt directly with it when he explained that "the States will retain, under the proposed Constitution, a very extensive portion of active sovereignty";[152] and further, in the same essay, he said:

> The powers delegated by the proposed Constitution to the federal government are few and defined. . . . The powers reserved to the several States will extend to all the objects which, in the ordinary course of affairs, concern the lives, liberties, and properties of the people, and the internal order, improvement, and prosperity of the State.[153]

When Barton spoke of states' interests and states' rights, he was explaining two features of the draft Bill that would secure the federal scheme with the separate sovereignties of the states and Commonwealth. He explained that the states' interests were to be secured in the Constitution by the coordinate powers of the Senate in which the states were equally represented: "But if you must have two Chambers in your Federation, it is one consequence of the Federation that the Chamber that has in its charge the defence of State interests will also have in its hands powers in most matters co-ordinate with the other House."[154]

States' *rights*, however, which depended on the powers by which the sovereign states regulated their own affairs, rested on the reservation to the states of the powers that remained after *limited* powers were vested in the Commonwealth. The adjective "limited," as used by Story,[155] did not qualify the number of powers enumerated. It qualified the ambit and extent of the powers which were enumerated by reference to their terms. The exclusive powers that were vested in the Commonwealth were actually withdrawn from the states, whose remaining powers continued. As Allan and Aroney acknowledge, "The framers of the Australian Constitution . . . deliberately chose to construct a system which presupposed the existing powers of the States (as self-governing political communities) and in which only specific, limited legislative powers were conferred upon the Commonwealth."[156]

The reservation of the remaining powers to the states after federation was justified during the Convention by the use of phrases such as "protecting the individualism of the States after federation"[157] or "for the internal management of the States."[158]

Isaacs's rejection of equal representation was matched by his rejection of the legislative elements of the federal scheme that the Barton-led Convention was framing. His own use of the word "federal" in various forms—which included, inter alia, "federation on a decentralising principle"[159] and "federal authority"[160]—appears to have been a rhetorical camouflage for the actual scheme he desired.[161] His proposal for exclusive federal powers and exclusive state powers appears to preserve the legislative position of the states but denies them any influence in government of the Commonwealth,[162] much like the Canadian Constitution. Isaacs said of Dicey's definition of federalism that it supported his view and cited Dicey speaking generally of a federal state as a contrivance "intended to reconcile national unity and power with the maintenance of state rights."[163] Isaacs interrupted the citation at this point to say: "These state rights . . . are those which are conserved by the constitution to the states separately."[164] Isaacs's interpolation therefore suggests that the only state rights that are conserved are exclusive rights conserved by exclusive powers without concurrent powers.

He continued with Dicey's definition of federalism in support of his argument that national and state sovereignty are reconciled by a constitution under which "the ordinary powers of sovereignty are elaborately divided between the common or national government and the separate states."[165] Isaacs then selectively cites Dicey's reference to the US Constitution[166] to explain a federal Constitution, but omits Dicey's statement that federalism is "the distribution among bodies with limited and co-ordinate authority of the different powers of government."[167] Isaacs goes on to argue that federalism does not consist of two chambers with different foundations, but rather "in having the powers and jurisdictions and the subject matter so divided that one part belongs entirely to the national sphere and the other part to the separate state spheres."[168] Isaacs's inaccurate citation is underlined by Dicey's own footnote, which distinguishes the US Constitution from the Canadian Constitution by the reservation of powers doctrine, with the Canadian Constitution reserving all powers to the Dominion not exclusively conferred upon the provinces.[169]

During the second session, Isaacs expressly rejected the place of the states in a federal Constitution when he responded to South Australian delegate Josiah Symon's comment that the Senate was representative of state interests,[170] with: "As I understand the matter, the visible sign of state autonomy consists in the reserved powers."[171] However, he implicitly rejected the notion of concurrent, overlapping powers and the coordinate powers of the states in the Senate when he said: "The states, as states, according to my view, have no place in the federation."[172] His two statements are reconciled only if the Commonwealth and states have mutually exclusive powers and the states have no coordinate powers in the Senate, as in the Canadian Constitution. Bernhard Wise identified this when he countered that Isaacs's clear division of exclusive powers was not possible to achieve, as the Canadian Constitution had demonstrated.[173] As states play no part in Isaacs's Commonwealth, the only powers that will be exclusive to the states will be the police powers.[174]

Deadlock: Dissolution and Referendum

The deadlock clause generated one of the longest debates of the Convention, occurring mostly in the first two sessions. Barton was opposed to its inclusion but it was an important clause for Isaacs who, through it, promoted the use of the referendum as a means of resolving legislative difficulties between the two Houses. While the referendum, in principle, allowed the government to appeal to the people, thus bypassing a Senate obstruction, in effect it undermined the states' influence on government and a defeat at a referendum did not result in a government's loss of office. While Isaacs's preference for a unitary Constitution was explicit in his debates of equal representation and the Senate's coordinate powers,[175] his endorsement of the referendum was a more subtle approach and only implicitly unitarian, since it appeared to concede the federal nature of the Senate while tacitly providing the means of undermining it. This was plain from his concession to federalism: "Allow equal representation and argue for a referendum of ascertaining the will of the majority."[176]

The need for a clause to resolve deadlock between the two Houses was first suggested by the Victorian Premier, George Turner, who thought the best solution was a direct referendum to ascertain "the wishes of the people by finding out whether a majority of the States are prepared to take a certain course, and see if they contain a majority of the people."[177] He thought either a double dissolution or referendum would ascertain the public's views. The ostensible reason for a deadlocks clause in the Constitution was the existence of coordinate legislative powers of the Senate.

It was, however, in the context of money bills that Richard O'Connor envisaged a deadlock occurring, and he distinguished "a deadlock which affects the carrying out of the daily business of Government—indeed its actual existence—and a deadlock which does not affect these matters."[178] He explained that it was necessary for the purpose of responsible government that the House of Representatives have the power to initiate all bills imposing taxation or appropriating revenue for supply purposes but "that no amendment of any of this class of measure should be allowed to the House which does not control the existence of Governments."[179]

Barton rejected a deadlock clause in the initial draft Bill, saying that "the Constitutional Committee have not found themselves in a position to accept any proposal made to them for the prevention of deadlocks."[180] When Turner commented on their absence from the draft Bill, Barton replied that there were clauses to prevent deadlocks "and the best there could be."[181]

Isaacs's demand for a clause to resolve deadlock in the draft Bill related initially to the resolution of a legislative deadlock[182] that paralyzed the Parliament. His purely democratic solution was a safety valve that "will give free play to the opinion of the majority."[183] He tied the issue of deadlock to equal representation, which he accepted as necessary for federation but insisted "that the will of the majority of the people on national questions . . . the will of the whole of the Federation collectively and proportionately shall be done."[184] He argued for a deadlock clause that was fair to the small states, for "ascertaining definitely and decisively the will of the majority of the people"[185] by the referendum.

Barton's responses assumed that the only deadlock to be considered was that related to financial clauses, which could paralyze a government. He argued that the Constitution did not need such a clause since the draft Bill prohibited tacking,[186] which was the historical cause of deadlock in the colonies. If the House sought to tack to supply, the legislation would be held unconstitutional by the High Court.[187]

Quick and Garran note that it was not generally recognized by the Convention at this time that a provision designed to resolve a deadlock could actually become a tactical instrument for creating deadlock.[188] Isaacs saw deadlock in much broader terms than just as a dispute over supply legislation: "While we provide here for the absence of tacking, we cannot provide for the rejection by one Chamber of the distinct proposals of the other."[189] While this would normally be expected in a federal Constitution, Isaacs attributed deadlock to a defective Constitution, one that did not provide for harmony between the two branches of the legislature, "as they are in a unitary government. The majority have rested these two Houses upon foundations of mutual hostility, mutual jealousy, and mutual distrust."[190] For Isaacs, the real culprit was equal representation and coordinate powers in the Senate, which "endowed these Houses with power to support the antagonism to which they have been invited."[191] When proposals from other delegates had been rejected by the Convention, Isaacs moved the insertion of his clause to deal with deadlock. The essence of Isaacs's proposal was that a House whose proposed law was rejected or was unacceptably amended by the other House might refer the proposed law to the people for their direct determination. The proposed law became law as if it had been passed by both Houses of Parliament if "the proposed law is affirmed by a majority of States containing also a majority of the population of the Commonwealth."[192] Had it been accepted, a second chamber would have been merely ornamental. Isaacs explained that his solution was available in every state Constitution in the United States except one. The referendum "would be a clear and decisive verdict on a matter on which the two branches of the Legislature had differed."[193]

Toward the end of the second session, the Convention debated a procedural motion which, based on a proposal for a new clause by the NSW Assembly, considered whether the draft Bill should include a deadlocks clause and the different methods for resolving a deadlock.[194] Victorian delegate Simon Fraser referred to the clause as a *mechanical means* for resolving deadlocks and warned the Convention that he could see it applied to disputes regarding "ordinary matters of legislation,"[195] which did not deadlock the Parliament. He repeated Barton's argument that that the Senate was elected by the whole people of a state and was more democratic than the House of Representatives.[196] Fraser concluded that a provision for a referendum in the Constitution would lead to a unified government: "As sure as we give the referendum to the federal government, so surely shall we make it a unified government."[197] Alfred Deakin agreed that "a national vote has to be rejected because it is not federal, and because it means unification."[198] Josiah Symon said of the referendum proposal that a matter decided by the people was inconsistent with government responsible to the House of Representatives, as it could continue to govern whatever the referendum decided.[199]

When Barton spoke against a deadlock clause in the second session, he was assuming that deadlock was a refusal of supply that would paralyze a government: "when the fuel of the machine of government is withheld that the machine comes to a stop; and that fuel is money."[200] Contrary to Isaacs's opinion that the two chambers were based on hostility, jealousy, and mistrust, Barton thought the two Houses would negotiate their way through differences and warned that the deadlock clause could be used to control one House.[201] Faced with the Convention's mood, however, he agreed that a provision to settle conflicts between the two Houses that was consistent with responsible government should be included. He argued that the referendum was appropriate for making a Constitution, but inappropriate for resolving deadlock. As both Houses were popularly elected, he suggested that a provision for deadlock should result in the dissolution of both Houses; however, "if the referendum is so safeguarded that a double dissolution precedes it, I believe its impingement on ministerial responsibility, and members' responsibility, will not be so severe."[202]

Isaacs thought the Constitution should be founded "on the lines of the British Constitution, so far as that is applicable."[203] That Constitution was and is unitary. He said he would insist on "a national referendum to settle deadlocks"[204] if the Constitution contained only exclusively national matters, but because of the smaller colonies' fears, the double dissolution and the dual referendum should be used. He warned that because of its rigidity, it would be unalterable, with disastrous consequences like civil war, at which point the two larger colonies would, with the support of a smaller colony, "avert the disastrous catastrophe by assenting to a change of the constitution."[205]

When the Convention resolved to include a deadlocks clause,[206] the debate was complicated by the number of different amendments that, coming forward at different times, overlapped with one another. The eventual solution came from Joseph Carruthers, who proposed the double dissolution of both Houses, followed if necessary by a "full conference of the two Houses of Parliament."[207] Isaacs dismissed the proposal as "so much waste of time,"[208] preferring the dual referendum requiring a majority of the electors of the Commonwealth and each state. Barton rejected the referendum in a federal Constitution, suggesting it might be applicable in a unitary Constitution like that of New South Wales.[209] He thought the Carruthers proposal for the deadlock to be resolved by a double dissolution, followed by the joint sitting of the two Houses requiring either a two-thirds or three-fifths majority acceptable because it was consistent with responsible government.[210] The Carruthers proposal was approved by the Convention.[211]

Amending the Constitution

The draft Bill initially provided that the Constitution would be altered by a proposed amendment that had first been passed by an absolute majority of each chamber and subsequently approved by the electors of a majority of the states, which also comprised a majority of the people of the Commonwealth.[212] Isaacs's initial contribution was to support an amendment to the clause proposed by Alfred Deakin, which would require the support of only a simple majority and not an absolute majority of each House of the Parliament.[213] He argued that a mere majority would not be sufficient on its own but, as the clause also required the sanction of the step two ratification, it was acceptable.[214] He warned against a rigid Commonwealth Constitution, citing criticism of the rigidity of the US Constitution:

> In America there are loud and frequent complaints concerning the difficulty of altering the Constitution. As Mr. Moncure Conway has lately pointed out, there exists an almost intolerable state of things there,[215] "arising," as Mr Stead has graphically phrased it, "from the iron grasp of the dead hand."[216]

Deakin's amendment was defeated.[217] Barton's proposed amendment, which would require that only one half of votes cast in a state with full male and female suffrage would be counted in any referendum until a uniform qualification prevailed in the Commonwealth, was approved by the Convention.[218] When the clause was reconsidered in the Third Session, the Convention rejected a proposal to strike out the word "absolute" from the clause where it required an absolute majority of each house for an amendment to proceed to a referendum.[219] Isaacs suggested that any proposed amendment that was rejected by one house should be submitted to the people for determination by a referendum.[220] He argued that the amendment was therefore consistent with the original clause and warned that the difficulty of amending the US Constitution was an inherent defect. He asked whether the Convention wanted a Constitution "loaded with inherent defects, which it may be practically, if not totally impossible, to remove hereafter?"[221] When the proposed amendment was criticized for abandoning the assent of the legislature, Isaacs countered that the submission to a joint referendum achieved that end.[222] He characterized the disagreement between the two Houses as a disagreement among agents, where "I say, come back to the principal who has appointed them both."[223]

Deakin's contribution to the debate was a subtle attack on Isaacs's proposal. He endorsed Isaacs's amendment for enlarging the "restricted scope" of clause 121 while cautioning against too frequent and too easy amendment. He thought Isaacs's amendment gave insufficient weight to the effect on responsible government;[224] however, he pointed out that the "measure for the settlement of dead-lock between the two Houses of the Federal Parliament would apply to any measure introduced for the amendment of the Constitution"[225] if the consent of both Houses was not required. Deakin suggested that if the particular measure was passed by an absolute majority of one House, "the honourable member will see that all the requirements of clause 121 have been fulfilled."[226] When Isaacs asked whether Deakin was suggesting that the amendment "only be resorted to after the double dissolution,"[227] Deakin responded that he was merely demonstrating that there was another process under the deadlock clause by which Isaacs's proposal could eventually be accomplished.[228] He denied any criticism of Isaacs's proposal. Deakin is implying that the effect of Isaacs's proposal would be that a proposed law to amend the Constitution which was rejected by one House could be the basis of a double dissolution and become effective at a joint sitting, pursuant to the deadlocks clause, thus bypassing section 121.

Symon suggested that Deakin had shown "that the provisions avoiding dead-locks applied as effectually to a difference between the two Houses with regard to a proposed amendment of the Constitution as to a difference in regard to anything else"[229] and he described Isaacs's response to that as "petulant."[230] He said, almost presciently, of Isaacs's proposal that it "is really an insidious attack on the rights and powers of the Senate. The result will be to paralyse the Senate in dealing with any fundamental alteration of the Constitution."[231] When Isaacs asked him to consider his argument where "the Senate initiates the reform and the Assembly rejects it," Symon implied that Isaacs had a different plan in mind to the one he was proposing—perhaps a plan to limit the power of the Senate:

> I do not say for a moment that my learned friend has advocated the amendment with that deliberate intention. But we must all reckon with our past history. I know the zeal and assiduity with which he has sought to secure all possible restrictions on the Senate.[232]

Barton stressed the likelihood of misuse if a ministry might avert some disaster to itself by amending the Constitution. He repeated his objection to the referendum as a proposal that undermined responsible government. The amendment sought was radically different from what was in the Bill "because it tends to make the existence of Parliament immaterial."[233] South Australian delegate James Howe was suspicious of Isaacs's amendment. He suggested that Isaacs intended to advocate proportional representation in the Senate. When Isaacs sought a reason for that view, Howe replied,

> I know the tenacity of purpose of the honourable member, and that he is one of those whom nothing less than an earthquake can extinguish when he has set his mind upon a certain course. I fully expect, therefore, that he will bring forward such a proposal as I have indicated.[234]

Isaacs dismissed Barton's arguments, characterizing the disagreement between the Houses in relation to constitutional amendment as an example of deadlock;[235] where the deadlock related to constitutional amendment, the people would not be afforded the opportunity of expressing their will.[236] He responded evasively to Howe's allegation stating that he had "from the first fought very hard to obtain equal representation in the Senate."[237] Howe was implicitly suggesting, however, that with Isaacs's amendment, the Constitution could easily be amended again after federation to introduce proportional representation for the Senate. Isaacs's amendment was defeated.[238] Quick and Garran report that a clause was added to what had become clause 128 by the1899 Premier's Conference, "providing for a reference to the electors notwithstanding the disagreement of one House."[239] All amendments to the Constitution required ratification by the consent of the governed.

Summary of the Federal Features

The federal scheme of the Constitution remained unaltered by its passage through the Imperial Parliament. In framing the federal scheme, the Convention generally followed the federal scheme of the US Constitution and maintained the separate sovereignties of the federal entity and the states, vesting limited and enumerated powers in the former[240] and reserving the powers not exclusively vested in the Commonwealth[241] to the states.[242] Where powers are shared and a valid law of the Commonwealth conflicts with that of a state, to the extent of the conflict, the state law is invalid.[243] The original states at federation were to be equally represented in a Senate,[244] which shared coordinate powers with the House of Representatives in relation to all legislation[245] other than proposed laws appropriating supply or imposing tax.[246] Such laws can only originate in the House of Representatives and cannot be amended by the Senate. The interests of the states were protected by the coordinate powers in the Senate.[247] In the event that a proposed law was twice rejected by the Senate, the Constitution prescribed that the Governor-General may dissolve both Houses simultaneously. If, after the dissolution, the House again passes the proposed law and the Senate rejects or fails to pass it, the Governor-General may convene a joint sitting of the two Houses and if an absolute majority agrees, it shall become law.[248]

FEATURES OF RESPONSIBLE GOVERNMENT IN THE DRAFT BILL

Neither the draft Bill nor the Constitution refers to responsible government or to the prime minister and cabinet. Nor can they be inferred from constitutional provisions unless it is first acknowledged that the intention of the Founders was to have a system of responsible government based on the Westminster elements melded into the federal scheme. Once it is noted that responsible government was intended, the provisions of the draft Bill are not only intelligible, but logical. The FEAs obliged the Convention to draft a federal Constitution under the Crown, and the relationship between the Crown and the legislature is established in a scheme of responsible government by the Executive, consisting of the Governor-General, prime minister, and cabinet, who wield the executive power of the Commonwealth.

Executive Power

The issue of whether the Governor-General possessed a discretion was alive from the first session. The executive power clause in the initial draft Bill stated that: "The executive power and authority of the Commonwealth is vested in the Queen, and shall be exercised by the Governor-General as the Queen's representative."[249] Speaking to the provision, George Reid stipulated what he said was the colonial practice:

> Now, I think we had better, since we are going to put in black and white the full functions of the Commonwealth, state what I deem will be the fact in practice, that the executive power is to be exercised *by and with the advice* of the Executive Council.[250]

After referring to clause 2 of the draft Bill, under which the queen appointed a Governor-General with such powers and functions as she thought fit, Reid distinguished the Crown prerogatives in the colonies from Crown prerogatives in the United Kingdom and explained that a refusal by the Crown to receive advice was not an executive act at all. "An executive act is something which affects the subjects of the country."[251] When Josiah Symon suggested that the appointment of a minister was a prerogative act, Reid argued that it would be an exercise of the prerogative only if that prerogative was vested in the Governor-General under clause 2 of the Constitution's Chapter 1.[252] Clause 2 stated:

> The Queen may, from time to time, appoint a Governor-General, who shall be Her Majesty's representative in the Commonwealth, and who shall have and may exercise in the Commonwealth during the Queen's pleasure, and subject to the provisions of this Constitution, such powers and functions of the Queen as Her Majesty may think fit to assign to him.[253]

In the belief that Her Majesty could, under clause 2, vest prerogative powers in the Governor-General, Reid questioned the necessity for the monarch's power but, given that it was there, "surely we can put in black and white the principle of executive action which always is that the Governor shall act with the advice of the Executive Council."[254]

Barton explained that there were two classes of Executive Acts of the Crown: those exercised by the prerogative and those that were ordinary Executive Acts, where it was prescribed that the Executive should act in Council and where, being the result of Statutes,[255] it was unnecessary to add the words "with the advice of the Governor in Council" because it was not possible for the prerogative to be exercised as a personal act of the Crown: "The prerogative is never in these days exercised as a personal act of the Crown as we understand it."[256] The significance of this statement should not be overlooked. It was not disputed by any delegate. Barton further explained that while the prerogative was expressed to be exercised with the consent of the Executive Council, the advice came from those answerable to the people:

> The point of the matter is that where the expression of the Act is in the form commonly used to indicate a prerogative act—that is without the addition of the words "in Council"—that does not indicate any real personal power in the depositary of the Crown's authority.[257]

In other words, what were in the unwritten British Constitution, referred to as prerogative powers exercisable only on advice, are expressed clearly in the Commonwealth's written Constitution by the presence or absence of the words "in council": still only exercisable on advice. In his review of a proposed law to amend the Commonwealth Constitution, Michael Crommelin[258] took issue with Barton's response to Reid, noting that:

> William [*sic*] Carruthers had made the point with devastating simplicity: Mr Barton first of all recites Dicey to show what occurs under the unwritten Constitution of England. But here we are framing a written Constitution. When once that Constitution is framed we cannot get behind it.[259]

Carruthers's argument was, like Reid's, a desire for the words to be introduced out of an abundance of caution, but not a fundamental disagreement with what the clause ought to say. Barton's response, however, was that if the words were inserted, Westminster should advise them "how the distinction would be made every time. The words: With the advice of the Federal Council would be struck out and the words: The Queen or The Governor-General would be left."[260]

As discussed in chapter 1, literalist and other rules for the interpretation of ordinary legislation such as *The Sale of Goods Act* have little need to consider the political scheme of the Act, but they are insufficient for construing a written Constitution that contains a political theory.[261] Such ordinary legislation is, or attempts to be self-explanatory so that the text suffices. Crommelin takes Carruthers's criticism much further than Carruthers, describing Barton's solution to constitutional design as obscurantist, evasive, and misguided for classifying

> the powers of the head of state in only two categories: those conferred on the Governor-General in Council; and those conferred simply on the Queen or the Governor-General as her representative. In a written constitution, function should prevail over form, as Carruthers had urged.[262]

Crommelin's description is, however, an inaccurate interpretation of the executive powers of the Commonwealth. Crommelin ignores much of Barton's explanation when he demands that the executive powers be classified in four categories:

> formal powers exercisable by the Governor-General; powers exercisable by the Governor-General upon the advice of the Federal Executive Council; powers exercisable by the Queen or the Governor-General only in accordance with Ministerial advice; and powers exercisable by the Queen or the Governor-General, in appropriate circumstances, without or contrary to Ministerial advice (reserve powers).[263]

He implicitly admits that the reserve powers are not in the Constitution, but laments that they should be. Crommelin's criticism of Barton is based upon two errors. First, he presumes that the Constitution is a piece of

Imperial legislation and seeks to interpret it without regard to the political scheme of responsible government. Second, he construes the Constitution in accordance with what he believes the executive power in the Constitution should contain, rather than what is there. Had he accepted that the Founders gave responsible government in the political scheme its legal meaning, he would not have assumed that the Governor-General held any powers that were exercisable without ministerial advice, let alone reserve powers. Crommelin's legal positivism compelled him to see only the text, to which he added his own political scheme. It is important to note that Joseph Carruthers, a solicitor, was not disputing the substance of Barton's explanation of the law: he was merely offering his drafting advice to the three members of the drafting committee, Edmund Barton QC, Richard O'Connor QC, and Sir John William Downer QC, in terms that he thought better expressed the same opinion. What can be concluded from the debate is that there were only two categories of executive powers in the Constitution, as Barton explained: there were prerogative acts, which were only exercised on advice, and there were statutory acts, which were also exercised on advice. The reason why Crommelin cannot find the other powers that he describes as formal powers of the Governor-General and the reserve powers for which advice is not required is because they were never part of the Constitution. They were not needed and were not consented to by the people at the referenda. Barton did not consider it necessary that Reid's amendment be made because "he admits that what he desires is secured by section 61"[264] of the Constitution.

When the executive power of the Commonwealth was considered during the second session, the Premier of Western Australia, Sir John Forrest, requested the use of the expression "the Governor" and the avoidance of the term "Governor in Council," because "'Governor' is well known, and is understood to mean the governor acting with the advice of his responsible ministers. If you use the words 'in council,' a doubt arises as to whether the Governor is expected to act on his own responsibility or with the advice of his ministers."[265]

Barton, in explaining why "the words 'in council' are sometimes used and sometimes omitted," said it was a fallacy to suppose that any act was "done by a Governor of a colony, even upon a prerogative with[out] the advice of ministers."[266] Forrest then asked where the prerogative was in clause 64 that provided,

> Until the Parliament otherwise provides, the number of Ministers of State who may sit in either House shall not exceed seven, who shall hold such offices and by such designation as The Parliament from time to time proscribes, or, in the absence of provision, as the Governor-General from time to time directs.

This aspect of the debate indicates a profound constitutional point. The powers vested in the Governor-General are vested only nominally in that office. They are not personal to the office, but can only legally be exercised when the ministers give advice, regardless of whether the words "in council" are used. The whole structure of section 61 suggests a metaphoric meaning consistent with the democratic nature of the House of Representatives and a government responsible to that chamber. During the third session of the Convention, Deakin reflected on clause 68, which stated: "The command in chief of the naval and military forces is hereby vested in the Governor-General as the Queen's representative."[267] Deakin objected because it seemed to confer "some additional personal power . . . in the Governor-General."[268] An amendment was moved that would replace the words "as the Queen's representative" with "acting under the advice of the Executive Council." Barton's reply disposed of the issue: "As it is now, the, Governor cannot act without the advice of the Minister any more than the Queen, can, even if not specified to, be 'in Council.'"[269] At a later stage of the debate, he added that

> it is laid down by every constitutional writer whose word is worth having that every prerogative of the Crown is now administered in trust for the people, which means, and is stated to mean, that it is administered by the advice of a responsible Minister.[270]

This statement of the law relating to the executive power that will be ratified by the people is critical to understanding how responsible government functions in conjunction with the Commonwealth Constitution.

Barton expressed the idea that responsible government (i.e., the responsibility of the executive) meant being responsible to the House of Representatives when he said: "I take it under the system of responsible government there is one power, and one only, that places it in the control of the *representatives* to demand the expulsion of the Government."[271] This statement was not disputed; indeed, it was even endorsed by Isaacs when he said: "Responsible government, as has been admitted on all hands, means the responsibility of the Ministry of the day to the Lower Chamber."[272] The only concern about that principle that arose during the Convention was how to reconcile that principle with the powers regarding money bills granted to the Senate.

Money Bills and Coordinate Powers

Barton confirmed that the system of government in the draft Constitution would be that of responsible government, requiring the ministers to sit in the Parliament.[273] The model for responsible government in the colonies at the time of the Convention was the Westminster Parliament in London, where the

Crown would commission a prime minister who had the confidence—that is, support—of a majority of the House of Commons to form government.[274] The legislative powers of the House of Lords with respect to laws appropriating revenue or imposing taxes, however, were subject to different complicating conventions. The conventions, like all the powers of the House of Lords, existed by agreement but had undergone significant changes since the passage of the Bill of Rights in 1689. In the speech that accompanied his resolutions "to enlarge the powers of self-government of the people of Australia,"[275] Barton said of the power to appropriate revenue or to impose taxation that "if we are to have responsible government carried on, that the ultimate control of taxation and expenditure must be in the hands of the National Assembly."[276] Barton had said of the finance provisions in the new draft Bill that "if government is finance and finance is government these clauses must be considered amongst the most important in the Bill."[277] The underlying assumption of the draft Bill was that responsible government meant the government was only accountable to the House of Representatives, which Barton expressed as: "I take it under the system of responsible government there is one power, and one only, that places it in the control of the representatives to demand the expulsion of the Government."[278] He identified that power as the power of the purse, which in the colonial Parliaments lay with the people:

> Because the power of the purse is given to the people in the Constitution of the colonies, and the existence of that power of the purse enables the people to indicate distrust of the Government by the refusal of supplies at the moment it becomes bereft of the confidence of the people.[279]

The draft Bill secured that power to the House of Representatives with clause 52, which required money bills to originate only in the House of Representatives: "Proposed laws having for their main object the appropriation of any part of the public revenue, or the imposition of any tax or impost, shall originate in the House of Representatives."[280] However, given the federal nature of the Constitution that the Convention was framing, and given that the Senate would have coordinate powers with the House of Representatives, the issue confronting the Convention was the extent of the Senate's powers over the government's finances.

At the beginning of the first session, Barton opined that the finance clauses of the 1891 draft Bill were consistent with a government responsible to the House of Representatives:

> If we are to have what we understand as responsible government, I am of opinion that if you made similar provision to that made in the Bill of 1891 it would be scarcely possible to carry on government except in that way. I take it under the

> system of responsible government there is one power, and one only, that places it in the control of the representatives to demand the expulsion of the Government.[281]

However, clause 55(1) of the draft 1891 Bill, while denying the Senate the power to amend money bills and those imposing taxation or appropriating supply,[282] still vested in the Senate a power to *affirm or reject* them. Barton credits the existence of this power to the view that it was possessed by the House of Lords. During the third session of the Convention, he relates that opinion to the work of jurist Thomas Erskine May and explains it in greater detail.[283] A major issue for the 1897 Convention was to determine the extent of the Senate's coordinate powers regarding money bills. Under clause 53 of the initial 1897 draft Bill, the Senate would have the power to amend taxation bills, but might only suggest amendments to appropriation Bills.[284] Isaacs had reluctantly accepted equal representation in the Senate, but he opposed the Senate having coordinate powers with regard to money bills. While he demanded either one or the other, his underlying argument was against both. The legislative powers of the Senate in relation to money bills were an important consideration of the Convention.

The scheme of clause 53(1) was to vest equal legislative powers in the Senate and the House of Representatives for all proposed laws other than those appropriating supply, which the Senate could expressly "affirm or reject," but could not amend. It could, however, amend laws imposing taxation. Clause 53(2) mandated that tax laws deal only with the imposition of tax, thus preventing tacking, and clause 53(5) permitted the Senate to return a proposed law that it could not amend to the House of Representatives with suggested amendments. Since the Senate under clause 53(1) might still amend taxation bills, it differed from the relevant clause in the Bill of 1891.[285] Barton explained that in the new Bill, the Senate would have a power to amend all taxation bills, but that it might only suggest alterations to appropriation Bills.

Reid sought to amend clause 53(1) to deny the Senate a power to amend both laws imposing taxation and laws appropriating supply.[286] Isaacs generally agreed with Reid's amendment because it reduced the Senate's powers.[287] He argued that unequal populations in the states should deny them equal power over money bills in the Senate, a problem that would not exist in a unitary Constitution: "In one country, with a *unitary Government*, there is no such serious difficulty if you have the Senate or the equivalent House elected upon as broad a basis as we are prepared to make it here."[288]

In a direct rebuttal of Isaacs's proposals, Barton reminded the delegates that they had been sent to promote federation, not retard it:

> The colony of every one of us has sent us here to perform a duty on its behalf, and that duty is to work out a practical scheme of Federation, and a scheme which can be accepted by every one of the colonies.[289]

In a statement that might have resonated in November 1975, he endorsed the sentiment of earlier speakers from the more populous colonies that the Senate should not have the power to destroy the financial policy of the government.[290] He confirmed that government responsibility was to the House of Representatives when he asked rhetorically: "where is the principle of responsibility,"[291] denying that a government could be responsible to both Houses: "Instead of Ministers being responsible to the people through the House of Representatives they are responsible, some may say, to the people through both Houses."[292] While it was the smaller states that wanted the power of amendment, he argued that all the colonies had accepted the 1891 compromise[293] and reminded the delegates that in 1891, there were those who "claimed entirely co-ordinate power of the Senate while the other side stipulated that the Senate should have practically none."[294] He described the compromise as a middle line, not to be departed from.[295] Despite opposing the clause, Isaacs voted with the majority in favor of Reid's amendment, thus denying the Senate the power to amend taxation laws.

The term "proposed laws" found in clauses 52 and 53(5) of the initial draft Bill was a reference to bills that were still to be dealt with by the second chamber. Barton explained that if a bill became law and contained anything other than the imposition of taxation, the High Court could decide whether "it will be unconstitutional and void."[296] The court could not, however, adjudicate regarding *proposed* laws:

> "Laws" means "enacted laws." "Proposed" laws are to originate in the House of Representatives. It is not intended . . . that the High Court of the Commonwealth should have under review such a question as whether a Bill originated in one House or another if passed into law. That is a question for the Houses to settle between themselves.[297]

Reid thought the issue should be up to the two Houses to determine, and intimated that he might move to insert the word "Proposed" before the word "Law" in clause 53(2), which required "Laws imposing taxation shall deal with the imposition of taxation only."[298] Barton sought to clarify the principles that were involved. The first principle was that questions of procedure were to be settled between the two Houses: "There never was a Constitution in the world which gave any judiciary the power to inquire into the manner in which the Houses settled their procedure in those matters."[299] The second principle applied where a law was passed properly but, on the face of it, "one House is deprived of its fundamental rights as a component part of the Constitution, that should be settled by the arbiter of the Constitution."[300] Reid withdrew his amendment.[301]

By the commencement of the third session, the Senate's express power to *affirm or reject* money bills in clause 55(1) had been deleted by the Drafting Committee without debate. The power remained, however, as an implication from subclause (5), which provided: "Except as provided in this section the Senate shall have equal power with the House of Representatives in respect of all proposed laws." Because the word "proposed" when it qualified the word "law" in the Constitution referred to a bill that had passed the House of Representatives only,[302] it denied a court the power of judicial review. Isaacs returned to the issue of a "proposed law" during the third session. The debate relating to the constitutional treatment of tax bills in clause 55 provided an opportunity toward the end of the third session for Isaacs to again attempt to reduce the power of the Senate. Isaacs objected to the High Court's judicial review power, which could determine a law imposing tax was unconstitutional even though passed by an agreement between both chambers. He challenged the idea of judicial review by suggesting that it was wrong that "a measure *within* the jurisdiction of the Parliament"[303] should afterward be challenged in the Supreme Court.[304]

Isaacs's proposal that the word "Bills" or the phrase "proposed laws" be used in clause 55 would prevent the High Court from reviewing the legislative conduct of two Houses regarding such laws. This weakened the Senate by abrogating the need for that House to comply with the Constitution, provided the Senate was agreeable.[305] Downer characterized Isaacs's proposal as a case of,

> Let the Houses of Parliament act capriciously and variously from day to day—allow this "tacking" to go on if the Houses choose to agree to it—let the Houses do one thing one day and another the next, and do not bother about altering the Constitution, but trust the Parliament.[306]

He argued that the Parliament was only to be trusted when it was within the Constitution. After asserting that Isaacs's proposal was intended to weaken the Senate—"The amendment the honourable member has moved is distinctly for the purpose of weakening the Senate"[307]—Downer concluded: "If you say 'Trust the Parliament,' no Constitution is required at all; it can simply be provided that a certain number of gentlemen shall be elected, and meet together, and, without limitation, do what they like."[308]

Barton explained that clause 55 related to the validity of a law, which would be clear on its face: "When it purports to impose taxation, it goes beyond that purpose, or whether the law deals with one subject of taxation only; you can see upon the face of the law whether an annual Appropriation Act deals with matters beyond the annual appropriation."[309]

Barton thought the matter was analogous to the legislative powers of the Commonwealth under then clause 52 and the powers reserved to the states:

> Take the case of a law passing beyond the powers given under clause 52, and which law does pass beyond those powers, and therefore, invades the domain of the states, which are protected under clauses 99 and 100. That is a matter which will be apparent on the face of the law in question, and therefore, there is material for the High Court to declare the law invalid.[310]

The provision against tacking he considered a protection of the public from one chamber obtaining the passage of a wrongful law. Isaacs's amendment was defeated. The consideration of clause 55 also provides an important insight into the Convention's understanding of responsible government and its source in the parliamentary conventions at Westminster.

As Chief Justice of Queensland, Sir Samuel Griffith did not attend the 1897 Convention, but his interest in cause of federation was evident in an opinion he authored,[311] which communicated his concern to the Convention that the Senate might interfere with a government's taxation laws by amending the assessment and collection provisions that were contained in a separate law.[312] Since laws imposing taxation could only deal with one subject, a second bill containing the machinery provisions would be needed to assess and collect the tax. NSW delegate Richard O'Connor reminded the Convention that with responsible government, the fixing of financial policy must be in the hands of the House of Representatives without the Senate "directly interfer[ing] with the financial policy of a Government."[313]

Barton had justified the denial to the Senate of a power to amend as being analogous with the convention at Westminster. In the process of explaining that convention, he tacitly demonstrated the danger of construing a Constitution without regard to the political scheme for which it was established. He cited the work of Thomas Erskine May,[314] who had traced the convention regarding money bills to the resolution of the House of Commons in 1678 during the reign of Charles II. That resolution read:

> That all aids and supplies, and aids to his Majesty in Parliament, are the sole gift of the Commons and all bills for the granting of any such aids and supplies ought to begin with the Commons; and that it is the undoubted and sole right of the Commons to direct, limit, and appoint in such bills the ends, purposes, considerations, conditions, limitations, and qualifications of such grants, which ought not to be changed or altered by the House of Lords.[315]

Following May, Barton concluded that, as a result of the 1678 resolution, "the Lords are excluded from the power of initiating and amending Bills dealing with expenditure and revenue."[316] He again cited from May. The House of Lords

> may not amend the provisions in Bills which they receive from the Commons dealing with the above mentioned subjects, so as to alter, whether by increase or reduction, the amount of a rate or charge, its duration, mode of assessment, levy, collection, appropriation, or management; or the persons who pay, receive, manage, or control it; or the limits within which it is leviable.[317]

With respect to the Senate, Barton, while admitting an imperfect analogy with the House of Lords, concluded,

> That the Senate shall not have the power to affect the amount and extent of the tax to be levied; that it shall have the power of suggestion; that it shall not have the power of amendment; and that it *shall have* the power of rejection, are principles which are laid down in the Constitution.[318]

However, Barton missed the preceding reference in May to an earlier (1671) resolution of the House of Commons, which acknowledged the Commons' right to give aid to the king but which specifically proscribed the Lords' right to amend the rate of tax. May had explained that the Commons had a right—then three centuries old—to tax members of the House of Lords as subjects of the Crown, and that in consequence of that right: "That in all aids given to the king by the Commons, the rate of tax ought not to be altered by the Lords."[319] Since aids to the Crown had to be paid for, the Lords could not alter the rate of tax and hence alter supply. It defies reason to assume that this interdiction against the Lords left it free to reject tax laws outright. If the power of rejection did exist, it would have been just as effective as the power of amendment, for the Lords could threaten rejection in order to secure an amendment by the Commons. Since the Lords were themselves subject to taxation,[320] a power of rejection would probably have been well used to secure their self-interest. May, however, asserted as a matter of construction of the 1678 resolution that "the functions of the House of Lords in the grant or imposition of supply and taxation are reduced to a simple assent or negative."[321]

When viewed in the context of the 1671 resolution, however, the 1678 resolution promotes a different result, one that the House of Lords honored until 1909.[322] May interpreted the 1678 resolution as if the second clause commencing "and that it is the undoubted right" was a limitation on the wider purpose of the first clause. Such an interpretation, however, is a misreading. In light of the political circumstances under which the resolution of 1671 was passed—that is, the necessity to pay supplies as demanded by an absolute monarch—the second clause can only be an addition of powers to the first clause. Understood in that way, the resolution of 1678 literally confers the sole power in relation to supply upon the Commons. This is the only meaning possible for the unique phrase, "All aids and supplies . . . are the sole gift of the Commons"; it implicitly deprives the Lords of a power regarding the granting of supplies to the Crown. The resolution of 1671 deprives the Lords of any power in relation to the imposition of Ways and Means—that is, of "the rate or tax"—to pay for the supplies. That this is the correct understanding of the Commons' resolutions is confirmed by the House of Lords. The Lords were entitled to suggest amendments, but took no action when those suggestions were disregarded.

Barton accepted May's statement that the Westminster convention had left the Lords with the power to assent or negate supply and tax bills, but then inquired "how far the power of dissent may be exercised without invading the privileges of the Commons."[323] In 1860, the Lords rejected the Paper Duties Repeal Bill; the Commons, by resolution, affirmed its right of granting aids and supplies to the Crown but appeared to accept the Lords' right to affirm or reject tax bills. In a passage cited by Barton, May attributes the Commons' resolution to its maintenance of its privileges

> to secure to the Commons their rightful control over Taxation and Supply, this House has it in its own hands the power so to impose and remit taxes, and to frame Bills of Supply, that the right of the Commons as to the matter, manner, measure, and time may be maintained inviolate.[324]

Barton relies on May to advise the Convention delegates of the solution adopted by the Commons; it included the duties repeal in the one bill together with a number of other tax measures to pay "for the service of the year; and this Bill the Lords were *constrained* to accept."[325] Neither Barton nor May explain why the Lords were "constrained"—that is, forced—to pass that Bill if they held the power of rejection that May asserted. Barton took care to say that the Senate under the Commonwealth Constitution would not be in the same position as the House of Lords:

> I wish to guard myself from being supposed that I place the Senate in the position of the House of Lords. I only wish to refer to the matter to this extent: That there is a point at which there might be a denial of responsible government, and I do not wish the powers of the Senate to extend to any point at which responsible government might be frustrated, or to take it up to that point.[326]

Barton thus explicitly states that the powers of the Senate as he has drawn them are not such as to defeat responsible government. He said of May's explanation of the relative powers of the Commons and the Lords that May distinguishes between the Commons' privileges and the Lords' legal rights, that it is inferred "that there may be an encroachment upon privileges, which is, nevertheless, the assertion of a legal right."[327] May, therefore, is implying that a Commons privilege would be defeated by the Lords' legal right. But this is to assume, against the immediate sense of the two seventeenth-century resolutions, that the Lords had a legal power to reject supply, even though by convention it had not exercised that power for more than 200 years. Further, May's argument characterized the Lords' power as a legal power, even though all the Lords' powers only existed by convention, by agreement between an absolute monarch and his peers; but suggested that the power exercised in the Commons' resolutions was not legal right but a privilege, although it too arose from the same conventional source. May's argument points to a legal power arising from the actions of a conventional House of Lords, which it denies to an equally conventional Commons. It might be answered that the House of Lords, as a part of the British Constitution, enjoyed legislative powers. It did; however, those powers were subject to the changing conventions that reflected the changing political scheme of the British Constitution during the nineteenth century.

The Commons' privilege as against that of the House of Lords is an alternative name for a constitutional convention. The assertion that the Lords could exercise a legal right that they had abandoned to a convention is to deny that conventions have the force of constitutional law.[328] Responsible government, however, is the product of conventions. Until the *Parliament Act 1911* (UK), the legislative powers exercised by the Lords and Commons were the product of Parliamentary conventions. May's (and Barton's) analysis of the legality of their actions relies on the opinions of Earl Grey and Viscount Eversley[329] that the Lords' legislative power in 1860 included a power to reject money bills it could not amend. That view ignored the conventional nature of the powers and the rebuke by the Commons of the Lords' breach of the convention to which it had acquiesced. The scheme of the British Constitution underwent major changes during the nineteenth century, largely due to electoral reform.[330]

If the Bill of Rights of 1688[331] can be said to have taken away the monarch's absolute power and made the monarch subject to the Parliament, the two *Electoral Reform Acts* of the nineteenth century completed a devolution of executive power from a Privy Council appointed from the House of Lords and responsible to the monarch, to a cabinet responsible to the people's representatives in the House of Commons. With those legislative measures, the conventional nature of a government responsible to the Crown was replaced by one responsible to an elected chamber and it retained control of the finances necessary for effective responsible government that it had acquired by convention. It must be borne in mind that the power of the House of Lords was itself only ever a convention that was secured originally by an absolute monarch. Whatever its power regarding supply had once been, it had by long-established convention abandoned that power to the Commons.

May's analysis of the Westminster conventions shows a failure to comprehend how the changing political scheme of the British Constitution was reflected in the changing conventions. It led Barton to conclude that the convention required the Senate to have a power to reject supply; and his insertion of the final sentence of clause 53—"Except as provided in this section, the Senate shall have equal power with the House of Representatives in respect of all proposed laws"—was an attempt to place what May believed to be the Westminster convention in the Commonwealth Constitution. It was, however, an error.

Despite the existence of the last sentence of section 53 of the Constitution, "Except as provided in this section, the Senate shall have equal power with the House of Representatives in respect of all proposed laws," the practice of the Commonwealth Senate after federation was actually consistent with the Westminster parliamentary convention as I have explained above, but was formalized in Britain by the *Parliament Act 1911*; that is, the Commonwealth Senate, from 1901 until November 1975, never rejected (or refused to consider) a budget of a government with the confidence of the House of Representatives, even when that government did not have the support of a majority of senators.

CONCLUSION

Original Intention of the Founders

One lesson of the 1897 Constitutional Convention is that the construction methodology to be adopted by the High Court is not a matter of judicial discretion. One particular feature, common to both the Constitution and the process mandated by the FEAs, implies the presence of a political imperative in the Constitution that makes it obligatory for the High Court to seek the meaning originally intended by the Founders in the scheme or theory of the Constitution. The existence of that imperative derives from the adoption by the Founders and the colonial parliaments of a fundamental principle of the United States' founding documents. That principle was explicated by Chief Justice Marshall in the seminal case of *Marbury v Madison*, where he said: "That *the people* have an original right to establish for their future government such principles as, in their opinion, shall most conduce to their own happiness is the basis on which the whole American fabric has been erected."[332]

This principle, whereby the people choose the scheme of their future government, is a necessary implication from the assumption of a natural equality among humans. The notion of the natural equality has been the subject of a number of explanations. Jaffa offers two explanations. His first relies on the words of Colonel Rumbold, which were delivered from the scaffold in 1685: "I am sure there was no Man born marked of God above another; for none comes into the World with a Saddle on his Back, neither any Booted and Spurr'd to ride him."[333] His second explanation exploits the perception that the natural inequality between man and the horse makes man the natural ruler of horses. However, while equality does not mean that all men are equal in intelligence, strength, beauty, or in moral or intellectual capacity: "It does mean that there is no natural difference between man and man, such as there is between man and every other species of animal, that makes one man *by nature* the ruler of another man."[334]

From that equality, it is an inescapable conclusion that a government and the Constitution that regulates its powers derive their authority to do so from the people's consent.[335] The political principle of consent found its most eloquent expression in the Declaration of Independence of the United States: "Governments are instituted among Men, deriving their just powers from the *consent of the governed.*"[336] That statement espouses the very principle from which the sovereignty of an equal people—that is, democracy—arises. As Story explained: "It was an act of original, inherent sovereignty by the people themselves, resulting from their right to change the form of government, and to institute a new government, whenever necessary for their safety and happiness."[337]

Story's single sentence expresses exactly the steps taken by the peoples of the Australian colonies toward federation. The exercise of the people's sovereignty was provided for in the FEAs enacted by the several colonies. The similarly worded provisions of those Acts required that the ten delegates from each colony to the Constitutional Convention be elected by the voters of the participating colonies. Other provisions of the FEAs provided that the Commonwealth Constitution, when drafted and approved by the Convention, be submitted to the peoples of the various colonies at referenda for their ratification. The relevant provision of the *Enabling Act* of each colony (NSW Act, s. 32) stated:

> 32. So soon as practicable after the close of the proceedings of the Convention the question of the acceptance or rejection of the Constitution shall be referred and submitted to the vote of all persons in New South Wales qualified and entitled to vote for the election of Members of the Legislative Assembly. The voting shall be taken throughout [the colony] as one electoral district.[338]

The presence of an equivalent section 32 in each of the colonial FEAs reflects the equality of the electors and implies that their ratification of the

Constitution was democratic and made on behalf of all the people of their colony. The referenda conducted by four of the colonies were not successful due to the failure in New South Wales of the yes vote to exceed the 80,000 that an amending statute[339] required. The Queensland Parliament enacted the *Australasian Federation Enabling Act (Qld)* in 1899 and participated in the referendum held that year when four of the other five colonies held their second referendum—Western Australia holding its in 1900. The people of each of the six colonies consented to the Commonwealth Constitution as original states. The fact that the Constitution, thus framed, was ratified signals both the people's consent and a sovereign act of the Australian people.[340]

That action in combination with the election of delegates to the Convention was something other than a precondition to the submission of the Bill to the Westminster Parliament for enactment. It was "an act of original, inherent sovereignty by the people,"[341] who had exercised their right to change the form of government, to institute a new form of government to which they consented. The sovereignty of the Australian people is expressed in the Preamble to the Constitution and was alluded to by the early court when Griffith for the majority asked rhetorically, "What did the 'people' agree to?"[342]

If it now seems merely axiomatic that democratic governments must regularly obtain the consent of the electorate if they are to continue to govern, it must be remembered that the United States of the eighteenth century was an experiment with an extended democratic republic[343] dedicated to the proposition that *all men are created equal.*[344] Many thought it would fail.[345] It has been said that "the United States of America may be said to be the only country in the world which was founded in explicit opposition to Machiavellian principles."[346]

The Commonwealth of Australia had its origins in the actions of six self-governing colonies, five of which began a process by which the colonies would unite and the powers of government would be shared in a federal system that reflected both the United States and the parliamentary conventions at Westminster. The founding principle was the natural equality of all and from that an appeal to the consent of the people of those colonies to so unite.

Harry Jaffa relates that when the two Founders, Thomas Jefferson and James Madison, were asked by the University of Virginia in 1825 what books and documents ought to be recommended as authoritative principles for the Faculty of Law, they responded that the best guide was the "Declaration of Independence as the fundamental act of union of the United States."[347] After remarking that Aristotle equated the intention of the legislator with the law, Jaffa relates that Madison thought the meaning of the Constitution to be:

> in the propriety of reasoning to the sense in which the Constitution was accepted and ratified by the nation. In that sense alone it is the legitimate

> Constitution. . . . If the meaning of the text be sought in the changeable meanings of the words composing it, it is evident that the shape and attributes of the government most partake of the change to which the words and phrases of all living languages are constantly subject. What a metamorphosis would be produced in a code of laws if all its ancient phraseology were to be taken in a modern sense![348]

The changeableness of meaning to which Madison refers is not only accelerated but facilitated by the literalism associated with legal positivism outlined in chapter 1. Following Jaffa, "the sense in which the Constitution was accepted and ratified by the nation" can have no other meaning but that explicated by the Founders of a Constitution. The principle that justifies the US Constitution is to be found in the natural equality of all men. The significance of consent as the founding principle of the Commonwealth Constitution crystallizes when it is noted that, in contrast, neither the Canadian nor New Zealand Constitutions of the nineteenth century—both pieces of Imperial legislation—were the product of their people's consent. The *New Zealand Constitution Act 1852* (UK) was enacted by the Imperial Parliament[349] and proclaimed by Sir George Grey, secretary of state for the Colonies. It was amended by the passing of the *New Zealand Constitution Amendment Act 1857* (UK) which granted limited powers of amendment to the local legislature.[350] No record could be found that the Constitution was submitted to the people of New Zealand for ratification. Similarly, the *British North America Act 1867* (BNA) was drafted in Whitehall to effect a union of four Atlantic provinces "into one Dominion, 'with a constitution similar in principle to that of the United Kingdom.'"[351] This was the request contained in resolutions carried at a conference of provincial delegates in Quebec in 1865.[352] Significantly, the BNA contains no provision whereby either the Canadian people or even the Canadian Parliament could amend it. It could only be amended by the Imperial Parliament.

The principle of consent of the governed that is explicit in the Constitution at section 128, and in the steps by which the delegates were called to the Convention and the ratification of the final draft, is explicit evidence of a political imperative in the Constitution: that it is the meaning to which the people consented, the meaning propounded by its representatives, the Founders in Convention, for which the High Court must seek in any construction. For the Commonwealth Constitution, the only meaning to which the people have consented is the meaning their Founders placed before them in the referenda of 1899.[353] The jurisprudence of original intention of the Founders is therefore the only methodology of construction that can be said to be implicitly mandated by both the form and content of the Commonwealth Constitution, and therefore should be adopted for the High Court.

Federal Structure

The vast majority of the Convention voted for a federal scheme. That scheme incorporated federal elements that were derived from the US Constitution and included the following: a bicameral parliament consisting of a House of Representatives to represent the whole people of the Commonwealth proportionate to the numerical strength of each state and a Senate where the states would be equally represented. The Senate shared equal coordinate legislative powers with the House, except for the powers regarding money bills.

The Constitution withdraws specific powers from the states and vests them exclusively in the Commonwealth; however, it vests limited and enumerated powers in the House that it shares concurrently with the Senate. Powers not withdrawn from the states or vested exclusively in the House are reserved to the states. Where there is a conflict between a concurrent state law and a valid Commonwealth law, the state law, to the extent of the conflict, is invalid. The Constitutions of the states continued after federation, subject to the Constitution.

Isaacs rejected the federal scheme and expressly preferred a unitary Constitution. His arguments to the Convention included attacks on the equality of representation of the states in the Senate and a rejection of the Senate's coordinate powers. He argued for exclusive legislative powers to be divided between the Commonwealth and the states similar to the division in the Canadian Constitution, thus obviating the need for the Senate to have any powers or any influence on a government formed in the House. He argued against the Senate's coordinate powers regarding money bills, and the reservation of powers to the states, and for the inclusion of a clause in the draft Bill that would resolve legislative deadlocks between the two Houses. He argued for a direct appeal to the people by referendum as a means of constitutional amendment if a Senate rejected a bill for such an amendment.

Responsible Government

The decision of the Convention that the Constitution would exercise executive power under a system of responsible government was made at an early stage and appeared in the April 1897 draft Bill. In order to give effect to that principle, the Constitution contained the following four elements.

Section 61 of the Constitution vested executive power of the Commonwealth in the queen, in trust for the people, to be exercised by the Governor-General. As no power was vested in the Governor-General, antecedent ministerial advice was necessary to effectuate the power. The significance of this wording was that it quarantined the Commonwealth's executive powers and executive government from any powers that the monarch might have chosen under section 2 of the Constitution to vest in the Governor-General.

Section 62 of the Constitution established a Federal Executive Council consisting of ministers of state to advise the Governor-General. This replicated the corresponding convention at Westminster, where it operated as part of the unwritten British Constitution. As I have shown, Barton explained to the delegates—an explanation from which there was no dissent—that the Governor-General possessed no personal prerogative powers and that they only ever acted on ministerial advice. The wording used in different provisions of the Constitution in which the Governor-General or the Governor-General in Council was said to act reflected the law at that time that a power was either subject to legislation or was prerogative in nature. In all cases, the Governor-General acts on the advice of ministers.

The Founders understood responsible government under the Westminster convention to mean a government that was responsible to the House of Commons as representatives of the people. That was the principle already practiced in the colonial Parliaments and the one approved by the Founders. Barton had said and the Convention subsequently approved: "I take it under the system of responsible government there is one power, and one only, that places it in the control of the representatives to demand the expulsion of the Government."[354] That view was echoed a number of times during the Convention, together with the requirement that the Governor-General only act on the advice of ministers.

While the Constitution vested an equal power in the Senate to reject appropriations for annual supply, the moderating factor on its exercise lies in the fact that senators were intended to represent the interests of their states, not those of a partisan political party, as occurred soon after federation in 1901. Senators' interests were never likely to coalesce across state lines to the point of threatening the government's supply. The power to propose amendments suggested that negotiations between the two Houses would remedy items in the government's money bills that adversely affected particular state interests.

When viewed in the jurisprudential light of original intent, Isaacs's reflection on the US Constitution is prescient of the danger to the Commonwealth Constitution of a judiciary that abandons the Founders' original intent:

> as in America so it will be here, that the makers of the Constitution were not merely the Conventions who sat and the states who ratified their conclusions, but the *Judges of the Supreme Court,* Marshall, Jay, Story, and all the rest of the renowned Judges who have pronounced on the Constitution, have had just as much to do in shaping it as the men who sat in the original Conventions.[355]

Chapter 3 will show that the early court of Griffith CJ, Barton, and O'Connor JJ enunciated a federal scheme consistent with that framed by the Founders and ratified at the subsequent referenda. It will also show that, after federation, Isaac Isaacs, both when acting as legal counsel and after his appointment to the High Court in 1906, interpreted the Constitution literally in order to advance arguments that denied a federal scheme and, with it, the separate sovereignties of the Commonwealth and states in order to promote a unitary scheme similar to that for which he argued during the Convention.

NOTES

1. The draft Constitution is referred to as a Bill due to its planned enactment by the Imperial Parliament.
2. The term "money Bill" as used in this essay refers generally to those Bills that either appropriate revenue or impose taxation.
3. John Quick and Robert Garran, *The Annotated Constitution of the Australian Commonwealth* (Angus & Robertson, 1901) p. 110.
4. Ibid., 111.
5. Ibid., 118.
6. Ibid., 113.
7. Ibid., 120
8. Ibid., 121.
9. Ibid., 125.
10. Ibid., 129.
11. Ibid., 130. Andrew Inglis Clark was knowledgeable about the US Constitution and had prepared a draft of a whole federal Constitution in preparation for the 1891 Convention in Sydney.
12. Ibid., 131.
13. Ibid., 143.
14. Ibid., 144.
15. Ibid., 147–8.
16. Ibid., 150.
17. Ibid., 152.
18. Ibid.
19. Ibid.
20. Ibid., 153.
21. Ibid., 153.
22. Ibid., 159.
23. Ibid., 160–1. The colonial legislation comprised the *Australasian Federation Enabling Act 1895* (NSW) No. XXIV; *Australasian Federation Enabling Act 1896* (Vic) No. 1143; *Australasian Federation Enabling Act 1895* (SA) No. 632; *Australasian Federation Enabling Act 1896* (Tas) No. 57; and *Australasian Federation Enabling Act 1896* (WA) No. XXXII.

24. As each of the colonial Acts bore the same name, they will be referred to hereinafter as FEA followed by the relevant colony contained in parenthesis; *Australasian Federation Enabling Act 1895* (SA) would be FEA1895 (SA).

25. s. 7.

26. s. 11.

27. s. 13.

28. s. 26.

29. s. 32.

30. s. 35

31. s. 36.

32. The equivalent provisions in the other colonial FEAs were FEA 1896 (Vic), ss. 7, 11, 33, 36 (needing 50,000 votes), 37 respectively; FEA(SA) ss. 18, 10, 33, 36 (only a simple majority), 37 respectively; FEA 1896 (TAS) ss. 19, 12 & 32, 36 (needing 6,000 affirmative votes), 37 respectively. Pursuant to the FEA 1896 (WA) ss. 17, 28 (needing 6,000 affirmative votes). Section 17 of FEA1896 (WA) provided for the Western Australian delegates to be elected by members of both Houses of that Parliament sitting and voting together and for the ratification of the draft Bill by the electors after it was approved by the Parliament.

33. See, for example, Anne Twomey, "Independence," in Cheryl Saunders and Adrienne Stone (eds), *The Oxford Handbook of the Australian Constitution* (Oxford University Press, 2018) p. 105; James Allen and N. Aroney, "An Uncommon Court: How the High Court of Australia Has Undermined Australian Federalism" (2008) 30(2) *Sydney Law Review* 245, 262; J.E. Richardson, "The Legislative Power of the Senate in Respect of Money Bills," 1976 50 *Australian Law Journal* 273.

34. Isaacs J makes this point explicitly in *Amalgamated Society of Engineers v Adelaide Steamship Co Ltd* (Engineers' case) (1920) 28 at 142. However, it will be argued that according to the accepted definition of sovereignty, in respect of the Commonwealth Constitution, the British Parliament was displaced by the Australian people.

35. Official Record of the Debates of the Australasian Federal Convention, Adelaide, 115 (Bernhard Wise).

36. Ibid.

37. Ibid.

38. John Quick and Robert Garran, *The Annotated Constitution of the Australian Commonwealth* (Angus & Robertson, 1901) p. 243 suggest that this point was considered distinctly possible by the British government during the parliamentary debate of the Bill in 1900. The assertion of Imperial sovereignty over the Constitution as Imperial legislation, however, is inconsistent with the power of amendment in section 128 being reserved to the Australian people but not the Imperial Parliament.

39. Official Record of the Debates of the Australasian Federal Convention, Adelaide, 1.

40. Official Record of the Debates of the Australasian Federal Convention, Adelaide, 432 (Edmund Barton). Almost immediately on the introduction of the draft Bill, the States Assembly was renamed the "Senate."

41. Official Record of the Debates of the Australasian Federal Convention, Adelaide, 1218.

42. Official Record of the Debates of the Australasian Federal Convention, Sydney, 1 and 1109.

43. Official Record of the Debates of the Australasian Federal Convention, Melbourne, 1 and 2521.

44. FEA 1895 (NSW) s. 7; FEA 1896 (Vic) s. 7; FEA 1895 (SA) Preamble; FEA 1896 (Tas) Preamble; FEA 1896 (WA) Preamble.

45. Official Record of the Debates of the Australasian Federal Convention, Adelaide, 11 (Edmund Barton).

46. Official Record of the Debates of the Australasian Federal Convention, Adelaide, 10 (Edmund Barton).

47. Official Record of the Debates of the Australasian Federal Convention, Adelaide, 17 (Edmund Barton).

48. Official Record of the Debates of the Australasian Federal Convention, Adelaide, 21 (Edmund Barton).

49. Official Record of the Debates of the Australasian Federal Convention, Adelaide, 21 (Edmund Barton).

50. Official Record of the Debates of the Australasian Federal Convention, Adelaide, 20 (Edmund Barton).

51. Official Record of the Debates of the Australasian Federal Convention, Adelaide, 21 (Edmund Barton).

52. Official Record of the Debates of the Australasian Federal Convention, Adelaide, 20 (Edmund Barton), emphasis added.

53. Official Record of the Debates of the Australasian Federal Convention, Adelaide, 21 (Edmund Barton).

54. Official Record of the Debates of the Australasian Federal Convention, Adelaide, 21 (Edmund Barton).

55. Official Record of the Debates of the Australasian Federal Convention, Adelaide, 20 (Edmund Barton).

56. Official Record of the Debates of the Australasian Federal Convention, Adelaide, 20 (Edmund Barton).

57. Official Record of the Debates of the Australasian Federal Convention, Adelaide, 21 (Edmund Barton).

58. Official Record of the Debates of the Australasian Federal Convention, Adelaide, 21 (Edmund Barton).

59. Official Record of the Debates of the Australasian Federal Convention, Adelaide, 22 (Edmund Barton). Barton preferred that the name of the House be "States Assembly," which gives an indication that the chamber's legislative powers would advance the states' interests.

60. Official Record of the Debates of the Australasian Federal Convention, Adelaide, 21–2 (Edmund Barton).

61. Official Record of the Debates of the Australasian Federal Convention, Adelaide, 22 (Edmund Barton). The US Constitution, Article 1, Section 7, vests a similar power in the House of Representatives.

62. Official Record of the Debates of the Australasian Federal Convention, Adelaide, 23 (Edmund Barton).

63. Official Record of the Debates of the Australasian Federal Convention, Adelaide, 23 (Edmund Barton), emphasis added.

64. Official Record of the Debates of the Australasian Federal Convention, Adelaide, 24 (Edmund Barton).

65. Official Record of the Debates of the Australasian Federal Convention, Adelaide, 170 (Isaac Isaacs).

66. Official Record of the Debates of the Australasian Federal Convention, Adelaide, 173 (Isaac Isaacs).

67. As Isaacs never specifically articulates the best regime, it is almost impossible to determine what would constitute a principle for deciding such issues. The inference from his contribution to the debates is that he thought a pure democracy was the only acceptable option.

68. Alexander Hamilton, *Federalist No. 62, The Federalist Papers*, ed. Clinton Rossiter (New American Library, 1961) p. 376, describes equal representation as a compromise "between the opposite pretensions of the large and small States." Referring to independent and sovereign states, unequal in size bound together by a simple league, Hamilton concludes that "it does not appear to be without some reason that in a compound republic, partaking both of the national and federal character, the government ought to be founded on a mixture of the principles of proportional and equal representation."

69. Joseph Story, *Commentaries on the Constitution of the United States Vol. 3* (Hilliard Gray & Co, 1833) p. 177 (695): "no person . . . can doubt, that the compromise actually made was well founded in policy, and may now be fully vindicated upon the highest principles of political wisdom." Isaacs was aware of Story's analysis. He refers to it *Commonwealth v New South Wales* (1923) 32 CLR 200 at 213.

70. Official Record of the Debates of the Australasian Federal Convention, Adelaide (1897), 174 (Isaac Isaacs). In the third session, Isaacs alludes to the diverse interests as being the proportional contribution of revenue to the Commonwealth.

71. Official Record of the Debates of the Australasian Federal Convention, Adelaide (1897), 174 (Isaac Isaacs). In the search for divergent state interests, one need go no further than the different views about slavery among US states.

72. Equal representation would be meaningless if the Senate had no legislative power.

73. Official Record of the Debates of the Australasian Federal Convention, Adelaide, 174 (Isaac Isaacs).

74. Official Record of the Debates of the Australasian Federal Convention, Adelaide, 175 (Isaac Isaacs).

75. Ibid. Isaacs's characterization of the Canadian and US Constitutions as being different degrees of centralization abolished any intrinsic differences between the two Constitutions with a quantitative distinction. If there are only quantitative differences of degree and not differences in kind between different Constitutions, every Constitution is more or less a federation. Isaacs's wish for federation after the US style is disingenuous. It was never his preference.

76. It is difficult to reconcile Isaacs's objections to compromises when he was prepared to accept equal representation, against his own principles, because he thought it was inevitable. It was inevitable that a Constitution decided at a Convention would involve compromises; but Isaacs's error lies in his belief that the resolution of two apparently conflicting positions was inferior to both. This suggests that his political "principle" was simply majority rule, but on a national scale.

77. Official Record of the Debates of the Australasian Federal Convention, Adelaide (1897), 173 (Isaac Isaacs), emphasis added. But see *Huddart Parker & Co Pty Ltd v Moorehead* (1909) 8 CLR 330, 388, where Isaacs used the term chronologically, in the sense of *first* intention, while denying the existence of such a purpose or "intention," describing it as subjective and, in *Baxter v Commissioners of Taxation (NSW)* (1907) 4 CLR 1088, 1170 as the "*supposed* object."

78. Official Record of the Debates of the Australasian Federal Convention, Adelaide (1897), 178–9 (Isaac Isaacs), emphasis added.

79. This would be consistent with the Benthamite notion of utilitarianism, where justice was the greatest good of the greatest number, implying a simple majority rule.

80. Official Record of the Debates of the Australasian Federal Convention, Adelaide (1897), 389 (Isaac Isaacs).

81. Official Record of the Debates of the Australasian Federal Convention, Adelaide (1897), 390 (Edmund Barton).

82. Official Record of the Debates of the Australasian Federal Convention, Adelaide (1897), 390–1 (Edmund Barton).

83. Thomas Jefferson, *Notes on the State of Virginia* (Lilly and Wair, 1832) p. 234.

84. A. Hamilton, J. Madison & J. Jay, *The Federalist Papers*, ed. Clinton Rossiter (New American Library, 1961) pp. 314–5.

85. Ibid., 315–6.

86. Official Record of the Debates of the Australasian Federal Convention, Adelaide (1897), 376 (Edmund Barton).

87. Ibid.

88. Official Record of the Debates of the Australasian Federal Convention, Adelaide (1897), 377 (Edmund Barton).

89. Ibid.

90. Official Record of the Debates of the Australasian Federal Convention, Adelaide (1897), 378 (Edmund Barton). Because Barton envisaged the second chamber as a permanent defender of states' interests from encroachment by federal powers, he wanted it named the States Assembly, to remind people of its purpose. As the Convention voted during the first session (p. 459) to call the chamber the Senate, it will be convenient from this point on to refer to the chamber as "the Senate" other than in citations.

91. Official Record of the Debates of the Australasian Federal Convention, Adelaide (1897), 378 (Edmund Barton).

92. Official Record of the Debates of the Australasian Federal Convention, Adelaide (1897), 379 (Edmund Barton).

93. Official Record of the Debates of the Australasian Federal Convention, Adelaide (1897), 380 (Edmund Barton).

94. Official Record of the Debates of the Australasian Federal Convention, Adelaide (1897), 382 (Edmund Barton).

95. Ibid.

96. Ibid. This was occasionally referred to as the 1891 compromise.

97. Official Record of the Debates of the Australasian Federal Convention, Adelaide (1897), 1152 (Edmund Barton).

98. Official Record of the Debates of the Australasian Federal Convention, Adelaide (1897), 383 (Edmund Barton).

99. Official Record of the Debates of the Australasian Federal Convention, Adelaide (1897), 386 (Edmund Barton).

100. Official Record of the Debates of the Australasian Federal Convention, Adelaide (1897), 432 (Edmund Barton).

101. Ibid.

102. Official Record of the Debates of the Australasian Federal Convention, Adelaide (1897), 432–3 (Edmund Barton).

103. Official Record of the Debates of the Australasian Federal Convention, Adelaide (1897), 435 (Edmund Barton).

104. The first draft Bill was tabled on April 12, 1897. At the conclusion of the debates during the first session, a second version of the draft Bill was printed, bearing the date April 23, 1897. While reference is made throughout this chapter to the numbered clauses in a draft Bill, it must be remembered that due to drafting requirements, as amendments and insertions were dealt with and clauses consolidated, added, or deleted, clause numbers changed; where possible, such changes are identified in the notes.

105. Draft of a Bill to Constitute the Commonwealth of Australia (12/4/97): cl. 9.

106. Draft of a Bill to Constitute the Commonwealth of Australia (12/4/97): cl. 67.

107. Draft of a Bill to Constitute the Commonwealth of Australia (12/4/97): cl. 99.

108. Official Record of the Debates of the Australasian Federal Convention, Adelaide (1897), 485 (George Turner).

109. Official Record of the Debates of the Australasian Federal Convention, Adelaide (1897), 486 (George Turner).

110. Official Record of the Debates of the Australasian Federal Convention, Adelaide (1897), 660 (Isaac Isaacs).

111. Official Record of the Debates of the Australasian Federal Convention, Adelaide (1897), 661 (Isaac Isaacs).

112. Ibid., emphasis added.

113. Ibid.

114. Ibid.

115. If it appears superfluous to have two chambers elected in proportion to population, the reason is because the second chamber becomes unnecessary. Isaacs attempts to cure this defect by a deadlock clause that will allow the government to appeal to the people.

116. Glynn's reference to the "seventy-second" essay should have been to No. 62. Alexander Hamilton, *The Federalist Papers, No. 62*, ed. Clinton Rossiter (New American Library, 1961) p. 376.

117. Alexander Hamilton, *The Federalist Papers, No. 62*, ed. Clinton Rossiter (New York: New American Library, 1961) p. 377.

118. Official Record of the Debates of the Australasian Federal Convention, Adelaide (1897), 641.

119. Official Record of the Debates of the Australasian Federal Convention, Adelaide (1897), 683: clause 23.

120. Official Record of the Debates of the Australasian Federal Convention, Adelaide (1897), 695–9 (Isaac Isaacs).

121. Official Record of the Debates of the Australasian Federal Convention, Adelaide (1897), 696 (Isaac Isaacs). "[Barton] seems to think it is essential that there should be this proportion between the Senate and the House of Representatives. But it does not exist in America, and if it does not exist there, on what principle can it be argued that it is essential?"

122. Official Record of the Debates of the Australasian Federal Convention, Adelaide (1897), 696–7 (Isaac Isaacs). The error in Isaacs's argument is in his implicit assumption that the federating states are not separately sovereign entities after federation; that is, he assumes the states and the federal scheme away.

123. Official Record of the Debates of the Australasian Federal Convention, Adelaide (1897), 696 (Isaac Isaacs).

124. Official Record of the Debates of the Australasian Federal Convention, Adelaide (1897), 703 (Edmund Barton).

125. Ibid.

126. Official Record of the Debates of the Australasian Federal Convention, Adelaide (1897), 704 (Edmund Barton). Barton implicitly recognizes and counters Isaacs's antifederal, pure democracy argument.

127. Official Record of the Debates of the Australasian Federal Convention, Adelaide (1897), 706 (Edmund Barton). Barton lists the argument as one of the three kinds of lies: "lies, adjective lies, and statistics" (at 705).

128. Official Record of the Debates of the Australasian Federal Convention, Sydney (1897), 256.

129. Official Record of the Debates of the Australasian Federal Convention, Sydney (1897), 258.

130. Official Record of the Debates of the Australasian Federal Convention, Sydney (1897), 260 (Henry Higgins).

131. Official Record of the Debates of the Australasian Federal Convention, Sydney (1897), 290 (Josiah Symon).

132. Ibid.

133. Ibid.

134. Official Record of the Debates of the Australasian Federal Convention, Sydney (1897), 305 (Isaac Isaacs). Isaacs is implying that an easier means of constitutional amendment would have outlawed slavery and prevented the Civil War. He ignores both the likelihood that the slave owner states would still have seceded

to defend their right in property (*Dred Scott* v *Sandford* 60 U.S. 393 (1857).) and the threat posed by President Abraham Lincoln with restoration of the Missouri Compromise. Harry V. Jaffa in *A New Birth of Freedom; Abraham Lincoln and the Coming of the Civil War* (Rowman & Littlefield, 2000) pp. 246–7 shows that the slave-state Democrats would have held a majority in the Senate had they not seceded from the Union and could block any legislation or constitutional amendment that Lincoln might have sought to introduce. That he undertook to do neither is indicative of how far-fetched Isaacs's theory was.

135. John W. Burgess, "Ideal of the American Commonwealth" (1895) 10 *Political Science Quarterly* 404, 410.

136. Official Record of the Debates of the Australasian Federal Convention, Sydney (1897), 308. Isaac Isaacs cites the *Political Science Quarterly Review*. The erosion of state sovereignty and states' reserved powers was effected by the constructions of its Constitution by the Supreme Court in the latter part of the nineteenth century. This was a generic source for one of the voices to which Isaacs referred above. Nicholas Aroney, "The Ghost in the Machine: Exorcising *Engineers*," Paper presented to Fourteenth Conference of the Samuel Griffith Society, Sydney, 14–16 June 2002, correctly identifies the role that Burgess played in Isaacs's definition of federalism "as essentially a unitary state" (p. 3).

137. Official Record of the Debates of the Australasian Federal Convention, Sydney (1897), 304 (Isaac Isaacs).

138. Official Record of the Debates of the Australasian Federal Convention, Sydney (1897), 304 (Isaac Isaacs).

139. *Dred Scott v Sandford* 60 U.S. 393, 426 (1857).

140. Harry V. Jaffa, *A New Birth of Freedom; Abraham Lincoln and the Coming of the Civil War* (Rowman & Littlefield, 2000) p. 175.

141. Official Record of the Debates of the Australasian Federal Convention, Sydney (1897), 304 (Isaac Isaacs): "I have supported equal representation, because I recognise, as a fact, that the smaller colonies so-called—the less populous colonies—will not come into a federation without it. I recognise that as a matter of fact; it is a political fact, and it is a fact that has the justification of expediency."

142. Official Record of the Debates of the Australasian Federal Convention, Sydney (1897), 420.

143. Official Record of the Debates of the Australasian Federal Convention, Adelaide (1897), 11 (Edmund Barton).

144. Official Record of the Debates of the Australasian Federal Convention Adelaide (1897), 377 (Edmund Barton).

145. Draft of a Bill to Constitute the Commonwealth of Australia, (12/4/97) cl. 97.

146. Geoffrey de Q Walker, "The Seven Pillars of Centralism: Engineers Case and Federalism" (2002) 76 *Australian Law Journal* 681.

147. *McCulloch v Maryland*, 17 U.S. (4 Wheat.) 316 (1819).

148. Joseph Story, *Commentaries on the Constitution of the United States Vol. 3* (Hilliard Gray & Co, 1833) p. 752 (1900). Story's reference to the sovereignty of the people has a particular relevance to the source of the Australian Constitution as a compact of the people of the several states.

149. Commonwealth of Australia Constitution, s. 51(i). Story's *Commentaries* appear to have been well known to the delegates, being cited on a number of occasions: Official Record of the Debates of the Australasian Federal Convention, Adelaide (1897), 171, 832 (Isaac Isaacs). Official Record of the Debates of the Australasian Federal Convention Sydney (1897), 294 (Josiah Symon); 306, 307 (Isaac Isaacs); 324, 325 (Bernhard Wise); 340 (Edmund Barton); 346 (Henry Higgins). Official Record of the Debates of the Australasian Federal Convention Melbourne (1898), 540 (Henry Higgins).

150. *D'Emden v Pedder* (1904) 1 CLR 91.

151. Ibid. at 105.

152. Alexander Hamilton, *Federalist No. 45, The Federalist Papers*, ed. Clinton Rossiter (New American Library, 1961) p. 290.

153. Ibid., p. 292.

154. Official Record of the Debates of the Australasian Federal Convention, Adelaide (1897), 22 (Edmund Barton).

155. Joseph Story, *Commentaries on the Constitution of the United States Vol. 1* (Hilliard Gray & Co, 1833) p. 410 (1900).

156. James Allan and Nicholas Aroney, "An Uncommon Court: How the High Court of Australia has Undermined Australian Federalism" (2008) 30(2) *Sydney Law Review* 245, 264–5.

157. Official Record of the Debates of the Australasian Federal Convention, Adelaide (1897), 21 (Edmund Barton).

158. Official Record of the Debates of the Australasian Federal Convention, Adelaide (1897), 1143 (Isaac Isaacs).

159. His disingenuousness was evident when he said of the United States as a federation on a decentralizing principle "the principle I hope we shall follow." Official Record of the Debates of the Australasian Federal Convention, Adelaide (1897), 175 (Isaac Isaacs).

160. Official Record of the Debates of the Australasian Federal Convention, Adelaide (1897), 543 (Isaac Isaacs).

161. Official Record of the Debates of the Australasian Federal Convention, Sydney (1897), 305 (Isaac Isaacs), emphasis added.

162. However, as his scheme of exclusive Commonwealth and state powers by definition includes taxation, Commonwealth taxation will of necessity tax only state assets, there being no federal assets other than state employees. This was the principle evident in Marshall CJ's statement that "the power to tax involves the power to destroy" *McCulloch v Maryland* 17 U.S. (4 Wheat) 316 at 431.

163. Official Record of the Debates of the Australasian Federal Convention, Sydney (1897), 312 (Isaac Isaacs).

164. Ibid. It is inconceivable that Dicey has missed the fact of the coordinate powers in the US Constitution.

165. Official Record of the Debates of the Australasian Federal Convention, Sydney (1897), 312 (Isaac Isaacs).

166. Official Record of the Debates of the Australasian Federal Convention, Sydney (1897), 312–3 (Isaac Isaacs). The passage from Dicey can be found in A.V.

Dicey, *Introduction to the Study of the Law of the Constitution*, 3rd ed. (Macmillan, 1889) p. 134.

167. A.V. Dicey, *Introduction to the Study of the Law of the Constitution*, 3rd ed. (Macmillan, 1889) pp.134–5, emphasis added.

168. Official Record of the Debates of the Australasian Federal Convention, Sydney (1897), 313 (Isaac Isaacs). The relationship between the two provisions is discussed at length in *Deakin v Webb* (1904) 1 CLR 585, 605.

169. A.V. Dicey, *Introduction to the Study of the Law of the Constitution*, 3rd ed. (Macmillan, 1889) p. 142 n. 1. The equivalent footnote in the 8th edition of Dicey's work (215), n 1 on p. 148, adds "The Constitution of the Australian Commonwealth follows in effect the example of the Constitution of the United States."

170. Official Record of the Debates of the Australasian Federal Convention, Sydney (1897), 300 (Josiah Symon), emphasis added.

171. Official Record of the Debates of the Australasian Federal Convention, Sydney (1897), 305 (Isaac Isaacs). By visible, I submit that he intended visible in the Constitution, as the reserve powers as a concept are invisible.

172. Official Record of the Debates of the Australasian Federal Convention, Sydney (1897), 305 (Isaac Isaacs).

173. Official Record of the Debates of the Australasian Federal Convention, Sydney (1897), 318 (Bernhard Wise). This difficulty was an implicit criticism of the unitary Canadian Constitution, which had been badly managed by the Privy Council.

174. This is consistent with his implicit argument for a unitary Constitution.

175. Official Record of the Debates of the Australasian Federal Convention, Adelaide (1897), 660–1 (Isaac Isaacs).

176. Official Record of the Debates of the Australasian Federal Convention, Adelaide (1897), 661 (Isaac Isaacs).

177. Official Record of the Debates of the Australasian Federal Convention, Adelaide (1897), 41 (George Turner).

178. Official Record of the Debates of the Australasian Federal Convention, Adelaide (1897), 54 (Richard O'Connor).

179. Official Record of the Debates of the Australasian Federal Convention, Adelaide (1897), 53 (Richard O'Connor).

180. Official Record of the Debates of the Australasian Federal Convention, Adelaide (1897), 455 (Edmund Barton).

181. Official Record of the Debates of the Australasian Federal Convention, Adelaide (1897), 580 (Edmund Barton).

182. Official Record of the Debates of the Australasian Federal Convention, Adelaide (1897), 41 (Sir George Turner).

183. Official Record of the Debates of the Australasian Federal Convention, Adelaide (1897), 656 (Joseph Carruthers).

184. Official Record of the Debates of the Australasian Federal Convention, Adelaide (1897), 661 (Isaac Isaacs).

185. Ibid.

186. Tacking was the practice of including expenditures which were not related to supply (and ostensibly able to be amended) in supply legislation that the Senate could

not amend. It was particularly problematic in the United States and could be used to confer benefits on political allies. If the legislation was rejected a deadlock resulted.

187. Official Record of the Debates of the Australasian Federal Convention, Adelaide (1897), 1152 (Edmund Barton).

188. John Quick and Robert Garran, *The Annotated Constitution of the Australian Commonwealth* (Angus & Robertson, 1901) p. 181. However, it appears to have gone unnoticed that a Senate might also create a deadlock for its own purpose by refusing to consider legislation.

189. Official Record of the Debates of the Australasian Federal Convention, Adelaide (1897), 1163 (Isaac Isaacs).

190. Ibid. This proposition is consistent with Isaacs's stated premise that only interests common to all are necessary in the federal Constitution. It permits him to characterize the federal structure as one of hostility, jealousy, and distrust.

191. Official Record of the Debates of the Australasian Federal Convention, Adelaide (1897), 1163 (Isaac Isaacs).

192. Official Record of the Debates of the Australasian Federal Convention, Adelaide (1897), 1169 (Isaac Isaacs). Given the proportion of population in the states of New South Wales and Victoria, a successful referendum would be carried by the addition of the smallest state. One aspect of Isaacs's proposal not debated was whether legislation could be approved by the people even though it was otherwise unconstitutional. According to the democratic assumptions underpinning the general thrust of Isaacs's views, any legislation approved by the people at a referendum would be constitutionally valid. In other words, once the referendum was accepted as the means of resolving disputes between the two Houses, the provisions in the Constitution relating to the passage of such legislation, including in the Senate, would be impotent.

193. Official Record of the Debates of the Australasian Federal Convention, Adelaide (1897), 1172 (Isaac Isaacs).

194. Official Record of the Debates of the Australasian Federal Convention, Sydney (1897), 541.

195. Official Record of the Debates of the Australasian Federal Convention, Sydney (1897), 565 (Simon Fraser). I submit that Fraser is actually challenging Isaacs's sincerity since no one had at that stage questioned it.

196. Official Record of the Debates of the Australasian Federal Convention, Sydney (1897), 566 (Simon Fraser).

197. Official Record of the Debates of the Australasian Federal Convention, Sydney (1897), 567 (Simon Fraser).

198. Official Record of the Debates of the Australasian Federal Convention, Sydney (1897), 588 (Alfred Deakin).

199. Official Record of the Debates of the Australasian Federal Convention, Sydney (1897), 596 (Josiah Symon).

200. Official Record of the Debates of the Australasian Federal Convention, Sydney (1897), 620 (Edmund Barton).

201. Barton did not anticipate the entrenchment of party politics in this country or, if he did, he still believed the Senate would represent state interests and not party interests.

202. Official Record of the Debates of the Australasian Federal Convention, Sydney (1897), 628 (Edmund Barton).

203. Official Record of the Debates of the Australasian Federal Convention, Sydney (1897), 660 (Isaac Isaacs).

204. Official Record of the Debates of the Australasian Federal Convention, Sydney (1897), 661 (Isaac Isaacs). A Constitution containing only exclusive matters would be unitary like the Canadian Constitution.

205. Official Record of the Debates of the Australasian Federal Convention, Sydney (1897), 663 (Isaac Isaacs), emphasis added. It cannot be a threat by the smaller states as the larger states would have nothing to fear from such a threat. Isaacs appears to have taken as a reference, an earlier comment by F. Holder: "Practically, the only thing which would justify the referendum would be a crisis threatening the existence of the commonwealth itself; when it might be the only alternative to a civil war." Official Record of the Debates of the Australasian Federal Convention, Sydney (1897), 563.

206. Official Record of the Debates of the Australasian Federal Convention, Sydney (1897), 709.

207. Official Record of the Debates of the Australasian Federal Convention, Sydney (1897), 863 (Joseph Carruthers).

208. Official Record of the Debates of the Australasian Federal Convention, Sydney (1897), 861 (Isaac Isaacs).

209. Official Record of the Debates of the Australasian Federal Convention, Sydney (1897), 907–8 (Edmund Barton).

210. Official Record of the Debates of the Australasian Federal Convention, Sydney (1897), 909 (Edmund Barton).

211. John Quick & Robert Garran, *The Annotated Constitution of the Australian Commonwealth*. (Angus & Robertson, 1901) p. 193.

212. Draft of a Bill To Constitute the Commonwealth of Australia, (12/4/97): cl. 121.

213. Official Record of the Debates of the Australasian Federal Convention, Adelaide (1897), 1021 (Isaac Isaacs). An "absolute majority" was defined as a majority of all the members of a House, whether they all voted or not.

214. Official Record of the Debates of the Australasian Federal Convention, Adelaide (1897), 1021 (Isaac Isaacs).

215. This is the only reference to Moncure Conway and his writings in the Convention records. A short autobiography of Moncure Daniel Conway exists in the Dickinson College Archives, Virginia (Dickinson College Archive (2005) *Moncure Daniel Conway (1832–1907)*), where Moncure lectured. It describes him as an American lawyer, a Methodist/Unitarian, and a leading abolitionist before and during the Civil War who was highly critical of the US Constitution. It is highly probable that the origin of most of Isaacs's views on the Senate and federalism, on equal representation of the states in the Senate, of the abolition of the states (p. 18), of states' rights (p. 9) on a unitary Constitution with a single chamber (p. 18), and on the Senate as a cause of the Civil War (p. 7) is to be found in the writings of Moncure Conway, especially his work, *Republican Superstitions as Illustrated in the Political History of*

America (1872), which holds all those views. Conway argued, like Isaacs, that equal representation of the states in the Senate was not one of principle but a compromise based upon the State's "relative power in the new government" (p. 8) and he implies (p. 9) that the doctrine of the reserved powers by which powers were reserved to the states was not part of the Constitution which is flatly contradicted by Marshall CJ in *McCulloch v Maryland* and James Madison, *Federalist No. 45, The Federalist Papers*, ed. Clinton Rossiter (New American Library, 1961) p. 288.

216. Official Record of the Debates of the Australasian Federal Convention, Adelaide (1897), 1021 (Isaac Isaacs). The analogy to a dead hand is misleading because a wisely considered, written Constitution contains permanent principles that survive the death of the authors. Construction of such a Constitution therefore requires knowledge of the sources of learning from which those principles were drawn and, in the case of the Commonwealth Constitution, that must necessitate an investigation of the US Constitution and the knowledge of its Founders—something that Edmund Barton had obviously done. The US Chief justice John Marshall, in his dissenting opinion in *Ogden v Saunders* (1827) 25 US 354, endorsed a construction of the Constitution that sought the original intention of the Nation's Founders.

217. Official Record of the Debates of the Australasian Federal Convention, Adelaide (1897), 1023.

218. Official Record of the Debates of the Australasian Federal Convention, Adelaide (1897), 1209.

219. An absolute majority is a majority of all members of a chamber entitled to vote. A simple majority is a majority of those who vote.

220. Official Record of the Debates of the Australasian Federal Convention, Adelaide (1897), 1169 (Isaac Isaacs).

221. Official Record of the Debates of the Australasian Federal Convention, Melbourne (1898), 718 (Isaac Isaacs).

222. Ibid.

223. Official Record of the Debates of the Australasian Federal Convention, Melbourne (1898), 724 (Isaac Isaacs). Isaacs's error is that he attempts to explain the political scheme of a polity as if it were the result of the common law, when in fact the reverse was true. His understanding of the "consent of the governed" is limited by the law of agency, which is consistent with elections and referenda to amend a Constitution, for wisdom. Implicit in the notion of the electorate's will to which Isaacs refers is that it is wise. This notwithstanding, members of Parliament are not elected as agents of the individual electors, but as preferred to other candidates according to some criterion of practical ability, that is, some notion of prudence. The principle of the referendum in respect of a written Constitution is not an appeal to wisdom, but an appeal for the consent of the governed to a wise law.

224. Official Record of the Debates of the Australasian Federal Convention, Melbourne (1898), 727 (Josiah Symon).

225. Official Record of the Debates of the Australasian Federal Convention, Melbourne (1898), 728 (Alfred Deakin).

226. Official Record of the Debates of the Australasian Federal Convention, Melbourne (1898), 729 (Alfred Deakin).

227. Official Record of the Debates of the Australasian Federal Convention, Melbourne (1898), 730 (Isaac Isaacs).

228. Official Record of the Debates of the Australasian Federal Convention, Melbourne (1898), 730 (Alfred Deakin). While Deakin's argument has the ostensible appearance of advancing Isaacs's proposal, it also has the effect of warning the Convention of a side issue of which it was unaware.

229. Official Record of the Debates of the Australasian Federal Convention, Melbourne (1898), 731 (Josiah Symon).

230. Official Record of the Debates of the Australasian Federal Convention, Melbourne (1898), 731 (Josiah Symon).

231. Official Record of the Debates of the Australasian Federal Convention, Melbourne (1898), 733 (Josiah Symon).

232. Official Record of the Debates of the Australasian Federal Convention, Melbourne (1898), 733 (Josiah Symon).

233. Official Record of the Debates of the Australasian Federal Convention, Melbourne (1898), 751 (Edmund Barton).

234. Official Record of the Debates of the Australasian Federal Convention, Melbourne (1898), 754 (James Howe).

235. Official Record of the Debates of the Australasian Federal Convention, Melbourne (1897), 757 (Isaac Isaacs).

236. Ibid.

237. Official Record of the Debates of the Australasian Federal Convention, Melbourne (1897), 759 (Isaac Isaacs).

238. Official Record of the Debates of the Australasian Federal Convention, Melbourne (1897), 765 (James Howe).

239. John Quick and Robert Garran, *The Annotated Constitution of the Australian Commonwealth* (Angus & Robertson, 1901) p. 988.

240. Commonwealth of Australia Constitution, ss. 51.

241. Commonwealth of Australia Constitution, ss. 52, 86, 90.

242. Commonwealth of Australia Constitution, s. 107.

243. Commonwealth of Australia Constitution, s. 109.

244. Commonwealth of Australia Constitution, s. 7.

245. Commonwealth of Australia Constitution, ss. 53.

246. Commonwealth of Australia Constitution, ss. 53.

247. Commonwealth of Australia Constitution, ss. 107

248. Commonwealth of Australia Constitution, s. 57.

249. Draft of a Bill To Constitute the Commonwealth of Australia, (12/4/97): cl.58. In the draft Bill produced by the Convention at the end of the first session, the clause remained unchanged, but had been renumbered as clause 60 and the Federal Executive Council (FEC) that the Governor-General chose and summoned to aid and advise him had become clause 61.

250. Official Record of the Debates of the Australasian Federal Convention, Adelaide (1897), 908 (George Reid), emphasis added.

251. Official Record of the Debates of the Australasian Federal Convention, Adelaide (1897), 909 (George Reid).

252. Ibid.

253. Commonwealth of Australia Bill, 22 March to 23 April 1897, cl. 2.

254. Official Record of the Debates of the Australasian Federal Convention, Adelaide (1897), 910 (George Reid).

255. Official Record of the Debates of the Australasian Federal Convention, Adelaide, (1897), 910 (Edmund Barton).

256. Official Record of the Debates of the Australasian Federal Convention, Adelaide, (1897), 910 (Edmund Barton), emphasis added.

257. Official Record of the Debates of the Australasian Federal Convention, Adelaide, (1897), 910–11 (Edmund Barton).

258. Michael Crommelin, "Governor-General and the Republic Powers of the Head of State" (2015) 38(3) *Melbourne University Law Review* 1118.

259. Ibid., 1122. Carruthers's name was Joseph Hector Carruthers.

260. Official Record of the Debates of the Australasian Federal Convention, Adelaide (1897), 913 (Edmund Barton). In his rush to attribute fear of Westminster's rebuke to Barton's response rather than knowledge of the law and correct drafting technique, Winterton missed the significance of Barton's statement and the Convention's acceptance of it. George Winterton, *Parliament, The Executive and the Governor General A Constitutional Analysis* (Melbourne University Press 1983) p. 3. Had he but reflected on Barton's words, he would have understood the intention of the Founders was to remove any semblance personal power from the Governor-General.

261. Story provides a guide to the rules for interpreting the US Constitution in which he also explains the dangers that can arise: Joseph Story, *Commentaries on the Constitution of the United States, Vol. 1* (Hilliard Gray & Co, 1833) pp. 383–442.

262. Michael Crommelin, "Governor-General and the Republic Powers of the Head of State" (2015) 38(3) *Melbourne University Law Review* 1118, 1122. It is difficult not to understand Crommelin's criticism of the need for more form in the draft Bill as a demand for greater detail—a demand that, if applied, generally would defeat the idea of a Constitution, by producing a code.

263. Ibid., 1118, 1122–3.

264. Official Record of the Debates of the Australasian Federal Convention, Adelaide (1897), 910 (Edmund Barton).

265. Official Record of the Debates of the Australasian Federal Convention, Sydney (1897), 804 (Sir John Forrest).

266. Official Record of the Debates of the Australasian Federal Convention, Sydney (1897), 805 (Edmund Barton). Without the alteration of the transcription of Barton's statement from "with" to "without," his response to Forrest would have contradicted every other explanation he had made. The essence of Barton's explanation, which is supported by other delegates, is that as the governor always acts with the advice of his ministers, so too will the Governor-General only act on ministerial advice.

267. Draft of a Bill to Constitute the Commonwealth of Australia (23/4/97): cl. 68.

268. Official Record of the Debates of the Australasian Federal Convention, Melbourne (1898), 2250 (Alfred Deakin).

269. Official Record of the Debates of the Australasian Federal Convention, Melbourne (1898), 2251 (Edmund Barton).

270. Official Record of the Debates of the Australasian Federal Convention, Melbourne (1898), 2252–3 (Edmund Barton).

271. Official Record of the Debates of the Australasian Federal Convention, Adelaide (1897), 23 (Edmund Barton), emphasis added.

272. Official Record of the Debates of the Australasian Federal Convention, Adelaide (1897), 1170 (Isaac Isaacs).

273. Official Record of the Debates of the Australasian Federal Convention, Adelaide (1897), 443 (Edmund Barton).

274. Attention to this connection will be given during consideration of the debates in the third session of the Convention. The system of responsible government had also been adopted in the colonial Parliaments.

275. Official Record of the Debates of the Australasian Federal Convention, Adelaide (1897), 17 (Edmund Barton).

276. Official Record of the Debates of the Australasian Federal Convention, Adelaide (1897), 22 (Edmund Barton).

277. Official Record of the Debates of the Australasian Federal Convention, Adelaide (1897), 441 (Edmund Barton).

278. Official Record of the Debates of the Australasian Federal Convention, Adelaide (1897), 23 (Edmund Barton).

279. Official Record of the Debates of the Australasian Federal Convention, Adelaide (1897), 23 (Edmund Barton).

280. Official Record of the Debates of the Australasian Federal Convention, Adelaide (1897), 442 (Edmund Barton). While the US Constitution, Article 1, section 7, vests a similar power in the House of Representatives, the "power to propose or concur with amendment" is vested in the Senate.

281. Official Record of the Debates of the Australasian Federal Convention, Adelaide (1897), 22–3 (Edmund Barton).

282. "Supply" in relation to the Finance clause of the draft Bills refers to the appropriation for the ordinary annual services of the government.

283. Official Record of the Debates of the Australasian Federal Convention, Melbourne (1898), 2064 (Edmund Barton). It is, however, anomalous. A Senate with the power to *affirm or reject* supply has only to threaten their use in order to compel a government to accede to its demands, that is, to be responsible to both Houses. It is clear that the Convention accepted the idea of the Senate as representing states' interests; however, the assumption that senators would represent their particular states precluded the idea that senators would owe allegiance to political parties whose interests transcended state interests.

284. Official Record of the Debates of the Australasian Federal Convention, Adelaide (1897), 443 (Edmund Barton).

285. Official Record of the Debates of the Australasian Federal Convention, Adelaide (1897), 471 (Richard O'Connor) and 489 (Charles Kingston); the 1891omprompromise.

286. Official Record of the Debates of the Australasian Federal Convention, Adelaide (1897), 484 (George Reid). He sought to restore the 1891 compromise.

287. Official Record of the Debates of the Australasian Federal Convention, Adelaide (1897), 543 (Isaac Isaacs).

288. Official Record of the Debates of the Australasian Federal Convention, Adelaide (1897), 545 (Isaac Isaacs), emphasis added. Isaacs had therefore proposed two essentially similar solutions: two chambers elected on a proportional basis, or equal representation without coordinate powers. Both solutions produced a unitary form of government. He endorsed a bicameral structure within the context of a unitary scheme where the states had no legislative influence on the Commonwealth.

289. Official Record of the Debates of the Australasian Federal Convention, Adelaide (1897), 552 (Edmund Barton).

290. Official Record of the Debates of the Australasian Federal Convention, Adelaide (1897), 554 (Edmund Barton).

291. Official Record of the Debates of the Australasian Federal Convention, Adelaide (1897), 554–5 (Edmund Barton).

292. Official Record of the Debates of the Australasian Federal Convention, Adelaide (1897), 555 (Edmund Barton).

293. Official Record of the Debates of the Australasian Federal Convention, Adelaide (1897), 555 (Edmund Barton)

294. Official Record of the Debates of the Australasian Federal Convention, Adelaide (1897), 555 (Edmund Barton).

295. Official Record of the Debates of the Australasian Federal Convention, Adelaide (1897), 556 (Edmund Barton).

296. Official Record of the Debates of the Australasian Federal Convention, Adelaide (1897), 575 (Edmund Barton).

297. Official Record of the Debates of the Australasian Federal Convention, Adelaide (1897), 576 (Edmund Barton); emphasis added ([*sic*]; read "is"). Barton's explanation of the word "proposed" is important, given the decision of Barwick CJ in *Victoria v Commonwealth* (1975) 134 CLR 81 at 118; (cf. *Sir John Did His Duty* (Griffin Press, 1983) p. 83). Barwick bases the court's power on the assertion that the "Court is the guardian of the Constitution," but he exercises the power as if it is actually the guardian of the Parliament whose processes it can review. Barton and the Convention deny that: the people are the guardian of the Parliament.

298. Official Record of the Debates of the Australasian Federal Convention, Adelaide (1897), 578 (George Reid).

299. Official Record of the Debates of the Australasian Federal Convention, Adelaide (1897), 584 (Edmund Barton).

300. Official Record of the Debates of the Australasian Federal Convention, Adelaide (1897), 584 (Edmund Barton).

301. Clause 53 was renumbered at the end of the first session as clause 55.

302. Official Record of the Debates of the Australasian Federal Convention, Adelaide (1897), 477 (Isaac Isaacs).

303. Official Record of the Debates of the Australasian Federal Convention, Melbourne (1898), 2000 (Isaac Isaacs).

304. Ibid. This was an express attack on the status of a written Constitution as itself a source of law with which the legislature and executive must comply,

as the "within jurisdiction" qualification would be ineffectual to render any law unconstitutional.

305. Official Record of the Debates of the Australasian Federal Convention, Melbourne (1898), 2002 (Isaac Isaacs). Downer remarked that if the Convention was to accept Isaacs's axiom, "trust the Parliament," there was no need for a Constitution: Official Record of the Debates of the Australasian Federal Convention, Melbourne (1898), 2006 (John Downer).

306. Official Record of the Debates of the Australasian Federal Convention, Melbourne (1898), 2005 (John Downer).

307. Official Record of the Debates of the Australasian Federal Convention, Melbourne (1898), 2006 (John Downer).

308. Official Record of the Debates of the Australasian Federal Convention, Melbourne (1898), 2006 (John Downer).

309. Official Record of the Debates of the Australasian Federal Convention, Melbourne (1898), 2015 (Edmund Barton).

310. Official Record of the Debates of the Australasian Federal Convention, Melbourne (1898), 2016 (Edmund Barton). Clause 52 was renumbered as clause 51, containing the heads of concurrent legislative powers.

311. Sir Samuel Griffith had attended the 1891 Convention. By 1897 he had become Chief justice of Queensland and had not sought to be a delegate to the Convention. He had nevertheless provided assistance to the Convention from time to time.

312. Official Record of the Debates of the Australasian Federal Convention, Melbourne (1898), 2049 (Isaac Isaacs).

313. Official Record of the Debates of the Australasian Federal Convention, Melbourne (1898), 2060 (Richard O'Connor).

314. Official Record of the Debates of the Australasian Federal Convention, Melbourne, (1898), 480 (Edmund Barton).

315. Thomas Erskine May, *A Treatise upon the Law, Privileges, Proceedings and Usage of Parliament*, 10th ed., eds. Reginald Palgrave et al. (William Clowes & Sons, 1844) p. 542. It needs to be recalled that Charles II was an absolute monarch who was not bound by the laws of England.

316. Official Record of the Debates of the Australasian Federal Convention, Melbourne (1898), 2061 (Edmund Barton).

317. Official Record of the Debates of the Australasian Federal Convention, Melbourne (1898), 2061 (Edmund Barton).

318. Official Record of the Debates of the Australasian Federal Convention, Melbourne (1898), 2061 (Edmund Barton), emphasis added.

319. Thomas Erskine May, *A Treatise upon the Law, Privileges, Proceedings and Usage of Parliament*, 10th ed., eds. Reginald Palgrave et al. (William Clowes & Sons, 1844) p. 541.

320. Ibid.

321. Ibid., 550.

322. In 1909, the House of Lords rejected the annual budget of the Asquith government. The motive to reject the budget was fear of a range of tax increases,

including a 20 percent tax on any increase "in the *site* value of land accruing *after* April 30, 1909 and payable on each occasion on which the property changed hands, whether by purchase or death." Sir J.A.R. Marriott, *Modern England 1885–1945*, 4th ed. (Methuen, 1948) p. 293. The conflict between the two Houses led to the passage of the *Parliament Act 1911*, which sought to codify the constitutional powers of the House of Lords in relation to supply.

323. Official Record of the Debates of the Australasian Federal Convention, Melbourne (1898), 2064 (Edmund Barton).

324. Thomas Erskine May, *A Treatise upon the Law, Privileges, Proceedings and Usage of Parliament*, 10th ed., eds. Reginald Palgrave et al. (William Clowes & Sons, 1844) p. 550.

325. Official Record of the Debates of the Australasian Federal Convention, Melbourne (1898), 2065 (Edmund Barton), emphasis added.

326. Official Record of the Debates of the Australasian Federal Convention, Melbourne (1898), 2064 (Edmund Barton).

327. Official Record of the Debates of the Australasian Federal Convention, Melbourne (1898), 2064 (Edmund Barton).

328. That denial is consistent only with the narrow definition of "law" in legal positivism which includes a sanction; see John Austin, *The Province of Jurisprudence Determined* (John Murray, 1861) p. xli. Also see J. Raz, The Concept of a Legal System, 2nd ed. (Oxford University Press, 1980) p. 3.

329. Official Record of the Debates of the Australasian Federal Convention, Melbourne, (1898), 2065 (Edmund Barton).

330. *Reform Act 1832* (UK) 2&3 Will. IV c.45 and the *Representation of the People Act 1867* (UK) 30&31 Vict. C. 102.

331. *Bill of Rights of 1688* 1 William & Mary Sess 2 c 2.

332. *Marbury v Madison* 5 U.S. at 176 emphasis added.

333. Harry V. Jaffa, *Original Intent & The Framers of the Constitution* (Regnery, 1994) p. 112.

334. H.V. Jaffa, *Equality & Liberty* (Oxford University Press, 1965) pp. 13–4.

335. The Commonwealth of Australia Constitution, ss. 7, 24 and 128.

336. Martin Diamond, W.M Fisk & H. Garfinkel, *The Democratic Republic* (Rand McNally, 1966) p. 543, emphasis added.

337. Joseph Story, *Commentaries on the Constitution of the United States Vol. 1* (Hilliard Gray & Co, 1833) p. 211.

338. The corresponding provisions in the other colonial FEAs were: FEA (NSW), s 32; FEA (Vic), s. 32; FEA (SA), s 32; FEA (TA), s 32; FEA (WA), s 28.

339. Act No. 34, 1897 (NSW), s 2.

340. This view needs to be contrasted with the view that the Constitution is an Act of the Imperial Parliament and that that Parliament is the sovereign body.

341. Joseph Story, *Commentaries on the Constitution of the United States Vol. 1* (Hilliard Gray & Co, 1833) p. 211.

342. *Baxter v Commissioners of Taxation (NSW)* (1907) 4 CLR 1087, 1112. Geoffrey de Q Walker cited this section of *Baxter* to demonstrate the early court's

"contextual approach": "The Seven Pillars of Centralism: *Engineers' Case* and Federalism" (2002) 76 *Australian Law Journal* 680.

343. James Madison, *Federalist No. 14 The Federalist Papers*, ed. Clinton Rossiter (New American Library, 1961) p. 104.

344. Leo Strauss, *Natural Right and History* (University of Chicago Press, 1953) p. 1.

345. James Madison, *Federalist No. 14 The Federalist Papers*, ed. Clinton Rossiter (New American Library, 1961) p. 100.

346. Leo Strauss *Thoughts on Machiavelli* (University of Washington Press, 1969) p. 13.

347. H.V. Jaffa, *Original Intent & The Framers of the Constitution* (Regnery, 1994) p. 22.

348. H.V. Jaffa, A New Birth of Freedom; Abraham Lincoln and the Coming of the Civil War (Rowman & Littlefield, 2000) p. 86.

349. *New Zealand Constitution Act 1852* (15 & 16 Vict. c. 72). Report of the Constitutional Arrangements Committee (Hon Peter Dunne, Chairperson) August 2005, Inquiry to Review New Zealand's Existing Constitutional Arrangements, p. 43.

350. Report of the Constitutional Arrangements Committee (Hon Peter Dunne, Chairperson) August 2005, Inquiry to Review New Zealand's Existing Constitutional Arrangements, p. 44.

351. W.H.P. Clement, *The Law of the Canadian Constitution* (Carswell, 1892) p. 2.

352. Ibid.

353. Section 74 was consented to by the delegates as representatives of the colonial governments in 1900 when the words of the section insisted upon by Imperial authorities rephrased the Convention's decision to leave construction of the Constitution with the High Court. There have been eight minor amendments of clauses consented to by the people since federation.

354. Official Record of the Debates of the Australasian Federal Convention, Adelaide (1897), 21 (Edmund Barton).

355. Official Record of the Debates of the Australasian Federal Convention, Melbourne (1898), 283 (Isaac Isaacs).

Chapter 3

The Early Court

INTRODUCTION

This chapter will argue that the decisions of the early court[1] sought to give effect to the original intention of the Founders that the Constitution was federal, and that it followed the division of powers of the US Constitution. It does this through an examination of a selection of judgments of the early court in which the constitutional relationship between the Commonwealth and the states is explained by the twin doctrines of noninterference (or immunity of instrumentalities) and states' reserved powers.

This chapter will show that the methodology of construction employed by the early court assumed the text to be informed by inferences from the political scheme that was known to have been agreed to by the Founders. These considerations included the federal nature of the Constitution, its source in the US Constitution, and the separate sovereignties of the Commonwealth and each of the several states in accordance with the Constitution. Haig Patapan specifically raises this point when he states, "This way of interpreting the Constitution, which looked to American precedents, was prepared to take into account the political and legal context of the founding, relying on the historical facts and circumstances to give meaning to the text."[2]

According to Patapan, the interpretative method implied "a political vision of a co-sovereign federalism that was largely consistent with the views of the framers of the Constitution."[3] The early court accepted that in a truly federal Constitution, the separate sovereignties of the Commonwealth and the states must imply the existence of limits to powers in order to protect each sovereign domain. In the Commonwealth Constitution, these rules were identified as the doctrines of noninterference (or immunity of instrumentalities) and the doctrine of states' reserved powers. As shown in chapter 2, the relevance of those doctrines to the Commonwealth Constitution was the result of the Founders' insistence that the federal scheme resemble that of the US Constitution. This chapter will show that the early court's method of construction relied, inter alia, on matters known by both "public notoriety"[4] and "common knowledge"[5] in order to establish that the Founders of the Commonwealth Constitution had based its federal character and its distribution of powers on that of the United States.[6]

The cases to be considered in this chapter also show how Isaacs, when appearing as legal counsel—even before the High Court was constituted in 1903—with *Wollaston's case*,[7] and after his appointment to the Bench in 1906, sought from the beginning to construe the Constitution so as to undermine the federal scheme. The constitutional scheme for which Isaacs implicitly argued was one that, by depriving the states of their legislative powers, resembled a unitary scheme similar to that for which he had argued during the Convention. As a result of Isaacs's activities, the early court was obliged on a number of occasions to reestablish the constitutional basis of the doctrines that Isaacs sought to undermine.

In 1902, before members of the High Court had been appointed, the Victorian Supreme Court determined *Wollaston's case*,[8] in which Isaacs appeared as legal counsel for the Victorian State Government. The Victorian Commissioner of Taxation had levied state income tax on a Commonwealth officer and Isaacs had submitted that the doctrine of immunities in *McCulloch v Maryland* had no application to the Commonwealth Constitution. That submission was accepted by the Victorian Supreme Court and cited in its judgment. *Wollaston's case* was applied by the Tasmanian Supreme Court in the case of *Pedder v D'Emden*[9] and by the Victorian Supreme Court again in *Webb v Deakin and Lyne*,[10] each of which came on appeal to the High Court when it was constituted in 1903.

In a series of cases between 1903 and 1908, beginning with *D'Emden v Pedder*,[11] the High Court laid down the two doctrines as being necessarily implied from the Commonwealth Constitution, which incorporated a federal scheme based on that of the United States, in which the Commonwealth and the states were separately sovereign.

DOCTRINE OF NONINTERFERENCE

Noninterference and Sovereignty

The doctrine of noninterference (or immunity of instrumentalities) was originally developed to protect the executive and legislative powers of the Commonwealth from interference by the executive and legislative powers of the states.[12] That doctrine was also held to be reciprocally true, protecting the states' sovereign executive and legislative actions from interference by the Commonwealth. The apparent contradiction of sovereignty divided between two distinct organs of government in a federal union, in which one is subject to the other in certain matters, was reconciled by Justice Story, who explained that the term *sovereignty* had a variety of meanings. Some meanings will be wide and will apply in an enlarged sense to the whole people exercising all the powers, both domestic and foreign, for their common benefit; others will have a lesser, more limited, sense of sovereignty—sovereign only in respect of specific powers within that overall framework:

> But the sovereignty of the government, organized within the state, may be of a very limited nature. It may extend to few, or to many objects. It may be unlimited, as to some; it may be restrained, as to others. To the extent of the power given, the government may be sovereign, and its acts may be deemed the sovereign acts of the state.[13]

The opportunity to explain how the sovereign powers of different sovereign entities might be protected or quarantined from interference by the other so that each remains sovereign under the Commonwealth's federal Constitution first came before the High Court when D'Emden, a Commonwealth officer in the recently transferred exclusive Commonwealth Department of Posts and resident in Tasmania, appealed his conviction by the Tasmanian Supreme Court. He was charged that he

> did on the 31st March, 1903, in Tasmania aforesaid give to the paying officer of the Commonwealth of Australia a receipt liable to duty . . . the said receipt when so given by the said H. L. D'Emden as aforesaid not being duly stamped.[14]

The unanimous decision of the Court in *D'Emden v Pedder*[15] affirmed that the Commonwealth and Tasmania, within the ambit of its authority, were separately sovereign, subject only to the restrictions imposed by the Imperial connection and provisions of the Constitution "either expressed or necessarily implied."[16]

The idea of separate sovereignties in the different senses meant by Story is expressed in the headnote of the case report of *D'Emden v Pedder* as follows:

> The Commonwealth and the States are, with respect to the matters which under the Constitution are within the ambit of their respective legislative or executive authority, sovereign States, subject only to the restrictions imposed by the Imperial connection and the provisions of the Constitution, either expressed or implied.[17]

Counsel for the State of Tasmania had submitted that the power of direct taxation was reserved to the States by section 107 of the Constitution and the authority of the Commonwealth Parliament ought to be read subject to this power of the states. The High Court held that it was an implication from the Commonwealth's and states' sovereignties that where the Constitution grants sovereignty it protects the instruments of sovereignty, the legislative and executive powers, from interference. The court stressed that this was not a doctrine of a special system of law, but a necessary rule of construction of all grants of power applying from the necessity of the case:

> In other words, where any power or control is expressly granted, there is included in the grant, to the full extent of the capacity of the grantor, and without special mention, every power and every control the denial of which would render the grant itself ineffective.[18]

In other words, it is an incident of sovereignty that the Commonwealth was entitled, within its own sphere, "to exercise its legislative and executive powers in absolute freedom, and without any interference or control whatever except that prescribed by the Constitution itself,"[19] a right of sovereignty subject to extrinsic control being a contradiction in terms. The court concluded that the incidents of Commonwealth sovereignty, absolute freedom from interference or control whatever except as provided for in the Constitution, "must be taken to be the essence of the Constitution."[20]

Chief Justice Griffith, who delivered the judgment of the early court, spoke of two circumstances that affected the legislative powers of the Commonwealth and the states. He identified the concurrent powers under section 51 of the Constitution as a large class of powers with respect to which a similar power is *for a time* reserved to the states and as a result conflict can occur for which section 109 is an appropriate cure.[21] While Griffith explained that the invalidity was only to the extent of the inconsistency, it is important to note that section 109 is said to resolve conflict only between concurrent powers. Where the Commonwealth law relates to an exclusive topic—for example, posts and telegraphs—the state is not competent to pass legislation on that topic,[22] "as from the point at which the quality of exclusiveness attaches to the federal power the competency of the State is altogether extinguished."[23] After referring to *McCulloch v Maryland* as the authority, Griffith summarized the doctrine of immunity of instrumentalities, which governs the mutual relations between the separate sovereign elements of the Constitution:

> When a State attempts to give to its legislative or executive authority an operation which, if valid, would fetter, control, or interfere with, the free exercise of the legislative or executive power of the Commonwealth, the attempt,

> unless expressly authorized by the Constitution, is to that extent invalid and inoperative.[24]

Griffith said that the Tasmanian Stamp Act's demand that a penalty be incurred unless duty is paid on a receipt given under the Federal Audit Act was an act of interference with the Commonwealth officer's duty:

> The attaching by a State law of any condition to the discharge of a federal duty is assuredly an act of interference or control. Moreover, any State enactment which on the face of it attempts to deal with a matter within the exclusive legislative power of the Commonwealth, and upon which the Commonwealth has legislated, is necessarily, so far as it purports to apply to that matter, inconsistent with the law of the Commonwealth.[25]

He thus provides two ways in which the rule applies: the state's law is invalid to the extent that it interferes with a Commonwealth officer's obligation to pay income tax, but it is also invalid as legislating for the exclusive Commonwealth, federal power over posts and telegraphs.[26] He acknowledges as "a fact of public notoriety" that the framers of the Constitution were familiar with the US Constitution so when provisions are discovered that are "undistinguishable in substance, though varied in form, from provisions"[27] of the US Constitution, it is reasonable to infer that the framers intended a similar interpretation. In this manner, the early court confirms that it is the "framers" intended meaning that the court construes. Griffith confirms that the court's acceptance of "the doctrines laid down by the United States Supreme Court [and] delivered by Marshall, CJ, in *McCulloch's Case*."[28]

Griffith rejected as a misapprehension a finding by the Tasmanian Supreme Court that the doctrine laid down in *McCulloch v Maryland* had been considerably modified by later decisions of the US Supreme Court. He accepted that the applicability of the case to different facts had been questioned; however, "neither the authority of the judgment nor the accuracy of the statement of the law contained in it has ever been questioned in the United States, nor have the doctrines enunciated in it ever been qualified."[29]

Griffith therefore had appealed directly to the principle espoused in *McCulloch v Maryland.* From that case, he also cited the three assumptions arising from the separate sovereignties of the federal scheme: that a power to create implies a power to preserve; that a power to destroy, if wielded by a different hand, is hostile to and incompatible with these powers to create and to preserve; and that, where this repugnancy exists, authority that is supreme must control, not yield to, that over which it is supreme.[30]

Griffith rejected the opinion of the Tasmanian Supreme Court that the doctrine of *McCulloch v Maryland* required the Court to answer "whether the attempted exercise of State authority actually impedes the operations of the Federal Government."[31] This, he responded, would depend on a question of fact to be determined by a jury. The issue before the court was "a conflict with the exclusive power of legislation given to the Commonwealth over its own Departments."[32] While the High Court was concerned with the interference by a state duties law with a Commonwealth officer and a Commonwealth law, it was not suggested that the state law was invalid. The issue between the Commonwealth and states was a matter inter se for which the High Court, pursuant to section 74(1) of the Constitution, was the court of exclusive, final appeal. The problem confronting the High Court was examining whether there was a limit on the extent, not the validity, of a state's law.

This was the first occasion when the early court stated that the objective when construing the Constitution was to reveal the intention of the Founders.[33] While the construction established the efficacy of the doctrine of noninterference, it arrived at that solution as an implication from the federal scheme,[34] but it derived the nature of the federal scheme and the separate sovereignties it represents from the authorities of the US Supreme Court. That source and those authorities were not evident on the face of the Commonwealth Constitution, but were readily identified from what was notoriously known. The High Court acknowledged the guiding authority of the US Supreme Court and Marshall CJ's doctrine of noninterference as the rule in *D'Emden v Pedder*.

That rule was challenged when the salaries of two members of the Federal Parliament, Alfred Deakin and William Lyne, who were in Melbourne for the sitting of Parliament, were held liable to income tax under the *Victorian Income Tax Act 1896*. *Deakin v Webb*[35] came on appeal from the Victorian Supreme Court, which applied its earlier decision in *Wollaston's case*.[36] Isaacs's submission in *Wollaston's case*, that in the United States "the Federation and the States there have no common authority and no common head—no power which can in any way control the operation of either,"[37] was an implicit denial of both the people as the source of political power, the Constitution, and the Supreme Court's power of judicial review.

The Federal Scheme

In *Deakin v Webb*, the relationship of the US Constitution with that of the Commonwealth was again challenged by Isaacs on various grounds. He submitted that the US Constitution and the case of *McCulloch v Maryland* were to be rejected as authorities for the Commonwealth Constitution;[38] he maintained that the principle of *McCulloch*—the power to tax is the power to destroy—"has no application to a constitution under the Crown"[39] and cited the Privy Council judgment in *Bank of Toronto v Lambe* (at p. 578)[40] as the authority. Their Lordships' judgment, which begins on that page, makes no mention of "the power to tax is a power to destroy"; however, it does discuss the doctrine of immunities as "the principles laid down for the United States by Chief Justice Marshall" at p. 587, by describing the "elaborate distribution of the whole field of legislative authority"[41] between the Dominion and Provinces, thus distinguishing only the Canadian Constitution from that of United States. Of greater significance, however, was Isaacs's submission that the Constitution must be dealt with as any other Imperial Act and no prohibitions can be implied.[42] In anticipation of his judgment in the *Engineers' case*,[43] Isaacs submitted that a court could look only at the Constitution's legal aspect[44]—that is, its legal text—and construe it literally.[45]

The court dealt at length with Isaacs's submission regarding the Privy Council decision in *Bank of Toronto v Lambe*.[46] The Privy Council had said in respect of the principle repeated above as "the power to tax is the power to destroy" that, with regard to the power stated in the Canadian law, it was what the Parliament had intended to give, and to place a limit on it because it might be used unwisely would lead to insuperable difficulties of construction.[47] The doctrine of *McCulloch v Maryland* could not apply to the Canadian Constitution since it was not federal. The High Court, however, explained that the Privy Council's argument was based upon the express words of the Canadian Constitution. Referring to the Commonwealth Constitution, it explained that where the existence of the power or the limits of its exercise "is a matter of inference and of implication depending upon a consideration of the whole of an instrument dealing with the relations of the several parts of a federated State,"[48] the possibility that it might be used to destroy or impair the efficiency of the government is very relevant when construing the whole document. This ruling reflected two facts about the Australian Constitution: first that, unlike the Canadian Constitution, the Australian was federal; and second, the readiness of the early court to identify the doctrine of immunities as an implication from the federal scheme of the Constitution. After indicating that the Commonwealth and Canadian Constitutions were fundamentally different in the distributions of respective legislative powers, and that the issue decided in *McCulloch v Maryland* did not in fact arise in the Canadian case,[49] the court concluded that the Privy Council decision had no bearing upon the questions before the court. It reaffirmed the decision in *D'Emden v Pedder* in the following words:

> When a State attempts to give to its legislative or executive authority an operation which, if valid, would fetter, control, or interfere with, the free exercise of the legislative or executive power of the Commonwealth, the attempt, unless expressly authorized by the Constitution, is to that extent invalid and inoperative.[50]

In expressing the result in this way, the early court again implicitly affirmed the federal nature of the Constitution and held that the legislative or executive power of the Commonwealth is free from interference unless "expressly authorized by the Constitution."[51] The court related the federal powers to sections 51 and 52 of the Constitution, and section 107 was again related to the Tenth Amendment of the US Constitution.[52] Section 51 enumerates the heads of legislative powers granted by the Constitution to the Commonwealth and shared concurrently with the states. Section 52 vests powers exclusively in the Commonwealth after federation.[53] In its response to the submission that the taxing power was reserved to the State of Victoria by section 107 of the Constitution, the court highlighted the need to consider the different sovereignties. It explained that the power of taxation was an attribute of sovereignty that was limited "to all persons to whom the sovereignty itself extends *quo ad hoc*;"[54] that is, it included people who were ordinary citizens but not those who were there by direction. The court concluded that the taxing power does not apply to a person "who is sent to live within a State by a paramount sovereignty without choice on his part."[55]

In his submission, Isaacs sought to distinguish the US and Commonwealth Constitutions on the ground that the source of power of the former was the people of the several states while the ultimate source of the latter was the Crown or Imperial Parliament. The court responded to this in the following terms: "It is a matter of *common knowledge* that the framers of the Australian Constitution deliberately adopted, with regard to the distribution of powers, the model of the United States, in preference to that of the Canadian Dominion."[56]

In doing so, the court explicitly appealed to the original intention of the Founders as the guiding purpose of construction and indicated the necessity of taking into account political considerations beyond the text as well as implications from the text. It added that as the distribution of powers followed that of the United States and "the respective powers of the Commonwealth and the States having been defined and distributed,"[57] the source of the distribution was irrelevant for interpretation.

Griffith used the term "common knowledge" in the same way that he used "public notoriety" as evidence of facts known to the Founders that related to the political scheme of the Constitution. The common knowledge and the public notoriety referred to in the two cases so far considered include knowledge available to or published in respect of the deliberations of the delegates to the Constitutional Convention. The extent of this knowledge might have been confirmed by reference to the Convention debates that were transcribed and circulated in the public domain and debated in the Parliaments of the states, and reported in the popular press.[58] Construction of the Constitution was also assisted by inferences drawn from the similarity of the provisions of the Commonwealth and US Constitutions. In the process of explaining the effect of this similarity, the court justified its approach by appealing to the original intention of the Founders:

> The American Constitution as to this point having been long since settled by judicial decision, it is a reasonable inference that it was intended by the framers of the Australian Constitution, when adopting similar language, that like provisions should receive like interpretation.[59]

The court rejected Isaacs's submission[60] that *McCulloch v Maryland* had no application to a constitution granted by the British parliament.[61] It explained that the scheme of the Constitution, like that of the United States, "is to confer certain definite and specified powers upon the Commonwealth and to leave the residue of power in the hands of the States."[62] The court recites the "reasons" furnished to it by Supreme Court Justice a'Beckett in relation to the decision[63] appealed from, namely, that the decision in *D'Emden v Pedder* "was not based upon the reduction of the officer's income by the amount of the stamp but on the requirement of a stamp being an interference."[64] In *Wollaston's case*, however, a'Beckett had suggested that US cases did not apply to the Commonwealth Constitution because section 109 would invalidate state laws, which were inconsistent with Commonwealth laws or had interfered with federal instrumentalities.[65] The High Court's response, after referencing where in *D'Emden v Pedder* to look, was a lengthy extract from the US case of *Dobbins v Commissioners of Erie County*[66] to confirm the reduction in income as the basis of the decision, concluding that that decision's interpretation had long been settled and it was reasonable to assume it was "a reasonable inference that it was intended by the framers of the Australian Constitution, when adopting similar language, that like provisions should receive like interpretation."[67]

When the court upheld the Commonwealth's appeal, Isaacs applied for a certificate from the Court pursuant to section 74 of the Constitution authorizing an appeal to the Privy Council. In rejecting the application, the three members of the early court delivered separate judgments. Griffith confirmed the Constitution provided that the High Court was the tribunal of ultimate appeal.[68] Griffith compared the Commonwealth Constitution with that of the United States[69] and, confirming his intention to construe the Constitution in accordance with the Founders' intention, advised that they "deliberately rejected the scheme of the Canadian Constitution, and deliberately accepted that of the United States Constitution."[70] He held that the effect of section 74 of the Constitution was to identify the *limit* of a power validly enacted, not its validity. In responding to Isaacs's application for a certificate, Griffith stated that the first question for the court to determine was whether the doctrine in

D'Emden v Pedder was actually part of the Commonwealth Constitution and questioned whether Isaacs accepted the court's decision: "As to the first question, the judgment in *D'Emden v Pedder* (*supra*) has not been objected to. I do not know now whether Mr Isaacs contends that that decision was wrong. I am unable to gather from him distinctly whether he does or does not."[71]

Barton J was more forthcoming about the necessity of the court to take notice of more than just the plain words of a provision when, in relation to the meaning of the words "any special reason" in section 74, he said "it is not unreasonable that I should say something about the *circumstances under which this section originated*."[72] He argued that the court could reasonably rely on facts relating to the circumstances in which a particular provision was drafted with an appeal to the "common knowledge on the subject."[73] Isaacs's application was rejected.

The decision in *Deakin v Webb* confirmed and explored the implicit attributes of the Constitution's federal scheme that had been previously enunciated in *D'Emden v Pedder* as resulting from the separate sovereignties of the Commonwealth and the several states. While the court confirmed as a basis for its construction of the Constitution that the Australian Founders used "language not verbally identical, but synonymous, for the purpose of defining that distribution"[74] of powers found in the US Constitution and the necessity for a consideration of implications from the text, Isaacs's submissions denied that the Constitution's federal scheme was based on the US Constitution. His submission to the Court in *Deakin v Webb*, requiring the court to have regard only to the "legal aspect" of the Constitution,[75] had no other purpose than to permit a literal construction that would isolate the Constitution from its political scheme.

In *D'Emden v Pedder*, the court held that the doctrine of noninterference protected Commonwealth legislative and executive powers from interference by validly enacted state taxing legislation. The question of whether the rule in *D'Emden v Pedder* had a reciprocal application to protect state executive and legislative powers from interference by the Commonwealth came before the High Court in *The Federated Amalgamated Government Railway and Tramway Service Association v New South Wales Railway Traffic Employees Association (Railway Servants' case)*.[76] As the decisions stood, it was clear that Commonwealth legislative and executive powers were immune to the interference of state authority; however, that might simply reflect the sovereignty of the Commonwealth over the states.

The Reciprocal Form of *D'Emden v Pedder*

This issue came before the High Court when the New South Wales Railway Traffic Employees Association applied to register their trade union under the

Commonwealth Conciliation and Arbitration Act 1904 (the Act). Registration would have made the NSW State Railways, a state government instrumentality, subject to the Act even where the railways were engaged in entirely intrastate trade and commerce. Only certain submissions that are summarized in Griffith's decision are relevant to this essay. The intervening states submitted that section 51(xxxv) of the Constitution did not authorize provisions in the Act that would operate "to interfere with the free State control of State railways."[77] The Commonwealth and the applicants, on the other hand, submitted that the legislation was valid since section 98 of the Constitution authorized laws made with respect to trade and commerce among the states to extend to the railways the property of any state.[78] The Commonwealth's submission would have extended its power by framing its industrial relations legislation as an extension of the trade and commerce power (Constitution, s. 51(1)) to state-owned railways under section 98.[79] It implicitly challenged the doctrine of immunities developed in *Deakin v Webb* and *D'Emden v Pedder*.

The decision of the court unanimously affirmed that the rule in *D'Emden v Pedder* also applied reciprocally and was "equally true of attempted interference by the Commonwealth with State instrumentalities."[80] The question for the court was whether the power asserted by the Commonwealth in the Act was conferred by the Constitution, and two aspects of the Constitution became pertinent: the Constitution was an Act of the Imperial Parliament, but it was also a compact, a fact "recited in the Preamble."[81] The court accepted that the Constitution was an Act of the Imperial Parliament, but ruled that its construction must have regard to the "facts and circumstances existing at the date of the contract."[82] Here the court has wrongly suggested that the compact was between "the six Australian Colonies"[83] when the Preamble states that it was between the "*people*" of those colonies, which suggests union prior to federation.

The judgment argued that, since the Constitution had been submitted to the voters of the states, it ought, prima facie, to be held that the purpose was to invite their attention to specific matters relating to respective powers of the states and Commonwealth and the proposed manner of dealing with it.[84] While this implies a construction of original intention, the court did not acknowledge the people as the immediate source of sovereignty, an argument that if made at that time would have negated the Imperial Parliament as that source as well as the source of Isaacs's literalism argument.

The court declared that the rule in *D'Emden v Pedder* consisted of two principles: that of the separate sovereignties of the Commonwealth and the states and its corollary, the doctrine of noninterference unless authorized by the Constitution. It then held, regarding the case then before it, that "the doctrine is equally applicable"[85] and that the rule in *D'Emden v Pedder* was reciprocally true "of an attempted interference by the Commonwealth with

State instrumentalities."[86] It cited a number of US Supreme Court decisions, but the principle on which the court relied was that expressed by Nelson J in *Collector v Day*[87] when he described the states, in respect of their reserved powers, "as sovereign and independent as the general government."[88] As a result, "the means and instrumentalities employed by that government to carry its powers into operation" are necessarily exempt from federal taxing powers.[89] To the submission that the doctrine only applied to the taxation power, the High Court replied that taxation was only an instance of interference and control, which could be effected by the Commonwealth upon the states and vice versa. The court's statement that "the foundation of the argument is the necessity for freedom from control, and taxation is only forbidden because it is an interference"[90] implies that the opposite of sovereignty is control.

Regarding the Commonwealth's submission that section 98 of the Constitution extended its trade and commerce power to state-owned railways, the court explained that the trade and commerce power was, within its ambit, unlimited but that the power's connection to trade and commerce must be direct, substantial, and proximate:

> But we think that the power of the Commonwealth Parliament to regulate interstate trade and commerce, although unlimited within its ambit, cannot as a mere matter of construction, be held to have so wide an ambit as to embrace matters the effect of which upon that commerce is not direct, substantial and proximate. And, in our opinion, the general conditions of employment are not of this character.[91]

The court confirmed that the purpose of the power in section 51(i) was the regulation of interstate trade so as to give effect to the freedom of trade requirement in section 92 and not the regulation of industrial relations. To the submission that the authority of the Commonwealth Parliament to interfere with state instrumentalities is that conferred in express words or by necessary implications, the court, referring to its decision in *D'Emden v Pedder*, held that it must be "expressly authorised."[92]

The reciprocity of the doctrine of noninterference that the court applied in favor of the states against Commonwealth interference was merely the court's recognition of the sovereignty of the states under the federal Constitution. The reciprocal application of the doctrine it had enunciated in D'Emden v Pedder represented the court's further elaboration of the federal scheme of the Commonwealth Constitution. The doctrine of noninterference or immunity of instrumentalities is the necessary implication from the political structure of a truly federal Constitution[93] consisting of separate sovereignties as originally intended by the Founders. A construction of the Constitution compatible with that intention will not permit the sovereignty of either the Commonwealth or the states to be interfered with unless expressly authorized. In the process of determining this case, the court reaffirmed the link between the Commonwealth Constitution and the federal structure of the US Constitution. The effect of the court's decision was the promotion of the political scheme of the Constitution over that view of the text as a piece of Imperial legislation.

Sovereignty, or an Act of the Imperial Parliament

The fact of the Constitution as an enactment of the Imperial Parliament can be said to have played no part—or at least no significant part—in the construction of the Constitution by the early court. The Imperial connection was referred to but was not thought relevant to the construction of the Constitution and the distribution of its powers. The early court sought the Founders' originally intended meaning for the text at each opportunity and was not reluctant to consider the significance of the political scheme.

That changed when, in 1906, Isaac Isaacs and Henry Higgins were appointed Justices of the High Court.[94] An appeal by a defendant who had been found liable before the District Court of New South Wales for income tax assessed on his income as a Commonwealth officer came before the High Court in *Baxter v Commissioners of Taxation (NSW)*[95] in 1907. The decision in *Baxter* was divided, with a single judgment by the Justices from the early court granting the appeal and the separate judgments of Isaacs and Higgins dismissing the appeal. Isaacs's opposition to the early court's interpretation of the Constitution continued in his dissenting judgments once he was on the Bench. He employed Privy Council judgments regarding Imperial legislation that were construed literally to undermine judgments of the early court and the federal scheme that the Founders intended. The Privy Council heard an appeal directly from the decision of the Supreme Court of Victoria in the matter of *Webb v Outtrim*. The significance of *Baxter's case* was that it provided the High Court with an opportunity to answer criticism leveled by the Privy Council at the High Court's jurisprudence.

HIGH COURT OR PRIVY COUNCIL

In December 1906, leave had been granted by the Victorian Supreme Court to the Victorian Government to appeal to the Privy Council regarding its decision in *Webb v Outtrim*.[96] The Supreme Court had applied the High Court's decision in *D'Emden v Pedder* in order to dismiss the income tax liability of a Commonwealth officer. The granting of leave by the Supreme Court avoided the constitutional restriction in section 74, which vested final appellate jurisdiction in the High Court to determine matters relating to inter se issues. The first paragraph of section 74 of the Constitution provides:

> No appeal shall be permitted to the Queen in Council from a decision of the High Court upon any question, howsoever arising, as to the limits inter se of the Constitutional powers of the Commonwealth and those of any State or States, or as to the limits inter se of the Constitutional powers of any two or more States, unless the High Court shall certify that the question is one which ought to be determined by Her Majesty in Council.

The case involved a question as to the limits inter se of the state law vis-à-vis Commonwealth executive powers. The Earl of Halsbury, on behalf of the Privy Council, adopted a literal construction of the Constitution and purported to overrule the doctrine of immunities as stated in *D'Emden v Pedder* and *Deakin v Webb*.[97] He disparaged the rules of construction employed by the early court in those cases by rejecting *McCulloch v Maryland* as an aid to construing the Constitution,[98] disparaging Griffith's reliance on the authoritative interpretation of similar provisions[99] and chiding him for relying on "the knowledge of those who framed the Constitution and their supposed preferences for this or that model"[100] as in turn relying on the supposed preferences of the Founders.[101] The judgment of the Victorian Supreme Court was reversed.

The effect of the Privy Council decision was to raise two questions for the High Court in *Baxter v Commissioners of Taxation*: whether the High Court or the Privy Council was, under the Constitution, "the ultimate arbiter upon questions as to the limits *inter se* of the constitutional powers of the Commonwealth and those of any State or States";[102] and whether the doctrine of immunities and its reciprocal application still existed. Griffith framed the question as whether "the conventional duty of one Court not in all respects the highest, to follow another Court of higher authority"[103] can be excluded by the Constitution. He argued that the meaning of the words might be clear and that whether "power was intended to be exercised must be discovered from . . . a consideration of the whole purview of the Constitution, and the answer . . . cannot be given without having regard to *its history*."[104]

The significance of the meaning of "its history" should not be overlooked. It was a direct rebuttal of the Privy Council's legal positivist approach to construction, and allowed the court to consider how the political scheme of the Constitution affected the text's meaning. While acknowledging that the mischief rule in *Heydon's case*[105] provided a solution to the construction of a written instrument, Griffith cited the four matters to be considered for "the sure and true interpretation of all Statutes in general":[106]

> to suppress the mischief and advance the remedy, and to suppress subtle inventions and evasions for continuance of the mischief, and *pro privato commodo*, and to add force and life to the cure and remedy, according to the true intent of the makers of the Act, *pro bono publico*.[107]

The phrase "makers of the Act" is ambiguous, since it could refer to either the Founders or even the Westminster Parliament, depending upon the meaning of "sovereignty." However, given previous statements by the early court, it is more likely to refer to the "true intent of the Founders" since the Founders were without doubt "the makers of the Act" in the complete sense of making. That construction is also supported by the consideration of the Constitution as a compact to which the early court referred in its decision.[108] It noted the difference in detail between an ordinary piece of legislation and "instruments which purport to call into existence a new State with independent powers of legislation and government,"[109] and cited the opinion of Story J in the US case of *Martin v Hunter's Lessee*[110] to explain the absence of detail in the Constitution as not suiting:

> the purposes of the people, in framing this great charter of our liberties, to provide for minute specifications of its powers, or to declare the means by which those powers should be carried into execution. . . . Hence its powers are expressed in general terms, leaving to the legislature, from time to time, to adopt its own means to effectuate legitimate objects.[111]

Having asserted that the Constitution did not provide minute specifications, the majority appealed to the knowledge of the Founders of the many forms of government, their incidents and attributes that had been discussed for more than 2000 years, and the doctrines applicable to them.[112] They suggested that the historical knowledge assumed to the Founders would be lost by a literal construction and contrasted a literal construction that relied only on a dictionary as a construction by an astral intelligence: "It is true that what has been called an 'astral intelligence', unprejudiced by any historical knowledge, and interpreting a Constitution merely by the aid of a dictionary, might arrive at a very different conclusion as to its meaning from that which a person familiar with history would reach."[113]

Having indicated the necessity of considering the historical facts associated with the Constitution, the majority related a brief statement of the history of the federal movement in the colonies and an historical survey of the choice of a federal structure that reflected the US Constitution rather than the Canadian Constitution.[114] However, according to the majority, knowing the local history of the origin of a new state is insufficient for understanding it. The majority, speaking generally, explained the necessity for a court to know what the Founders could be expected to know in order to fashion a federated Commonwealth and stated that "the application of this doctrine is not excluded or weakened by its notorious historical truth as to the members of the Convention."[115]

In this case, the majority relies on notorious historical truths in order to reveal the original intention of the Founders. When the intention of the Founders regarding the federal scheme is known, it directs construction back to the federal scheme of the US Constitution and the relevant decisions of the US Supreme Court. The majority judgment again repeated its warning of the danger of a literal construction undertaken by the aid of a dictionary as if it was "a mere decree of the Imperial Parliament without reference to history."[116] Even if relevant, the court advised, such a construction is negatived by the Preamble: "How, then, can the facts known by all to have been present to the minds of the parties to the agreement be left out of consideration?"[117]

Baxter v Commissioners of Taxation (NSW) provides the final step in the explication of the doctrine of noninterference by the early court. It also provides an explanation of other provisions in the Constitution. However, its most important contribution is a more complete explanation of the knowledge and sources of knowledge that a court vested with the power of constitutional review in a federal scheme must possess and that is necessary for a sufficient understanding of the Constitution to permit accurate and valid interpretations.

Summary—Immunities Doctrine

Each of the cases considered in this section demonstrates a consistency of purpose by the early court to articulate the federal scheme of a Constitution that divided legislative and executive powers between the Commonwealth and the states as the Founders had originally intended. Recognizing the influence of the United States on the Founders' deliberations, the early court sought to protect the sovereign powers of each entity from interference by those of the other by the application of the doctrine of noninterference. Isaacs, on the other hand, argued for a literal construction of what he termed Imperial legislation, cited Privy Council judgments that emphasized literalism and rejected US Supreme Court decisions. His rejection of the federal doctrines would, if accepted, have left the states' executive and legislative powers subject to being overpowered by the Commonwealth and by the eventual centralization of legislative and executive powers in the Commonwealth.

States' Reserved Powers

The reservation of powers to the states that were not vested exclusively in the Commonwealth or withdrawn was that part of the Commonwealth

Constitution's scheme that was modeled by the Founders on the Tenth Amendment of the US Constitution. It was given effect by section 107 of the Commonwealth Constitution, which states that

> every power of the Parliament of a Colony which has become or becomes a State, shall, unless it is by this Constitution exclusively vested in the Parliament of the Commonwealth or withdrawn from the Parliament of the State, continue as at the establishment of the Commonwealth.

While section 107 reserves powers to the states that are not vested exclusively in the Commonwealth (or withdrawn), the effect of the reserve powers doctrine was to protect the powers of the separately sovereign states in relation to the management of their internal or private affairs from being overborne by the extension of Commonwealth powers that exceeded their limits. Regarding the provision in the US Constitution, James Madison described the object of the powers reserved to the states: "The powers reserved to the several States will extend to all the objects which, in the ordinary course of affairs, concern the lives, liberties, and properties of the people, and the internal order, improvement, and prosperity of the State."[118]

The doctrine of states' reserved powers was applied by the majority judgment of the early court in *R v Barger*[119] when the Commonwealth legislated to impose excise, a power exclusive to the Commonwealth, under the *Excise Tariff Act 1906* (Cth) (ETA) on Australian manufacturers who paid labor below a rate authorized by the ETA. The Commonwealth sought to sue Mr. Barger for penalties imposed under the ETA. The early court formed a majority and gave judgment for Barger; Isaacs and Higgins gave separate judgments for the Commonwealth.

Barger had objected that, despite the title and phraseology of ETA, "it is, in substance, not an exercise of the power of taxation conferred on the Parliament by the Constitution, but an attempt to regulate the internal trade and industry of the States . . . which is reserved to the States."[120] Barger had argued "that in determining whether a particular law is or is not within the power of the Parliament, regard must be had to the substance of the legislation rather than to its literal form,"[121] otherwise the Commonwealth could enact legislation under a constitutional head of power in order to achieve an object that was not within power. Griffith, speaking for the early court, cited the Privy Council case of *Attorney-General for Quebec v Queen Insurance Co*,[122] which supported such an inquiry, and therefore Barger's submission. He also cited the early court's own decision in *Peterswald v Bartley*[123] to the same effect when it said, "In considering the validity of laws of this kind, we must look to the substance and not the form. If the Statute is good in substance, the Court will regard the substance, and hold the law to be valid, whatever the form may be."[124]

He said that the issue before the court related to the nature of the Commonwealth's taxation power and whether "the ambit of the power is circumscribed by any, and what limits."[125] Griffith rejected Barger's submission that, as excise was a tax, the doctrine of noninterference prohibited interference by the Commonwealth power of taxation with trade and commerce internal to the state. In explaining the ambit of a Commonwealth legislative power, Griffith distinguished the doctrine of noninterference from the reserved powers doctrine and explained that the rules were related but that applicability to the present case was different, although founded upon the same principles: "The Constitution contains no provisions for enabling the Commonwealth Parliament to interfere with the private or internal affairs of the States, or to restrict the power of the States to regulate the carrying on of any businesses or trades within their boundaries, or even, if they think fit, to prohibit them altogether."[126]

Griffith explained that, regarding certain provisions in section 51 of the Constitution: "In some instances, when it was intended to allow the Parliament to regulate the domestic affairs of the States, the power was conferred by express words."[127] These powers, expressed generally, remain unqualified as to the extent of their effect and can be compared to the express limitation of the power to legislate directly for trade and commerce in section 51(i) of the Constitution: "Trade and commerce *with other countries, and among* the States," which precludes the internal affairs of a State.

Barger had submitted that the ETA was not a taxing statute, "but an attempt to regulate the internal trade and industry of the States, which, it is said, is not within the powers of the Parliament but is reserved to the States."[128] The issue for the court was to determine whether the ETA was a taxing statute or intended for some other purpose, and hence invalid.[129] The essence of the early court's decision was an acknowledgment that a Commonwealth Government might use an unrelated head of legislative power in order to obtain an indirect effect under that power that it could not obtain directly by the dedicated power. Griffith explained the crucial issue as being one of deciding "between the ends that can be attained by exercise of the legislative power and the means that can lawfully be adopted to attain those ends."[130] The fact that a taxing statute could produce indirect effects was not the issue. The issue was "whether the legislature is competent to prescribe the same result by a direct law."[131]

In its construction of the Commonwealth Constitution, Griffith accepted that the possibility of indirect effects from an exercise of the taxation power was recognized by the Founders of the Constitution,[132] who drafted the provisions so as to prevent the Commonwealth using its taxing power to discriminate between the states and between different parts of states.[133] After a consideration of the powers of taxation in section 51(ii) and uniform customs duties in section 88 of the Constitution, Griffith concluded that the power of taxation was subject to some limits. The Commonwealth had argued that as the limits were only those of the express words of section 51(ii), the persons on whom a tax or excise fell "may be made to depend upon any other condition whatever."[134] On the other hand, the defendant Barger had argued that the limitation of the power was not only in the express words of the sections, but also in other parts of the Constitution. Construction of the power of taxation must therefore be consistent with the other provisions of the Constitution, otherwise the Parliament could invade any area "by the simple process of making liability to the taxation depend upon matters within those regions."[135]

Griffith again turned to *Peterswald v Bartley*, where the early court had explained that, when construing the Constitution with respect to establishing where a particular power to act lay, it was necessary to consider all the provisions of the Constitution—those that applied generally as well as the particular provisions under consideration: "it is necessary to have regard to its general provisions as well as to particular sections, and to ascertain from its whole purview whether the power to deal with such matters was intended to be withdrawn from the States, and conferred upon the Commonwealth."[136]

Peterswald v Bartley was the first of the cases relating to the states' reserve powers to come before the High Court, and the facts were in a sense the reverse of those in *R v Barger*, in that it was the *Liquor Act 1898* (NSW) that imposed license fees on beer brewers, which were held by that State's Supreme Court to be an excise that infringed the exclusive Commonwealth power over excise. On appeal, the early court overturned the Supreme Court's decision, explaining that it looked at the Act "to see whether it was passed for the purpose of regulating or controlling the manufacture of this particular article, beer"[137] and held that the license fee was "one of several conditions imposed upon the manufacturer for regulating the trade, which is one of the primary functions of a State legislature."[138] The early court concluded that the license fee was not a duty but a valid exercise of the state's police powers for the control and regulation of the trade. Griffith explained that, if the Supreme Court had been correct, the Commonwealth would have the power to regulate the states' internal affairs. In denying that result, Griffith said that it is "altogether contrary to the *spirit* of the Constitution."[139] What Griffith meant by "spirit of the Constitution" can only have been the whole political scheme of the federal Constitution, the separate sovereignties of the Commonwealth and the states, the distribution of powers between the two sovereign bodies, and the scheme of responsible government.

The statements by the early court regarding the doctrine of states' reserve powers and their construction of the Constitution have received support in the analysis of the doctrine by James Allan and Nicholas Aroney.[140] They note concerning the reserve powers that: "Reference to the doctrine is often made, but its textual foundations and precise meaning are not always clearly explained or well-understood"[141] and they identify references in the literature to "the amorphous idea of fields reserved to the States,"[142] which fields are then illuminated by references to the matters to be regulated as "'internal' or 'domestic affairs.'"[143] Allan and Aroney appear to accept Isaacs's characterization of the reserved powers as "fields" rather than specific powers, even acknowledging his responsibility for the doctrine of "covering the field."[144] Covering the whole field was devised by Isaacs[145] as a test for inconsistency between federal and State laws. It achieved two purposes from Isaacs's point of view: it expanded Commonwealth power by substituting a new test for inconsistency that did not address any inconsistency in powers and which the Commonwealth legislature could appropriate on its own say-so; and, it eventually confirmed the superiority of all Commonwealth laws over State laws pursuant to section 109 of the Constitution even where both laws could be obeyed.

Allan and Aroney do not reference the criticism of it by Evatt J, who described covering the field as a cliché.[146] Their analysis concludes that the illumination of the issue by reference to fields is insufficient because section 107 does not provide "any clear guidance as to what exactly is reserved to the States."[147] Their criticism seems to overlook the fact that an inconsistency will only arise between Commonwealth and State concurrent powers and as, according to the Constitution, the subject matter of each Commonwealth power is limited, inconsistency with a State law will be evident on its face. A construing court would have no need to investigate if the State held a power since only a Commonwealth law exercising an exclusive power would be prima facie supreme. While Allan and Aroney rely on a legal positivist jurisprudence in their analysis, their conclusions actually reflect their concern with the exercise of Commonwealth legislative powers since the explosion[148] of the reserved powers doctrine by the *Engineers' case*.[149]

What Allan and Aroney describe as the second or negative view of the Commonwealth's legislative powers, where the words of a legislative power are the limit on that power under all heads of power, "is the proposition that the limited terms in which each head of power is conferred upon the Commonwealth has implications for how each other head of power is to be interpreted. Most strongly put, this amounts to a negative implication and a strict reservation of power."[150]

The significance of their proposition is evident in the judgment of Griffith CJ in *Huddart Parker & Co Pty Ltd v Moorehead*,[151] where the appellant company was convicted for refusing to answer the respondent's questions. The Commonwealth argued that the power to legislate under section 51(xx) for "foreign corporations and financial and trading corporations formed within the limits of the Commonwealth" included the power to create corporations since that power would permit the Commonwealth "to attach to the corporation when created any condition whatever that Parliament may think fit."[152] Griffith rejected that submission, saying that the words of the section did not deal with the creation of corporations and "the Commonwealth must take [corporations] as it finds them."[153] In his separate judgment, Barton thought the words of section 51(xx) could bear either meaning, but argued that for it to be an exception to the reservation of powers: "it would, as its framers must have known, have had to be expressed in language which admitted only of the former of these exceptions."[154] O'Connor came to the same conclusion that the power referred to corporations "formed under the laws of any State"[155] and assumed that was what "the framers of the Constitution intended."[156] Each of the early court justices asserted that the doctrine of reserve powers was consistent with what the Founders intended.[157]

Summary of Reserve Powers

The Tenth Amendment to the US Constitution, which was the source of the doctrine of states' reserved powers for the Convention, was not cited by any member of the High Court in *Peterswald v Bartley*,[158] *R v Barger*,[159] or *Huddart Parker & Co Pty Ltd v Moorehead.*[160] Yet the appeal to the "Founders" by all members of the early court implicitly recognizes the source of the reserve powers doctrine was the Tenth Amendment. When Isaacs corrected Josiah Symon during the Constitutional Convention to declare, "As I understand the matter, the visible sign of state autonomy consists in the reserved powers,"[161] he acknowledged that the states' separate sovereignties were inextricably linked to the powers reserved to the states by section 107 of the Constitution. This implies that his attack on the states' reserve powers doctrine was an attack on the visible sign of state sovereignty.

CONCLUSION

This chapter has demonstrated that the decisions of the early Court interpreted the Constitution so as to reveal details of the federal structure as the Founders at the Convention had intended and that the people in their several referenda had ratified. It showed that the early court identified the source of that structure in the federal doctrines of the US Supreme Court in relation to the immunity of instrumentalities and states' reserve powers and identified the intentions of the Founders by drawing on matters in relation to the Constitutional Convention that were known either notoriously or from common knowledge. Such matters included the choice of the US Constitution as a template for the Commonwealth Constitution and the presence of similarly worded provisions in the Commonwealth Constitutions necessitating a similar construction in both the Commonwealth and US Constitutions.

While the judgments on which Isaacs deliberated have not received the same degree of analysis as those of Griffith, Barton, and O'Connor, this chapter's purpose is to understand the methodology of the early court and its fidelity to the political scheme of the Constitution as intended by the Founders and ratified by the people. In that respect, the early court complied with the Constitution's inherent construction principle to reveal the Founders' original intention.

Isaacs rejected both the doctrine of immunities and that of states' reserved powers, and therefore the federal scheme after that of the United States as intended by the Founders and ratified by the people. To achieve that, Isaacs adopted a literal construction of the text of what he termed "Imperial legislation,"[162] cited Privy Council cases that endorsed that view,[163] and rejected US Supreme Court cases[164] that sustained the federal scheme. Of particular relevance to this essay is Isaacs's rejection in *R v Barger* of the authority of the Privy Council case *Attorney-General for Quebec v Queen Insurance Co* for construing legislation according to its substance rather than its form so as to prevent the legislature from encasing the substance of a law in a different form in order to disguise its purpose and to extend Commonwealth powers beyond that intended by the Founders.[165]

As the court sought to reveal the original intention of the Founders of the Constitution, we are obliged to consider what Isaacs said of this intention since his construction of the same document arrived at what is a diametrically opposite view of the Constitution. In *Huddart Parker & Co Pty Ltd v Moorehead*, Isaacs presents a concise rejection of the majority's resort to the reserve powers doctrine, explaining that a literal construction of the text was a universal rule of the highest authority:

> that though we are to examine every part of the instrument we must be guided by its language alone as applied to the subject matter, and it is not permissible to wander at large upon a sea of speculation searching for a suitable intent by the misty and uncertain light of what is sometimes called the spirit of the document, for that is largely fashioned subjectively by the preconceptions of the individual observer.[166]

This statement is a concise affirmation of Isaacs's legal positivism, in which there is no such thing as the political scheme, theory, or spirit of the constitution. These, he asserts, are "largely fashioned subjectively by the preconceptions of the individual observer."[167] The supreme paradox, however, is that whether the scheme reflects the spirit of the Constitution or reflects Isaacs's own construction, which rejects that concept, his own is subject to the same criticism; it is a scheme fashioned subjectively with no rational basis. His argument fails completely once it is recalled that he attended the Constitutional Convention and participated vigorously in the debates. As chapter 2 demonstrated, he also argued for a specific unitary scheme for the Constitution. His argument that there is no object, real or supposed, is self-serving and indefensible. His fellow Victorian delegate, Alfred Deakin, thought Isaacs unfortunate at the Convention in "the impression he created, for though his acuteness and research soon won remark, his endeavour to command attention by force and his constant appeal to the general principles of democracy fell flat upon his hearers."[168]

Isaacs maintained his objection to the scheme of the Constitution as explicated by the early court when he delivered the judgment of the High Court in the *Engineers' case* and took the opportunity to reject the doctrines associated with the early court's decisions with countervailing arguments that extolled the very spirit of the Constitution for which he had argued during the Convention and of which he denied any existence in *Huddart Parker & Co Pty Ltd v Moorehead.* The scheme that resulted from his judgment in the *Engineers' case* was essentially unitary.

On March 17, 1898, at the conclusion of the Convention, Edmund Barton speaking to a motion that invited the colonial Premiers to provide copies of the draft of the Constitution Bill to the electors of their colonies, added the need for an authoritative statement of the principles of the draft Constitution. Yet, when Isaac Isaacs spoke in support of Barton's motion, he said of the Constitution:

> Whatever may be thought of the measure which we are about to place before the people of Australia, little fault can be found with the way in which the intentions and resolutions of the Convention have been expressed in actual words.[169]

NOTES

1. As mentioned previously, the phrase "early court" is used to refer to the first three appointments to the High Court of Australia, the Chief Justice Sir Samuel Griffith, Sir Edmund Barton, and Richard O'Connor, which were made in 1903. The phrase "early court" also refers to decisions of the court when the original appointments of Griffith CJ, Barton, and O'Connor JJ comprised a majority on the Bench. Isaac Isaacs and Henry Higgins were appointed to the Bench in 1906; Justice Richard O'Connor died in 1912.

2. Haig Patapan, 'Politics of Interpretation' (2000) 22(2) *Sydney Law Review* 247, 248.

3. Ibid.

4. *D'Emden v Pedder* (1904) 1 CLR 91 at 113.
5. *Deakin v Webb* (1904) 1 CLR 585 at 596.
6. The *British North America Act* 1867 (UK) 30&31 Vict. c3 (BNA=).
7. *In re Income Tax Acts (No. 4) (Wollaston's case)* 28 VLR 357.
8. Ibid.
9. *Pedder v D'Emden* (1903) TLR 146.
10. *In re Income Tax Acts (No. 4) (Deakin's and Lyne's cases)* 29 VLR 748.
11. *D'Emden v Pedder* (1904) 1 CLR 91.
12. *McCulloch v Maryland*, 17 U.S. (4 Wheat.) 316, 405 (1819).
13. Justice Joseph Story, *Commentaries on the Constitution of the United States Vol. 1* (Hilliard Gray & Co, 1833) p. 196 (208).
14. *D'Emden v Pedder* (1904) 1 CLR 92. This statement of the information alleged (the omission excepted) faithfully reproduces the information cited in the judgment of the Tasmanian Supreme Court. The statement of offence is identical with that in *Pedder v D'Emden* (1903) TLR 146 at 147. The Tasmanian Supreme Court applied *In re Income Tax Acts (No. 4) Wollaston's case* 28 VLR 357.
15. *D'Emden v Pedder* (1904) 1 CLR 91.
16. Ibid., 109. The Imperial connection was of minor importance.
17. Ibid. at 109.
18. Ibid., 110. The court referred to the maxim *quando lex aliquid concedit, concedere videtur et illud sine quo res ipsa valere non potest.*
19. Ibid., 110.
20. Ibid., 110.
21. Ibid., 111.
22. The Commonwealth law under which salaries are paid to an employee of the then Post Master General's Department is not a law with respect to posts and telegraphs as Griffith implies.
23. *D'Emden v Pedder* (1904) 1 CLR 91 at 111.
24. Ibid., 111.
25. Ibid., 118.
26. The Department of Posts and Telegraphs had been transferred as an exclusive power to the Commonwealth under section 69 of the Constitution.
27. *D'Emden v Pedder* (1904) 1 CLR 91 at 113.
28. Ibid., 113.
29. Ibid., 116.
30. Ibid., 117.
31. Ibid., 118.
32. Ibid., 118.
33. Ibid., 113.
34. Ibid., 113. The court's reference to its assumption of the framers' knowledge, which was also known by public notoriety, is indicative of the need to discover the original intention of the Founders of the Constitution.
35. *Deakin v Webb* and *Lyne v Webb* (1904) 1 CLR 585. Both cases involved similar facts and were heard together by the Victorian Supreme Court. Both appeals

came before the High Court raising identical issues. The two cases will be referred to in this essay as *Deakin v Webb*.

36. Mr. Isaac Isaacs KC (as he then was) appeared for the State of Victoria before the Victorian Supreme Court in *In re Income Tax Acts (No. 4) Wollaston's case* 28 VLR 357, *In re the Income Tax Acts (No. 4) Deakin and Lyne's cases* 29 VLR 748, and for the State of Victoria in *Deakin v Webb* at the High Court.

37. *In re Income Tax Acts (No. 4) Wollaston's case* 28 VLR 357 at 371. This submission misleads the Supreme Court and cannot be excused as advocacy but it also demonstrates the importance in constitutional matters of a consideration of the character of the political scheme.

38. *Deakin v Webb* (1904) 1 CLR 585 at 595–6.

39. Ibid., 596–7. Isaacs substitutes the words "the Crown" for the Privy Council's more precise reference to the *Federation Act*. There was, in fact, no attempt by the Privy Council to generalize its judgment from the Canadian Constitution to all Imperial legislation.

40. *Bank of Toronto v Lambe* (1887) 12 App. Cas. 575. The reference to *McCulloch v Maryland* at p. 578 was a submission made by legal counsel to the Privy Council, not part of the decision.

41. Ibid., 587.

42. *Deakin v Webb* (1904) 1 CLR 585 at 596.

43. See Chap. 4.

44. *Deakin v Webb* (1904) 1 CLR 585 at 597.

45. Ibid., 597.

46. Ibid., 606–11.

47. Ibid., 606–8.

48. Ibid., 608.

49. Ibid., 606.

50. Ibid., 623.

51. Ibid., 623.

52. Ibid., 605.

53. Examples of powers in the *Australian Constitution* regulated by s. 52 include those under ss. 69 and 86.

54. *Deakin v Webb* (1904) 1 CLR 585 at 617.

55. Ibid., 605. This conclusion appears to be erroneous, however, as Alfred Deakin was a resident of Victoria by choice and stood for elected office for that state. If consistency with *D'Emden v Pedder* was required, the court should have held the state's taxing power to be an interference with the contract of employment between the Federal Parliament and Mr. Deakin on which his salary was drawn.

56. Ibid., 606, emphasis added. Griffith enlarges on this response in *Federated Amalgamated Government Railway & Tramway Service Association v New South Wales Railway Traffic Employees Association* (1906) 4 CLR 488 at 534 and moves the Constitution closer to that of the United States when he refers to the Constitution as a compact of the Australian colonies rather than an agreement of the peoples of the several Australian colonies. He is more accurate in *Baxter v Commissioners of*

Taxation (NSW) (1907) 4 CLR 1087 at 1104 where, on behalf of the majority, he describes the Constitution as an agreement between the people of the colonies.

57. Ibid., 606.

58. *Sydney Municipal Council v Commonwealth* (1904) 1 CLR 208 at 213; a decision was made by the Court early on not to admit statements made at the Convention, although Barton's rejection of the idea is ambiguous. It must be noted that both Barton and O'Connor were active participants in the 1897–1898 Convention and Griffith and Barton were active participants in the 1891 Convention. What they knew as public notoriety consisted of the whole of the Convention together with the history of the Convention. Reliance on the 1897–1898 Constitutional Convention debates as a source for construing the Constitution was finally authorized by the High Court in *Cole v Whitfield* (1988) 165 CLR 360.

59. *Deakin v Webb* (1904) 1 CLR 585 at 616.

60. Ibid., 605.

61. Ibid., 595.

62. Ibid., 605. *R v Barger* (1908) 6 CLR 41 at 67. This statement of principle needs to be contrasted with that of Barwick CJ in *Victoria v Commonwealth* (1971) 122 CLR 353 at 371.

63. *In re the Income Tax Acts (No. 4) (Deakin and Lyne's cases)* 29 VLR 748.

64. *Deakin v Webb* (1904) 1 CLR 585 at 604.

65. *In re Income Tax Acts (No. 4) (Wollaston's case)* 28 VLR 357 at 395.

66. *Deakin v Webb* (1904) 1 CLR 585 at 613–5.

67. Ibid., 616.

68. Ibid., 622.

69. Ibid., 624.

70. Ibid., 624.

71. Ibid., 623. Isaacs's refusal to accept the decision should have placed everyone on notice as to his intentions.

72. Ibid., 626, emphasis added. Barton appears to make a direct appeal if not to the debates of the Convention then at least to his knowledge of the debates.

73. Ibid., 626.

74. Ibid., 606.

75. Ibid., 597.

76. *The Federated Amalgamated Government Railway and Tramway Service Association v New South Wales Railway Traffic Employees Association (Railway Servants' case)* (1906) 4 CLR 488.

77. Ibid., 533. Section 51(xxxv) limited the Commonwealth's industrial relations power to the prevention and settlement of industrial disputes extending beyond the limits of any one state.

78. Ibid., 533.

79. While this argument was held to be valid in *New South Wales v Commonwealth* (*Work Choices case*) (2006) HCA 52, the two differ only in respect of the head of power relied on in each case. The *Work Choices case* purported to regulate the industrial relations of corporations under the power in section 51(xx). The legislation in *Railway Servants* case purported to use the trade and commerce power (s. 51(1)).

80. *The Federated Amalgamated Government Railway and Tramway Service Association v New South Wales Railway Traffic Employees Association* (1906) 4 CLR 488.

81. Ibid., 534.

82. Ibid., 534. Griffith refers to the compact in the Constitution's Preamble as being between the six colonies when the Preamble states that the compact is between "the people of New South Wales, Victoria, South Australia, Queensland and Tasmania." That fact is fundamental to comprehending the legal status of the Constitution as a sovereign act of the people of the colonies. While Griffith and other members of the Court appeal to the intention of the framers, they implicitly predicate the sovereignty of the people. Their acknowledgment of the Constitution as Imperial legislation, however, suggests the court is attempting to reconcile two irreconcilable sovereignties.

83. Ibid., 534.

84. Ibid., 534.

85. Ibid., 537.

86. Ibid.

87. *The Collector v Day*, 78 U.S. 11 Wall. 113 113 (1870).

88. Ibid.

89. *The Federated Amalgamated Government Railway and Tramway Service Association v New South Wales Railway Traffic Employees Association* (1906) 4 CLR 488 at 537.

90. Ibid., 538.

91. Ibid., 545. This construction is not unlike that necessitated by the states' reserve powers in which the validity of a law is tested by a consideration of its substance rather than its form.

92. Ibid., 537.

93. Viscount Haldane, speaking for the Privy Council, used the term "truly federal" in respect of the US and Commonwealth Constitutions: *Attorney-General (Cth) v Colonial Sugar Refining Company Limited* (1913) 17 CLR 644 at 652.

94. See Former Justices of the High Court, http://www.hcourt.gov.au/justices/former-justices/former-justices.

95. *Baxter v Commissioners of Taxation (NSW)* (1907) 4 CLR 1087.

96. *Webb v Outtrim* (1906) 4 CLR 356. As a result of the Privy Council's decision in this case, the *Judiciary Act 1903* was amended in 1907 by the *Judiciary Act No. 8*, which vested sole authority to determine inter se matters in the High Court and expressly removed the authority for state Supreme Courts to hear such matters.

97. The Privy Council decision also overturned the reciprocal immunity established in *The Federated Amalgamated Government Railway and Tramway Service Association v New South Wales Railway Traffic Employees Association* (1906) 4 CLR 488.

98. *Webb v Outtrim* (1906) 4 CLR 356 at 358.

99. Ibid.

100. Ibid., 360.

101. Ibid.

102. *Baxter v Commissioners of Taxation (NSW)* (1907) 4 CLR 1087 at 1100.
103. Ibid., 1103.
104. Ibid., 1103–4.
105. Ibid., 1104.
106. Ibid., 1104.
107. Ibid., 1104.
108. Ibid., 1104–5. While the Preamble names only five states, Western Australia was also an original state.
109. Ibid., 1105. This implies that a valid construction of the Constitution must reference the omitted substance implied by the form.
110. *Martin v Hunter's Lessee* 14 U.S. (1 Wheat.) 304 (1816).
111. *Baxter v Commissioners of Taxation (NSW)* (1907) 4 CLR 1088 at 1105.
112. Ibid., 1106.
113. Ibid., 1106.
114. Ibid., 1107–12.
115. Ibid., 1109.
116. Ibid., 1109.
117. Ibid., 1109.
118. James Madison, *Federalist* No. 45, *The Federalist Papers*, ed. Clinton Rossiter (New American Library, 1961) p. 376. In *Sydney Municipal Council v Commonwealth* (1904) 1 CLR 208 at 213, *The Federalist* was ruled admissible by the High Court as an expert opinion or textbook.
119. *R v Barger* (1908) 6 CLR 41.
120. Ibid., 64.
121. Ibid., 64.
122. Ibid., 65.
123. *Peterswald v Bartley* 1 CLR 497 at 511.
124. *R v Barger* (1908) 6 CLR 41 at 65.
125. Ibid., 66.
126. Ibid., 72.
127. Ibid., 69. Griffith referred specifically to the following powers in section 51: Currency, coinage, and legal tender (xii); the incorporation of banks and the issue of paper money (xiii); weights and measures (xv); Bills of exchange and promissory notes (xvi); Bankruptcy and insolvency (xvii); and Foreign corporations, and trading or financial companies formed within the limits of the Commonwealth (xx).
128. Ibid., 64.
129. Ibid., 65; notably the opinion of Harlan J in *Guy v Baltimore*.
130. Ibid., 66.
131. Ibid., 67.
132. Ibid., 69.
133. Ibid., 70.
134. Ibid., 71.
135. Ibid., 71.
136. *Peterswald v Bartley* (1904) 1 CLR 497 at 507.
137. Ibid., 511.

138. Ibid., 511.

139. Ibid., 507, emphasis added. Isaacs's legal positivist response was that the spirit of the Constitution was subjective (388).

140. James Allan and Nicholas Aroney, 'An Uncommon Court: How the High Court of Australia Has Undermined Australian Federalism' (2008) 30(2) *Sydney Law Review* 244, 267–8.

141. Ibid., 267. The authors ignore the reference to the people (singular) in the Preamble as the source of authority for the Constitution and describe the Constitution as a "creature of the States."

142. Ibid., 268.

143. Ibid.

144. Ibid., 260 n 71.

145. *Clyde Engineering Co. Ltd v Cowburn* (1926) 37 CLR 466 at 489.

146. *Stock Motor Ploughs Ltd v Forsyth* (1932) 48 CLR 128 at 147; Evatt J provides a cogent criticism of the ambiguous phrase "cover the field," describing it as "no more than a *cliché*" and saying of previous decisions relying on the phrase: "These conclusions have, in the main, been reached, by ascribing 'inconsistency' to a State law, not because the Federal law directly invalidates or conflicts with it, but because the Federal law is said to 'cover the field.'" It is difficult to understand how "cover the field" became a test when it is not supported by the text or by the political context of the Constitution.

147. James Allan and Nicholas Aroney, 'An Uncommon Court: How the High Court of Australia Has Undermined Australian Federalism' (2008) 30(2) *Sydney Law Review* 268. This suggests Allan and Aroney are suggesting that the state powers be enumerated.

148. Ibid., 271. The authors qualify their reference to the doctrine being "exploded by the *Engineers' case*" by stating that it "is often said."

149. Ibid., 288. Their reference to inviolable "sovereignty" is actually closer to Isaacs's criticism of sovereignty than to the mutual sovereignties articulated by Marshall CJ and Story J.

150. Ibid., 269.

151. *Huddart Parker & Co Pty Ltd v Moorehead* (1909) 8 CLR 330.

152. Ibid., 348.

153. Ibid.

154. Ibid., 363, emphasis added.

155. Ibid., 371.

156. Ibid., 373.

157. Ibid., 363, per Barton J; and at 373 per O'Connor J.

158. *Peterswald v Bartley* (1904) 1 CLR 497.

159. *R v Barger* (1908) 6 CLR 41.

160. *Huddart Parker & Co Pty Ltd v Moorehead* (1909) 8 CLR 330.

161. Official Record of the Debates of the Australasian Federal Convention, Sydney (1897), 305 (Isaac Isaacs). By visible, he meant visible in the Constitution, since the concept of the reserve powers is invisible.

162. *Huddart Parker & Co Pty Ltd v Moorehead* (1909) 8 CLR 330 at 388–9.

163. *R v Barger* (1908) 6 CLR 41 at 85.

164. Ibid., 83.

165. Ibid., 95–6. His actual rejection of the ratio, that the Privy Council did not "assume an equivalent," is unintelligible. Isaacs used the opposite argument when, during the Constitutional Convention in 1898, he debated a constitutional amendment that would have permitted the Inter-State Commission to investigate differential rail transport rates that interfered with interstate trade, he protested: "Therefore, we say, let us look to the substance, not merely to the form, and consider what is just and fair." Official Record of the Debates of the Australasian Federal Convention, Melbourne (1898), 1459 (Isaac Isaacs).

166. *Huddart Parker & Co Pty Ltd v Moorehead* (1909) 8 CLR 330 at 388.

167. Ibid., 388. Isaacs' is the advanced stage of legal positivism, which posits the objectivity of science and the subjectivity of all values, choices, and preferences. While legal positivism is usually attributed to John Austin, the more complete form emerged after the fact value distinction of Auguste Comte from Carl Bergbohm and the Austrian legal positivists in 1892. That school recognized that only the fact of the law was objective; all else was subjective and hence unintelligible.

168. Alfred Deakin, *Federal Story: The Inner History of The Federal Cause*, ed. Herbert Brookes (Robertson & Mullens, 1944) p. 78.

169. Official Record of the Debates of the Australasian Federal Convention, Melbourne (1898), 2484 (Isaac Isaacs).

Chapter 4

The *Engineers' Case*

INTRODUCTION

This chapter argues that the majority judgment in the *Amalgamated Society of Engineers v Adelaide Steamship Co Ltd* (the *Engineers' case*)[1] that was written by Isaacs[2] construed the Constitution in a way that was designed to replace the federal scheme that the Founders intended and the people ratified, one commensurate with decisions of the early Court, with Isaacs's long-preferred unitary scheme. He achieved this by making all powers reserved to the states subject to invalidity pursuant to section 109 of the Constitution while abolishing doctrines that assumed the separate sovereignties of the Commonwealth and states in the Constitution. The effect of his judgment was not to abandon original intent as a method of construction, but rather to replace the original intent of the Founders with Isaacs's own original intent.

Isaacs's judgment not only changed the manner in which the Commonwealth Constitution was to be understood and construed, but it also changed the political scheme of the Constitution and therefore the way in which the Australian people lived together. This chapter will show that it was the political scheme that Isaacs was intent on replacing. While it has been regarded as a crucial decision in Australian constitutional jurisprudence, different commentators have given different reasons for the change.[3] Barton died on January 18, 1920, and the *Engineers' case* was heard over the last week of July and the first week of August 1920.[4] Sir Samuel Griffith died on August 9, 1920,[5] and Isaacs authored and delivered the majority judgment twenty-two days later.[6] His judgment in the *Engineers' case* has been regarded as bitter and disrespectful of Griffith and the early court.[7] Griffith had resigned from the Bench due to ill health and Sir Adrian Knox had been appointed as Chief Justice on October 18, 1919. Griffith is reputed to have suggested Knox in order to prevent Isaacs from being appointed.[8] None of the new appointees, Knox CJ or Gavan Duffy, Rich, and Starke JJ, had been delegates to the Constitutional Convention, and therefore lacked the passing familiarity with the Constitution that the original members of the High Court had as delegates to the Conventions.[9]

The *Engineers' case* involved an industrial dispute between the claimant Society and 843 respondents, among whom were a number of Western Australian government trading businesses. The amended questions considered by the court were as follows:

(1) Has the Parliament of the Commonwealth power to make laws binding on the States with respect to conciliation and arbitration for the prevention and settlement of industrial disputes extending beyond the limits of one State?
(2) As to each of the respondents named in the *special case*—Is the dispute which has been found to exist in fact between the claimant and the Minister for Trading Concerns (WA) an industrial dispute within the meaning of sec. 51(xxxv)?[10]

The Commonwealth had power under section 51(xxxv) of the Constitution to legislate for industrial disputes extending beyond the limits of a state. The "special case" was the submission of the Western Australian government that there could be no industrial dispute (as per section 51(xxxv)) between the claimant Society and the government's business enterprises.[11] While chapter 2 showed that the Convention incorporated the separate sovereignties of the states and Commonwealth into a federal scheme, similar to that of US Constitution, it was the analysis of the cases in chapter 3 that showed how the early court, guided by US Supreme Court authorities, protected the separate sovereignties by applying the doctrines of implied immunities and of states' reserved powers.[12]

Isaacs's judgment in the *Engineers case* rejected the federal nature of the Constitution and those doctrines that assumed the separate sovereignties of the Commonwealth and states, the immunity of instrumentalities, and states' reserved powers. The *Engineers case*, Haig Patapan explains, fundamentally changed the co-sovereign federalism view of the Constitution, overturning the doctrines of implied prohibition and reserve powers of the early court.[13] Another major contribution of the case was its formulation of "a new basis for interpreting the Constitution that was to exercise far-reaching influence on the High Court's jurisprudence."[14] That the decision of the court in the case was revolutionary[15] has been widely recognized, albeit in different ways. William Anstey Wynes thought "the *Engineers case* properly decided" and the principles of construction the only ones "upon which a written Constitution can properly and with any certainty be interpreted."[16] From another perspective, Leslie Zines observed in regard to the *Engineers' case* that: "Political scientists noted the trend towards centralisation" while the "refusal to look at implications was treated by many lawyers as establishing a simpler and more certain method of interpretation."[17]

The principal effect of the judgment was to render all the states' legislative powers, and not simply the powers shared concurrently with the Commonwealth,[18] conditional upon the legislative action or inaction of the Commonwealth pursuant to section 109 of the Constitution.[19] Zines referred to this aspect of the revolution as *centralization*, which is not dissimilar to Isaacs's description of the BNA at the Constitutional Convention: "It is a Federation upon the centralisation principle."[20] Jeffery Goldsworthy referred to Isaacs's view as "centralising nationalism," and speculated that Isaacs was motivated by a "personal political" view.[21] Gregory Craven called it "centralisation of power."[22] This notion of a sliding scale of power, however, obscures the issue by implying a sliding scale of sovereignty rather than discrete issues of complete sovereignty. While these commentators have recognized this shifting of power, they have not all necessarily seen it as a loss of sovereignty. The notion of a sliding scale of sovereignty is inaccurate regarding a federal system since it denies concurrent sovereignty over the same objects. Joseph Story, speaking of sovereignty in the US Constitution, suggested that the sovereignty of a nation could be absolute, while the sovereignty of a government within it "may extend to few or many objects. It may be unlimited, as to some; it may be restrained, as to others."[23] In other words, it would relate to discrete objects rather than operating on a sliding scale.

The quality of the judgment in the *Engineers' case* has been questioned.[24] Its legacy, however, has been more than the destruction of the doctrines that protect a truly federal Constitution. It was also responsible for entrenching a literalist methodology of construction in the High Court's jurisprudence. Isaacs's distinction between the Commonwealth Constitution and that of the United States was described by Sir Owen Dixon as irrelevant.[25] Isaacs's insistence on a literal construction[26] of the Constitution merely applied Dicey's legal positivist distinction between the legal and political sovereign that he had linked to the legislative powers of the British Parliament as distinguished from the political powers of the people. Chapter 1 of this essay disputed the validity of Dicey's theoretical distinction and its application to a Constitution in which sovereignty rested with the people. While Isaacs's legal positivism might imply that his use of a literal construction was doctrinaire, this chapter will show that its use and the case law he cited in support facilitated a conclusion that replaced the constitutional scheme originally intended by the Founders with a scheme similar to that for which Isaacs had argued at the Convention. He relied, in the majority judgment, on the authority of legal positivist decisions of the Privy Council that asserted a consideration only of the legal text without regard for the political scheme in respect of noncomparable constitutions. It might be thought that the precedent value of the previous seventeen years of High Court decisions would have been sufficient to prevent such a wholesale reinterpretation of the Constitution as to deprive the States of their federal powers. Isaacs argued, as he had done previously, that Privy Council authorities were binding on the ground that the Commonwealth Constitution was an Act of the sovereign Imperial Parliament and that Privy Council rules of statutory construction were mandatory. "That instrument is the political compact of the whole of the people of Australia, enacted into binding law by the Imperial Parliament."[27] This argument ignores the real ground of sovereignty in the Australian people.[28]

Isaacs employed a number of different devices in his judgment in the *Engineers' case*. As already noted, following Privy Council authority, he prescribed a literal construction of the Constitution that he equated with the natural meaning of words; he rejected any appeal to decisions of the US Supreme Court although he availed himself of them in support of his arguments; he altered the facts in cases in order to bring them within the compass of his argument; and he abused the citation of a Privy Council case that had rejected his argument by citing the ex-curial Westminster Parliamentary speech of the same Lord Chancellor.[29]

LITERALISM

While literalism is the common face of a legal positivist construction of a Constitution, Isaacs's justification for a literal construction begins with his statement of the special duty of the court to find the intention of the Constitution "from the words of the compact"[30] without any reference to the underlying scheme. He links his demand for a literal construction to specific decisions of the Privy Council and the House of Lords, which he describes as "the highest tribunals of the Empire,"[31] purposefully ignoring those of the High Court. The first of the citations relied on was that of Lord Macnaghten in *Vacher & Sons Ltd v London Society of Compositors*,[32] whose decision denied the judiciary authority to question the policy of any Act of the Parliament:

> A judicial tribunal has nothing to do with the policy of any Act which it may be called upon to interpret. That may be a matter for private judgment. The duty of the Court, and its only duty, is to expound the language of the Act in accordance with the settled rules of construction.[33]

While Macnaghten explicitly directed the court toward a consideration of the text of an Imperial Act, his reference to the restraint prescribed for a tribunal from considering the policy of any Act implicitly challenged the High Court's duty under the federal Constitution to consider the policy of Acts to determine whether they were valid pursuant to a constitutional head of power as demonstrated in chapter 3. Isaacs's citation implied that the High Court did not have a power of judicial review, whether of inter se questions (regardless of section 74 of the Constitution) or even the constitutionality of any legislation. Isaacs reinforced this conclusion when he later turned to *Vacher*, where the court had cited the settled rules of construction "very distinctly enunciated"[34] by the highest tribunals, the "golden rule or universal rule"[35]—and the warning by Lord Haldane not to go astray in the labyrinth of interpreting the "motives of the Legislature."[36] Walker accurately identifies Isaacs's purpose when he remarks that "the 'Golden Rule' is about altering the natural meaning of legislation where it is apparent that an error has been made and an absurdity would otherwise result."[37] While this anticipates Isaacs's intention to alter the meaning of the Constitution, it must be stressed that there was no warrant for that alteration and the Golden Rule is otherwise inapplicable to the Commonwealth Constitution, since the power of alteration is denied to the judiciary and vested in the people by section 128 of the Constitution.[38] Isaacs's Imperial authorities are premised on the ground that the court is construing an ordinary law of the Imperial Parliament rather than a federal Constitution.[39] He cites Lord Selborne's judgment on behalf of the Judicial Committee in *R v Burah*[40] with approval. In that decision, His Lordship advocated a literal construction where a question arose about whether any given legislation exceeded the power granted:

> The established Courts of Justice, when a question arises whether the prescribed limits have been exceeded, must of necessity determine that question; and the only way in which they can properly do so, is by looking to the *terms* of the instrument by which, affirmatively, the legislative powers were created, and by which, negatively, they are restricted. . . . It is not for any Court of Justice to inquire further, or to enlarge constructively those conditions and restrictions.[41]

Lord Selborne's dictum was given in a case challenging legislation enacted by a nonelected Indian legislature, in a "unitary" government whose powers were, according to Lord Selborne, "expressly limited by the Act of the Imperial Parliament which created it."[42] While his dictum relates to the powers in the Imperial Act, the prescribed limits he mentions relate to the powers of the unitary Indian legislature that passed the challenged Act. Isaacs's application of the dictum at once assumes the sovereignty of the Imperial Parliament, but it also authorizes only express limitations or enlargements.[43]

Selborne's judgment is only applicable, however, if the Commonwealth Constitution is unitary and not federal, for a federal division of powers after that of the United States, as the Founders knew, necessarily has implied limits. Selborne's dictum supports Isaacs's literalism: it is irrelevant to the Commonwealth Constitution whose federal scheme was intended by the Founders to incorporate the separate sovereignties as shown in chapters 2 and 3 and a High Court jurisdiction to resolve conflicts between them.[44] Such a jurisdiction necessitates a consideration of the nature and limits of powers of each sovereign body, having regard to the federal structure in the context of the whole Constitution. This requirement was alluded to by Griffith in *Deakin v Webb* when explaining the necessity of considering specific matters in the context of the whole scheme of the Constitution when a power or a limit thereto was a matter of inference and implication.[45] Selborne's dictum is only relevant to the Commonwealth Constitution, if that Constitution is unitary. Isaacs confirms this purpose by linking the principle in Selborne's judgment to the Canadian Constitution with a reference to the Privy Council judgment of Lord Loreburn, who said:

> In the interpretation of a completely self-governing Constitution founded upon a written organic instrument, such as the *British North America Act, if the text is explicit the text is conclusive, alike in what it directs and what it forbids*. When the text is ambiguous, as, for example, when the words establishing two mutually exclusive jurisdictions are wide enough to bring a particular power within either, recourse must be had to the context and scheme of the Act.[46]

This passage was also cited by Isaacs in the High Court case of *Colonial Sugar Refining Co Ltd v Attorney-General of the Commonwealth*,[47] where he asserts that Lord Loreburn's dictum is applicable simply by "Altering 'Canada' to 'Australia.'"[48] In that case, Isaacs implied that the Commonwealth Constitution, like its Canadian counterpart, established "two mutually exclusive jurisdictions." Loreburn, on the other hand, argues that where powers overlap, as they did in that case and do in the Commonwealth Constitution, a court can have resort to "the context and scheme" of the Constitution. Given Dixon's warnings against the use of Canadian cases to interpret the Commonwealth Constitution,[49] it is useful to set out some of the significant differences between the two Constitutions, which militate against resorting to cases construing the Canadian Constitution without a consideration of the different political schemes:

- The Commonwealth Constitution's federal scheme is a compact of the Australian people to which they consented. The Canadian Constitution is a confederacy of unitary schemes[50] imposed by Westminster.

- The Commonwealth Constitution vests both exclusive and concurrent powers in the Commonwealth, reserving those not exclusive to the Commonwealth to the states.[51] The BNA vested mutually exclusive powers in each of the dominion and the provinces.[52]
- Australian states are represented equally in the Senate by elected senators. Canadian senators[53] who meet a property qualification are appointed[54] for life.[55]
- The High Court of Australia[56] is an independent and coordinate branch of the federal power.[57] The Canadian Supreme Court is a product of the Canadian legislature in 1875.[58]
- The High Court is a Court of final appeal for the interpretation of the Constitution. The Privy Council was the Court of final appeal for all Canadian civil matters until 1949.[59]
- The sovereign power to amend the Commonwealth Constitution is vested in the Australian people. The power to amend the BNA law lies with the Imperial Parliament.

Quick and Garran considered the US cases more valuable as aids to the interpretation of the Commonwealth Constitution than Canadian cases because of the federal nature of the relationship between the Commonwealth and the states and the mutually exclusive relationship between the two Canadian constitutional entities: "The States of the Commonwealth occupy positions corresponding to those of the American Union, the mode of distribution of powers under the Constitution of the Commonwealth resembling the American rather than the Canadian model."[60]

While the early court acknowledged the possibility of conflict arising as a result of the separate sovereignties, Isaacs mischaracterized this as abuse[61] and cited the Privy Council decision in *Bank of Toronto v Lambe* in support, asserting that "the ordinary meaning of the terms employed in one place may be restricted by terms used elsewhere"[62] was pure legal construction. However, an examination of the decision in *Lambe* shows that the judgment's author, Lord Hobhouse, was referring to the moral quality of a valid, *exclusive* law:

> But whatever power falls within the legitimate meaning . . . is, in their Lordships' judgement, what the Imperial Parliament intended to give; and to place a limit on it because the power may be used unwisely, as all powers may, would be an error.[63]

This rule is irrelevant where a valid law of one sovereign entity interferes with the legislative or executive power of another sovereign entity; it is only applicable in Isaacs's judgment because he has already assumed that the federal division does not exist.[64] The Canadian jurist Vincent C. MacDonald documented a well-recognized problem with the Canadian Constitution which was exemplified in *Bank of Toronto v Lambe*. The Constitution, ostensibly having no overlapping powers, gives no indication of which unitary entity is dominant or where the implied limits lie, and the Privy Council decisions actually distorted the Constitution in "the process of judicial fabrication of a constitution alien to that desired and enacted."[65] It is reasonable to conclude from Isaacs's silence on the effect of fundamentally different Constitutions on constitutional decisions that he had simply assumed the states were not sovereign and that his methodology and his arguments merely gave effect to this premise.

As explained in chapter 3, when representing the Victorian government before the High Court in *Deakin v Webb*, Isaacs had submitted to the court that in construing the Constitution, the court could only look at the "legal aspect."[66] The demand for an interpretation of a Constitution's "legal aspect," or text, is implicitly a legal positivist argument for a literal construction in isolation from the political scheme. The inherent errors resulting from such a construction were explored at length in chapter 1. There it was shown that, as sovereignty in the Commonwealth is vested in the people, who alone are authorized by the Constitution to alter the text and therewith the legislative powers and laws of the Parliament, a construction of the text must seek the meaning to which the sovereign people have consented. Dicey's concept of the "legal" therefore has no relevance to the interpretation of the Australian Constitution, the political scheme of which is inseparably joined to the text.

As the political and the legal are united in the Commonwealth Constitution, the majority judgment's insistence upon a consideration of a literal interpretation of the text in its natural meaning without considering the political scheme is to deny access to the natural meaning that such a context provides. As an exercise of judicial fiat, it severs the link between the political schemes to which the text was joined, permitting the scheme to be altered in line with the interpretation of the text. John Nethercote observed the shift in the High Court from a federalist perspective of the early court which maintained the autonomy of both Commonwealth and state governments to the centralist perspective of the *Engineers' case*.[67] This objective, Nethercote thought, "was achieved by returning the Constitution to British methods of statutory interpretation, by treating it as an ordinary statute of the Imperial Parliament."[68] While this is true, Nethercote's argument made no attempt to reconcile Isaacs's choice of authorities with his participation in the Convention, where his arguments for a unitary scheme were rejected.[69]

On the other hand, although Marshall CJ stated that the words of the US Constitution were employed by the framers "in their natural sense,"[70] he implies that the natural sense of the words of the US Constitution must be construed to support the political theory of the Constitution, rather than being "in support of some theory not to be found in the Constitution."[71] Marshall's principles of construction therefore align closely with that of the early court, which referenced that theory to the framers' intention.

US DECISIONS

Isaacs confronted the problem that US Supreme Court decisions posed for his arguments by the simple expedient of banning them from the court. Chapters 2 and 3 discussed how the Founders adapted the US Constitution's federal scheme and chapter 3 looked at how the early court articulated the principles upon which it relied in US Supreme Court cases, initially those of Marshall CJ, which provided the analytic doctrines related to true federalism. On the other hand, the Privy Council cases that Isaacs cited endorsed a literal construction of a law enacted by the Imperial Parliament. While his choice of Privy Council cases could direct the court's attention to the text, they had nothing to say about the federal doctrines that were relevant to the Constitution's political scheme. That Isaacs's choice of authorities was directed against the US-styled constitutional federalism can be inferred from his treatment of Viscount Haldane LC, whose judgment for the Privy Council in *Attorney-General (Cth) v Colonial Sugar Refining Company Limited* (*Colonial Sugar case*)[72] declared the Commonwealth Constitution truly federal after that of the United States, whereas the BNA "departs widely from the true federal model adopted in the Constitution of the United States, the tenth amendment to which declares that the powers not delegated to the United States by the Constitution, nor prohibited by it to the States, are reserved to the States."[73]

He held that when the Founders framed the Australian Constitution, "the principle established by the United States was adopted in preference to that chosen by Canada."[74] Isaacs, however, ignored His Lordship's curial statement on this issue but quoted from a speech in 1900 when, as Sir Richard Haldane MP, he spoke in the Westminster Parliament to the *Commonwealth of Australia Constitution Act*. Commenting that the Commonwealth shared responsible government with the Westminster Parliament, he added: "Therefore, what you have here is nothing akin to the Constitution of the United States except in its most superficial features."[75] It was an unfortunate choice of words by Haldane the Parliamentarian, and Isaacs cited them to his advantage. He calls the Privy Council an august body and the method of its judicial investigation legally binding without mentioning that its method in the *Colonial Sugar case* was directed to understanding the powers of a federal government and that it found them by "examining the *scheme* of the Act of 1900, which established the Commonwealth Constitution."[76] By "scheme" it can be inferred that Haldane meant the federal scheme, and the arguments of the Convention from which the principles of the scheme were known notoriously, for His Lordship found as a matter of law that in framing the Commonwealth's scheme, "the principle established by the United States was adopted in preference to that chosen by Canada"[77] and that principle—being from the United States—is not evident on the face of the Constitution's text.

Isaacs's argument against US Supreme Court decisions was based on what he calls the two cardinal features of the Commonwealth's political system: "Pervading the instrument, they must be taken into account in determining the meaning of its language. One is the common sovereignty of all parts of the British Empire; the other is the principle of responsible government."[78]

The irony of this statement must surely be that since neither is mentioned in the Constitution, they can only pervade the instrument as its spirit, something that Isaacs had previously denied existed.[79] Sir Owen Dixon dismissed Isaacs's explanation as irrelevant:

> We are next exhorted by the judges to bear in mind two cardinal features of our political system, namely the unity of the Crown and the principle of responsible government, and these are said to distinguish it radically from the US Constitution—and so of course they do, *but in no relevant respect.*[80]

Isaacs was unperturbed by this irony. Because of those two features, he declared that the use of decisions of the US Supreme Court in the determination of Australian cases would be a profound error:

> No more profound error could be made than to endeavour to find our way through our own Constitution by the borrowed light of the decisions, and sometimes the dicta, that American institutions and circumstances have drawn from the distinguished tribunals of that country.[81]

This reinforced his earlier statement to the same effect that the US cases were not applicable to the Commonwealth Constitution: "But we conceive that American authorities, however illustrious the tribunals may be, are not a secure basis on which to build fundamentally with respect to our own Constitution."[82] By this means, he not only prevented parties from citing US Supreme Court decisions to the High Court, but also prevented the court from any future reconsideration of the *Engineers' case* based on US decisions. As final as his stricture was, it did not prevent him from citing decisions of the US Supreme Court including *Keller v The United States*, *Virginia v West Virginia*, and *Gibbons v Ogden*[83] in support of aspects of his own argument.

Although the *Engineers' case* fell for consideration in accordance with the rule in *McCulloch v Maryland*,[84] the majority judgment does not mention the case once. As referred to previously, it cites Marshall's caution in *Gibbons v Ogden* that construction of the extent of constitutional powers should be "by the language of the instrument that created them, taken in connection with *the purposes* for which they were conferred."[85] Isaacs's construction, however, avoided any consideration of the actual purpose of the Constitution.[86] *Keller v The United States*[87] was given as an authority for the proposition that state police powers—those reputed to be exclusive to the states—"must yield whenever Congress, in the exercise of the powers granted to it, legislates upon the precise subject matter."[88] That particular passage, however, was a submission by the US Assistant Attorney General to the Supreme Court. It was repeated in Justice Brewer's judgment for the majority, only to be rejected when he said of the conflict between the federal law and the police power:

> Although Congress has not largely entered into this field of legislation, it may do so, if it has the power. Then we should be brought face to face with such a change in the internal conditions of this country as was never dreamed of by the framers of the Constitution. While the acts of Congress are to be liberally construed in order to enable it to carry into effect the powers conferred, it is equally true that prohibitions and limitations upon those powers should also be fairly and reasonably enforced.[89]

Isaacs's rejection of cases decided by the US Supreme Court was selective insofar as it only prevented the citation of cases, such as *McCulloch v Maryland* and *The Collector v Day*, that were sources of the doctrines that had sustained the federal scheme in the decisions of the early court—the same doctrines that he intended to abolish.

DOCTRINE OF IMPLIED IMMUNITIES

While Isaacs was able to proscribe the drawing of necessary implications that arise from the separate sovereignties in US Supreme Court cases by denying those cases' admissibility, he was obliged to give reasons for rejecting them where they had been raised in the decisions of the early court. In order to understand how the majority judgment in the *Engineers' case* achieved such a fundamental change to the political scheme of the Constitution from the meaning originally intended by the Founders, attention must also be paid to the many seemingly inconsequential points that Isaacs raises, which are often not in their proper context, for these comprised the incremental steps necessary for him to bring his intention to effect. The reason for that attention is underlined by recalling how, during the Convention, he attributed great changes to the US Constitution from the interpretations of the US judges.[90]

Isaacs asserts that the decisions of the early court contained no clear principle but were at variance with the natural meaning of the text of the Constitution;[91] and that some rested on reasons not founded on the words of the Constitution but "on implication drawn from what is called the principle of 'necessity,' being itself referable to no more definite standard than the personal opinion of the Judge who declares it."[92] This, however, is to divide Griffith's argument and to substitute necessity as the principle rather than the implication the doctrine represented. The personal opinion to which Isaacs refers in the context of "necessity" was the existence of the separate sovereignties and the federal scheme. Griffith attributed the implication to "the necessity to preserve the Constitution as granted,"[93] where the Commonwealth and states were separately sovereign, a condition associated with a federal scheme.[94] A necessary implication from the text would be a question of constitutional law, not personal opinion, yet Isaacs states that necessity is employed in "a political sense"[95]—presumably in reference to the federal scheme and therefore in the extended sense by which Dicey meant "political."

The separate sovereignties of the Commonwealth and states, expressed for the states in the reserved powers, constituted a fundamental legal principle of the Constitution and was intended by the Founders, as acknowledged by Isaacs and shown in chapter 2. It was a continuing concern of most delegates that the sovereignty of the states be protected throughout the Convention, as Barton explained:

> It must be recollected that the ordinary rights of liberty and protection by the laws are not among the subjects confided to the Commonwealth. The administration of the laws regarding property and personal liberty is still left with the states. We do not propose to interfere with them in this Constitution. We leave that amongst the reserved powers of the states.[96]

As the necessary implication from separate sovereignties is a doctrine derived from a construction that protects the scheme of the Constitution, it is therefore a matter of the law of the Constitution. Isaacs repeats what he refers to as the states' argument in the case before him: viz., that they were protected from the Commonwealth's industrial relations power by the doctrine of immunities laid down in *D'Emden v Pedder*: "The chief contention on the part of the States is that what has been called the rule of *D'Emden v Pedder* justifies their immunity from Commonwealth control in respect of State trading."[97] This, however, is less a gloss on the states' submissions[98] than a reformulation of them. The states, in response to a submission by the applicant Association that the real *ratio decidendi* of *D'Emden v Pedder* was the supremacy of Commonwealth powers under section 109,[99] submitted that section 109 applied only to concurrent powers and denied that the rule in *D'Emden v Pedder* was based on section 109 of the Constitution; they submitted that the rule was *reciprocally* true, citing *Federated Amalgamated Government Railway and Tramway Service Association v New South Wales Railway Traffic Employees' Association* (the *Railway Servants case*) to that effect.[100]

Isaacs cited the rule in *D'Emden v Pedder*,[101] commenting that the rule did not actually support the states' case but, rather destroyed it. This is *literally* true, since the rule invalidated state laws to the extent that they interfered with Commonwealth powers. But it was untrue of the states' case, which was based on the *reciprocal* of the rule, that found in the *Railway Servants case*, that the Commonwealth law was invalid to the extent it interfered with a state executive function. Isaacs had therefore misrepresented the states' argument. He denied that the reciprocal rule could be found in *D'Emden v Pedder*; "it would be *obiter* if found,"[102] which is a straw-man argument since *D'Emden v Pedder* was not concerned with a Commonwealth law interfering with a state legislative or executive function but with a state law interfering with a Commonwealth power. Isaacs misstates the issue in the *Engineers' case* as if to show that the state executive is interfering with a Commonwealth law: "An authority has been set up by a State which is claimed to be an executive authority and which, if exempt from Commonwealth legislation, does fetter or interfere with free exercise of the legislative power of the Commonwealth under pl. XXXV of sec. 51."[103]

The case was not about the state executive interfering with a Commonwealth legislative power. Isaacs's statement in this form, however, points to the difficulty he faces in bringing the case within section 109, with which he will purport to solve his problem, for that section requires a conflict between a Commonwealth law and a state law, and nowhere in the case is the particular state law cited. Further, the case is about Commonwealth interference with a state executive power, which invites the rule in the *Railway Servants' case*. Isaacs's statement of the issue, however, enabled him to attack the rule in *D'Emden v Pedder*[104] which, if the issue in the *Engineers' case* was accurately stated, would not have been possible. In common sense terms, if a state authority were exempt from Commonwealth legislation, it would be impossible to interfere with the Commonwealth legislation. Isaacs therefore attempted to substantiate his statement by arguing that the state's executive authority did fetter or interfere with Commonwealth legislative power under section 51(xxxv):

> Unless that placitum is not as complete as its words in their natural meaning indicate, or since sec. 107 applies to State concurrent powers equally with its

> exclusive powers, unless every Commonwealth legislative power, however complete in itself, is subject to the unrestricted operation of *every* State Act.[105]

While these two qualifications are syntactically difficult to follow, they refer respectively to the doctrines of immunities and states' reserved powers, and he used this same argument in his rejection of both. By referring to the words' *natural* meaning, the first clause purports to prove that there is no interference because the power, construed literally, is complete. The word "complete" seems to suggest that his literal construction excludes even the express qualification "extending beyond the limits of any one State,"[106] which is the factor that enlivens the Commonwealth head of power. The second qualification argues that only states' exclusive powers are reserved from Commonwealth interference; a state concurrent power cannot exist concurrently with the complete Commonwealth power. On this last point, he is implying his "cover the field" test of a Commonwealth power even if the power is limited by its express terms. The Commonwealth's industrial relations power in section 51(xxxv) of the Constitution was limited to "disputes extending beyond the limits of any one State."

The decision cites the Preamble to the Commonwealth Constitution and concludes that: "'The Crown' is one and indivisible."[107] It purports to summarize an argument of the Western Australian government asserting that it distinguishes the Imperial King, the Commonwealth King, and the State King and that "the Commonwealth King has no power to bind the first and the last, and, reciprocally, the last cannot bind either of the others."[108] It rejects that argument, however, since

> the Crown is ubiquitous and indivisible in the King's dominions. Though the Crown is one and indivisible throughout the Empire, its legislative, executive and judicial power is exercisable by different agents in different localities, or in respect of different purposes in the same locality, in accordance with the common law, or the statute law there binding the Crown.[109]

At this point, the judgment tends toward dogmatism by asserting that laws made by the Commonwealth under the Constitution necessarily bind the Crown, peoples of the states and the states themselves: "laws validly made by authority of the Constitution, bind, so far as they purport to do so, the people of every State considered as individuals or as political organisms called States—in other words, bind both Crown and subjects."[110]

As this statement makes no mention of implied limits to Commonwealth powers and assumes that a validly made Commonwealth law is necessarily valid against the states now described as "political organisms," Isaacs implicitly declares the disappearance of sovereign states. Their "people" become "subjects" and the sovereign states become the "Crown." At this point, it is useful to recall his statement that the Crown is "one and indivisible throughout the Empire."[111] When taken together, these statements implicitly abolish the federal scheme, with all entities suddenly united under the one Crown.

While the cited passage qualifies the Commonwealth law as one "validly made," the law will always be valid because the legislative authority of sovereign states has been deposed. The sovereign states are no longer states but "political organisms" under the one Crown, and laws passed by the Commonwealth bind the peoples and state "political organisms" that no longer hold independent sovereign legislative powers. As he provides no reasons based on the Constitution to limit a valid Commonwealth law, Isaacs's argument resembles a truncated version of section 109 of the Constitution—truncated, because a conflict of Commonwealth law with state law was always the condition precedent to the jurisdiction of section 109 of the Constitution. Isaacs's judgment has altered the case before the court from a Commonwealth law interfering with a state executive function, which raised an inter se issue and the remedy under section 74, to one of inconsistency for which section 109 provides the remedy. The doctrine of immunities arose as a necessary implication from the separate sovereignties. However, if the state has no sovereign legislative power, its laws can offer no resistance to a Commonwealth law.

Isaacs facilitated his attack on the doctrine of immunities (or noninterference) with a condemnation of all implications, including necessary ones from the Constitution's federal scheme. Referring to Griffith CJ's resort in *Attorney-General for Queensland v Attorney-General for the Commonwealth* to implications that the states are "based on a vague individual conception of the spirit of the compact"[112] but not on any specific language or principle of constitutional interpretation, Isaacs argues that "this method of interpretation cannot, we think, provide any secure foundation for Commonwealth or State action, and must inevitably lead—and in fact has already led—to divergencies and inconsistencies more and more pronounced as the decisions accumulate."[113]

While *D'Emden v Pedder* was the Australian case that expressed the doctrine of immunities, Isaacs asserted that the rule found "its most distinct formulation in *Attorney-General for Queensland v Attorney-General for the Commonwealth.*"[114] At issue in that case was whether states' Crown land leased to private interests was exempt from a Commonwealth land tax under the doctrine of immunities. Griffith had held that the doctrine of immunities did not apply. The tax would only fall on the private leasehold interest in the land,[115] but the Crown's interest in reversion would be tax free.

The chief focus of Isaacs's attention to the *Goldsbrough case*, however, was not that decision but Griffith's explanation of the rule in *D'Emden v*

Pedder; he also took issue with Griffith's reasons in the *Goldsbrough case*. He said that Griffith,

> assuming the implication of non-interference to arise *prima facie* from necessity *in all cases* and then to be subject to *exclusion* where the necessity ended,[116] proceeded to say: "It is manifest that, since the rule is founded upon the necessity of the implication, the implication is excluded if it appears upon consideration of the whole Constitution that the Commonwealth, or, conversely, the State, was intended to have power to do the act the validity of which is impeached."[117]

Isaacs employs the literary device here by adding his own emphasis to terms that aren't actually present. Although the first two lines purport to summarize Griffith's interpretation of the rule in *D'Emden v Pedder* appearing in the *Goldsbrough case*, the italicized words are actually Isaacs's. None of them appears in any Griffith judgment since noninterference does not arise in "all cases" from the separate sovereignties. Griffith's statement in the *Goldsbrough case* was:

> In *Deakin v Webb* it was contended that the rule, being based upon necessary implication, could not be *extended* beyond the necessity, and that upon a consideration of the whole Constitution, it would be found that the rule did not *extend* to the interference with the Commonwealth power then in question.[118]

Griffith cites *Deakin v Webb* as the source of the first two lines, but says of them that "it was contended,"[119] meaning it was a submission. Actually, the submission was Isaacs's; he appeared as counsel in *Deakin v Webb*. Moreover, Griffith's statement in both *Goldsbrough* and *Deakin v Webb* of Isaacs's contention was *not* that the rule of noninterference was subject to *exclusion* where the necessity ended; rather, Griffith said that it could not be *extended* beyond the necessity, and he accepted that in the *Goldsbrough case*.[120] The more telling aspect of Isaacs's argument is that in *Deakin v Webb*, Griffith stated that Isaacs's contention was premised on an admission that the rule in *D'Emden v Pedder* was sound:

> It was also contended that, *admitting the soundness* of the rule in *D'Emden v Pedder* (*supra*), yet that rule, being based upon necessary implication, could not be extended beyond the necessity, and that its application to any particular case might be excluded by a contrary and controlling implication to be found in the Constitution.[121]

By selectively editing Griffith's citation to include words that exclude the implication if the necessity ends, Isaacs suggests that Griffith's argument agreed that "in *all cases*" that the rule of noninterference ended where the necessity ended. Since the necessity arose from the federal scheme, Isaacs's argument appears to be that Griffith's argument implicitly abolished the federal scheme. In the last four lines of Griffith's reasons cited above, Griffith explained the limit to the doctrine as "the Commonwealth, or, conversely, the State, was *intended* to have power to do the act the validity of which is impeached."[122] In that circumstance, no necessity can arise. Regarding the *Goldsbrough case*, Isaacs asserted that Griffith ascertained the intention "by reference to outside circumstances, not of law or constitutional practice, but of fact such as the expectations and hopes of persons undefined that Crown lands then leased would become private property."[123] Isaacs then asserts in the next sentence that Griffith's interpretation of the Constitution depended on an implication that was

> formed on a vague individual conception of the *spirit* of the compact, which is not the result of interpreting any specific language to be quoted, nor referable to any recognised principle of the common law of the Constitution, and which, when stated, is rebuttable by an intention of exclusion equally not referable to any language of the instrument or acknowledged common law constitutional principle.[124]

This misstates Griffith's reasons, which direct the inquiry as to whether the intended power resides in the Commonwealth or the states, to a "consideration of the whole of the Constitution."[125] Other aspects of Isaacs's statement are also misleading. Walker remarked:

> Indeed, for the first 20 years of the Commonwealth, all the High Court Justices claimed to be applying the ordinary rules of interpretation, as Professor Leslie Zines has pointed out, and Griffith had repeatedly enunciated all the interpretative principles mentioned in *Engineers*.

The *vague* spirit to which Isaacs referred was, in fact, the intention of the Founders that the Constitution should embody a federal scheme after that of the United States, from which the doctrine of immunity of instrumentalities arose. Isaacs asserted that Griffith's method of interpretation was not dependable for construing the Constitution as it had led to divergences and inconsistencies,[126] the cause of which lay with Griffith's reliance on implications. As Griffith's interpretation was said to be not the "result of any specific language" nor "referable to any language of the instrument,"[127] Isaacs has endorsed his own argument for literal constructions of the Constitution's text without implications.[128]

While the states submitted that the case was controlled by the *reciprocal* of the rule in *D'Emden v Pedder*—that is, the rule in the *Railway Servants' case*—Isaacs's analysis focused almost entirely on *D'Emden v Pedder* to provide an alternative explanation for why a state could not impose a tax on a Commonwealth officer's salary. As shown in chapter 3, *D'Emden v Pedder* followed the US Supreme Court decision in *McCulloch v Maryland.* Isaacs stated the passage in *D'Emden v Pedder*: "When a State attempts to give to its legislative or executive authority an operation which, if valid, would *fetter, control, or* interfere with, the free exercise of the legislative or executive power of the Commonwealth, the attempt, unless expressly authorised by the Constitution, is to that extent invalid and inoperative."[129]

The practical effect of the rule is not to invalidate a valid law, but to impose a limit on its application. The legal argument for the decision was based on the US case *McCulloch v Maryland.* As chapter 3 showed, the early court confirmed this interpretation in *Deakin v Webb*[130] as known notoriously (and intended by the Founders) in response to the argument of a'Beckett J in *Wollaston's case* that section 109 would invalidate state laws inconsistent with Commonwealth laws.[131] Without acknowledging his own role as legal counsel for Victoria in *Wollaston's case*, Isaacs sets out to show that *Wollaston's case* was the correct basis for the decision in *D'Emden v Pedder*, and that a situation where a state law interferes with a Commonwealth law is to be resolved by section 109 of the Constitution. That provision states that "when a law of a State is inconsistent with a law of the Commonwealth, the latter shall prevail, and the former shall, to the extent of the inconsistency, be invalid."[132]

As the facts before the court in *D'Emden v Pedder* did not support that construction of section 109, Isaacs changed the facts and argued an inconsistency[133] between the Tasmanian *Duties Act*[134] and the Commonwealth *Audit Act*,[135] which would be dealt with by section 109 of the Constitution. Isaacs states the facts of *D'Emden v Pedder* as follows:

> The Commonwealth law (*Audit Act* 1901) made provision as to how public moneys of the Commonwealth were to be paid out: written vouchers were required for all accounts paid. . . . The irresistible construction of the Act is that these vouchers, which the law requires for the protection of the Commonwealth Consolidated Revenue Fund are to be under the sole control of Commonwealth authorities.[136]

From this statement of the facts, Isaacs concludes that

> a State Act making it an offence to give such a voucher except on a condition imposed by the State Parliament, namely, a tax in aid of the State revenue, was, so far, manifestly inconsistent with the Commonwealth law. Sec. 109 of the Constitution applies to such a case, and establishes the invalidity to that extent of the State law.[137]

Isaacs's construction of section 109 is made in isolation from the theory of the Constitution as the Founders intended. However, it must be asked in any event how the two Acts are inconsistent, let alone manifestly inconsistent. Since it is possible to obey both Commonwealth and state laws, "there is no inconsistency between the laws in the sense of direct repugnancy, conflict or collision"[138] and inconsistency was expressly denied by the early court.[139] Of greater importance for Isaacs, however, is that implicit in his argument is the proposition that if section 109 of the Constitution applies to every Commonwealth law, the basis for the doctrine of implied immunities disappears.

Isaacs's restatement of the facts in *D'Emden v Pedder* purports to demonstrate the existence of an inconsistency between Commonwealth and state laws that he describes as "an offence to give such a voucher except on a condition." Isaacs's argument, however, does not sustain that conclusion. First, the Tasmanian *Duties Act*[140] did not—and in fact could not—make it an offence to "give a voucher," as Isaacs asserted, as the giving of the voucher was always a matter of Commonwealth law. The actual offence for which D'Emden was charged and convicted was not paying duty, having been charged in Tasmania that he "[gave] to the paying officer of the Commonwealth of Australia a receipt liable to duty . . . the said receipt . . . *not being duly stamped.*"[141] The stamp was not a precondition for issuing the voucher: it was evidence of the fact that duty had or had not been paid.

Second, what Isaacs recited as a sign of inconsistency—"A State Act making it an offence to give such a voucher except on a condition imposed by the State Parliament, namely, a tax in aid of the State revenue"—is not inconsistent with the Commonwealth law, but instead is an attempt through taxation to fetter or control or interfere with a Commonwealth power,[142] precisely as the early court held. The objects of the Tasmanian *Duties Act* were never inconsistent with those of the Commonwealth *Audit Act*, there was no prohibition on the Commonwealth giving the voucher and, as there was never an offence for giving the voucher, the Tasmanian law was never *inconsistent* with the Commonwealth *Audit Act*. Although they did not occupy the same field, the effect of a criterion such as "field" for identifying inconsistency is readily seen. *D'Emden v Pedder* was a High Court appeal from a fine imposed by a state court for not paying a state tax on a Commonwealth salary, which was held to be an interference. As D'Emden was not fined for issuing a voucher, Isaacs's argument was an invention. The basis of the High Court decision was that a valid Tasmanian *Duties Act* had exceeded its constitutional limit by imposing a tax that interfered with an exclusive Commonwealth power and was "to that extent invalid and inoperative."[143] When the facts of the case are accurately stated, it is clear that the matter had nothing to do with an inconsistency and section 109.

Isaacs's argument concluded that section 109 of the Constitution was paramount. He denied any observation in *D'Emden v Pedder* suggesting the doctrine was reciprocally true: "that observation must be considered as unwarranted by the Constitution, and overruled."[144] This statement appears to be little more than prejudicial, since the reciprocity of the rule was not part of the judgment in *D'Emden v Pedder*. However, with regard to the reciprocal rule found in the *Railway Servants' case*, the judgment dismisses it without giving any reasons when it says that "the true basis of *D'Emden v Pedder* is the supremacy of Commonwealth law over State law where they meet on any field, there can be no possible reciprocity. Mutual supremacy is a contradiction of terms."[145]

Having abolished the doctrine of implied immunities and established the supremacy of all Commonwealth law over state law pursuant to section 109 of the Constitution, Isaacs returned to the issue of the reciprocal immunity of a state authority from Commonwealth interference later in his reasons, when he attempted to reconcile his argument relating to *D'Emden v Pedder* with the true basis of the states' argument in the *Railway Servants' case*.[146] While it was a reciprocal rule of that in *D'Emden v Pedder*, the rule in the *Railway Servants' case* was based on the US decision in *Collector v Day*.[147] As with *McCulloch v Maryland*, Isaacs does not refer to *Collector v Day* and he attempts no analysis of the *Railway Servants' case*.

We are obliged to ask, however, why Isaacs did not attempt to counter the argument where it occurs in the *Railway Servants' case*, which was the main authority for the states' case. One possible answer is that the *Railway Servants' case* relied upon a Commonwealth law interfering with the state executive authority. Since there was no state law in conflict with the Commonwealth law, section 109 of the Constitution could not apply. The *Railway Servants' case* could not be manipulated as *D'Emden v Pedder* could. Isaacs stated that as "the true basis of *D'Emden v Pedder* is the supremacy of Commonwealth law over state law where they meet on any field, there can be no possible reciprocity."[148] Isaacs's argument can be stated briefly: the states' right under the *Railway Servants' case* did not exist because he had abolished the reciprocal right under *D'Emden v Pedder*.

The true authority for the *Engineers' case* was always the *Railway Servants' case*. In both cases, the *Commonwealth Conciliation and Arbitration Act* interfered with a state government's executive authority. Like the *Railway Servants' case*, the *Engineers' case* did not involve an inconsistency between concurrent Commonwealth and state laws, so could never have properly been resolved by section 109 of the Constitution, as the Founders intended it to apply "in cases of concurrent legislative jurisdiction,"[149] that is, in respect of two laws that each dealt with the same subject matter. Isaacs's assertion that *D'Emden v Pedder* was a case of conflict,[150] and hence came within the scope of section 109 of the Constitution, was not correct, as Evatt J explained in the later case of *West v Commissioner of Taxation (NSW)*[151] when analyzing the theory of section 109 of the Constitution. Evatt said of Isaacs's analysis of the case that "*D'Emden v Pedder* shows how little historical warrant there is for the statement in the *Engineers' case* that the former decision 'rests on the supremacy created by sec. 109.'"[152]

Although the reserved powers doctrine of the early court was never an issue raised by the parties in the *Engineers' case*, it was part of the federal scheme intended by the Founders, so Isaacs could not leave it in the Constitution without implicitly questioning his removal of immunities.

DOCTRINE OF STATES' RESERVE POWERS

As shown in chapter 2, during the Convention Isaacs felt obliged to correct Josiah Symon's assertion that the Senate represented states' interests by retorting: "As I understand the matter, the visible sign of state autonomy consists in the reserved powers."[153] The cases considered in chapter 3 showed that section 107 of the Constitution, by which powers not vested exclusively in the Commonwealth were vested in the states, was inserted by the Founders in order to protect the rights of the states to regulate their own internal affairs. Griffith linked the meaning of the section to the Tenth Amendment of the US Constitution in at least two cases.[154] During the Constitutional Convention, Barton explained that powers were included in the Constitution to protect states' rights.[155] States' interests, however, were preserved by equal representation in the Senate and its coordinate powers.[156] While, after federation, the rise of disciplined political parties had replaced that duty with party loyalty,[157] until the *Engineers' case* it was still possible for the High Court to protect the states' interests against Commonwealth laws.

Section 107 reserved the colonial powers to the states not withdrawn or vested exclusively in the Commonwealth:

> Every power of the Parliament of a Colony that becomes a State, shall, unless it is by this Constitution exclusively vested in the Parliament of the Commonwealth or withdrawn from the Parliament of the State, continue as at the establishment of the Commonwealth.[158]

Walker draws attention to the capriciousness of Isaacs's judgment in the *Engineers' case* when he says of its treatment of the reserved powers doctrine:

> But in a brief passage that was unnecessary for the decision and therefore not strictly authoritative, the majority went further and sidelined the reserve powers

doctrine, and s 107 with it. They simply asserted that s 107 did not support a general reserved powers implication.[159]

While this comment is accurate, it overlooks the political necessity for the demise of the reserve powers doctrine if the new unitary political scheme was to be completed. The separate sovereignties could not be abolished simply by ending the doctrine of immunities, if the states were left with an indicia of sovereignty in the form of reserved powers. Allan and Aroney reinforce Walker's comment when they remark:

> Nothing in the language of the *Australian Constitution*, or its structure, or the process that was used to adopt it, or the basis upon which its approval by the voters was promoted, or the likely original understandings of most of those voters, or anything else at the time would have suggested that the States would become the enfeebled, emasculated creatures they have become.[160]

However, their description of the states as "enfeebled and emasculated" could also have been applied accurately to the whole political scheme intended by the Founders for the Constitution.

The majority judgment in the *Engineers' case* attacks the reserve powers doctrine associated with section 107 in two places, but begins as follows. It first asserted that the court must, when construing Commonwealth legislative powers in section 51, consider "whether there is anything in the Constitution which falls within the *express* limitation referred to in the governing words of sec. 51."[161] The Commonwealth legislative powers are expressed in section 51, to be subject to "one general express limitation, namely 'subject to this Constitution.'"[162] As that is an express limitation, he argued that a construction of the legislative powers should only be concerned with "anything in the Constitution which falls within the *express* limitation referred to in the governing words of sec. 51."[163] While this does not preclude a consideration of implied limitations, it must be noted that he demands that the inquiry into express limitations "must proceed consistently with the principles upon which we determine *this* case, for they apply generally to all powers contained in that section."[164] Through this device, all limitations implicit in constitutional federalism have been excluded. He also ensured, as already stated, that such federal implication could not be brought indirectly before the court by his prohibition on US Supreme Court decisions.[165]

The majority judgment describes the Western Australian government business as a state authority, which, as previously cited, if it is exempt from Commonwealth legislation actually fetters or interferes with the Commonwealth's legislative power regarding industrial relations under section 51(xxxv).[166] It is therefore arguing that the criterion for inconsistency with section 109 of the Constitution is that a state *authority* actually fetters or interferes with Commonwealth *legislative* power unless it is exempt from Commonwealth legislation. The argument therefore asserts that the rule in *D'Emden v Pedder* has become the criterion for inconsistency within section 109 of the Constitution. The argument also reverses the whole case, since the issue before the court was interference by the Commonwealth industrial relations law with a state executive power. The relevant passage in which Isaacs recasts the issue as a state power interfering with a Commonwealth law, part of which I have already cited, occurs much earlier in his judgment. The full citation follows:

> An authority has been set up by a State which is claimed to be an executive authority and which, if exempt from Commonwealth legislation, does fetter or interfere with free exercise of the legislative power of the Commonwealth under pl. XXXV of sec. 51, unless that placitum is not as complete as its words in their natural meaning indicate or, since s 107 applies to State concurrent powers equally with its exclusive powers, unless every Commonwealth legislative power, however complete in itself, is subject to the unrestricted operation of *every* State Act.[167]

His argument involves a sleight of hand. It begins with a state executive authority that, part way through, becomes "State concurrent powers equally with its exclusive powers"; that is, an executive authority has changed into legislative powers. Without actually specifying the applicable legislative power he has only then to bring that state legislative power under the authority of section 109 of the Constitution to resolve the problem. Isaacs's proposition in the clause commencing "since s 107" is not limited to concurrent powers reserved by section 107 to the states, for he asserts that all state legislative powers fetter or interfere with Commonwealth legislative powers; however, as the Commonwealth power is *complete in itself*, he is suggesting that Commonwealth powers are supreme. Isaacs's definition of states' powers as exclusive or concurrent gives an insight into the direction of his argument for a unitary Commonwealth Constitution. It will not necessarily be like the Canadian Constitution, for that would vest mutually exclusive powers in the states and the Commonwealth. Isaacs's argument suggests his preferred scheme is a pure unitary Constitution. If all state powers are vulnerable to total invalidity pursuant to section 109 of the Constitution, Commonwealth concurrent powers, always being supreme, will become exclusive once enacted.[168] Isaacs understood this, and assumed it to be true when he explained that a state legislative power would be invalidated by repugnant Commonwealth legislation in the same field.

> The effect of State legislation, though fully within the powers preserved by sec. 107, may in a given case depend on sec. 109. However valid and binding on

> the people of the State where no relevant Commonwealth legislation exists, the moment it encounters repugnant Commonwealth legislation operating on the *same field* the State legislation must give way.[169]

Isaacs's statement redefines "inconsistency" in section 109 by asserting that whenever Commonwealth legislation "operates" in the same field as the state legislation, the latter is invalid. Since "operation" can be defined broadly, it can mean that a law is inconsistent or that it fetters, interferes with, or controls. His new definition has rejected the Founders' originally intended meaning for section 109 that the Commonwealth and states may each legislate on the same matter without inconsistency.

When Isaacs turned again to the reserve powers of the states, he restated the principle of section 107 by differentiating state exclusive and concurrent powers from Commonwealth concurrent powers. He explained that the limits on Commonwealth concurrent powers are only those that can be identified in the express terms of the Constitution. While section 107 of the Constitution reserves legislative and executive powers to the states that are not exclusively vested in the Commonwealth, Isaacs's analysis has changed the character of what is reserved. As the Constitution is silent about any *exclusive* state powers, it is reasonable to conclude that if all concurrent state powers will potentially conflict with a Commonwealth power, the states would still have their exclusive powers including, at a minimum, states' police powers. Even these, however, are discarded:

> But it is a fundamental and fatal error to read sec. 107 as reserving *any* power from the Commonwealth that falls fairly within the explicit terms of an express grant in sec. 51, as that grant is reasonably construed, unless that reservation is as *explicitly* stated.[170]

As mentioned previously, Isaacs first excluded all implications from the Constitution and recognized only the express limitation in section 51 of the Constitution on Commonwealth legislative powers, that they are all "subject to this Constitution,"[171] as the benchmark and then construed the Constitution literally while having regard only to express limitations. His judgment had earlier (and incorrectly) relied on *Keller v The United States of America* in order to leave even the police powers subject to invalidity under section 109. There are no limitations expressly stated because the limiting doctrines were understood to be implications from the separate sovereignties. Isaacs had already precluded any consideration of implications, so in their absence his decision abandoned the effect of section 107, leaving all state powers vulnerable to invalidation by an exercise of a Commonwealth legislative power under section 109 of the Constitution. The judgment concluded that all

Commonwealth powers would become exclusive at the expense of all state powers:

> The principle we apply to the Commonwealth we apply also to the States, leaving their respective acts of legislation full operation within their respective areas and subject matters, but, in case of conflict, giving to valid Commonwealth legislation the supremacy expressly declared by the Constitution, measuring that supremacy according to the very words of sec. 109.[172]

The supremacy was unqualified. After citing section 109, Isaacs concluded that the section

> gives supremacy, not to any particular class of Commonwealth Acts but to *every* Commonwealth Act, over not merely State Acts passed under concurrent powers but *all* State Acts, though passed under an exclusive power, if any provisions of the two conflict; as they may—if they do not, then *cadit quæstio*.[173]

This passage therefore confirms that, according to Isaacs's construction, there are not actually any exclusive state legislative powers since they can all be invalidated by Commonwealth legislative power, should the Commonwealth decide to legislate in the same field. In that context, the political scheme of the Constitution resembles the unitary English scheme rather than the Canadian one. Isaacs's reference to "exclusive powers" was only ever a diversion, as the Constitution is silent on their existence. Nicholas Aroney refers to the survival of a "resilient core"[174] of the *Engineers' case* that he describes as "the proposition that federal legislative powers are to be interpreted in priority to, and without substantial consideration of, the 'remaining' legislative capacities of the States. Such a proposition was a direct challenge to the doctrine of State reserved powers."[175]

While this sums up the practical effect of Isaacs's judgment on the doctrine of states' reserve powers, it cannot be said that Isaacs's arguments were either accurate or sufficiently cogent to support his conclusion, relying as they do on a number of specific assertions with no substantive reasons other than judicial fiat. The implicit rejection of the sovereignties of the separate states in the *Engineers' case* was expressly challenged three years later in *Commonwealth v New South Wales*,[176] in which Isaacs expressed his opinion of the idea of separate sovereignties in the context of the Commonwealth Constitution in a joint judgment with Rich and Starke JJ. After explaining the Australian character of the High Court, Isaacs rejected any similarity between the representative of an independent sovereign in a foreign tribunal and a state of Australia in the High Court, Australia's highest Australian tribunal.[177] Unfortunately, Isaacs's example demonstrates the same limited concept of sovereignty as that held by Dicey, and his assertion of the existence of states' exclusive powers[178] contradicts the example he gives of sovereignty. Isaacs has defined sovereignty in the absolute narrow sense used by Dicey to reflect the unitary government of Britain. He supported his version with a reference to the Story's *Commentaries on the United States Constitution*:[179]

> [Story] says: "In the first place, antecedent to the Declaration of Independence none of the colonies were, or pretended to be, sovereign States, in the sense in which the term 'sovereign' is sometimes applied to states. The term 'sovereign' or 'sovereignty' is used in different senses, which often leads to a confusion of ideas, and sometimes to very mischievous and unfounded conclusions."[180]

Isaacs concluded from this that the "assumption that New South Wales is a 'sovereign State' would be both mischievous and unfounded."[181] This, however, is another example of Isaacs's capacity to selectively cite passages from authors, which are either taken out of context or omit significant qualifications, or that he adapts to his own purpose. The passage he cites from Story refers to the condition of the American colonies "antecedent to the Declaration of Independence,"[182] when the colonies were subject to the direct rule of the British monarch, George III. Story's understanding of sovereignty is more complete than that of Isaacs, as demonstrated by a subsequent passage to which Isaacs did not refer. It shows not only that Story did not endorse Isaacs's opinion, but that Isaacs misstates Story's concept of sovereignty. Story understood the term "sovereignty" in a much wider sense than the narrow, unitary, concept preferred by Isaacs. Story explained sovereignty as:

> In its most enlarged sense it means the people composing a particular nation or community. . . . But the sovereignty of the government, organised within the state, may be of a very limited nature. It may extend to few, or to many objects. It may be unlimited, as to some; it may be restrained, as to others. To the extent of the power given, the government may be sovereign, and its acts may be deemed the sovereign acts of the state.[183]

Story's comment, cited above by Isaacs, related to an incorrect assumption by some at the time that the early American colonies were sovereign in the largest sense of "supreme, absolute, uncontrollable power, the *jus summi imperii*, the absolute right to govern."[184] After the *Declaration of Independence*, however, Story argues that the American states were sovereign in a limited sense, thus denying the basis for Isaacs's conclusion regarding New South Wales.

None of the facts that arose to be litigated in the *Engineers' case* raised any questions that might have required the High Court to consider the application of the reserve powers doctrine. Nor did Isaacs attempt to show that it was a relevant consideration of the court. Although his argument is clearly false, the decision can be described as *obiter*. Nevertheless, it has been said to be the most successful part of the *Engineers' case* judgment and has rarely been criticized.[185] Isaacs rejected the reserve powers doctrine on the ground that all state legislative powers were subject to invalidation at the hands of the Commonwealth pursuant to section 109, should the Commonwealth exercise its legislative powers.

The *Engineers' case* was not well received at the time. It attracted significant criticism, especially from state politicians, "with the South Australian Premier stating that he would fight it to the last ditch and that it undermined responsible government"[186] and from lawyers such as T. C. Brennan KC, who made sustained attacks[187] upon it. An application by the states for special leave to appeal to the Privy Council was rejected by Lord Haldane.[188] *The Argus*, a Melbourne newspaper, turned to the very principle that this essay argues is the foundation stone of the Commonwealth Constitution to criticize the decision:

> One of the fundamental principles of the Constitution is that it cannot be altered except by the consent of a majority of the people, voting as Commonwealth and as State citizens. It is infinitely preferable that such alterations should be made by the people rather than by the justices of the High Court.[189]

Anne Twomey relies on a historical analysis to identify the political forces then at work at the time. She places the *Engineers' case* into the context of a period of strong nationalism that outweighed federalism.[190] As most referenda to increase Commonwealth power had failed, she implies that there was a causal link between the growing nationalism and the reinterpretation of the Constitution by the Knox Court.[191] The problem with Twomey's reliance on such historical forces as nationalism is that it does not give Isaacs, the author of the judgment, credit for having a rational purpose that preexisted the historical events she posits as determinative historical forces. The causal forces of nationalism and federalism are insignificant when Isaacs's consistency of purpose—in the Convention, as Counsel for the State of Victoria, in his dissenting judgments on the High Court and in his judgment in the *Engineers' case*—is considered objectively. All were intended to achieve the political scheme implicit in the arguments regarding the text of the Constitution that he advanced during the 1897–1898 Constitutional Convention, arguments that were rejected by the Convention and the people.

In his critical analysis of the *Engineers' case*, Walker said of its conclusion that federal industrial law would bind state government enterprises, thus overturning the doctrine of implied immunities, that "it could have reached the same result by simply holding that a business operated by the state was not a function of government and that the doctrine therefore did not apply to it."[192] That conclusion, however, would have made the case an explicit question of states' reserved powers and that doctrine, being a rule of construction, was vulnerable—like any other doctrine or theory of the Constitution—to Isaacs's literalist methodology.

CONCLUSION

Chapter 2 showed Isaacs's full participation in the Constitutional Convention, in which—despite his preference for a unitary scheme—the delegates framed a federal scheme that sustained the separate sovereignties of the Commonwealth and the states, one that was consented to by the colonial people and originally intended by the Founders. Given his knowledge of that federal scheme and its origin, the arguments he advances in the majority judgment and his construction of constitutional provisions can be presumed to reflect his own political preference. The difficulties encountered in following his arguments appear to be deliberate, to present a judgment in which his reasons are made opaque by arguments that are misleading or based on doubtful assumptions of fact and with relevant considerations dismissed by judicial fiat.

The judgment abolished the doctrine of immunity of instrumentalities that arose as a necessary implication from the separate sovereignties of the Commonwealth and states. The doctrine in the case rested on the decision in the *Railway Servants case*. Isaacs denied the existence of the doctrine where it was found in *D'Emden v Pedder* by altering the facts and the decided law, then sophistically asserted that the converse of that doctrine found in the *Railway Servants case* could not exist. He refused to consider any implications from the text and further entrenched the majority's denial of the federal doctrines by refusing with irrelevant reasons to consider US Supreme Court authorities that articulated the federal doctrines. In an otherwise doctrinaire explanation of the demise of the twin sovereignties, Stephen Gageler, now Justice Gageler of the High Court, confirmed both his own legal positivism and the success of Isaacs's intention in regard to section 109 of the Constitution when he said: "The High Court in 1920 recognised that express provision as a declaration of Commonwealth legislative supremacy."[193] In fact, all implied limitations were abolished by the simple act of demanding that only express limits on Commonwealth powers would be recognized. Contrary to the Founders' intentions for the shared concurrent powers, the judgment denied that any powers were reserved to the states and rendered them subject to invalidity by Commonwealth legislation pursuant to section

109 of the Constitution, a decision that had no relevance to the issues before the court.

Isaacs questioned decisions of the early court in relation to the federal scheme and the separate Commonwealth and state sovereignties and dismissed them with inadequate and spurious examinations based upon arguments that assumed the unitary scheme constitution to which he intended to give effect. He expressly adopted a literal method of construction for interpreting the Constitution on the basis of Privy Council decisions that espoused Dicey's legal positivist distinction between the text and the political scheme—decisions that were distinguishable despite his contrived arguments to support their relevance. As the political scheme and the Commonwealth Constitution's text are inseparably united, Isaacs was able to effect a construction of the text knowing that it would alter the political federal scheme by which the Australian people had agreed to live together. The result of Isaacs's judgment, as he well understood, was the production of a political scheme in which the major federal elements had been destroyed, leaving behind the unitary scheme for which he had argued at the Convention. The truly federal[194] political scheme originally intended by the Founders was replaced by the political scheme originally intended by Isaacs. The only possible conclusion that can be drawn from the evidence of the four chapters is that Isaacs's judgment in the *Engineers' case* was a sham.[195] In effect, the judgment rewrote the Commonwealth Constitution from that consented to by the Australian people without changing a single word.[196]

Isaacs's legacy to High Court jurisprudence cannot be overstated. It has been the singular most successful vehicle by which the legal positivist separation of the text from the political scheme was absorbed into constitutional interpretation. This legal positivist legacy continued in the High Court through to 1975, despite Sir Owen Dixon's efforts to mitigate its effect. His *strict and complete legalism*, however, was another example of the literalism that prospered in the work of Sir Garfield Barwick.

NOTES

1. *Amalgamated Society of Engineers v Adelaide Steamship Co Ltd* (1920) 28 CLR 129. The Amalgamated Society of Engineers, when mentioned separately from the case, will be referred to as the "Society."

2. Sir Owen Dixon, 'Marshall and the Australian Constitution' (1955) 29 *Australian Law Journal* 423. For simplicity's sake, the judgment will be attributed to Isaacs, as Dixon understood him to be the author for the majority: Knox CJ, Isaacs, Rich, Starke JJ.

3. Greg Craven, "After Literalism, What?" (1992) 18(4) *Melbourne University Law Review* 875—"political and social developments." Anne Twomey, "The Knox Court," in Rosalind Dixon and George Williams (eds), *The High Court, the Constitution and Australian Politics* (Cambridge University Press, 2015) p. 106—"growing independence and . . . greater national powers." Greg Craven, "Heresy as Orthodoxy: Were the Founders Progressivists?" (2003) 31 *Federal Law Review* 87, 126—"out of step with contemporary needs." James Allan & Nicholas Aroney, "An Uncommon Court: How the High Court of Australia has Undermined Australian Federalism" (2008) 30(2) *Sydney Law Review* 271–2—"a certain kind of textual formalism." Geoffrey de Q Walker, "The Seven Pillars of Centralism: Engineers case and Federalism" (2002) 76 *Australian Law Journal* 684—"reflecting a conscious centralist agenda."

4. *Amalgamated Society of Engineers v Adelaide Steamship Co Ltd* (1920) 28 CLR 129.

5. Sir Samuel Griffith, Former Justices of the High Court, at http://www.hcourt.gov.au/justices/former-justices/former-justices.

6. *Amalgamated Society of Engineers v Adelaide Steamship Co Ltd* (1920) 28 CLR 129.

7. Sir Owen Dixon, *Marshall and the Australian Constitution* (1955) 29 ALJ 423; Nicholas Aroney, "The Ghost in the Machine: Exorcising Engineers," *Proceedings of Fourteenth Conference of the Samuel Griffith Society*, Sydney, 14–16 June 2002, Ch. 2.

8. Roger B. Joyce, *Samuel Walter Griffith* (University of Queensland Press, 1984) p. 357.

9. O'Connor J died in 1912 and was replaced in 1913 by Gavan Duffy J. In 1913, Powers and Rich JJ were appointed. Griffith CJ retired in 1919 (replaced by Knox CJ) and Barton J died in 1920 (replaced by Starke J). The ages of the new appointments at the time of appointment were Knox, 56; Gavan Duffy, 61; Powers, 60; Rich, 50; Starke, 49.

10. *Amalgamated Society of Engineers v Adelaide Steamship Co Ltd* (1920) 28 CLR 129 at 132; emphasis added. The respondents named in the "special case" were state government businesses that were found to perform work for the public.

11. Ibid., 176; emphasis added. Gavan Duffy says that if the Western Australian Crown conducted its businesses in South Australia, it "must be deemed to have submitted itself to the laws of South Australia, as if it were a *private* person," an argument that implies a solution to the case.

12. *Deakin v Webb* (1904) 1 CLR 585 at 605: "In our judgment the schemes of these two Constitutions are, in this respect, identical. In neither case is any new power conferred upon the States, nor is there any exclusive distribution of powers, except as to a limited class of cases." James Madison, "*Federalist* No. 45," *The Federalist Papers*, ed. Clinton Rossiter (New American Library, 1961) p. 292 said of the Tenth Amendment: "The powers delegated by the proposed Constitution to the federal government are few and defined. Those which are to remain in the State governments are numerous and indefinite."

13. Haig Patapan, "Politics of Interpretation" (2000) 22(2) *Sydney Law Review* 247, 248.

14. Ibid., 249.

15. Leslie Zines, "Sir Owen Dixon's Theory of Federalism" (1965) 1(2) *Federal Law Review* 222.

16. As reported in Leslie Zines, "Sir Owen Dixon's Theory of Federalism" (1965) 1(2) *Federal Law Review* 222 n 6. Anstey Wynes' comment is an endorsement of Isaacs's methodology but sits oddly with the judgments of Marshall CJ, who also construed a written Constitution. Anyone remotely familiar with High Court revisionist decisions over the past century and the court's readiness to dispute, refine, and overturn previous decisions must doubt his political judgment on this point. Knowledge of the Constitution's scheme would provide certainty.

17. Leslie Zines, "Sir Owen Dixon's Theory of Federalism" (1965) 1(2) *Federal Law Review* 222. This is another endorsement of the legal positivist methodology, which does not question why the exceptions to literalism were needed if literalism was the best methodology.

18. *Baxter v Commissioners of Taxation (NSW)* (1907) 4 CLR 1087.

19. Official Record of the Debates of the Australasian Federal Convention, Melbourne (1898), 1912–1913 (George Reid). This was precisely the issue about which George Reid sought clarification from Edmund Barton in the final session of the Convention.

20. Official Record of the Debates of the Australasian Federal Convention, Adelaide (1897), 175 (Isaac Isaacs). The meaning of Isaacs's assertion is that there is only a difference in degree between the Canadian and US Constitutions. His assertion of his intention to follow the US federation is deceptive, since he only ever advocated a unitary Constitution for Australia.

21. Jeffrey Goldsworthy, "Justice Windeyer on the *Engineers' Case*" (2009) 37(3) *Federal Law Review* 363, 364. He did not, however, draw any adverse inference from Isaacs's "personal political view."

22. Gregory Craven, "Cracks in the Facade of Literalism: Is there an Engineer in the House?" (1992) 18(3) *Melbourne University Law Review* 540, 552.

23. Justice Joseph Story, *Commentaries on the Constitution of the United States Vol. 1* (Hillard Gray & Co, 1833) pp. 196 (210).

24. John Nethercote, "The *Engineers' Case*: Seventy Five Years On" (1995) Sixth Conference of the Samuel Griffith Society. See also Sir Owen Dixon, "Marshall and the Australian Constitution" (1955) 29 *Australian Law Journal* 423 (1).

25. Sir Owen Dixon, "Marshall and the Australian Constitution" (1955) 29 *Australian Law Journal* 423 (1).

26. *Amalgamated Society of Engineers v Adelaide Steamship Co Ltd* (1920) 28 CLR 129 at 144, 150, 158. A legal positivist insistence on "words in their natural meaning" should not be confused with Marshall CJ's the "natural and obvious import" of words, for he implicitly qualifies the meaning of the words with a reference to the "theory found in the Constitution": *Gibbons v Ogden* 22 U.S. (9 Wheat.) 1, 188 (1824).

27. *Amalgamated Society of Engineers v Adelaide Steamship Co Ltd* (1920) 28 CLR 129 at 142. Isaacs's description of the compact as political is self-serving

for the legal/political distinction permits him to ignore its status as a compact or agreement.

28. Greg Craven says of the debates of the Imperial Parliament concerning the Commonwealth Constitution "that Parliament was concerned not to debate the Bill before them, but to give effect to it as an expression of the will of the colonial populations. . . . The deliberations behind the Bill are those of the Founding Fathers." Greg Craven, 'Original Intent and Australian Constitution' (1990) 1 *Public Law Review* 166, 180–1.

29. *Amalgamated Society of Engineers v Adelaide Steamship Co Ltd* (1920) 28 CLR 129 at 147.

30. Ibid., 142.

31. Ibid., 148.

32. *Vacher & Sons Ltd v London Society of Compositors* (1913) AC 107.

33. *Amalgamated Society of Engineers v Adelaide Steamship Co Ltd* (1920) 28 CLR 129 at 142.

34. Ibid., 148. These tribunals were the House of Lords and the Judicial Committee of the Privy Council.

35. Ibid., 148.

36. Ibid., 148–9.

37. Geoffrey de Q Walker, 'The Seven Pillars of Centralism: Engineers case and Federalism' (2002) 76 *Australian Law Journal* 678, 687. It is not clear whether Isaacs meant only to dissemble or whether he was seeking an authority to alter the wording of the Constitution. However, if the latter, it is inconsistent with his assertions elsewhere that the construction placed upon the Constitution by the early court was incorrect.

38. A belief in a judicial power of amendment appeared recently in the High Court case of *Nationwide News Pty Ltd v Wills* (1992) 177 CLR 1 at 47, per Brennan J: "It is a Constitution the text of which the people alone can change." But note Brennan's judicial silence about *his* power to change the meaning of the text.

39. This is said to "sound a quaint note" by Greg Craven, "Cracks in the Facade of Literalism: Is There an Engineer in the House?" (1992) 18 *Melbourne University Law Review* 540, 543.

40. *Amalgamated Society of Engineers v Adelaide Steamship Co Ltd* (1920) 28 CLR 129 at 149. Burah's case was concerned with an Imperial Act that imposed a Constitution on an Indian state.

41. Ibid., 149.

42. *R v Burah* (1878) 3 App Cas 889 at 904.

43. See also Ibid., 905.

44. Commonwealth of Australia Constitution, ss. 74 & 75.

45. *Deakin v Webb* (1904) 1 CLR 585 at 608.

46. *Attorney-General for Ontario v Attorney-General for Canada* (1912) AC 571 at 583. *Amalgamated Society of Engineers v Adelaide Steamship Co Ltd* (1920) 28 CLR 129 at 150; emphasis in original. As chapter 2 demonstrated, Isaacs is merely asserting a Privy Council authority that provides a scheme for which he originally argued at the Constitutional Convention, a scheme the Convention rejected.

47. *Colonial Sugar Refining Co Ltd v Attorney-General of the Commonwealth* (1912) 15 CLR 182 at 213–4.

48. Ibid., 214.

49. *West v Commissioner of Taxation (NSW)* (1937) 56 CLR 657 at 679.

50. See BNA ss. 91 and 92, which vest mutually exclusive powers in the Dominion and Provinces, but do not unify them federally. Edmund Barton considered the Canadian Constitution not as a federation but rather as tending toward unification. Official Record of the Debates of the Australasian Federal Convention, Adelaide (1897), 951 (Edmund Barton).

51. Commonwealth of Australia Constitution s. 107.

52. BNA ss. 91 & 92. This mutually, exclusive scheme is the context of Lord Loreburn's reference above to "ambiguous" text.

53. BNA s. 23.

54. BNA s. 24.

55. BNA s, 29.

56. Commonwealth of Australia Constitution Chapter III,

57. B. Schwartz, (1955) *American Constitutional Law* (Cambridge University Press, New York, 1955) p. 126. Section 74 of the Commonwealth Constitution was unique in its establishment of the High Court as the final arbiter of the Constitution rather than Privy Council or another Court of a foreign jurisdiction.

58. Supreme Court of Canada, Creation and Beginnings of the Court.

59. Ibid. If, as Vincent C. MacDonald has observed, "At all events the ability to regulate judicial appeals is indeed, as the Privy Council has observed, 'a prime element in Canadian sovereignty,'" then according to the Privy Council, that "prime element" of sovereignty was apparent in the Australian Constitution from the beginning: Vincent C. MacDonald, "The Privy Council and the Canadian Constitution" (1951) 29(10) *The Canadian Bar Review* 1021.

60. John Quick and Robert Garran, *The Annotated Constitution of the Australian Commonwealth* (Angus & Robertson, 1901) p. 554.

61. *Amalgamated Society of Engineers v Adelaide Steamship Co Ltd* (1920) 28 CLR 129 at 151.

62. Ibid., 151.

63. *Bank of Toronto v Lambe* 12 App. Cas. 575 at 586.

64. Isaacs's argument is identical with the one he made to the Victorian Supreme Court (*In re Income Tax Acts (No. 4) (Wollaston's case)* 28 VLR 357) and, as counsel for that state, made again to the High Court. Griffith CJ dealt extensively with it and rejected it on numerous grounds: *Deakin v Webb* (1904) 4CLR 585 at 605–6. In a general sense, Isaacs argues that the early court had misconstrued the Constitution and that no opportunity for abuse actually existed because the Constitution was unitary.

65. But see Vincent C. MacDonald, "The Privy Council and the Canadian Constitution" (1951) 29(10) *The Canadian Bar Review* 1021, 1026, where MacDonald, after reflection on the Colonial Secretary, Lord Carnarvon's comments that the Privy Council "was external to Canada provided a detachment from local affairs that made for impartiality, sound judgment and the protection of minority interests," says of that body's decisions [at 1031]: "Contrary to Lord Carnarvon's hopes, the Privy Council

has not been a protector of minorities so much as it has been a protector of the provinces, and in that endeavour has distorted the whole scheme of legislative powers in the process of *judicial fabrication of a constitution alien to that desired and enacted*" (emphasis added).

66. *Deakin v Webb* (1904) 1 CLR 585 at 597.

67. John Nethercote, "The *Engineers' Case*: Seventy Five Years On," Sixth Conference of The Samuel Griffith Society, Melbourne, 17–19 November 1995) p. 116.

68. Ibid., 118.

69. As I have previously shown, Isaacs gave advance notice of the power of High Court Justices during the third session of the Constitutional Convention: Official Record of the Debates of the Australasian Federal Convention, Sydney (1897), 308 (Isaac Isaacs).

70. *Gibbons v Ogden* 22 U.S. (9 Wheat.) 1, 188 (1824).

71. Ibid.

72. *Attorney-General (Cth) v Colonial Sugar Refining Company Limited* (1913) 17 CLR 644.

73. Ibid., 652.

74. Ibid., 652.

75. *Amalgamated Society of Engineers v Adelaide Steamship Co Ltd* (1920) 28 CLR 129 at 147. It must surely suggest mendacity when Isaacs cites content from a speech by a member of Westminster Parliament because it supports his argument, while knowing that the same gentleman, in his judicial capacity as Lord Chancellor after deliberating on the same issue on the Privy Council, expressly contradicted his own speech. The only reason for it, I submit, is that His Lordship's opinion was such an embarrassment to Isaacs's argument that he "verballed" the Lord Chancellor.

76. *Attorney-General (Cth) v Colonial Sugar Refining Company Limited* (1913) 17 CLR 644 at 651, emphasis added. That Lord Haldane meant by "scheme of the Act" the political scheme of the Constitution is evident from the description and explanation he provides of the formation and interaction of specific elements of the Canadian, Australian, and US Constitutions. Of the Canadian Constitution, he concludes that it "departs widely from the true federal model adopted in the Constitution of the United States" [at 652].

77. Ibid., 652.

78. *Amalgamated Society of Engineers v Adelaide Steamship Co Ltd* (1920) 28 CLR 129 at 146.

79. *Huddart Parker & Co Pty Ltd v Moorehead* (1909) 8 CLR 330 at 388.

80. Sir Owen Dixon, "Marshall and the Australian Constitution" (1955) 29 *Australian Law Journal* 423, emphasis added. A similar sentiment is expressed by the Court in *Deakin v Webb* (1904) 1 CLR 585 at 606.

81. *Amalgamated Society of Engineers v Adelaide Steamship Co Ltd* (1920) 28 CLR 129 at 148.

82. Ibid., 146.

83. Ibid., 145–6.

84. *McCulloch v Maryland*, 17 U.S. 4 Wheat. 316 316 (1819).

85. *Amalgamated Society of Engineers v Adelaide Steamship Co Ltd* (1920) 28 CLR 129 at 146.

86. Ibid., 142.

87. *Keller v The United States* 213 U.S. 138 (1909).

88. *Amalgamated Society of Engineers v Adelaide Steamship Co Ltd* (1920) 28 CLR 129 at 146.

89. *Keller v The United States* 213 U.S. (1909) 138, 148–9. The leading judicial positivist on the bench, Holmes J, dissented.

90. Official Record of the Debates of the Australasian Federal Convention, Sydney (1897), 308 (Isaac Isaacs), emphasis added.

91. *Amalgamated Society of Engineers v Adelaide Steamship Co Ltd* (1920) 28 CLR 129 at 141–2.

92. Ibid., 142. See *D'Emden v Pedder* (1904) 1 CLR 91 at 110.

93. *Baxter v Commissioners of Taxation (NSW)* (1907) 4 CLR 1087 at 1130.

94. See *D'Emden v Pedder* (1904) 1 CLR 91 at 109 and *Federated Amalgamated Government Railway and Tramway Service Association v New South Wales Railway Traffic Employees' Association* (1906) 4 CLR 488 at 537.

95. *Amalgamated Society of Engineers v Adelaide Steamship Co Ltd* (1920) 28 CLR 129 at 151.

96. *Official Record of the Constitutional Convention, Melbourne* (1898), 1765–6 (Edmund Barton).

97. *Amalgamated Society of Engineers v Adelaide Steamship Co Ltd* (1920) 28 CLR 129 at 144.

98. Ibid., 135.

99. Ibid., 133.

100. Ibid., 135–6.

101. Ibid., 144.

102. Ibid., 145.

103. Ibid., 144.

104. *Deakin v Webb* (1904) 1 CLR 585 at 600. Isaacs as counsel for the respondent asserts the supremacy of Commonwealth powers under section 109.

105. *Amalgamated Society of Engineers v Adelaide Steamship Co Ltd* (1920) 28 CLR 129 at 144, emphasis in original.

106. Commonwealth of Australia Constitution s. 51(xxxv).

107. *Amalgamated Society of Engineers v Adelaide Steamship Co Ltd* (1920) 28 CLR 129 at 152.

108. Ibid., 152.

109. Ibid., 152. This argument has the sound of a political slogan and had a medieval appeal when applied to God as one in the form of the Holy Trinity, but it is unintelligible when directed, in the twentieth century, to the Crown in the United Kingdom, self-governing dominions, and an independent nation with a federal Constitution. Sir Owen Dixon says of Isaacs's claim that unity of the Crown and responsible government are two cardinal features distinguishing our political system from the American Constitution, that they do so "but in no relevant respect"; "Marshall and the Australian Constitution" (1955) 29 *Australian Law Journal*, 420, 423 (1).

110. Ibid., 153.

111. Ibid., 152.

112. Ibid., 145. The case is reported as *Attorney-General for Queensland (ex rel Goldsbrough, Mort & Company Limited) v Attorney-General for the Commonwealth* (1915) 20 CLR 148. It might be considered strange that Isaacs would refer to this case as its most distinct formulation when that attribute would by general consensus apply to *Deakin v Webb.* However, Isaacs's method of dealing with the rule in the Goldsbrough case explains his purpose quite clearly.

113. Ibid., 145.

114. *Amalgamated Society of Engineers v Adelaide Steamship Co Ltd* (1920) 28 CLR 129 at 145.

115. *Attorney-General for Queensland (ex rel Goldsbrough, Mort & Company Limited) v Attorney-General for the Commonwealth* (1915) 20 CLR 148 at 162. By chance, the facts of this case were raised hypothetically at the first session of the Constitutional Convention: Official Record of the Debates of the Australasian Federal Convention, Adelaide (1897), 1001–2 (Edmund Barton). Barton's explanation, that the Commonwealth could tax the difference between the value of the land and the value of the Crown interest in the reversion, although signifying the reserve powers doctrine, was not challenged by Isaacs.

116. *Amalgamated Society of Engineers v Adelaide Steamship Co Ltd* (1920) 28 CLR 129 at 145, emphasis in Isaac's original. None of the italicized phrases, however, appear in Griffith's judgment; they are all Isaacs's additions.

117. Ibid., 145, italics in original.

118. *Attorney-General for Queensland (ex rel Goldsbrough, Mort & Company Limited) v Attorney-General for the Commonwealth* (1915) 20 CLR 148 at 163.

119. Ibid., 163.

120. *Amalgamated Society of Engineers v Adelaide Steamship Co Ltd* (1920) 28 CLR 129 at 163.

121. *Deakin v Webb* (1904) 1 CLR 585 at 603, emphasis added.

122. *Amalgamated Society of Engineers v Adelaide Steamship Co Ltd* (1920) 28 CLR 129 at 145, emphasis added.

123. Ibid., 145.

124. Ibid., 145. Isaacs was contradicted by his own quotation of Sir Richard Haldane's speech, which referred to the Commonwealth Constitution "modelled on our own model, pregnant with the same spirit" (p. 147). As Viscount Haldane LC, he corrected himself in the decision *in Attorney-General (Cth) v Colonial Sugar Refining Company Limited* (1913) 17 CLR 644.

125. Ibid., 145.

126. Ibid., 145.

127. Ibid., 145.

128. Ibid., 157.

129. Ibid., 144; emphasis added. The rule in *D'Emden v Pedder* referred only "to interfere" invalidated action in the former but did not include to fetter or control.

130. *Deakin v Webb* (1904) 1 CLR 585 at 616.

131. *In re Income Tax Acts (No. 4) (Wollaston's case)* 28 VLR 357 at 395.

132. Commonwealth of Australia Constitution, s. 109, emphasis added.

133. *Amalgamated Society of Engineers v Adelaide Steamship Co Ltd* (1920) 28 CLR 129 at 156.

134. *Duties Act* (Tas) 2 Edw. VII. No. 30.

135. *Audit Act* (Cth) No. 4 of 1901.

136. *Amalgamated Society of Engineers v Adelaide Steamship Co Ltd* (1920) 28 CLR 129 at 156. We note the rhetorical skill with which Isaacs describes his own construction of the Act as irresistible when it is rebuttable as either inaccurate or untrue.

137. Ibid., 156. But see *Baxter v Commissioners of Taxation (NSW)* (1907) 4 CLR 1087 at 1129 where Griffith CJ states "sec. 109 only applies in cases of concurrent legislative jurisdiction."

138. *West v Commissioner of Taxation (NSW)* (1937) 56 CLR 657 at 690 per Evatt J.

139. *D'Emden v Pedder* (1903) 1 CLR 91.

140. Act of the State of Tasmania, 2 Edw. VII. No. 30 (Tasmanian Duties Act); see *Pedder v D'Emden* (1903) TLR 146.

141. *D'Emden v Pedder* (1904) 1 CLR 91 at 92; emphasis added. See also, *Pedder v D'Emden* (1903) TLR 146.

142. *Federated Amalgamated Government Railway and Tramway Service Association v New South Wales Railway Traffic Employees' Association* (1906) 4 CLR 488.

143. *D'Emden v Pedder* (1904) 1 CLR 91 at 92 at 111.

144. *Amalgamated Society of Engineers v Adelaide Steamship Co Ltd* (1920) 28 CLR 129 at 156.

145. Ibid., 156.

146. *Federated Amalgamated Government Railway and Tramway Service Association v New South Wales Railway Traffic Employees' Association* (1906) 4 CLR 488. Isaacs appeared in the case (at 516) as Attorney-General for the Commonwealth.

147. *The Collector v Day*, 78 U.S. (11 Wall.) 113 (1870).

148. *Amalgamated Society of Engineers v Adelaide Steamship Co Ltd* (1920) 28 CLR 129 at 156, emphasis added.

149. *Baxter v Commissioners of Taxation (NSW)* (1907) 4 CLR 1087 at 1129.

150. *Amalgamated Society of Engineers v Adelaide Steamship Co Ltd* (1920) 28 CLR 129 at 156.

151. *West v Commissioner of Taxation (NSW)* (1937) 56 CLR 657.

152. Ibid., 690.

153. Official Record of the Debates of the Australasian Federal Convention, Sydney (1897), 305 (Isaac Isaacs). By visible, I submit that he intended visible in the Constitution, since the reserve powers as a concept is invisible.

154. *D'Emden v Pedder* (1904) 1 CLR 91 at 111; *Baxter v Commissioners of Taxation (NSW)* (1907) 4 CLR 1087 at 1112–3.

155. Official Record of the Debates of the Australasian Federal Convention, Adelaide (1897), 377 (Edmund Barton).

156. Official Record of the Debates of the Australasian Federal Convention, Adelaide (1897), 22 (Edmund Barton).

157. James Allan and Nicholas Aroney, "An Uncommon Court: How the High Court of Australia Has Undermined Australian Federalism" (2008) 30(2) *Sydney Law Review* 263.

158. Commonwealth of Australia Constitution, s. 107.

159. Geoffrey de Q Walker, "The Seven Pillars of Centralism: Engineers case and Federalism" (2002) 76 *Australian Law Journal* 682. Walker rightly points out that the court could have rejected the West Australian government's case by "simply holding that a business operated by the State was not a function of government and that the doctrine therefore did not apply to it" (682).

160. James Allan and Nicholas Aroney, "An Uncommon Court: How the High Court of Australia Has Undermined Australian Federalism" (2008) 30(2) *Sydney Law Review* 245, 247. I submit that the main reason why this collapse of State powers and with it Australian federalism was the result of the High Court's predominant legal positivist jurisprudence and its construction of the text without regard to the political scheme.

161. *Amalgamated Society of Engineers v Adelaide Steamship Co Ltd* (1920) 28 CLR 129 at 144, emphasis added.

162. Ibid., 144.

163. Ibid., 144; emphasis added.

164. Ibid., 144; emphasis added.

165. Ibid., 146.

166. Ibid., 144.

167. Ibid., 144. It should be noted that the Constitution does not mention the nature of the states' powers that continue after federation. That is an addition that Isaacs makes. It is also distracting to his argument.

168. This view is implicit in the wide constructions he made of the concurrent legislative powers in section 51 in his minority judgments for the early court, for example, *R v Barger* (1908) 6 CLR 41 at 82 and *Huddart Parker & Co Pty Ltd v Moorehead* (1909) 8 CLR 330 at 388 *et seq.*

169. *Amalgamated Society of Engineers v Adelaide Steamship Co Ltd* (1920) 28 CLR 129 at 154, emphasis added. Repugnancy remained an undefined term but is not necessarily coeval with conflict.

170. Ibid., 154, emphasis added.

171. Ibid., 144, emphasis in original.

172. Ibid., 155.

173. Ibid., 154.

174. Nicholas Aroney, "The Ghost in the Machine: Exorcising *Engineers*," Fourteenth Conference of the Samuel Griffith Society, Sydney, 14–16 June 2002, 62.

175. Ibid.

176. *Commonwealth v New South Wales* (1923) 32 CLR 200. I assume that the joint judgment was written by Isaacs, given the similarity in sources and argument to submissions made during the Constitutional Convention.

177. *Commonwealth v New South Wales* (1923) 32 CLR 200 at 210.

178. *Amalgamated Society of Engineers v Adelaide Steamship Co Ltd* (1920) 28 CLR 129 at 144, although at 155 Isaacs abandons the notion of exclusive state powers.

179. Joseph Story, *Commentaries on the Constitution of the United States Vol. 1* (Hillard Gray & Co, 1833). Justice Story was a colleague of Marshall CJ, to whom he dedicated the work with the following: "From two great sources, however, I have drawn by far the greatest part of my most valuable materials. These are *The Federalist*, an incomparable commentary of three of the greatest statesmen of their age and the extraordinary Judgments of Mr Chief Justice Marshall upon constitutional law" (p. v).

180. *Commonwealth v New South Wales* (1923) 32 CLR 200 at 210.

181. Ibid.

182. Joseph Story, *Commentaries on the Constitution of the United States Vol. 1* (Hilliard Gray & Co, 1833) pp. 191 (207).

183. Ibid., 193–4 (208). It is more than noteworthy that Story remarks about a limited sense of sovereignty that "it is in this sense that Blackstone employs it," 192 (207).

184. Ibid., 191 (207).

185. Nicholas Aroney, "The Ghost in the Machine," Fourteenth Conference of the Samuel Griffith Society, Sydney, 14–16 June 2002, 62. Haig Patapan recounts the cases in which, to that time, "The *Engineers* decision regarding reserved powers has been followed" by the High Court, in "Politics of Interpretation" (2000) 22(2) *Sydney Law Review* 35 n 29.

186. Anne Twomey, "The Knox Court," in Rosalind Dixon & George Williams (eds), *The High Court, the Constitution and Australian Politics* (Cambridge University Press, 2015) pp. 98, 105.

187. Ibid., 98, 104–5.

188. H.V. Evatt, *The King and his Dominion Governors*, 2nd ed. (Frank Cass, 1967) p. 311. The decision was unreported.

189. *The Argus* (Melbourne: 1848–1957) Trove, National Library of Australia, 1 September 1920, p. 8.

190. Anne Twomey, "The Knox Court," in Rosalind Dixon & George Williams (eds), *The High Court, the Constitution and Australian Politics* (Cambridge University Press, 2015) pp. 98, 99. Such an argument would obviously not apply to the United States.

191. Ibid., 98, 100.

192. Geoffrey de Q Walker, "The Seven Pillars of Centralism: Engineers case and Federalism" (2002) 76 *Australian Law Journal* 682.

193. Stephen Gageler, "The Federal–State Balance in Federal Systems," in Gabrielle Appleby, Nicholas Aroney and Thomas John (eds), *The Future of Australian Federalism* (Cambridge University Press, 2012) p. 29. In a legal positivist sense, Gageler's comment is correct, but it is an understatement of Isaacs's real purpose and is inaccurate when compared with Griffith's statement in *Baxter*.

194. *Attorney-General (Cth) v Colonial Sugar Refining Company Limited* (1913) 17 CLR 644 at 652. It is surprising that little has ever been made of Viscount Haldane's reference to the Tenth Amendment of the US Constitution as representative of a true federal Constitution. His subsequent reference to section 107 of the Commonwealth Constitution contradicts Isaacs's rejection of the doctrine of the states' reserved powers.

195. A majority of the High Court in a recent case approved of the statement: "that where there was a 'sham'; the term, when '[c]orrectly employed', denoted an objective of deliberate deception of third parties." *Raftland Pty Ltd v Commissioner of Taxation* (2008) 238 CLR 516 at 532. And, in *Jacques v Federal Commissioner of Taxation*, Isaacs J. said, "A sham transaction is inherently worthless, and needs no enactment to nullify it. [*Jacques v Federal Commissioner of Taxation* (1924) 34 CLR 328 at 358.]"

196. That judges on the High Court are aware of this is evident in the words of one of the most liberal High Court Justices who said of sec. 128 of the Constitution: "It is a Constitution the *text* of which the people alone can change." *Nationwide News Pty Ltd v Wills* (1992) 177 CLR 23 at 47; emphasis added.

Chapter 5

The High Court after *Engineers*

INTRODUCTION

This chapter argues that Isaacs's literalism from the *Engineers' case* and its justification in the legal positivist separation of the text of the Constitution from its political scheme continued to dominate the jurisprudence of the subsequent High Court. Focusing on the leading constitutional judgments of Sir Owen Dixon and Sir Garfield Barwick, it shows that literalism, and its jurisprudential commitments, became the orthodoxy. Dixon's contribution to this essay is important for two reasons. He is the only Justice of the High Court to expressly reject essential methodological elements of Isaacs's argument in the *Engineers' case*, even if he accepted its conclusion.[1] Walker thought Dixon did much "to wind back the approach it [the *Engineers' case*] stood for."[2] However, Dixon's legalism was only a legal positivist literalism, differently named which maintained an overriding concern with the text of the Constitution while ignoring the scheme intended by the Founders. It was this that provided the convenient hook on which Barwick, in his judgments, could hang the more doctrinaire literalism of Isaacs.

SIR OWEN DIXON

This section shows that Dixon was aware of some of the deficiencies in Isaacs's reasons in the *Engineers' case* and sought to give effect to some changes that he hoped would provide a better ground for interpreting the Constitution. He expressed concern in *West v Commissioner of Taxation (NSW)*[3] for Isaacs's denial of implications, as a limitation on the text's meaning. It did not, however, cause him to consider the political scheme of the Constitution that the

Founders had intended. Yet this chapter shows that when Dixon attempted to articulate the federal scheme of the Constitution in *The Lord Mayor, Councillors and Citizens of the City of Melbourne v Commonwealth*,[4] he did so without referencing the condition of state sovereignty that would impose specific reservations upon constitutional construction. His method was to construe the Constitution as one political scheme, federal only in name, in which powers were shared under the Commonwealth's umbrella. His appeal to American authorities as a reason for dismissing the Marshallian federal doctrines was an implicit recognition of the power of a court of review (implicitly, as demonstrated by Isaacs) to change the Constitution from what was approved by the authorizing body—the people—to one that the court thought was best.

The Isaacs's Influence

While Dixon's judgments can be read as laying out his own methodology for construing the Constitution as an articulation of his complete legalism, his judgments are confined to the text of the Constitution without regard to the Founders' political scheme. In *West v Commissioner of Taxation (NSW)*,[5] the High Court was asked to consider whether a pension payable under the *Superannuation Act 1922* (Cth) was liable to state income tax. Prima facie, this would have been answerable by application of the doctrine of immunities in *Deakin v Webb*. Dixon's reasons commenced with a caution of the danger of applying decisions from the Canadian Constitution to questions regarding the Commonwealth Constitution:

> Much caution should be used in applying decisions upon the *British North America Act* to questions arising upon the Commonwealth Constitution. The instruments are very different and few or none of the difficulties to which secs. 91 and 92 of the Canadian Constitution continue to give rise have any real counterpart in the Australian Constitution.[6]

His argument is a subtle attack on Isaacs's judgment in the *Engineers' case*, where legal positivist judgments of Privy Council cases were cited to reject the analysis of the early court. As shown in chapter 4, Isaacs's use of those cases also provided support for his literalist construction. Dixon states expressly that the instruments are very different, but does not suggest that the difference manifests itself in the political scheme. His legal positivism confines the difference to the juridical difficulty of interpreting the different and theoretically mutually exclusive powers of sections 91 and 92 of the BNA, but which in practice actually overlapped. Dixon ignores his own caution to suggest that "there is not much danger" in applying Canadian decisions "to the present case"[7] because of the "the manner in which the Commonwealth legislation deals with the liability of the pension to State taxation."[8] Dixon notes that the Commonwealth law controls whether the pension is subject to a state income tax law. As he has therefore imputed a power to the Commonwealth by which it subjects itself to or protects itself from state taxes, he has already conceded Isaacs's conclusion in the *Engineers' case* that the federal scheme of the Constitution was not one of separate sovereignties. Dixon's construction ignores the theory of the Constitution. He recognizes that the Commonwealth Constitution is federal, but his federalism does not involve sovereignty. In fact, he does not mention the word at all. He accepts that the doctrine of immunities does not apply and, like Isaacs, looks to invalidate state law pursuant to section 109 of the Constitution:

> The State tax would be inconsistent with the law of the Commonwealth in making enjoyment of the right or benefit conferred by the latter the special occasion of a burden. The invalidity of the State law would then be a result of sec. 109 of the *Constitution*.[9]

His qualification of this statement, "that this is [not] the only ground upon which a discriminatory State tax on salaries, pensions or other payments received from the Commonwealth would be invalid,"[10] should not be taken to suggest that the doctrine of immunities was still operational. Dixon confirmed Isaacs's view that only an express provision could limit a Commonwealth power as well as implicitly endorsing Isaacs's literalism and rejecting the federal scheme of the Founders. He approvingly cited Isaacs's statement in *Pirrie v McFarlane* that

> the natural and fundamental principle that, where by the one Constitution separate and exclusive governmental powers have been allotted to two distinct organisms, neither is intended, in the absence of distinct provision to the contrary, to destroy or weaken the capacity or functions expressly conferred on the other.[11]

While Dixon explicitly rejected Isaacs's demand that no implications be made in interpreting the Constitution, his statement that "such a method of construction would defeat the intention of any instrument, but of all instruments a written constitution seems the last to which it could be applied"[12] was merely a literary truism that implications are as much a part of literalism as are connotations and denotations. Both Philip Ayres[13] and Geoffrey de Q Walker[14] credited Dixon's judgment in *West's case* for having restored the drawing of implications from the Constitution but, like Dixon, they did not connect with Isaacs's ulterior purpose in the *Engineers' case*, which was to deny the existence of the federal scheme that he was determined to abolish. Dixon's obligation to Isaacs's judgment in the *Engineers' case* is evident when he says that a constitutional power prima facie enables the Commonwealth "to make laws affecting the operations of the States and their agencies."[15] He expresses this rule to be subject to exceptions, these being "the nature or the subject matter of the power"[16] or the language of the power or some other constitutional provision; however, he does not mention the necessary implications from a federal scheme. With a reference to *Deakin v Webb*, where Commonwealth law fixed a salary and state law taxed it, Dixon said "the scope and purpose of the law which secures the payments must be ascertained."[17] This means, however, that he accepts Isaacs's rationale that there is no implied limit as between Commonwealth and state legislative powers. The only limit on a Commonwealth power is the one expressed in the Commonwealth law made pursuant to that particular power. The Commonwealth *Superannuation Act* contained no express protection from state tax.

The Commonwealth legislation in the present case clearly meant to leave the pension without any protection unless the Executive Government thought fit to confer it. This circumstance completely distinguishes the case from *Deakin v Webb*, as explained in the *Engineers' Case*.[18]

Under Dixon's brand of federalism, the implied limits of the early court have been replaced by an implied constitutional power in the Commonwealth to authorize or prevent interference. Despite an attempt to differentiate his method from that of Isaacs, Dixon shares Isaacs's legal positivism and its commitment to a text unrelated to the political scheme of the Founders. His literalism, albeit enlarged by literary implications, confirms Isaacs's decision and his indebtedness to the *Engineers' case*.

Dixon's Nonfederal Scheme

The issue before the court in *The Lord Mayor, Councillors and Citizens of the City of Melbourne v Commonwealth* (*State Banking case*)[19] was whether the Commonwealth's *Banking Act 1945* was unconstitutional in its attempt to regulate where states could bank, given the express exclusion of state banking from Commonwealth legislative power in relation to banking by section 51(xiii) of the Constitution. Dixon's analysis takes issue with reasons in the *Engineers' case* only to the extent that he provides his own legal vision of the federal scheme, drawn not from the original intention of the Founders or as necessary implications from the true federal scheme identified by the Privy Council,[20] but from his consideration of the text of the Constitution informed by perceived differences between a federal and unitary Constitution.[21] He acknowledges that policies can be accomplished under a unitary scheme that are not possible under a federal scheme, but he fails to explain the necessary elements of the federal scheme.[22] He asserts without reasons that state and federal governments are "separate bodies politic and prima facie each controls its own moneys,"[23] but in the absence of separate sovereignties (a term totally absent from his judgment), he provides no reason why a separate body politic even has its own money.[24] He argues that for the Commonwealth to control where the states can bank, "there must be found in the Constitution a definite legislative power of sufficient amplitude."[25] By "definite," he seems to suggest a specific legislative power that correlates with the object of where a state can bank. Section 51(xiii) of the Constitution, which refers to "banking other than State banking," is not apparently of "sufficient amplitude," suggesting that something more authoritative than a named power is required. He notes that the Commonwealth power under section 51(xiii) of the Constitution in relation to banking expressly excludes state banking, but includes "State banking which extends beyond the limits of the State concerned"[26] and reasons that "state banking was contemplated as a possible function of government which should be excluded from the operation of federal law within the territorial limits of the authority of the government concerned."[27] He thus proposes an area of state law "within the territorial limits" that is untouchable by the Commonwealth; according to Story's *Commentaries*, this is a criterion of sovereignty; except for the fact that Dixon does not recognize state sovereignty—although he does recognize territorial limit. His difficulty is that there is nothing in the Constitution that recognizes territorial limit that does not imply sovereignty.

He announced that "the Court has adopted a rule"[28] for construing how the Commonwealth's powers applied to the States and he sourced the rule to the *Engineers' case*: "The prima-facie rule is that a power to legislate with respect to a given subject enables the Parliament to make laws which, upon that subject, affect the operations of the States and their agencies. That, as I have pointed out more than once, is the effect of the *Engineers' case*."[29]

In this reference, he has not only accepted Isaacs's rejection of the doctrine of immunities but also Isaacs's rejection of state sovereignty. It is not apparent exactly what status Dixon accorded a state except that, under his rule, a Commonwealth power can affect the operations of the states and their agencies. He identified three exceptions to the rule: the prerogative, a tax law, and a law discriminating against the states. While the prerogative and tax are not involved in the *State Banking case*, Dixon describes discrimination as "a law which discriminates against States, or a law which places a particular disability or burden upon an operation or activity of a State, and more especially upon the execution of its constitutional powers."[30]

Discrimination is therefore a Commonwealth law having "an immediate object of controlling the State in the course which otherwise the Executive

Government of the State might adopt."[31] Such a law has two facets: the first prescribed the course that the executive government of the State must take.[32] The irony of this rule can be seen if the concept of state sovereignty is not included when executive power is considered. In that circumstance, the state as an entity does not exist. The second facet of Dixon's rule applies when the connection between the Commonwealth law and the head of power is

> so insubstantial, tenuous or distant by the character of the control or restriction the law seeks to impose upon State action that it ought not to be regarded as enacted with respect to the specified matter falling within the Commonwealth power.[33]

This second aspect only makes sense if it posits a law that has two objects, one constitutional and the other not. It suggests that a Commonwealth law would be invalid if, for example, the connection with the head of power were tenuous or insubstantial; such an attempt might seek to regulate industrial relations through the Commonwealth powers regarding "lighthouses, astronomical observations, fisheries, weights and measures, bills of exchange or marriage"[34]—something that Dixon himself postulates. He implies, however, that the law would be valid if it sought to regulate industrial relations with a substantial connection to another head of power, for example, through the exclusive power to levy excise duties (section 90 of the Constitution). The Commonwealth's attempt to do that was rejected by the early Court in *R v Barger*.[35] In rejecting the Commonwealth's legislation, the early court examined the substance of legislation rather than its form. Thus, Dixon's second aspect not only extends Commonwealth powers but also places the powers reserved to the states liable to invalidity, which explains why Dixon described Commonwealth powers as enumerated[36] but not limited. Limited and enumerated defined Commonwealth powers when the Commonwealth was federal after the United States. A confusion emerges in Dixon's federal scheme when he has to sacrifice the states' powers, and hence federalism. The confusion appears when he confirms that a law could not be held invalid if it "discloses another purpose and that the purpose lies outside the area of federal power."[37] The only areas outside of federal powers are states' powers, but he confirms that if a Commonwealth law is operating within a field "assigned to the Commonwealth as a subject of legislative power,"[38] the direct connection to the legislative power would be sufficient to validate the law.[39] Thus, he confirms the triumph of form over substance and by construing the "field" instead of the head of power in section 51, he authorizes the demise of powers reserved to the states.

Dixon's criterion for a connection between a federal law and a legislative power was that it be of sufficient amplitude, but his explanation—that the connection be not tenuous, distant, or insubstantial—is vague. In comparison, the early court in *R v Burah*, as shown in chapter 3, distinguished between the literal form of a law and the substance of the law to ensure that the law did not seek to achieve by indirect means what it could not achieve directly.[40] The doctrine of immunities that Dixon sought to replace cast a strict obligation on the High Court to protect the powers of each from encroachment by the other unless it was permitted explicitly or by necessary implication. The court was expected to find the limit of a power on each occasion. Under Dixon's new formulation, the court would determine whether the Commonwealth's invasion of a state power was tenuous or insubstantial—a political judgment for the court, which had to consider which of the different objects of the law was sought and to what degree.

He said of the federal taxing power and its interference in state government functions that it had been taken to extravagant lengths and applied artificially, which led to "the making of untenable distinctions."[41] Citing *New York v United States*,[42] Dixon identified the US Supreme Court as the cause of the immunities doctrine being "applied artificially to notionally and abstract interferences"[43] and going to extravagant lengths in that jurisdiction. As a result, the Supreme Court had abandoned both doctrines, as it had in Australia[44]—something of which Dixon approved. Frankfurter J in *New York v United States* thought Marshall's maxim that "the power to tax involves the power to destroy" a rhetorical absolute with unrevealed practical limitations,[45] which suggests that Frankfurter had already abandoned the separate sovereignties for a lesser notion of federalism.[46] Dixon did not contemplate the possibility that Frankfurter's "practical limitations" were the result of US jurists' legal positivist interpretations of the Constitution's text in isolation from the political scheme intended by the US Founders, including Marshall CJ. Dixon's argument has the effect of accepting decisions of the Supreme Court that prevent "juristic principle designed for the practical affairs of government" from becoming abstract extremes. Dixon says approvingly:

> The notion of a reciprocal immunity from which it arose has been condemned as fallacious and the constitutional law of the United States now gives as little countenance to the extreme applications made of the principle of non-interference as does the constitutional law of Australia.[47]

The problem, though, is actually different from that to which Dixon refers. Reciprocal immunity was as much a necessary corollary of a Constitution with separate sovereign entities as doctrine of immunities, and if the separate sovereignties are a part of the Constitution ratified by the people, a court charged to defend the Constitution would have taken a political decision were it to change its meaning, despite its claim to only interpret the law.

The *New York v United States* decision suggested social complexity as the reason for the alteration in the United States, even though no complexity was actually cited. Dixon implied that Isaacs's judgment in the *Engineers' case* was a necessary correction of "extreme applications of the principle of non-interference." As shown by previous chapters, that view was misconceived. His own rejection of the federal scheme as enunciated by the early court's judgments is equally so. This is all the more telling, given Dixon's conclusion to his paper, "Marshall and the Australian Constitution," where he said: "His [Marshall's] judgments have that rarest of properties; when you read them they appear always to be right."[48] In that article, Dixon expresses concern that the word "inconsistent" in section 109 "received a pedantic construction drawn from a verbal formalism."[49] He thought that before declaring a state law invalid, the court should ask "whether the paramount legislature in Australia has dealt with a topic falling within a field of its power in a manner showing that it has undertaken to determine what the *condition of the law* shall be on the subject."[50] Dixon's reference to the Commonwealth as the "paramount legislature" and his characterization of a head of power as "a field of its power" concede Isaacs's view that the Commonwealth requires each legislative power to be broadly construed. It shifts construction from an examination of a limited power to an examination of what constitutes the "field." However, the Commonwealth legislature determining what "condition the law shall be" appears to be no different from Isaacs's test of whether the Commonwealth "evinces an intention to cover the whole field,"[51] and hence to exclude states' reserved powers.

In a number of extra-curial writings, Dixon made much of his own methodology for construing the Constitution. When he took his oath of office as Chief Justice of the High Court on April 21, 1952, he articulated his methodology for the construction of the Constitution as "strict and complete legalism."[52] He is reported to have told an associate that he regretted having used that phrase. It was misunderstood that he was using it "of specifically Constitutional matters."[53] He explained that the court's sole function was to interpret a constitutional power or restraint upon power, and to say whether a given measure fell on one side of a line consequently drawn or on the other:

> Such a function has led us all I think to believe that close adherence to legal reasoning is the only way to maintain the confidence of all parties in federal conflicts. It may be that the Court is thought to be excessively legalistic. I should be sorry to think that it is anything else. There is no other safe guide to judicial decisions in great conflicts than a strict and complete legalism.[54]

While Dixon's legal reasoning has not been equated with Isaacs's literalism, there are few differences between them when the two cases that have been examined are considered in light of the *Engineers' case*. His legal reasoning is legal positivism that interprets the text from the text alone and, although informed by US decisions, he infers an explanation of federalism that was not intended by the Founders and ignores the federal scheme that the Founders intended. His federalism resembles Isaacs's scheme, where sovereignties are subsumed under the single Commonwealth, even if Dixon's construction method was differently expressed. Dixon's political scheme, like that of Isaacs, was not the one consented to by the Australian people, which is the one he was expected to uphold.

Dixon's complete legalism aligned itself with the common law, but his methodology was not from the common law. In his article, "Approaches to Constitutional Interpretation in Australia: an American Perspective,"[55] William Rich said of *legalism*, "Legalism is one of the terms often used to characterise the tradition of Australian constitutional jurisprudence. It belongs in a larger family of approaches including literalism, positivism, formalism, textualism and in the United States, strict construction."[56] He described Dixon's opinions as reflecting "a framework built upon the Supremacy of the Parliament of the United Kingdom and the common law as an 'Ultimate Constitutional foundation.'"[57] This conclusion is borne out by Dixon's own statement when he ignored Chapter III of the Commonwealth Constitution and the Australian people and asserted that the common law was the source of Commonwealth juristic authority, having been brought ashore by Governor Phillip in 1788 and imposed by Imperial law, the *Australian Courts Act 1828*,[58] on the colonies of New South Wales and Van Diemen's Land.[59]

Anthony Mason thought it unjust to describe Dixon as a "legalist": "Dixon J's contribution was to inject more of a federal balance into constitutional interpretation after the *Engineers case* by developing what have been called 'the federal implications.'"[60] Mason's notion of a "federal balance" is very general. He suggests that Dixon gave extra weight to the Constitution's federalism when compared with the *Engineers' case*—which, in a small way, he did. But the question that Mason never addressed was "the source of the federalism" that Dixon injected into the Constitution. Had he asked, "Whose federalism?", he could only have answered, "Dixon's federalism."[61]

In "Concerning Judicial Method," a paper delivered at Yale University in 1955,[62] Dixon asserted that the High Court's desire for consistency in the law was inherited from its links with the common law and English precedent of authority, and that it is what the courts in the hierarchy say that determines the law.[63] Consistency is, of course, important; however, to fulfill its purpose the court must seek to be consistent with the authoritative opinion of the Constitution's meaning. That meaning was the one originally intended by the Founders. Dixon places too much faith in the process of the hierarchical determination of the law, and hence of stare decisis. He explains that the validity of a judicial decision is determined according to an external standard that is not personal to the judge:

> It is taken for granted that the decision of the court will be "correct" or "incorrect," "right" or "wrong" as it conforms with ascertained legal principles and applies them according to a standard of reasoning which is not personal to the judges themselves.[64]

While the external standard is Dixon's demand that constitutional construction be applied impersonally—meaning, presumably, without bias—it implies that constitutional construction is ultimately a matter of trust, whether it is personal or impersonal. The High Court is the final appellate court for the Constitution. There is no appeal if a judge manipulates construction to achieve a personal preference in order to shoehorn the Constitution. That Dixon was unaware of that defect is apparent in the external matters that he claimed assisted his judicial reasoning. They included the argument of appeals at length in open court, which argument "is dialectical and the judges engage in the discussion";[65] a resort to case law in the course of argument, the courts having distinguished between persuasive and imperative authority; and the use of textbooks and other works of authority.[66] He considered these external matters "a definite system of accepted knowledge or thought and that judgments and other legal writings are evidence of its content."[67] The defect in his list, which results from his legal positivism, is the absence of any consideration of the political scheme of the Constitution as intended by the Founders. This defect arises because of his failure to acknowledge that the source of political and legal sovereignty in the Constitution was not the Imperial Parliament, but the Australian people, and as such he was obliged to discover the nature of the political scheme of the Constitution to which they consented.

Conclusion—Dixon

Dixon's objections to Isaacs's judgment in the *Engineers' case* set out in this section show that his objections to that judgment are not evidence of any substantial disagreement with Isaacs's literalism. His argument in *West* reveals a minor disagreement with Isaacs's exclusion of implications from the interpretation of the Constitution but an implicit acceptance that the necessary implications had no basis in the Constitution. What he did not see was Isaacs's ulterior motive in the *Engineers' case*, a decision that replaced the Founders' original intention with Isaacs's own original intention. Dixon had a legal positivist methodology in common with Isaacs, which was the basis of his implicit acceptance of Isaacs's literalism. Further, since he did not detect the purpose of Isaacs's construction devices, he accepted Isaacs's rejection of the doctrines of the federal Constitution and his use of section 109 to invalidate state laws when Commonwealth laws purported to cover the field.

Dixon's judgment in the *State Banking case* made the same methodological assumptions as were evident in *West's case*, and the cause was the same: his acceptance of Isaacs's literalist construction methodology. The difficulty imposed by this methodology became apparent when he rejected Isaacs's unitary scheme and attempted to articulate his own federal scheme. He dismissed the US Constitution as an exemplar because later Supreme Courts had abandoned the Constitution of their Founders and dismissed the doctrines associated with Chief Justice Marshall and the Tenth Amendment in preference for Commonwealth supremacy under section 109 of the Constitution. Rather than defend the Commonwealth Constitution as it was intended by the Founders, Dixon continued with the abandonment of the separate sovereignties and related principles, and consequently could not provide a firm basis on which a federal scheme could exist.

Sir Owen Dixon was obliged to retire from the High Court in 1964 due to ill health. That same year, Prime Minister Robert Menzies, who in 1920 had appeared for the applicant Association in the *Engineers' case*, appointed the then minister for external affairs, Sir Garfield Barwick, Chief Justice of the High Court of Australia. While Barwick agreed with Dixon's assertion of the correctness of a method of constitutional construction that adopted complete legalism, his own methodology of construction went beyond that of Dixon.

SIR GARFIELD BARWICK

This section will argue that, although Barwick adopted Dixon's terminology in his own jurisprudence, he openly avowed Isaacs's judgment in the *Engineers' case* and adopted its literalist construction methods. This indebtedness was openly declared in the *Payroll Tax case*[68] when he endorsed Isaacs's judgment and construed the Constitution citing Isaacs's authorities for his own,[69] but it was implicitly evident in his judgment in *Attorney-General (Cth); Ex rel McKinlay v Commonwealth.*[70] Whereas Dixon is reported to have despised much of the reasoning in the *Engineers' case*,[71] Barwick's opinion of it was the opposite. His jurisprudence espoused a complete return to Isaacs's literalist methodology of the *Engineers' case*, and hence Isaacs's unitary scheme, when he said: "The basic principles of construction of the Constitution were definitively enunciated by the Court in *Amalgamated Society of Engineers v Adelaide Steamship Co Ltd.*"[72] Isaacs's literalism was the sine qua non of his destruction of the federal scheme and its replacement by a unitary scheme.

Understanding Barwick's literalism is an essential step to understanding the nature of the advice he gave the Governor-General, Sir John Kerr, on November 10, 1975, and his ex post justification[73] of that advice: that Kerr held a constitutional power to dismiss an Australian prime minister who had the support of a majority of the House of Representatives. Unlike Dixon, Barwick was not given to lengthy extra-curial essays. A consideration of two cases is sufficient to identify his preferred jurisprudence. Those two cases are *Victoria v Commonwealth*[74] and *Attorney-General (Cth); Ex rel McKinlay v Commonwealth.*[75]

Barwick and Isaacs

In *Victoria v Commonwealth*, the State of Victoria sought a declaration from the High Court that so much of the Commonwealth *Payroll Tax Act*,[76] by which a tax was levied upon the wages paid or payable by a state to its employees, was invalid. Victoria's principal argument was that the Commonwealth's legislative power of taxation was subject to a limitation derived by implication from the federal nature of the Constitution:[77] "the States cannot tax the Commonwealth and the Commonwealth cannot tax the States."[78] It sought to base its argument on Dixon's reasons in *Melbourne Corporation v The Commonwealth*[79] rather than the reciprocal doctrine of immunities in the *Railway Servants' case.*[80]

After stating the facts of the case, Barwick addressed the method he would employ to construe the Constitution. He explained that the "question was a legal question. It was to be resolved by legal consideration alone, that is to say, by the construction of the Constitution according to legal principle."[81] These principles of legal construction were to be found in the *Engineers' case*: "The basic principles of construction of the Constitution were definitively enunciated by the Court" in the *Engineers' case.*[82] When he endorsed Isaacs's principal assumption in the *Engineers' case*, as applying "the ordinary rules of statutory construction as appropriate to an organic instrument to which the Crown was a party,"[83] he implicitly rejected Dixon's argument that the Crown, like responsible government, was irrelevant to the issues before the court in the *Engineers' case.*[84]

Barwick cited the same Privy Council cases as authorities for the principles of construction of a written Constitution as Isaacs had in the *Engineers' case*. An identical passage from Lord Selborne's judgment in *R v Burah* was cited and applied, as was an identical passage from Earl Loreburn in *Attorney-General (Ontario) v Attorney-General (Canada).*[85] Ignoring Dixon's warning of the irrelevance of Privy Council decisions to the Canadian Constitution, he cited the passage from *Attorney-General (Ontario) v Attorney-General (Canada)*, which directed a court to make a literal construction.[86] It was noted in chapter 4 that the literalist methodology evident in the two Privy Council cases was the doctrinaire face of legal positivism, which interpreted the legal text without any consideration of the political scheme to which the text was purposed.

As Victoria had argued that the Commonwealth payroll tax legislation did not bind it, Barwick imitated Isaacs by stating that the question was whether the Crown in the right of the Commonwealth could legislatively bind the Crown in the right of the state. He cited the legal axiom that "the Crown is ubiquitous and indivisible in the King's dominions"[87] as Isaacs had in the *Engineers' case*, ignoring Dixon's opinion that it was irrelevant.[88] He cited from the *Engineers' case* that "laws validly made by authority of the Constitution bind, so far as they purport to do so, the people of every State considered as individuals or as *political organisms called States*."[89]

To the proposition that there was an implied limitation on the legislative powers of the Commonwealth that excepted the Crown in right of the state, Barwick cited directly from the *Engineers' case* the passage that referenced Lord Selborne that no such limitation existed, before stating: "These principles were not only stated in universal terms but, in my opinion, are by their very nature of universal validity."[90] The Victorian submission implicitly questioned the correctness of Isaacs's conclusion in the *Engineers' case*, and in doing so had raised the issue of the nature of the Constitution's federal scheme. Barwick rejected Dixon's view that Isaacs's dictum in the *Engineers' case* of Commonwealth legislative supremacy was to be understood as only prima facie, but subject to being displaced by a range of other considerations.[91] He argued that a legislative power, if construed by ordinary methods, "extends to authorise legislation binding the Crown in right of a State."[92] When he explained his "ordinary methods" of construction, he implicitly rejected Dixon's restoration of implications from the text. He confirmed that his "ordinary methods" was Isaacs's literalism found in the dicta of Lord Selborne and Lord Loreburn in *R v Burah* and *Attorney-General (Ontario) v Attorney-General (Canada)*.[93] Again following Isaacs's judgment in the *Engineers' case*, he held that the court must look only for express limitations on Commonwealth powers:

> Section 51(xiii) is an obvious example of such an *express* limitation of subject matter. But if there be no such *express* limitation, the legislative power to bind the Crown in right of a State by a valid law with respect to a subject matter within s 51(ii).[94]

When he denied that the *Engineers' case* was authority for a rule "that in interpreting the Constitution no implications can be made,"[95] Dixon was mitigating the effect that Isaacs's refusal to draw implications would have.

However, his statement of the principle of construction, that a Commonwealth power prima facie will affect the states unless displaced by consideration of "the nature or subject matter of the power or the language in which it is conferred or on some other provision in the Constitution,"[96] was received cautiously by Barwick, who countered:

> The erection of a prima facie meaning of constitutional provision with provision for displacing considerations, though not an approach to construction which I would myself prefer, is after all but a form of expression and, as I understand it, not intended to depart from ordinary methods of construing constitutional provisions.[97]

Since every statement in a Constitution has a prima facie meaning that can be altered by other express or implied provisions, Barwick's statement effectively feigns support for Dixon's rejection of Isaacs's methodology only to preserve Isaacs's methodology and its source in the Privy Council.

The Victorian Government had submitted that the limitation on the Commonwealth's taxing power, section 51(ii), was a result of the federal nature of the Constitution,[98] which implicitly suggested that the rule in *McCulloch v Maryland* applied. In a lengthy argument muddied with ambiguity, Barwick began by stating that the Commonwealth Constitution

> does not represent a treaty or union between sovereign and independent States. It was the result of the will and desire of the people of all the colonies expressed both through their representative institutions and directly through referenda to be united in one Commonwealth with an agreed distribution of governmental power.[99]

It is difficult to see the relevance of the first sentence, since it was never part of Victoria's case, but it bears a striking resemblance to a passage from Story's *Commentaries*.[100] Barwick concedes in the second sentence that the Commonwealth Constitution was an agreement by the people of the several colonies uniting in a federal Commonwealth. Some light is shed on this passage when it is recalled that the Preamble to the US Constitution vests the founding principle of the Constitution in "We the people of the United States of America." The underlying constituent principle was expressed by Hamilton in the following way: "The fabric of American empire ought to rest on the solid basis of THE CONSENT OF THE PEOPLE."[101] Story (anticipating Griffith CJ in *Baxter's case*)[102] explained that the Union was an agreement of the people, the supreme authority in the US Constitution. Commenting on the Preamble to that Constitution, he said,

> "The language is, "We, the people of the United States," not, We, the states, "do ordain and establish;" not, do contract and enter into a treaty with each other; "this constitution for the United States of America," not this treaty between the several states.[103]

If the similarity in language of the two constitutional preambles points to the same founding authority, the similarity between Barwick's explanation to Story's attribution of authority to "the people" and his denial of any contract or treaty between the states points to the unreferenced source of Barwick's comment. Having identified the actual source of the Constitution in the US Constitution, Barwick asserts that the Constitution was made an Act of the Imperial Parliament and cites Isaacs's judgment in the *Engineers' case* to support it. He concedes a paragraph later that the Commonwealth Constitution was federal—although exactly what is meant by "federal" is ambiguous:

> The Constitution granted by the Imperial Act was "federal," not in the sense of a union of previously existing States surrendering powers to that union but in the sense that the powers of government were distributed, some by nomination of subject matter and others as residues.[104]

Having already stated that the Constitution was federal, he omitted to explain, as section 107 of the Constitution makes clear, that the residue of powers remained with the states. The effect of his explanation was the removal of sovereign states from the Commonwealth. Powers are distributed, but not between sovereign bodies subject to the Constitution, and what he meant by federal was never clearly stated. This might suggest that he was unable to reconcile powers held by two different entities without conceding sovereignty to each; or it might suggest that he was content to adopt Isaacs's argument without giving it much thought. According to Isaacs's argument the states were not sovereign, since their powers were subject to invalidity if the Commonwealth legislated to cover the field. Barwick had a contradictory explanation for the Commonwealth and states under the Constitution in an earlier case, where he explained the difference between the Commonwealth and US Constitutions as the former being composed of the states while the latter was a union of the states: "Each State is a part of the Commonwealth: see covering cl. 6. This situation is different from that arising under the Constitution of the United States which is as its name implies a union of States to which union certain powers are conceded."[105]

Barwick followed Isaacs faithfully, and dismissed the usefulness of "analogies drawn from situations in the United States of America and from judicial conclusions and observations upon the Constitution of that country."[106] Neither of his attempts to explain the Constitution by political science was accurate or successful. He seems to have realized this by following Isaacs's lead and describing the Constitution as the legislative Act of the Imperial Parliament, which "alone expresses the will of the Imperial Parliament which alone had legislative power to alter the colonial status."[107] Referring to the Constitution as the Act, he invokes the principle of literalism when he cites the *Engineers' case*, where it was said that "it must be read naturally in the light of the circumstances in which it was made."[108]

Given that he began that explanation by referring to Dixon's judgments in the two cases dealt with above, it is reasonable to conclude that Barwick's argument concerning the Constitution was an attempt to repudiate Dixon so as to justify Isaacs's explanation of the Constitution. That explanation and the literalism associated by the Privy Council with the interpretation of Imperial legislation were the cornerstones of Barwick's judgment in *Victoria v Commonwealth.* His use of literalism to construe the Constitution for a particular result is more conspicuous in the later case of *Attorney-General (Cth); Ex rel McKinlay v Commonwealth.*[109]

Barwick's Literalism

McKinlay's case commenced in the High Court on November 3, 1975, eight days before the dismissal of the Whitlam government. Judgment was handed down on December 1, 1975, dismissing the plaintiffs' claims. The election of both the House and the Senate following a double dissolution pursuant to section 57 of the Constitution was held on December 13, 1975. While the most obvious feature of Barwick's judgment in the *Payroll Tax case* was its express adoption of all the elements of Isaacs's construction methodology, the repetition of Privy Council authorities, and citations from the *Engineers*, the most striking feature of Barwick's judgment in *McKinlay's case* is the absence of any explicit reference to Isaacs or the *Engineers' case*—or to any authority for his decision, for that matter. Nevertheless, the judgment in *McKinlay's case* is pregnant with the same methodology. Barwick refers to only one Australian case,[110] *King v Jones*,[111] which was not cited in relation to any issue before the court. Four US cases were referred to but dismissed as irrelevant in his judgment.[112]

McKinlay was one of three plaintiffs whose main appeal challenged the constitutional validity of the *Commonwealth Electoral Act 1918–75* (the Act). The principal submission for McKinlay was stated thus: "Section 24 of the Constitution commands equality of representation for equal numbers of all the people of the Commonwealth both among the States (except for Tasmania) and within the States."[113]

The principal ground for the challenge was stated by Barwick to be that section 19 of the Act was ultra vires section 24 of the Constitution, "because it enables an electoral division to be under-represented and/or permits discriminatory representations and purports to fix the weight and composition of the electoral divisions within the State."[114] The relevant paragraph of section 24 of the Constitution states:

> The House of Representatives shall be composed of members directly chosen by the people of the Commonwealth, and the number of such members shall be, as nearly as practicable, twice the number of the senators.[115]

Barwick stated that the principal submission that was common to all the appeals

> was that there is to be found or implied in s 24 of the Constitution a *guarantee* that if the States of Australia should be divided into divisions for the purpose of choosing members of the House of Representatives, such divisions shall comprise an equal number of people or, as it was put, such divisions shall be of "practical equality" in numbers of people.[116]

He begins his analysis of section 24 by examining the submission that the implied guarantee is

> to be derived either by implying the word "all" before the word "people" in the first paragraph of s 24 or by regarding the total expression "directly chosen by the people" as necessarily involving the concept of each person having an equal vote in an election.[117]

McKinlay had sought to consult the Constitutional Convention debates to demonstrate the Founders' intention. Barwick rejected the submission, stating that "it is settled doctrine in Australia that the records of the discussions in the Conventions and in the legislatures of the colonies will not be used as an aid to the construction of the Constitution."[118] The objectivity of this statement can be measured against his judgment in *Re Webster*,[119] handed down less than four months previously, where, despite apologizing for having read the Convention debates, he nevertheless cited passages from them that supported his argument.[120] Before commencing his construction of the word "people" in section 24, he states that it is one of legal construction of the Constitution, which he describes as an Act of the Imperial Parliament:

> The problem which is thus presented to the Court is a matter of the legal construction of the Constitution of Australia, itself a legal document; an Act of the Imperial Parliament. The problem is not to be solved by resort to slogans or to political catch-cries or to vague and imprecise expressions of political philosophy.[121]

This implicit endorsement of Isaacs's literalist methodology excludes any consideration of a theory regarding this aspect of the Constitution, which Barwick attributes to "vague and imprecise expressions of political philosophy." He adds that the meaning of the *Electoral Act* depends on "the meaning of the relevant text of the Constitution, having regard to the historical context in which the Constitution was created and the terms and operation of the Act"[122]—the Act being the legislation of the Commonwealth Parliament. While the context in which the Constitution was created seems to suggest otherwise, it does not include the Founders' intention for the Constitution. Barwick characterizes the true guide for construction as being to produce stability in constitutional law by reading "the language of the Constitution itself no doubt generously and not pedantically, but as a whole: and to find its meaning by *legal reasoning*."[123] "Stability" in that context has an identical connotation with Isaacs's demand for consistency in interpretation.[124] The problem with stability as an object of construction, however, is that stare decisis does not distinguish between the construction employed in the *Engineers' case* and that employed in *Deakin v Webb*. His demand for legal reasoning is linked to Dixon's strict and complete legalism: "I respectfully agree with Sir Owen Dixon's opinion that 'there is no other safe guide to judicial decisions in great conflicts than a strict and complete legalism.'"[125] However, as already shown, Dixon's legalism—whether complete or strict—was another term for his legal positivist interpretation of the Constitution, unrelated to the meaning of the Founders. Despite linking his legal reasoning to that of Dixon, Barwick's legal reasoning was in fact not Dixon's but rather Isaacs's literalism.

Barwick's interpretation of the words "chosen by the people of the Commonwealth" in section 24 of the Constitution takes an unusual turn when he seeks to derive the meaning from its counterpart in section 7, where the expression is "directly chosen by the people of the States."[126] Section 24 also contains the words "*directly* chosen by the people"[127]—albeit of the Commonwealth. It might appear strange that he would seek the meaning of identical words by a consideration of them in another section, until he confirms that although the states had vastly different numbers of peoples, they were nonetheless equally represented in the Senate.[128] He concludes that the unequal numbers of people in the states provided evidence that "there could be no question that equality of voting strength throughout Australia was intended or provided for in s 7."[129] While this truism is literally true, his argument is irrelevant to the meaning of those words in section 24, for section 24, as shown in chapter 2, was intended by the Founders to provide representation for the people of the whole Commonwealth in the House of Representatives in proportion to the population of each state. Section 7 provides for equal representation, despite population differences, of each individual sovereign state in the Senate, as intended by the Founders. This feature implies, at a minimum, a practical equality of electorates.

His literal interpretation of the word "people" in section 7 gives two possible meanings: people, meaning the population; or people, meaning the electors. However, because he has adopted a literal construction of the provision, he concludes that it does not mean population of the state: "It would be both an unreasonable and impractical interpretation of the expression to read it as securing the franchise to every child and teenager in the population."[130] Instead, he assumes that the word "people" in section 7 means electors of the state and concludes that "it is quite evident from other provisions of Pt III [of the Constitution] that adult suffrage in each State was not intended or required by the expression 'directly chosen by the people.'"[131]

His literalist approach to construction precludes a consideration of the wider, metaphorical meaning of "people" in its denotation as the "demos,"[132] a meaning that was consistent with the same word in the Preamble. That meaning would include men, women, and children, as the Preamble implies. Electors would then comprise a class of the "people" identified with the franchise by the legislature to choose senators on the one hand and representatives on the other. When the word "people" is understood in the metaphorical sense of the Preamble, the adults to whom the franchise is granted by the legislature will represent "the people," equally of the whole Commonwealth or equally of each state, as originally intended. If, as Barwick asserts, "chosen by the people" means "chosen by the electors," then whomever the Parliament directs will be electors will be justified by sections 7 and 24 of the Constitution.

As the very first federal election was conducted under the varying franchises of each colony, Barwick concludes that "the existing franchises were constitutionally acceptable,"[133] meaning that the Founders had no preference for a democratically elected Parliament. This must be doubted. The initial elections after federation in 1901 were conducted on colonial franchises because there was no federal Parliament in existence to legislate for a uniform Commonwealth franchise or a distribution of electorates for the House. Further, for the first election, section 29 of the Constitution left the drawing of electoral divisions to the laws of the separate states only until the Commonwealth otherwise provided,[134] while section 26 provided a means of calculating how many representatives each state was entitled to while mandating the number of members to be elected in each state.[135] A *Commonwealth Electoral Act* was passed by the new Parliament within two years of federation.[136] While Barwick surmised that, since universal adult suffrage was unknown in the majority of the colonies, it was not intended by the Constitution, he makes an appeal to the original intention of the Founders:

> It is certain to my mind that the politically experienced members of the constitutional conventions, from which the terms of the Constitution emerged, would not have left the prescription of adult suffrage to be found in the expression "directly elected by the people" or that they would have recognised that expression as so providing.[137]

He concludes: "What I have so far written on the expression 'directly elected by the people' in s 7 is equally applicable to the same expression in s 24, though in that section it relates to the people of the Commonwealth."[138]

McKinlay had submitted that, as the US Constitution had been a pattern for the Australian Founders, the court should look to the decisions of the US Supreme Court in relation to "the expression 'directly chosen by the people' in Art. 1 of the Constitution of that country."[139] While four Supreme Court cases are cited, Barwick concludes that only *Wesberry v Sanders*[140] is current. He distinguishes it "upon the view taken by the majority of American history and of statements made in the constitutional conventions preceding the adoption of that Constitution."[141] He distinguishes the US Constitution from the Commonwealth's implicitly on the basis of Isaacs's distinction in the *Engineers' case* of responsible government—what Barwick calls the sovereignty of "Parliament in the scheme of government."[142] If the US Constitution consists of checks and balances that deny complete confidence in any single arm of government,[143] he again echoes Isaacs when, regarding the Commonwealth Constitution, he states that "where confidence in the parliament prevails, express words are regarded as necessary to warrant a limitation of otherwise plenary powers."[144] He rejects US Supreme Court decisions because "the two Constitutions have radical differences,"[145] giving as his reasons the concepts of the sovereignty of Parliament and ministerial responsibility;[146] a Presidential system;[147] the Commonwealth Constitution as an Act of the Imperial Parliament;[148] and the American Bill of Rights.[149] While Isaacs's unity of the Crown[150] is missing from this list, and the American Bill of Rights has been added, Barwick's reasons are merely a variation on Isaacs's. Having listed what he claimed were the distinguishing features of the American Constitution, all of which would fall within Dixon's description of Isaacs's ubiquitous Crown as irrelevant, Barwick concludes that "these provisions render quite impossible the construction of those words in the sense adopted in *Wesberry v Sanders*."[151] The Supreme Court in that case had held that the requirement of Article 1, section 2 that representatives be chosen by the people of the several states "means that as nearly as is practicable, one man's vote in a congressional election is worth as much as another's."[152]

Barwick's conclusion that "there is no constitutional guarantee of a universal franchise of equal voting strength or value, nor of practical equality in electoral divisions either in numbers of people or of electors"[153] is consistent with his legal positivist assumption that "the Australian Constitution is built upon confidence in a system of parliamentary Government,"[154] an assumption that obviates the need for any written Constitution. Despite Barwick's notion of the Constitution's value neutrality regarding democratic elections, he opines that the *Electoral Act* achieves equality of voting value because section 19:

> in not insisting on practical equality in numbers in divisions, accepting a tolerance of inequality of numbers expressed in a percentage, and in nominating the various considerations to be regarded when effecting a distribution, in my opinion, represents a practical endeavour to solve the problem and does represent a scheme designed to produce equality of voting value.[155]

Conclusion—Barwick

As shown in this section, the clearest expression of Barwick's literalism was contained in his express endorsement in *Victoria v Commonwealth* (*Payroll Tax case*) of Isaacs's judgment in the *Engineers' case* and his Privy Council authorities. It was clear and express. His citation of Isaacs's extracts from Privy Council authorities related to that court's analysis of Imperial legislation that imposed legislative and executive powers on what were at the time British colonies. The citations purported to impose a duty on a court to interpret Imperial legislation literally and, like Isaacs, Barwick adopted that approach, construing the words of the relevant provisions without regard to the political scheme while demanding that the court only take cognizance of express limitations in the Constitution of Commonwealth powers. He rejected any consideration of the federal scheme intended by the Founders, which necessarily implied the existence of limits on the extent of sovereign powers that were not exclusive.

Barwick's judgment in *McKinlay's case* differed from that in the *Payroll Tax case* in a number of ways. However, he still preserved the underlying legal positivist methodology and its concern with the text of the Constitution without regard to the political scheme of the Constitution. He did not cite any authorities in support of his decision, neither the *Engineers' case* nor the Privy Council. He confirmed his endorsement of Isaacs's literalism and its legal positivist assumptions in more subtle ways: his referral to the Constitution as a piece of Imperial legislation and his literal construction of the text. He construed the Constitution without any reference to its political scheme, rejecting American authorities and, in contradiction of his own actions, rejecting a resort to the Convention debates that might have illuminated the Founders' intended meaning.

The essence of McKinlay's submission was that the words "chosen by the people" in section 24 of the Constitution implied that the choosing of members of the House of Representatives should be made by electoral divisions whose voting strength was equal or practically equal.[156] Section 19 of the *Electoral Act* was therefore unconstitutional. Barwick's construction of the word "people" in "chosen by the people" of section 24 of the Constitution involved not only a literal interpretation of that provision, but a literal interpretation of the same words in section 7 of the Constitution when a consideration of the word's dictionary meaning of "demos" would have alerted him to a democratic connotation that supported McKinlay's submissions. Whereas restrictions on legislative powers were sought and applied in the US Constitution, Barwick argued that the Commonwealth Constitution revealed a confidence in the Parliament. The irony is that, although McKinlay sought to prove that electorates with unequal numbers of electors, which resulted from the provisions of the *Electoral Act*, were undemocratic, Barwick concluded that the *Electoral Act* produced an "equality of voting value."

CONCLUSION

While Dixon and Barwick approached construction of the Constitution with different objectives, the dependence of both jurists on legal positivism and its practical implementation through a focus on a literal construction of the text of the Constitution is evident. Dixon's jurisprudence has the appearance of an honest attempt to understand a Constitution that purports to be federal while compelled by the text to ignore the most obvious source of that theory in the decisions of the early court. His acceptance of aspects of Isaacs's decision in the *Engineers' case*, despite his criticism of it, reveals a blindness to Isaacs's purpose but a faithful adherence to a stare decisis, moderated accordingly. As a result of the limitations associated with literalism and despite acknowledging that the Constitution is federal, he is obliged to give it some form that it was never intended to have. He accepted the decisions of the US Supreme Court, which denied the true federal form of that nation's Constitution without a proper consideration because he had already accepted Isaacs's arguments. As a result, his federal scheme has no relationship to the political scheme intended by the Founders.

Barwick's judgment in *Melbourne Corporation v The Commonwealth* (*Payroll Tax case*) openly acknowledged his indebtedness to Isaacs's decision in *Engineers* and the Privy Council authorities from which Isaacs inferred the necessity of adopting a literal interpretation of the text of the Constitution without regard to the political scheme of the Founders. Having established that dependency, he refused to allow any political scheme to intrude into his construction of the text of the Constitution. He accepted Isaacs's denial of state sovereignty. His literalism was again apparent in his judgment in *McKinlay's case*. His construction of the phrase "chosen by the people" in section 24 of the Constitution was to focus solely on the trees while implying that the woods did not exist. The prejudicial character of his literal construction was palpable when he ignored the dictionary meaning of "people" as the demos or a unity of persons in order to deny the Constitution's democratic character and the legal obligation that the electoral distribution of voting power be practically equal.

As chapter 6 will show, Barwick used the devices found in his two judgments that have been discussed in this chapter when he advised Kerr regarding the Governor-General's powers and his ex post justification of the actions of both the Governor-General and the leader of the opposition, Malcolm Fraser.

NOTES

1. Grant Anderson and Daryl Dawson, "Sir Owen Dixon (1886–1972)," in *Australian Dictionary of Biography Vol. 14* (Melbourne University Press, 1966).
2. G. De Q Walker, "The Seven Pillars of Centralism: *Engineers case* and Federalism" (2002) 76 *Australian Law Journal* 686 (2).
3. *West v Commissioner of Taxation (NSW)* (1937) 56 CLR 657 at 682.
4. *The Lord Mayor, Councillors and Citizens of the City of Melbourne v Commonwealth* (1947) 74 CLR 31.
5. *West v Commissioner of Taxation (NSW)* (1937) 56 CLR 657.
6. Ibid., 679.
7. Ibid., 680.
8. Ibid., 679–80.
9. Ibid., 681.
10. Ibid., 681.
11. Ibid., 682.
12. Ibid., 681.
13. Philip Ayres, "Federalism and Sir Owen Dixon," Eleventh Conference of The Sir Samuel Griffith Society, Melbourne, 9–11 July 1999, 139.
14. Geoffrey de Q Walker, "The Seven Pillars of Centralism: Engineers Case and Federalism" (2002) 76 *Australian Law Journal* 678, 686 (2).
15. Ibid., 682.
16. Ibid., 682.
17. Ibid., 683.
18. Ibid., 683, emphasis added.
19. *The Lord Mayor, Councillors and Citizens of the City of Melbourne v Commonwealth* (State Banking case) (1947) 74 CLR 31 at 79–80.
20. *Attorney-General (Cth) v Colonial Sugar Refining Company Limited* (1913) 17 CLR 644 at 652.
21. *The Lord Mayor, Councillors and Citizens of the City of Melbourne v Commonwealth* (1947) 74 CLR 31 at 77.

22. Ibid., 77.

23. Ibid., 77.

24. This is noticeable in light of the express Commonwealth powers in the Constitution of section 51(xii), "currency, coinage, and legal tender"; and section 51(xiii), "the issue of paper money."

25. *The Lord Mayor, Councillors and Citizens of the City of Melbourne v Commonwealth* (1947) 74 CLR 31 at 77.

26. Commonwealth of Australia Constitution, s. 51(xiii).

27. *The Lord Mayor, Councillors and Citizens of the City of Melbourne v Commonwealth* (1947) 74 CLR 31 at 78.

28. Ibid., 78.

29. Ibid., 78.

30. Ibid., 79.

31. Ibid., 79.

32. Ibid. This rule faintly resembles the doctrine of immunities, except the law no long interferes with state legislative or executive powers, but rather limits the freedom only of the state executive.

33. Ibid., 79.

34. Ibid., 80.

35. *R v Barger* (1908) 6 CLR 4.

36. *The Lord Mayor, Councillors and Citizens of the City of Melbourne v Commonwealth* (1947) 74 CLR 31 at 79, 83.

37. Ibid., 79–80.

38. Ibid., 79.

39. His qualification reflects a similar qualification by White J in *McCray v United States* 195 US 27, 64 (1904).

40. *R v Barger* (1908) 6 CLR 41 at 65.

41. *The Lord Mayor, Councillors and Citizens of the City of Melbourne v Commonwealth* (1947) 74 CLR 31 at 80.

42. *New York v United States* 326 U.S. 572, 577 (1946).

43. *The Lord Mayor, Councillors and Citizens of the City of Melbourne v Commonwealth* (1947) 74 CLR 31 at 80.

44. Ibid., 80.

45. *New York v United States* 326 U.S. 572, 576 (1946).

46. Ibid., 576 (1946).

47. *The Lord Mayor, Councillors and Citizens of the City of Melbourne v Commonwealth* (1947) 74 CLR 31 at 80.

48. Sir Owen Dixon, "Marshall and the Australian Constitution" (1955) 29 *Australian Law Journal* 420.

49. Ibid., 427 (1).

50. Ibid., emphasis added.

51. *Clyde Engineering Co Ltd v Cowburn* (1926) 37 CLR 466 at 489.

52. Sir Owen Dixon, "Concerning Judicial Method," in Judge Woinarski (ed), *Jesting Pilate and Other Papers and Addresses* (Melbourne University Press, 1965) pp. 245, 247.

53. Fiona Wheeler, "Book Review: Owen Dixon" (2003) 31(2) *Federal Law Review* 415, 417.

54. Sir Owen Dixon, "Address Upon Taking the Oath of Office in Sydney as Chief Justice of the High Court of Australia on 21st April 1952" "Concerning Judicial Method," in Judge Woinarski (ed), *Jesting Pilate and Other Papers and Addresses* (Melbourne, 1965) p. 247.

55. William Rich, "Approaches to Constitutional Interpretation in Australia: An American Perspective" (1993) 12(2) *University of Tasmania Law Review* 150.

56. Ibid., 152.

57. Ibid., 173.

58. 9 Geo. IV c. 83

59. Owen Dixon, "The Common Law as an Ultimate Constitutional Foundation," in Judge Woinarski (ed), *Jesting Pilate and Other Papers and Addresses*, (Melbourne, 1965) p. 203.

60. Anthony Mason, "The High Court of Australia: A Personal Impression of Its First 100 Years" (2003) 27(3) *Melbourne University Law Review* 864, 878.

61. The irony of those who argue against the original intention as a moral imperative for constitutional construction is that they are only arguing for their own intention. Dixon's federalism was replaced by Barwick's, which was replaced by Brennan's, and so on.

62. Sir Owen Dixon, "Concerning Judicial Method" (1956) 29 *Australian Law Journal* 468.

63. Ibid., 470.

64. Ibid.

65. Ibid. Dixon's reference to the argument being dialectical is not correct, since argument at court is not a discussion whose purpose is to discover the truth, but a form of forensic rhetoric for the purpose of persuading the court; see Plato, *Gorgias*, 452e–457c. The distinction between the two is often made in reference to judges who continue to advocate once they are appointed to the Bench.

66. It should be noted here that had the early court accepted references to the Constitutional Convention record, the debate about construction method would have been much simpler and much more dialectical, and the outcome more reasonable.

67. Sir Owen Dixon, "Concerning Judicial Method" (1956) 29 *Australian Law Journal* 468, 470.

68. *Victoria v Commonwealth (Payroll Tax case)* (1971) 122 CLR 353.

69. Ibid., 364.

70. *Attorney-General (Cth); Ex rel McKinlay v Commonwealth* (McKinlay's case) (1975) 135 CLR 1.

71. Philip Ayres, "Federalism and Sir Owen Dixon," (1999) Eleventh Conference of The Sir Samuel Griffith Society 140; see also Nicholas Aroney, "The Ghost in the Machine: Exorcising *Engineers*," Fourteenth Conference of the Samuel Griffith Society, Sydney, 14–16 June 2002.

72. *Victoria v Commonwealth* (1971) 122 CLR 353 at 364.

73. Sir Garfield Barwick, *Sir John Did His Duty* (Griffin Press, 1983).

74. *Victoria v Commonwealth* (1971) 122 CLR 353.

75. *Attorney-General (Cth); Ex rel McKinlay v Commonwealth* (1975) 135 CLR 1.

76. Two Commonwealth laws were involved: The *Pay-roll Tax Act 1941–67* (Cth) and the *Pay-roll Tax Assessment Act 1941–69* (Cth).

77. *Victoria v Commonwealth* (1971) 122 CLR 353 at 356.

78. Ibid., 356.

79. *The Lord Mayor, Councillors and Citizens of the City of Melbourne v Commonwealth* (1947) 74 CLR 31 at 50, 55, 65–67, 70, 77 & 83.

80. *Federated Amalgamated Government Railway & Tramway Service Association v New South Wales Railway Traffic Employees Association* (1906) 4 CLR 488.

81. *Victoria v Commonwealth* (1971) 122 CLR 353 at 363.

82. Ibid., 364. His preference for the principles enunciated in the *Engineers' case* over other cases is evidenced by the fact that of the sixty-two case citations in his judgment, Barwick cites twenty-two from the *Engineers' case*.

83. Ibid., 366.

84. Sir Owen Dixon, "Marshall and the Australian Constitution" (1955) 29 *Australian Law Journal*, 420, 423.

85. *Victoria v Commonwealth* (1971) 122 CLR 353 at 364.

86. Ibid., emphasis added. Again it should be noted that Loreburn's exhortation only applies to the Canadian Constitution, which established two mutually exclusive jurisdictions.

87. *Victoria v Commonwealth* (1971) 122 CLR 353 at 366.

88. Sir Owen Dixon, "Marshall and the Australian Constitution" (1955) 29 *Australian Law Journal* 423.

89. *Victoria v Commonwealth* (1971) 122 CLR 353 at 367, emphasis added. The implications from this reference were dealt with in chapter 4.

90. Ibid., 367.

91. Ibid., 368. Perhaps Barwick's concern was that Dixon's *other considerations* could include necessary implications from the federal scheme.

92. Ibid., 368.

93. Ibid., 364.

94. Ibid., 368; emphasis added.

95. *West v Commissioner of Taxation (NSW)* (1937) 56 CLR 657 at 681.

96. Ibid., 682.

97. *Victoria v Commonwealth* (1971) 122 CLR 353 at 368.

98. Ibid., 369.

99. Ibid., 370.

100. Joseph Story, *Commentaries on the Constitution of the United States Vol. 1* (Hilliard Gray & Co., 1833) p. 446. Story denies that the American Constitution is a compact, describing it as "an ordinance or establishment of government and not a compact, though originating in consent and it binds as a fundamental law promulgated by the sovereign authority." Griffith's reference to the Australian Constitution as a compact reflects the limitation of his common law principle.

101. Alexander Hamilton, *Federalist No. 22, The Federalist Papers*, ed. Clinton Rossiter (New American Library, 1961) p. 152.

102. *Baxter v Commissioners of Taxation (NSW)* (1907) 4 CLR 1087 at 1104.

103. Joseph Story, *Commentaries on the Constitution of the United States Vol. 1* (Hilliard Gray & Co., 1833) p. 446.

104. *Victoria v Commonwealth* (1971) 122 CLR 353 at 371.

105. *Worthing v Rowell & Muston Pty Ltd* (1970) 123 CLR 89 at 100.

106. *Victoria v Commonwealth* (1971) 122 CLR 353 at 371.

107. Ibid., 371. The American colonies found their own source of power to alter their colonial status in the sovereign will of the people.

108. Ibid., 371.

109. *Attorney-General (Cth); Ex rel. McKinlay v Commonwealth* (1975) 135 CLR 1.

110. Ibid., 18.

111. *King v Jones* (1972) 128 CLR 221.

112. *Attorney-General (Cth); Ex rel McKinlay v Commonwealth* (1975) 135 CLR 1 at 22; *Baker v* Carr 369 U.S. 186 (1962); *Wesberry v Sanders*, 376 U.S. 1 (1964); *Kirkpatrick v Preisler*, 394 U.S. 526 (1969); *White v Weiser*, 412 U.S. 783 (1973).

113. *Attorney-General (Cth); Ex rel McKinlay v Commonwealth* (1975) 135 CLR 1 at 4.

114. Ibid., 16. The details of section 19 of the Act are not repeated in Barwick's judgment.

115. Commonwealth of Australia Constitution, s. 24. The following paragraph of section 24 commences "the number of members chosen in the several States shall be in proportion to the respective numbers of their people" and provides a means of calculating a quota of people for determining the number of representatives in each state so that the number of Commonwealth representatives shall be twice the number of senators. The steps prescribed (for which Parliament may otherwise provide) are not relevant to this investigation of Barwick's construction methodology.

116. *Attorney-General (Cth); Ex rel. McKinlay v Commonwealth* (1975) 135 CLR 1 at 16–17, emphasis added. The implication of this submission was that the Constitution implicitly provided democratic criteria for the election of representatives.

117. *Attorney-General (Cth); Ex rel. McKinlay v Commonwealth* (1975) 135 CLR 1 at 17.

118. *Attorney-General (Cth); Ex rel. McKinlay v Commonwealth* (1975) 135 CLR 1 at 17.

119. *Re Webster* (1975) 132 CLR 270.

120. *Re Webster* (1975) 132 CLR 270 at 279.

121. *Attorney-General (Cth); Ex rel. McKinlay v Commonwealth* (1975) 135 CLR 1 at 17.

122. Ibid., 17.

123. Ibid., 17, emphasis added. A similar declaration was made by Isaacs in *Amalgamated Society of Engineers v Adelaide Steamship Co Ltd* (1920) 28 CLR 129 at 141–2.

124. "The attempt to deduce any consistent rule from them has not only failed": *Amalgamated Society of Engineers v Adelaide Steamship Co Ltd* (1920) 28 CLR 129 at 142.

125. *Attorney-General (Cth); Ex rel McKinlay v Commonwealth* (1975) 135 CLR 1 at 17.

126. Ibid., 18.

127. Commonwealth of Australia Constitution, s. 24, emphasis added.

128. *Attorney-General (Cth); Ex rel McKinlay v Commonwealth* (1975) 135 CLR 1 at 18.

129. Ibid.

130. Ibid.

131. Ibid.

132. This is the political meaning given to the word "people" by the *Shorter Oxford English Dictionary*, 3rd ed. (Oxford University Press, 1964) p. 1468 (1).

133. *Attorney-General (Cth); Ex rel McKinlay v Commonwealth* (1975) 135 CLR 1 at 19.

134. Commonwealth of Australia Constitution, ss. 10 and 29.

135. Commonwealth of Australia Constitution, s. 26.

136. *Electoral Divisions Act 1903* (No. 9 of 1903). In *Attorney-General (Cth); Ex rel McKinlay v Commonwealth* (1975) 135 CLR 1 at 19, Barwick refers indirectly to the circumstances of the first election.

137. *Attorney-General (Cth); Ex rel McKinlay v Commonwealth* (1975) 135 CLR 1 at 19.

138. Ibid., 19.

139. Ibid., 22.

140. *Wesberry v Sanders* (1964) 376 US 1. The majority relied in this case on the opinions of James Madison. The contribution of Edmund Barton to the Commonwealth Constitution was of a similar size.

141. *Attorney-General (Cth); Ex rel McKinlay v Commonwealth* (1975) 135 CLR 1 at 23.

142. Ibid., 24.

143. Ibid., 23.

144. Ibid., 24. This is merely to repeat, without crediting, Isaacs's argument (*Engineers' case* at p. 144) that Commonwealth powers are subject only to "express limitation."

145. Ibid., 23.

146. Ibid., 23.

147. Ibid.

148. Ibid., 24.

149. Ibid., 23–4.

150. *Amalgamated Society of Engineers v Adelaide Steamship Co Ltd* (1920) 28 CLR 129 at 152.

151. *Attorney-General (Cth); Ex rel McKinlay v Commonwealth* (1975) 135 CLR 1 at 24–5.

152. *Wesberry v Sanders* 376 US 1, 7–8.

153. *Attorney-General (Cth); Ex rel McKinlay v Commonwealth* (1975) 135 CLR 1 at 25.

154. *Attorney-General (Cth); Ex rel McKinlay v Commonwealth* (1975) 135 CLR 1 at 24.

155. *Attorney-General (Cth); Ex rel McKinlay v Commonwealth* (1975) 135 CLR 1 at 25.

156. See also Official Record of the Debates of the Australasian Federal Convention, Adelaide (1897), 703 (Edmund Barton).

Chapter 6

Governor-General's Reserve Powers

INTRODUCTION

This chapter argues that the reasons advanced by both Sir John Kerr, the Australian Governor-General, and Sir Garfield Barwick, former Chief Justice of the High Court, do not establish that the Governor-General possessed discretionary powers—either prerogative or statutory—with which to dismiss the Whitlam government on November 11, 1975, in order to commission the Fraser-led opposition as government. It maintains that both men construed the relevant provisions of the Constitution literally without regard to the political conventions that operated in relation to responsible government in Australia, and that they articulated an understanding of the conventions of responsible government without regard to their actual substance as they were practiced in Australia. Their errors stemmed mainly from their literal constructions of the text of the Constitution, which distorted both the objects of the powers and the functions of the respective parties. On each occasion, their arguments implied the existence of a political scheme of the Constitution that was different from the scheme originally intended by the Founders. The literalist jurisprudence prevented the Governor-General's actions from being adequately considered, disguising what was a vice-regal usurpation of powers that the Founders intended to be exercised by the House of Representatives.

It is necessary to examine Kerr's argument first. Barwick does not descend to a forensic analysis of the totality of Kerr's argument, but rejects its legal basis of a prerogative power and substitutes a statutory power in its place. Barwick's analysis is shorter and consists of a literal construction of the text of the Constitution bolstered by unwarranted assumptions and an idiosyncratic explanation of the conventions of responsible government.

Kerr's argument is contained in his autobiography, *Matters for Judgment*,[1] which documents his life to 1978, including the events of 1975. Barwick's argument in defense of the Governor-General's actions is contained in a book described as "little more than pamphlet form,"[2] *Sir John Did His Duty*.[3] The difference between the two accounts was Barwick's belief that the Governor-General's power of dismissal was statutory and hence constitutional. Kerr, on the other hand, considered that his was a reserve power, a vice-regal prerogative, an area of law he describes as "recondite"[4] and unfamiliar to both the public and too many lawyers, including academic lawyers[5]—and, it seems, Barwick.

As chapter 2 explained, the executive power of the Commonwealth was subject to the conventions of responsible government as understood at the time of federation. Those conventions usually are attributed to the Westminster Parliament, but responsible government was also practiced in the Australian colonies. Dicey describes the conventions that were part of the British Constitution as a body of political ethics: "the 'conventions of the constitution,' which, consisting (as they do) of customs, practices, maxims, or precepts which are not enforced or recognised by the Courts, make up a body not of laws, but of constitutional or political ethics."[6]

Conventions can change over time, even quite rapidly, and with them the nature of the political scheme they support also alters. This helps to explain the change in conventions that attended the nineteenth-century democratic electoral reforms of the House of Commons. While the principles sustaining the conventions of responsible government as the Founders intended them to be understood are explained in chapter 2, the parliamentary practice of the Commonwealth Senate after federation became subject to its own convention in regard to supply, a convention that reflected responsible government as the Founders had intended. It is this practical context that must be understood if the variances proposed by Kerr and Barwick are to be properly assessed.

RESPONSIBLE GOVERNMENT IN THE COMMONWEALTH OF AUSTRALIA

The principle of responsible government as understood by the Founders was stated by Barton as follows: "I take it under the system of responsible government there is one power, and one only, that places it in the control of the representatives to demand the expulsion of the Government."[7] In 1981, the Clerk of the Commonwealth House of Representatives prepared the first edition of *House of Representatives Practice*[8] (the "Manual") to explain his knowledge of the actual practices of the Members of Parliament that together comprise the conventions of responsible government in the Commonwealth of Australia. The Manual explains that the authority of the prime minister to form a government arises from the support he or she has from a majority of the Members of the House of Representatives. The following is a brief summary of those essential matters:

- The party (or parties) having the support of the majority of Members becomes the government party.
- The party, or the largest party . . . opposed to the party supporting the government forms the "official" opposition.
- The party having the support of the majority of Members elects one of its members as leader. He is commissioned by the Governor-General as Prime Minister to form a Government on the basis that of all Members he is best suited to maintaining stability in government.[9]

The Manual explains that the members appointed by the prime minister to be ministers of state form the cabinet: "The full Ministry, or a selected group from within the Ministry, becomes the principal policy and decision-making group of government which is commonly known as the Cabinet."[10]

The Manual reaffirms the principle that governments are responsible only to the House of Representatives: "The Government can only maintain office while it retains the confidence of the House of Representatives."[11]

While the concentration of Members of Parliament into political parties after 1910 provided for stability of government,[12] the process for forming government remained largely unchanged from the date of the first Parliament. It is common knowledge that the prime minister is the leader of the party or parties in the House of Representatives, which comprise a majority of that chamber's members. The leader with that support traditionally is called upon by the Governor-General to form a government, which by convention requires the prime minister to choose his or her cabinet colleagues and then to tender those names to the Governor-General, who appoints them as officers pursuant to section 64 of the Constitution to administer the Departments of State as Ministers of the Crown. The Constitution is actually silent about both the prime minister and the cabinet, yet their existence is intrinsic to the conventions of responsible government. Barwick describes this process in similar terms, referring to it as "conformity with Australian practice."[13]

Chapter 2 confirmed that the procedures outlined in the Manual were well known to the delegates at the 1897 Constitutional Convention. Barton, in fact, had expressed the same opinion at the Convention when he explained that the executive in responsible government can only be responsible to one House, the people's chamber, for it is the people in their national character who pay the taxes and who should therefore have control of its expenditure.[14] This principle was underlined by the decision of the Convention's drafting committee to remove an express statement of the Senate's power to *affirm or reject*[15] supply bills during the second session of the Convention, leaving behind a muted power as an inference from the procedural clause in section 53: "Except as provided in this section, the Senate shall have equal power with the House of Representatives in respect of all proposed laws." Further, it should be recalled that senators were never intended by the Convention to represent the interests of particular political parties; instead, they were expected to represent and protect the interests of their own states. The Founders intended the Commonwealth's executive power to be exercised in accordance with the conventions of responsible government as they understood them. They could not have anticipated that responsible government could be transformed to a scheme more monarchical by a literal interpretation of the Executive Government chapter of the Commonwealth Constitution.

The facts leading up to the dismissal of the Whitlam government on November 11, 1975, are common to the accounts of both Kerr and Barwick, and were stated in chapter 1.

KERR'S DEFENSE

Kerr resigned as Governor-General in December 1977. His autobiography, *Matters for Judgment*,[16] first published in 1978, was reprinted in 1988,[17] five years after the publication of Barwick's book, *Sir John Did His Duty*. In the Preface, Kerr says of his reserve powers: "These have been generally referred to as the reserve powers of the Crown, although in Australia they derive from the Australian Constitution."[18] The issues this raises are whether he can provide a cogent explanation for the existence of reserve powers as powers of the Crown that is consistent with responsible government and a cogent construction of their existence in the Constitution. The later edition includes extracts from the reports of the 1985 Constitutional Commission and its Advisory Committee on Executive Government, which he suggests should be kept in mind when considering "the 1975 deadlock."[19] According to Kerr, the Commission concluded that the Senate, by refusing to pass the budget or supply, can in effect pass a "no-confidence motion in the government and force it into an election."[20] As demonstrated in chapter 2, the Founders made it clear that a Commonwealth government was responsible only to the people's chamber, the House of Representatives.

His analysis in support of his theory of the reserve powers as prerogative powers of the Crown relies principally on theories of two legal scholars, that of the Canadian parliamentarian, jurist, and academic Eugene Forsey, and that of the Australian parliamentarian, cabinet minister, and Justice of the High Court Herbert Vere Evatt. He devotes one chapter of *Matters for*

Judgment to Forsey's theory,[21] but two chapters to Evatt.[22] Kerr relates his personal contact with Forsey during the crisis and while writing his autobiography.[23] Evatt first published his study of the reserve powers, *The King and His Dominion Governors*,[24] in 1936. Evatt's work was well known to Forsey, who makes numerous references to it in his own work, *The Royal Power of Dissolution of Parliament in the British Commonwealth*.[25] Kerr recounts a personal association with Evatt that preceded Kerr's legal education and more than a passing familiarity with *The King and His Dominion Governors* that led him to say of Evatt that he occupied

> a key position as an authority on the reserve powers of the Crown; and his scholarly views not only were of great importance to me as the views of a distinguished lawyer and judge but were real and alive to me.[26]

Forsey's disagreements with Evatt relate only to the latter's evaluation of facts that led to the particular exercise of a "reserve power" by the Crown or its representative;[27] there was, however, no disagreement between them regarding the existence of the reserve powers or whether the powers were a Crown prerogative.

As Kerr's theory relies on the existence of the reserve powers that are a Crown prerogative, it is necessary to examine both Forsey's and Evatt's arguments regarding their existence, since both authors rely on examples that do not relate to a federal Constitution. Kerr's task, on the other hand, is to reveal his prerogative powers in the context of the written Commonwealth Constitution, a task at which he fails since he merely asserts a personal discretion to exercise constitutional powers without antecedent ministerial advice. Both Forsey and Evatt presume to examine the regal and vice-regal exercise of powers in isolation from a consideration of the political scheme in which the powers occur. This reflects their legal positivist methodology.

Reserve Power of Forced Dissolutions—Kerr and Forsey

In a chapter entitled "Consent of the Governed," Kerr states that the people were an important element in the constitutional apparatus, "not as legal sovereign or original constituent authority as in the United States but by virtue of the fact that upon their consent—the consent of the governed—depended . . . changes in the Constitution."[28] Chapter 2 showed, however, that the Constitution *was* a constituent act of the peoples of the colonies, whose power of amending the Constitution was a sign of their legal sovereignty.

Kerr explains that his reserve powers are "reserve powers of the Crown, exercisable by the Governor-General, to dismiss a government and force a dissolution of the Parliament."[29] He then qualifies this by explaining that the reserve powers "can nowadays be used, in exceptional and critical circumstances, only to obtain the decision of the people as to a solution of that crisis."[30] In normal times, "the principles of responsible government require the Governor-General normally to act upon the advice of the Ministry and in practical terms in the vast majority of cases he will undoubtedly do so."[31] Kerr's reference to "nowadays," however, implies that the reserve powers existed in period prior to the Constitution, and he seems to have missed the significance of this point. Kerr appeals to Forsey, who he says "deals at several points with the subject of what he calls 'forced dissolutions.'"[32] Forced dissolution is the dismissal of a ministry that has the support of the popularly elected chamber and accurately describes Kerr's dismissal of the Whitlam government. While Kerr cites Forsey, concluding that a forced dismissal by the Crown or its representatives "is now scarcely conceivable,"[33] he is encouraged by Forsey's argument that the reserve powers of the Crown to force or refuse dissolution are a safeguard against

> dictatorship by "the leader of the junta wielding for the moment the power of office." If, for example, a Cabinet with a majority in both Houses tried to use that majority to prolong the life of a Parliament indefinitely, a forced dissolution could be the only constitutional means of preserving the rights of the people.[34]

Forsey's hypothetical example, however, is irrelevant in Australia since the Constitution limits the term of the House of Representatives to three years, a fact acknowledged by Kerr.[35] Forsey's example is antidemocratic and based on the unlikely assumption that a majority of the elected members of a Parliament are more likely to act in a despotic way than the single unelected occupant of a ceremonial office. In fact, an Australian Governor-General must be considered a greater threat to democratic institutions when the Constitution is read literally, since he is vested by the Constitution as the commander in Chief of the armed services[36] and is therefore in a better position to use that power to become the leader of the junta.

Forsey's rejection of the Governor-General as a rubber stamp of ministerial advice reassures Kerr that the office of Governor-General retains a discretion, "to grant or refuse a dissolution"[37] and that she is not obliged to accept the advice of her ministers. Kerr repeats Forsey's argument that the Crown is the embodiment of the interests of the whole people, the indispensable center of the whole parliamentary democratic order:

> the guardian of the Constitution, ultimately the sole protector of the people if MPs or MLAs or ministers forget their duty and try to become masters, not servants. The Crown's reserve power to refuse the advice of ministers when the advice imperils the Constitution still remains.[38]

Kerr does not provide an example of which part of the Constitution is imperiled, but given the situation with which he believed he was dealing, it can safely be assumed that he is implicitly referring to the Westminster convention. Forsey's argument, however, assumes a hypothetical chaos where the government and the members of Parliament form an elected tyranny that threatens the political order of society. From this, Forsey—and therefore Kerr—claims the right of an unelected official to usurp power, take control, and restore order in the out of the ordinary times. It is impossible to read Forsey's theory and not find Carl Schmitt's critique of liberal democracy hiding behind it. Schmitt's disagreement with the liberal politics of the Weimar Republic in the interwar years was related to what he called its "entertainment and the abandonment of seriousness in the political."[39] While Schmitt would later be a prominent intellectual jurist in the National Socialist movement,[40] as early as 1922 he had published *Political Theology*,[41] defining the sovereign as "he who decides on the exception."[42] Sovereignty for Schmitt is about who decides in a conflict "what constitutes the public interest or interest of the state, public safety and order. . . . The exception, which is not codified in the existing legal order, can at best be characterized as a case of extreme peril, a danger to the existence of the state."[43]

Schmitt also distinguished between the legal in ordinary and in abnormal or "out of the ordinary" circumstances. He recounts that absolute monarchs distinguish between laws (measures and orders) and acts that are only legal by the monarch's fiat:

> This distinction is badly needed in the exceptional case, when an abnormal situation needs to be resolved through measures. . . . From the standpoint of legal theory, it is not enough here to repeat the formula—no doubt correct—that extraordinary situations require extraordinary means.[44]

Applying Schmitt's theory to the Australian Commonwealth would place the Governor-General's actions above the law and the Constitution, since his own fiat would be legally binding, even in the absence of an express power. Forsey's theory of the sovereign monarch using their reserve power as "the guardian of the Constitution . . . the sole protector of the people" imitates Schmitt's sovereign who, as guardian of the Constitution, seizes absolute power at a critical moment and defends the people by wresting power from the elected representatives—according to Schmitt, Forsey, and Kerr, all perfectly supra legal. Melo Cartaxo identifies Schmitt as the first to equate the head of state in parliamentary systems with "the guardian of the Constitution": "After the Germanic experience of the Constitution of the Weimar Republic (1919–1933), the head of state in parliamentary systems started to be regarded as a 'guardian of the constitution'—an expression introduced by Carl Schmitt."[45]

Forsey incorporated that concept of the guardian of the Constitution into his political theory:

> The Crown is the embodiment of the interests of the whole people, the indispensable centre of the whole parliamentary democratic order, the guardian of the Constitution, ultimately the sole protector of the people if MPs or MLAs forget their duty and try to become masters, not servants.[46]

To the response that the High Court is the guardian of the Constitution, Kerr responds that the courts guard the *law* of the Constitution, which is not what Forsey is talking about:

> He is referring to an area of decision making for the guardianship and protection of the whole Constitution, not just . . . constitutional law. He is talking about the "whole parliamentary democratic order" part of which rests . . . upon convention and customary usage.[47]

It has been remarked that "Schmitt's theory of the political was the obverse of his critique of liberalism,"[48] that is, of liberal democracy. Schmitt was not a democrat in the popular sense.[49] The same is true of Forsey and Kerr. Kerr paints the Governor-General as a supra-legal and supra-political figure, monarchical in essence, able under the pretext of protecting democracy to wrest control from a democratically elected government on the strength of nothing more than his opinion that these are exceptional times. Forsey does not acknowledge Schmitt's intellectual influence upon his ideas. Schmitt's call for political action by the individual and its higher moral justification than the law are analogous to Forsey's political theory and his appeal to the same higher moral cause as Schmitt's "guardian of the Constitution." These similarities permit the reasonable conclusion that Schmitt's theory was the origin of Forsey's. To the notion that the High Court was the guardian of the Constitution, Kerr responds that the courts only guard the law of the Constitution:[50]

> [Forsey] is referring to an area of decision making for the guardianship and protection of the *whole* Constitution not just that part of it which consists of constitutional law. He is talking about "the whole parliamentary democratic order," part of which rests not upon law at all but upon convention and customary usage. It is an area of decision making in which the reserve powers may be engaged and in which decisions will generally be non-justiciable. It is an area in which the Constitution, in the sense in which Forsey is using the word, can be, in proper cases, guarded by the Governor-General.[51]

Forsey's theory that a king or other vice-regal occupant of an unelected office is more trustworthy when there is a political crisis than the elected representatives, who must confirm their continued public support at each election, justified Kerr's view of his own supra-legal powers as the head of state of the Commonwealth of Australia. There is, according to Kerr's theory, no express legal limit to the Governor-General's power of intervention. The rule of power trumps the rule of law. As the power of guardianship is an unwritten, supra-constitutional power, it can be applied to any organ of government, including the real guardian of the Constitution, the High Court.

It is ironic that the weakness of Forsey's and Kerr's reserve powers theory is exemplified by one Canadian example to which neither of them refers. Evatt, however, explains it at length.[52] The facts briefly stated concerned the 1878 dismissal of the De Boucherville Ministry by the provincial Quebec lieutenant-governor Letellier, who was upset that his recommendations on public affairs "had not received proper consideration from Ministers [who] both in regard to administration and legislation, acted not only against the Lieutenant-Governor's will but often without his knowledge."[53] Letellier appointed the leader of the opposition to form a ministry and when he couldn't secure supply, granted him a dissolution from which process he eventually achieved a majority. The lieutenant-governor had exercised what the British Colonial Office[54] considered to be a valid power, and Evatt seemed to agree.[55] Letellier had exercised it to achieve his own personal wish, which if Forsey's theory and the Colonial Office is accepted was perfectly legal. Forsey's and Kerr's theory therefore implies that government is responsible to the monarch or its representative, not to the House of Representatives. Letellier was dismissed from office by the Dominion government in accordance with the Canadian Constitution. Prime Minister Sir John MacDonald remarked at the time in relation to Letellier's action in dismissing the ministry:

> In England the power of dismissal of a government having the confidence of parliament is gone for ever, and that, if it is gone there, it ought never to have been attempted to be introduced in a colony under the British Crown.[56]

Why this example is important is almost self-explanatory. There was no crisis or constitutional threat. There was only a vice-regal appointee who believed that the representative provincial government should implement his wishes and dismissed the democratically elected representative government to achieve his own end. The existence of such a power in an unelected official denies the need for elected representatives, as Letellier proved by appointing someone who agreed with him, who would "take responsibility" for his action. It depends, therefore, on the validity of the argument for justification by ex post ratification, which was an element of British parliamentary practice in the eighteenth century before the democratization of the House of Commons in the nineteenth century. Thomas Erskine May says of the principle: "Power proceeding from the king, and exercised by himself in person, is irreconcilable with popular government."[57]

Forsey's explanation of the existence of reserve powers as prerogative powers personal to the Crown that still existed in the twentieth century is an assertion rather than a proof. He cites examples of the actions of vice-regal appointments that are successful, but must assume that the governor or Governor-General concerned is legally entitled to exercise those powers despite the convention that obliges the office holder to act on ministerial advice. It is an assertion made possible by ignoring the democratic change of the political scheme whereby governments during the nineteenth century became responsible to the popularly elected chamber.

This defect is also evident in Evatt's forensic examination of the circumstances surrounding the exercise of reserve powers in his work *The King and his Dominion Governors*, which is also conducted in isolation from the identifiable political scheme in which the act occurred. Both Forsey's and Evatt's analyses reflect their legal positivism. Evatt's analysis, however, is more useful for its one reflection on the reserve powers that demonstrates how his legal positivism imposed an implicit limit on his analysis—a limit that prevents him seeing a superior legal interpretation.

Reserve Powers—Kerr and Evatt

Responsible government in parliamentary systems is conducted by means of conventions or unwritten rules, but responsible government is the only manner by which the executive is held responsible. It does not tell us whether the political scheme is democratic, monarchical, or even a mixture of these. Knowing the political scheme requires a consideration of the person or persons to whom responsibility is owed. When a government can be held accountable by a democratically elected chamber of representatives, it can be said to be democratic.[58]

Evatt takes for granted that the reserve powers are prerogative when he describes them as such: "And even those who have devoted considerable time, labour, and skill to the effort of explaining the mysteries of these reserve prerogatives become dogmatic upon the questions."[59] He goes so far as to caution that "it may be that certain powers and prerogatives have not been committed to the Dominions at all, because reserved for Imperial control."[60] In *The King and His Dominion Governors*, Evatt examines a variety of examples throughout the British Empire in which the monarch or its representative has acted without or contrary to the advice of ministers, but without providing the context of the particular political scheme in which those examples occurred. His analysis is limited to establishing if the facts related to each regal or vice-regal action are sufficient *in his judgment* to justify the particular action. While his conclusions are merely his opinions, they would have been on firmer ground if, for example, he had identified how the democratization of the House of Commons during the nineteenth century transferred political power from the monarch to the Members of that House of Commons. The effect of that change of political authority would have obliged him to at least consider whether a monarch's action, acceptable in a monarchy, would be unacceptable—even unconstitutional—where a government was responsible to a democratically elected chamber. It would also explain the change in the conventions of responsible government during the reign of Queen Victoria, who acted only on antecedent ministerial advice. Such an analysis would also have provided the benchmark for judging the acts of dominion and colonial governors in such political schemes.

With that knowledge, Evatt would have seen the action of King Edward VII, who refused the advice of his prime minister Asquith in 1909 and sent him to the people, as unconstitutional and a breach of a House of Commons, as democratic convention. Evatt cites from the speeches and notes of the main protagonists to show what each sought to achieve, but without articulating the different political schemes of the Houses of Commons and Lords in the twentieth-century Constitution, he was unable to deduce which of those claims was entitled to succeed and which was not. Evatt attributes Asquith's opinion that a constitutional monarch was not an arbiter between the different parties and did not take advice from both sides[61] as an accurate statement of the Whig view of the Constitution, "which in many quarters had become accepted; but such a theory is and will be regarded by many as an attempt to reduce the power of the Monarch to a nullity in those very times of great crisis when his intervention alone might save the country from disaster."[62]

However, Evatt omits from this description an explanation of the political scheme associated with the Whig view, including whether that view was shared by the relevant parties concerned. Had he made reference to the principle inherent in the Whig view that Parsons describes as the "doctrine of the divine right of the people,"[63] he may have been better able to judge the constitutionality of the actions of the House of Lords and King Edward VII.

The King and His Dominion Governors contains only one example of a Commonwealth Governor-General granting a double dissolution to a government: that of Governor-General Ferguson in 1914, who satisfied himself that the conditions for a double dissolution pursuant to section 57 of the Constitution had been met.[64] Ferguson had originally announced that he accepted the advice of his ministers in order to grant a double dissolution of the Parliament. In a later paper,[65] Evatt explains that then Chief Justice Griffith had provided an interpretation of the double dissolution provision, section 57 of the Constitution, for the Governor-General. Evatt recites from Griffith's advice "that the Governor-General cannot act except on the advice of ministers" but that "he is not bound to follow that advice but is in the position of an independent arbiter."[66] He advised that the Governor-General could accede to the request of the prime minister "only in cases in which the Governor-General is *personally satisfied, after independent consideration of the case*"[67] of two factors: first, whether the proposed law is publicly important; or, second, whether there is a practical legislative deadlock. In a theoretical sense, Griffith is correct, but the practicality of Griffith's advice can be seen in the fact that he fails to explain by what power a Governor-General can establish the facts by which to judge whether either of the two criteria has been satisfied other than by ministerial advice. He has no ability to enter into the debate or to conduct a poll, or to consult the Opposition. While Evatt concluded that all governors-general possess a "duty of independent exercise of discretion,"[68] he thought that the Ferguson case established four propositions, the principal and only positive one being his first: "That so long as the conditions mentioned in Section 57 are complied with, the Governor-General will grant a double dissolution to Ministers who possess the confidence of the House of Representatives."[69] In practical terms, the Attorney-General can be expected to provide the necessary legal advice that the conditions of section 57 have been met. Griffith's legal advice regarding section 57, which assumes an inquiry by the Governor-General, is only capable of being satisfied by ministerial advice. If the prime minister or Attorney-General advises that either of the conditions are met, the Governor-General has a minister who is responsible to the House of Representatives, and ultimately the people, for the decision. That is responsible government.

That practical solution proposed was inadvertently confirmed by Kerr's commentary on the example of Governor-General McKell, who acceded to a request by Prime Minister Menzies for a double dissolution in 1951.[70] McKell's actions are cited by Kerr as an example of "the Governor-General's discretion and his right to outside advice on the exercise of his discretionary powers."[71] Kerr explains that the outside advices to McKell were provided by Prime Minister Menzies.[72] The advices were provided to "the Governor-General by the Attorney-General, Senator Spicer and the Solicitor General, Professor KH Bailey."[73] These advices consisted of a ministerial advice and the advice to a ministerial adviser. Zelman Cowen, in his Introduction to Evatt's second edition, confirms that the duty of the Governor-General is to act on the advice of his ministers when he says: "In fact the Governor-General did not seek independent advice and accepted the advice of the Prime Minister supported by the opinions of the Attorney-General and Solicitor-General."[74] Kerr refers to the fact that Menzies had obtained "the *oral* advice of Mr Garfield Barwick, KC."[75] He also relates that by the time Menzies saw Barwick, the latter had stated his opinion to the Attorney-General and the solicitor-general.[76] Menzies himself said in his Foreword to the documents when they were tabled in the Parliament in 1957:

> On the evening of March 15th, I also saw Mr. Barwick who had, by that time, stated his opinion to the Attorney-General and the Solicitor-General after a complete examination of the records. When Mr Barwick saw me, I showed him the draft letter to the Governor-General. . . . Having perused this, he advised orally that, in his opinion, the submission I was making was completely justified on the facts, and in the terms of the Constitution.[77]

Cowen opined that the facts of the 1951 double dissolution "satisfy the propositions formulated by Evatt from the 1914 case."[78] In particular, the 1951 case satisfies Evatt's first proposition.[79]

While the other examples that Evatt analyses can be distinguished as being unrelated to a written, federal Constitution like that of the Commonwealth,[80] Kerr acknowledged that Evatt was unsure about whether the Governor-General had a discretionary power to dismiss a government that enjoyed the confidence of the House of Representatives: "Evatt . . . points out that 'the power of dismissal of Ministers possessing the confidence of the majority of the popular Assembly is not precisely ascertained';[81] and that 'the power of the Crown or its representative to insist upon a dissolution against the will of Parliament and Ministers alike . . . is also undefined.'"[82]

Evatt was also "not certain to what extent, and under what conditions, the Sovereign or his representative possesses the right to refuse a dissolution of Parliament to Ministers."[83] Evatt had therefore expressed reservations in respect of all the powers said by Kerr to be reserve powers, including whether a Governor-General has a discretion to refuse a dissolution. However, Evatt's theory of the reserve powers contained a more important concern, which casts a long shadow over any literal, legal positivist interpretation of the Commonwealth Constitution. The particular matter raised by Evatt occurs when he explains that there can be no legal repercussion from the king's or his representative's exercise of a reserve power to dismiss ministers or dissolve the Parliament. Evatt explains that

> whatever the "convention" or rule on the point may be, mere legal requirements have nothing to do with the matter. The reason is plain. The common law, in the case of Britain, and the Statute law, in the case of most of the Dominions, vests the relevant legal power in the King or the Governor. If the conventional rule is broken by the decision to dissolve, the legal power is merely applied. No question *of its* breach can arise.[84]

Evatt's explanation demonstrates that, if the Commonwealth Constitution is construed literally, powers that could only be exercised with ministerial advice in the political scheme of responsible government may be exercised legally by the Governor-General with no legal repercussions. What is only nominally available to be exercised by the Governor-General in light of the political scheme becomes a legal defense to any charge of misuse when viewed literally and in isolation of the political scheme. Such was the case when Lieutenant-Governor Letellier, for personal political reasons, dismissed a government that had the confidence of the popular assembly. The power once assumed to exist either as a positive law or prerogative might in reality only vest nominally in the head of state, yet it acquits the occupant of that position of culpability because literalism robs it of the political convention that determines proper or improper use. Whatever the king or Governor-General does is legally correct because all power appears, literally, to be exercisable by that person. Evatt's theory implies that there can be no legal dispute if the Governor-General exercises a power to advance their own policy because the power is theirs to exercise. Legal positivism therefore promotes a fundamental breach of the rule of law by assuming that nominal figureheads in democratic regimes are free to usurp the powers for their own use. The danger of Evatt's doctrine arises from the theoretical separation of the fundamental political structure of the Commonwealth government, the democratic conventions of a responsible ministry, from the text of the Constitution[85] which is indicative of his legal positivist methodology.

Ex-Governor-General, law professor, and university vice chancellor, Sir Zelman Cowen[86] inadvertently revealed a juristic propensity to accept the enlargement of a Governor-General's limited discretion into broadly based discretionary powers that could be exercised without ministerial advice regardless of the evidence:

> By 1901, when the Constitution came into operation, Westminster principles had established that the Governor-General normally acted on ministerial advice and further that this did not necessarily depend on whether a particular function was assigned, in terms, to the Governor-General in Council. At the same time it was clear that there were powers which in law might be exercised by the Governor-General in his own, independent, discretion.[87]

Cowen's statement expresses perfectly the non sequitur on which such legal positivist scholarship has been built in explaining the Governor-General's reserve powers. His first sentence, that the Constitution was framed with the need for ministerial advice in mind, actually repeats the opinion acted on by the Constitutional Convention. It is also consistent with the democratic and representative character of the House of Representatives. The second sentence, which posits a Governor-General's personal discretionary or reserve powers, was not "at the same time" clear. As will also be shown, its existence was expressly dismissed by the Convention as inconsistent with responsible government, which raises a most important jurisprudential question: viz., the binding nature of the Founders' intention for constitutional interpretation, that is, originalism. Cowen's second sentence implies accurately that Australian jurists have furnished the Governor-General with expanded discretionary powers simply by an exercise of their own fiat. Understanding how this happened is important for understanding the arguments that justify the actions of the Governor-General in November 1975.

Cowen defends this view that discretionary powers exist by citing Dr. Herbert Vere Evatt, the Australian jurist, Commonwealth Minister, and High Court Justice.[88] Other than the events of 1975, however, there is no example of a Governor-General exercising discretionary powers to dismiss a government that enjoys the support of a majority of the House of Representatives. Evatt cites many examples of vice-regal discretions in relation to foreign jurisdictions with unitary constitutions[89] or with Constitutions imposed upon their peoples by the Westminster Parliament[90] but never ratified by the people.

Cowen, like other jurists, inferred the existence of reserve powers from examples where the Governor-General obtained independent advice rather than accept ministerial advice to dissolve the House of Representatives. He refers to the same three examples in the first decade of federation to which Evatt refers[91] where the ministerial advice of a minority government to dissolve the House and call an election was rejected and a new government representing the majority was commissioned. As these examples all occurred at a time when political parties were unstable and were regularly unable to maintain the loyalties of members, the validity of ministerial advice required that it meet the first criterion of responsible government, that the minister has the confidence of the House of Representatives.[92] Both Cowen and Evatt infer the existence of much wider discretionary powers from specific examples of governors-general who did not accept ministerial advice without first clarifying such particulars. This suggests that both men confused the form of the advice for the substance of "ministerial." For the conventions of responsible government to function adequately and not merely formerly, a minister must have the authority of the House of Representatives and his advice must also be constitutionally valid. Academic jurists have rested their belief in reserve powers, powers that usurp those of the House's democratic representatives by abstracting from vice-regal questioning of ministerial advice. Despite Cowen's above quoted first sentence, a literal reading of the Commonwealth Constitution's text divorced from the Founders' scheme of responsible government would find certain executive powers that could be "lawfully" exercised by a Governor-General without ministerial advice. Evatt alludes to this issue in his book, *The King and His Dominion Governors*, but his legal positivist analysis causes him to misunderstand the insight that he actually had.

Richard Staveley correctly asked: "Is not responsible government denoted by established conventions which give coherence to certain formal provisions in the Constitution?"[93] In other words, the Constitution is subject to the conventions as they were understood by the Founders and not the other way around. This relationship is consistent with the jurisprudence originally intended by the Founders, as shown in chapter 3.

A vice-regal discretion to refuse a dissolution was the starting point for Kerr (and Forsey),[94] from which—having, he believed, established a discretion to refuse a dissolution—he extrapolated to conclude the existence of reserve powers. Evatt concludes his work by calling for a codification of the reserve powers, even though, as explained above, he was unsure about whether the reserve power to dismiss a government that had the support of the House of Representatives actually existed.[95] Evatt's codification proposal was not the conclusion of a man who set out to codify the common practice in the Commonwealth of Australia, for there was no evidence to support his theory. It is more likely to have been the result of his fear of a head of state absolved from liability for an exercise of nominally vested powers for personal reasons. Such absolution is inconsistent with the rule of law but is consistent with absolute monarchy.

Kerr and the Constitution

The idea of the reserve powers being prerogative has to be significantly qualified by Kerr's narrative in order to link his analysis of Forsey and Evatt to the discovery of reserve powers in the Commonwealth Constitution. Kerr does this in a gradual fashion in his explanation of the actual Dismissal. He begins with section 61 of the Constitution: "The executive power of the Commonwealth is vested in the Queen and is exercisable by the Governor-General as the Queen's representative, and extends to the execution and maintenance of this Constitution, and of the laws of the Commonwealth."[96] He speaks of the reserve powers under the Commonwealth Constitution as discretionary but only incidentally as prerogative, although that is apparently how he thought of them:

> The system of responsible government in Australia embraces and includes the discretionary power of the Crown—of the Governor-General—just as it . . . includes the Cabinet system, the role of the Prime Minister and the notion that a Government must have the confidence of the Lower House.[97]

Under this guise, the reserve powers are unwritten powers (the cabinet is not mentioned in the Constitution), but seemingly prerogative in character.

However, he contradicts this and suggests that they might be constitutional when he speaks of the conventions making responsible government work "because of section 61 and the extension of that section to embrace the prerogative powers of the Crown."[98] After citing section 61 of the Constitution, he adds: "'The laws of the Commonwealth' include the common law and hence the prerogative,"[99] thus implying that the reserve powers are constitutional, for he says of the Founders: "In drafting the Constitution they had seen fit to give all the prerogative powers relevant to handling a supply crisis and its resolution to the Governor-General."[100] Kerr states that attempts to include the reserve powers in the emerging written Constitutions of the old British Empire were attempts "to put into written form the conventions of the Constitution as they operated under the Westminster system,"[101] which implies that the powers previously were powers of the office of Governor-General by convention, though subsequently constitutional. Each of these descriptions of the reserve powers, whether as prerogative, constitutional, or conventional, implies a different legal character. Kerr suggests that the power is related to the "constitutional dicta and principles concerned with 'Constitution preservation,'"[102] which suggests the phrase "maintenance of this Constitution" in section 61 of the Constitution and reflects Forsey's (and Schmitt's) notion of constitutional guardian. He describes the power: "I had an active duty, by the exercise of my powers under the Constitution, to preserve it by preventing the effective smashing of the power of the Senate on supply, and of the reserve powers of the Crown."[103]

This statement suggests that Kerr identified his reserve powers as *conventional* "reserve powers of the Crown," which were vested by section 61 of the Constitution in him personally—he identifies them as "my powers"—to prevent, inter alia, "the smashing of the reserve powers of the Crown." The problem with this argument is that, as shown in chapter 2, the executive powers of the Commonwealth are vested in the Queen for the Australian people, that is, for their representatives, not the Governor-General. Further, it would seem hyperbolic to refer to the reserve powers being smashed, since if they exist by virtue of section 61, they are a constitutional power and will exist until the Constitution is amended to remove them. His construction, however, is contradicted by the Founders as expressed by Barton and discussed in chapter 2; namely, that the Governor-General acts only with ministerial advice. In that light, Kerr's power is only the assertion of a right to exercise constitutional powers without ministerial advice, that is, regal prerogative powers that are personal to the Governor-General and exercisable at his discretion. The impediment to this type of power, however, is the Commonwealth Constitution.

As Kerr's arguments for the Governor-General's powers are tied to a justification of the steps that he took during the Dismissal, it is necessary to examine the reasons he gives in relation to the following actions: the Senate's power to reject or defer supply; the Governor-General's power to withdraw a government's commission that enjoyed the confidence of the House of Representatives; and the Governor-General's power to dissolve the Parliament without ministerial advice.

Senate's Power to Reject or Defer Supply

When Kerr dismissed Whitlam on November 11, 1975, he handed him a letter to which was annexed a document entitled "Statement by the Governor-General." Both the letter and the Statement, which run to about four and a half pages in total, are reproduced in Kerr's book.[104] The Statement is divided into two sections: the Summary of his reasons for terminating Whitlam's commission; and a section entitled Detailed Statement of Decisions. I summarize the salient points of the Summary as follows:[105]

- The Constitution was federal.
- Responsible government requires a prime minister who cannot obtain supply to resign or advise a general election.
- The Governor-General has the authority and duty under the Constitution to withdraw the Commission of a prime minister who refuses to resign or advise a general election.
- In Australia, the confidence of both Houses is necessary.
- The Governor-General has the authority to ask the leader of the opposition, Malcolm Fraser, to form a caretaker government and to give undertakings that he would advise a double dissolution and guarantee supply.

The substance of Kerr's Summary consists of: a Senate determined to refuse or defer supply, and therefore a deadlock between the two chambers needing prompt resolution; a belief in parliamentary control of appropriation and that expenditure is a fundamental feature of our system of responsible government; and "generally accepted" knowledge that a government that has been denied supply by the Parliament cannot govern.[106]

Kerr asserts that the position of the government in Australia is quite different from that in the United Kingdom: "Here the confidence of both Houses on supply is necessary to ensure its provision. In the United Kingdom the confidence of the House of Commons alone is necessary."[107] As a result of these considerations, he informs Whitlam that "there will be an early general election for both Houses and the people can do what, in a democracy, such as ours, is their responsibility and duty and theirs alone."[108] He states that "the principle that a government which has been denied supply by the Parliament should resign or go to an election must still apply."[109]

Kerr's argument presents this conclusion as a mandatory "principle," which "must" apply. However, as with the rest of responsible government, what he has stated as a mandatory principle is, in fact, a convention that he asserts controls the situation—the convention being that a government denied supply by the Senate must abide by the conventions of responsible government, and resign or call an election. Thus, he asserts that obedience to the conventions is mandatory, as is obedience to the Constitution. The difficulty for Kerr's argument is that he states in his Detailed Statement of Decisions that the Constitution controls the conventions,[110] except that there is nothing in the Constitution requiring a government to obey the conventions or take either of the actions Kerr demanded. The convention is there to be broken, or obeyed, as a government wishes; the government might resign, call an election, or sit tight and negotiate with the Senate. It might place the bureaucracy on a skeleton staff and fight it out.[111] It might dismiss the Governor-General, for which it has plenary power. There is no law requiring anything to be done because, as Kerr asserts, the Constitution controls the conventions. That approach is actually the more attractive, given that the Senate had itself breached a convention it willingly entered into of never refusing supply to a government that had the confidence of the House of Representatives. The Senate's action until 1975 in this regard was consistent with the English practice after the passage of the *Parliament Act 1911*, which formalized the Westminster convention in that country after the parliamentary crisis of 1909.[112]

In his Detailed Statement of Decisions,[113] Kerr notes that the public had questioned whether responsible government obligated a Senate never to reject an appropriation bill. His rebuke of the public's suggestion indicates the confusion in his thoughts: "The Constitution must prevail over any convention because, in determining the question how far the conventions of responsible government have been grafted onto the Federal compact the Constitution must in the end control the situation."[114]

To the suggestion that a convention can grow and limit or qualify a constitutional provision, Kerr responds: "but this, in the case of section 53, is very doubtful and in any case it has not happened."[115] Stanley Bach reports, however, that the Commonwealth Senate had passed money bills prior to 1975 on 139 occasions without ever rejecting any—even when the government of the day lacked a majority in the Senate.[116] Kerr's argument is incorrect on two levels. First, the Constitution is silent about what happens when a government is refused supply by the Senate, so it cannot be said to control the conventions. Second, there was a convention that had bound the Senate since 1901 whereby the Senate had never refused to pass a government's supply bills. That convention was broken by the Coalition parties in the Senate. Having themselves breached that convention, there was no constitutional, legal principle that could oblige Whitlam to comply with Kerr's statement of another convention.

Staveley described the above statement by Kerr as "the axiom of judicial positivism."[117] This suggests that conventions are animated by a constitution, not the other way around. It implies that written constitutions are self-sufficient—an idea that is denied by the fact that the meaning of the Constitution had to be construed and that meanings differ with construction. However, if the Constitution prevails over conventions, and neither responsible government nor the reserve powers are mentioned in the Constitution, how can it be asserted that the reserve powers exist or that they permit Kerr to control responsible government? Staveley highlights the conundrum for Kerr when he asks rhetorically:

> Is not responsible government denoted by established conventions which give coherence to certain formal provisions in the Constitution? Where are the "reserve powers" of the Governor-General elaborated in the Constitution? Kerr relied on convention to over-ride convention and yet asserts that convention was controlled by the Constitution.[118]

Kerr repeats that the parliamentary control of appropriation is a fundamental feature of the system (i.e., convention) of responsible government, so when Parliament denies supply to a ministry, it cannot govern. He draws a parallel with Westminster by stating that this is *always* the case when a government has been denied supply by a popularly elected Lower House and the Upper House does not possess the power to reject money bills.[119] Kerr then states that it is mandatory, a matter of principle, that a government should "resign or go to an election" when an Upper House, which possesses the power to reject money bills, denies supply. While this implies that the government is responsible to the Upper House—he adds that "It is a necessary consequence of Parliamentary Control"[120]—his reasons involve no compelling legal point because the Constitution is silent on the issue. While Barton and the vast majority of delegates at the Constitutional Convention held that the government was only responsible to the House of Representatives, as detailed in chapter 2, a number of delegates expressed their concern about the idea that the Senate might reject a government's supply by describing it as: revolutionary[121] and inconceivable.[122] It might be trite to repeat the popular slogan "no taxation without representation," but it explains why supply and taxation laws were under the control of the British House of Commons and why they were placed under the control of the House of Representatives as the chamber in which the people were equally represented.

Kerr attempts to add democratic credibility to the financial powers of the Senate under the Constitution by attributing democratic status to it as a popularly elected chamber like the House of Representatives.[123] However, he is unable to maintain this argument when in the next sentence he admits that the Senate represents the equality of the states—which have unequal numbers of people—electing equal numbers of senators, and that the states do not pay tax.[124] Kerr's attempt to provide a "democratic" justification for the Senate's actions, and hence indirectly his own, confirms the most important argument of this essay: that the Constitution cannot be interpreted properly without a full understanding of the political scheme intended by the Founders. In the context of his confused and confusing explanation of the Senate and democratic representation, Kerr speaks of the Senate's power to reject bills or defer them under section 53 of the Constitution:

> [The Senate has] by Sec. 53 equal powers with the House with respect to proposed laws, except in the respects mentioned in the section. It was denied the power to originate or amend appropriation bills but was left with the power to reject them or defer consideration of them.[125]

Kerr's construction of the section is an example of how he interprets the reference to "equal power" in section 53 by including the power to "reject them or defer consideration" to justify the Senate's actions. As detailed in chapter 2, the power to affirm or reject as a legislative power of the Senate in relation to supply bills was included in the draft clause, but was removed during the second session of the Convention without debate or objection. The power to defer a bill, however, is not a legislative power at all, but rather a rule in respect of the order and conduct of business and proceedings of the Senate. The power to make such rules was granted to the Senate by section 50 of the Constitution. However, Kerr's assertion of the Senate's power ignores the fact that the Senate never actually rejected supply. Its deferral was the Opposition's parliamentary strategy to force an election. It achieved its aim when Kerr declared that he held reserve powers, dismissed the prime minister, and appointed the opposition leader as prime minister. At that time, the Senate passed the Whitlam Government's appropriation bills without amendment. It could never have been the Opposition's strategy to reject supply: first—even with its own control of the government—it did not have the numbers in the House of Representatives to originate its own supply bills; and second, without supply it was thought that there were insufficient funds for the Commonwealth to hold an election.[126] The object of the next section is to examine what Kerr meant by the term "reserve power."

The Reserve Power to Dismiss a Government

Kerr asserts that he possessed a reserve power "to dismiss a Ministry which has been refused supply by the Parliament and to commission a Ministry, as a caretaker ministry which will secure supply and recommend a dissolution, including where appropriate a double dissolution."[127] It is not clear that Kerr completely understood what he meant when he spoke of his reserve powers, because he relates them both to the Commonwealth executive power in section 61 of the Constitution and to an independent Crown prerogative. It was established in chapter 2 that the executive power referred to in section 61 contains prerogative powers but, given the wording of the section, they can only be the prerogative powers of the Commonwealth. The question to be addressed is who is authorized to exercise them. It is important in that context to keep in mind that Kerr has already posited that under certain circumstances they are exercised by the elected representatives—the cabinet ministers—but in other circumstances they can be exercised by the Governor-General. Kerr explains that there is a relationship between the executive power and the system of responsible government that works when the parliamentary conventions are observed. Kerr's system of responsible government includes "the discretionary powers of the Crown—of the Governor-General—just as it embraces and includes the Cabinet system, the role of the Prime Minister and the notion that a Government must have the confidence of the Lower House."[128] He refers to section 61 and declares that the "laws of the Commonwealth include the common law and hence the prerogative."[129] He refers to an advice given by the Solicitor General, Sir Maurice Byers, to Whitlam that the "the Queen's powers have been handed over to the Governor-General by the Constitution,"[130] with which he says he agrees but does not cite the advice. It is not immediately clear whether Kerr is here referring to the executive powers of the Commonwealth being handed to the Governor-General, for he also believes that the powers of the British monarch have been handed to the Governor-General along with the executive powers of the Commonwealth. Kerr's assent to Byers's proposition is therefore ambiguous, since he argues later that he holds a discretionary power that was exercisable by the Queen. Strictly speaking, his nomenclature has confused the matter. Under section 61, the executive powers of the Commonwealth, which are vested in the monarch, are exercisable by the Governor-General but have not been "handed over."[131] The executive powers include the Commonwealth's prerogative powers, not those of the monarch, even assuming the monarch has some. Kerr adopts a literal construction to interpret Sir Maurice Byers's advice to mean that the prerogative includes the power to dismiss ministers under section 64 of the Constitution:

> The executive power of the Commonwealth exercisable by the Governor-General under chapter II of the Constitution (including the power of dismissing Ministers under section 64) and also the powers relating to the dissolution of

Parliament conferred by section 5 and section 57 could not be made the subject of instructions from the Queen.[132]

Section 61 makes clear that the executive power is not exercisable by the monarch, but the power to appoint ministers under section 64 is expressly stated as "The Governor-General may appoint," so it cannot be a prerogative power. Kerr explains that the government and "Ministers are sworn in to serve the Crown."[133] It is that conception of himself as a viceroy with royal authority that guides Kerr's construction of the Constitution and his decisions. The direction of Kerr's argument becomes clear when he attempts to distinguish the Crown from the "Government" but not *government*:

> The *Government* has two separate relationships: one, with the Parliament from which it has to obtain the money it wants; and secondly with the Crown because it is the Crown's Ministers who constitute the Government and to whom the Crown has to look to ensure that moneys are provided to enable *government* to be carried on.[134]

Kerr makes the same distinction again when, after stating in relation to section 61 of the Constitution that the laws of the Commonwealth include the common law and hence the prerogative, he says: "A primary, indeed the primary duty of a Government is to ensure the provision of supply to the Crown."[135] After explaining the procedure by which Parliament controls revenue and spending, he explains that "vast sums are necessary to enable the Crown to carry on the complex executive government of modern times" before concluding: "This duty is a fundamental one without which government could not be carried on."[136] It is noteworthy that he refers to "government" and not *the* government, for he is in the process of distinguishing what he does from what the minister does. Kerr has, in this way, distinguished the Crown from the government—the government being the Parliamentarians who obtain the funds that Kerr, the Crown, requires in order to *govern*. Kerr, it seems, claims to *govern* the Commonwealth as the Crown and he places his stamp, or rather seal, on it. The ministers are not the executive, but administrators: "A Government is not a committee of the House of Representatives. Ministers are sworn in to serve the Crown. . . . They are the Queen's Ministers with duties to administer her government, the departments of State within her executive."[137]

This, of course, would have come as an enormous surprise to many people—particularly any Australian who has voted. Kerr confirmed this elevated opinion of the Governor-General (and himself) when he said that Whitlam believed that "all the powers of a legal and prerogative kind *devolve upon* the Governor-General under the Constitution."[138] The second definition of "devolve" in the *Shorter Oxford English Dictionary* is "to roll or flow down on."[139] Since executive power is vested in the monarch but only exercisable by the Governor-General, the power is not vested in the Governor-General. Of Whitlam, however, Kerr said: "He believed that under our Constitution the Governor-General is a viceroy. It was a mistake if he thought that I was *his* viceroy."[140]

This statement helps us to understand the gulf that existed between Kerr's understanding of the Governor-General's authority and the understanding of those who comprised the government. The people whom Kerr calls the government are the ones who are ultimately responsible to the people for the decisions taken and choices of policy made. That is the meaning of responsible government. If Kerr is the Crown and the Crown governs, then Kerr is not responsible to anyone for what he does. He thus resurrects the ancient rule of the monarch who could do no wrong,[141] a monarch surrounded by advisers who will accept responsibility for his decisions.[142] If his advisers could not obtain the necessary funds—in Whitlam's case, because of the Senate—the Governor-General could dismiss those advisers and obtain new ones who agreed to be responsible for the Governor-General's actions. Kerr's idea of his own position is like that of King George III, who governed with the advice of his hand-picked Privy Councillors while relying on funds provided by the Commons. When or if those funds were not forthcoming because the Commons rejected some action of the king, he changed advisers.[143] By accepting the role as Privy Councillors, the incoming Councillors agreed to accept responsibility for the king's actions.[144] In this way, the king could do no wrong. Such was the scheme of the aristocratic government of the United Kingdom in the eighteenth century.[145] That Kerr actually believed that the Governor-General of Australia in the twentieth century was the ruling monarch or viceroy of Australia says much about his conduct in November 1975. He went so far as to construe the words of section 61 of the Constitution literally to give the Governor-General even greater authority: an executive power exercisable by the Governor-General (without ministerial advice) with which even the Queen could not interfere: "As the Queen could not validly give me instructions as to how I should exercise my powers under section 64, I must not burden her with prior knowledge of my actual intention to act under that section."[146]

His argument in support of the power to dismiss the government is based upon a literal interpretation of section 64 of the Constitution, which states where relevant that:

> The Governor-General may appoint officers to administer such departments of State of the Commonwealth as the Governor-General in Council may establish. Such officers shall hold office during the pleasure of the Governor-General.

> They shall be members of the Federal Executive Council, and shall be the Queen's Ministers of State for the Commonwealth.[147]

He provides no explanation of his power under this section, merely implying that it is discretionary. It can be inferred, however, that the discretion exists because of a literal interpretation of section 64 wherein the power is exercised by the Governor-General, not the "Governor-General in Council." He assumes that it means a discretion to act without any ministerial advice. He relates that his action is based on an agreement he made with Whitlam regarding the previous termination of two ministerial commissions, in which he denied the relevant ministers a legal right to be heard. "In dismissing Mr Whitlam and his Government I was acting at my own discretion, but the law applied in all three cases was the same."[148] He simply does not accept that his actions were authorized by Whitlam's advice, for he says that he well understood "the nature of *my dismissal powers* under s 64, later to be used against him and his Government,"[149] where he acted without any advice.

Kerr supports his claim for a prerogative power to dissolve the Parliament against the wishes of the government that had the support of the House of Representatives with the opinion of Forsey, who based his argument on an example of this power exercised in a Canadian province in 1856.[150] The Australian Crown solicitor general, Maurice Byers, on the other hand, advised that there had been no true forced dissolution by the sovereign—that is, one against the advice of the ministry since 1783—and he doubted whether that power still existed. Kerr, preferring Forsey's opinion, replied ambiguously:

> Whether a verbal distinction is or is not to be made in referring to the one type of dissolution as a "true" forced dissolution is quite irrelevant to the existence, in other cases of the prerogative of dismissal with consequent dissolution.[151]

In the overall context of his analysis of executive powers, Kerr's reference to them as "my powers," exercisable on his own initiative, suggests that the Governor-General was not only equal with the monarch but, under the Constitution, was superior to the monarch since his powers were exercisable by him but not by the monarch. However, this window into Kerr's opinion reveals that the prerogative power that he sought to exercise was not, in fact, a prerogative power to dismiss a prime minister, but a power to govern like an absolute monarch. This view is reinforced by his actions surrounding his dissolution of the Parliament. He insisted that he received advice from Fraser even though the powers that he claimed were reserved to him, including the power of dismissal under section 64 of the Constitution and the power of dissolution of Parliament under section 57, were powers already in the Constitution.

Reserve Power to Dissolve Parliament

With regard to the power of dissolution of the Parliament under section 57 of the Constitution, Kerr cannot say he exercised a prerogative power of dissolution since he sought and obtained Caretaker Prime Minister Fraser's advice before acting on it. While Kerr speaks of the power that he purports to exercise to dissolve the Parliament as a prerogative power, if it were indeed a personal prerogative he would have had no need for Fraser's advice according to his theory. In fact, he demanded that Fraser provides a "formal undertaking to advise a double dissolution"[152] before he appointed the caretaker prime minister. Fraser advised him that he would obtain legal advice for advising a double dissolution, regarding which Kerr said: "Mr Fraser had no problems with what I proposed and I was able to achieve all of this without obstacle. I next said, 'I think it important to swear you in immediately and I will do that now.'"

When he had commissioned Fraser as his caretaker prime minister, Fraser replied with a letter to the effect that he accepted the commission. He also confirmed in writing

> that I have given you an assurance that I shall immediately seek to secure the passage of the Appropriation Bills. . . . I further confirm that, upon the granting of supply, I shall immediately recommend to Your Excellency the dissolution of both Houses of Parliament.[153]

Despite his lengthy analysis of the reserve powers doctrine in relation to the dissolution of Parliament as a prerogative power that could be exercised without antecedent ministerial advice, Kerr claimed to be able to dissolve the House of Representatives by reserve power,[154] but dissolved the whole Parliament by Proclamation pursuant to the power in section 57 of the Constitution on the advice of Fraser.[155] Kerr obtained the advice from Caretaker Prime Minister Fraser that he could sign the Proclamation and dissolve the Parliament since the Proclamation met the conditions imposed by section 57. Since a formal undertaking to render the advice had been demanded by Kerr as a precondition to his appointing Fraser caretaker prime minister, Kerr had in effect given himself that advice, a practice whose precedent during the reign of King George III was disapproved by the Westminster Parliament as contrary to the Westminster convention.

The proscription against a demand by the king for an undertaking to give specific advice arose during the reign of King George III when the Prime Minister, Lord Grenville, introduced into Parliament the Army Navy Service Bill, in which some of the disqualifications of Roman Catholic officers were removed.[156] The Bill offended the staunchly Protestant king, who—despite the withdrawal of the bill—insisted on the ministry giving a written declaration "that they would never, under any circumstances, propose to him further concessions to the Catholics, or even offer him advice upon the subject."[157] Thomas Erskine May reports that the ministers refused the pledge and were dismissed; the Prime Minister, Lord Grenville, was replaced by Spencer Perceval. The Commons, however, saw "the constitutional dangers involved in such an exercise of the prerogative."[158] A resolution was moved by Mr. Brand MP on April 9, 1807:

> That it is contrary to the first duties of the confidential servants of the Crown to restrain themselves by any pledge, expressed or implied, from offering to the king any advice which the course of circumstances may render necessary for the welfare and security of the empire.[159]

May reported that Spencer Perceval considered that in requiring the pledge, the king had acted without any advice whatsoever. However, this was said to be impossible since what would stop a king from simply giving himself advice in respect of any subject. May recounts that:

> In the debate it was argued, that as the king was not responsible by law, if the ministers should also claim to be absolved from responsibility, by reason of pledges given to the king, there would be no security for the people against the evils of bad government. Had the ministers agreed to such a pledge, they would have violated their oaths as privy councillors, and the king would have become absolute.[160]

This supports the argument that Kerr merely assumed he held the power to rule as an absolute monarch by obtaining advice he had guaranteed to himself. What is also clear from his very act of linking his action to the constitutional power in section 57 of the Constitution, however, is that Kerr was not exercising a prerogative power.[161] By prerogative, he appears to mean a power to govern either with or without ministerial advice according to his own discretion—much like an absolute monarch who was "not responsible by law." The power that Kerr claimed to dismiss a prime minister was last exercised by King William IV.[162] The argument of this essay, which is sustained by Barton's arguments during the Constitutional Convention, is that no such personal discretion exists in the Governor-General. Kerr says of the situation that confronted him regarding supply:

> a deadlock over supply is too serious especially in modern times to be dealt with under the provisions of section 57 which would require many months to elapse and an election to be held at the end of the period for both houses.[163]

As general as this statement appears to be, it does not explain the need for a dissolution after the crisis had passed for, if the crisis was deadlock over supply, Kerr had no need to dissolve the Parliament once the Senate acted to grant supply. Kerr proceeded to dissolve the Parliament pursuant to section 57 *after* the Senate had granted supply, and therefore after the deadlock had abated. His rationale of having the majority of the people sitting in judgment of the various parties' actions suggests that he sought to wash his hands of the event since he believed the public judgment would attend only on Fraser or Whitlam.[164]

Fraser kept his promise to Kerr by securing the passage of the supply bills through the Senate; however, the failure of supply was never going to be a trigger for the dissolution of both Houses under section 57 of the Constitution, since they did not satisfy that section's requirements. Kerr relied instead on twenty-one pieces of legislation that the Senate, under the control of the Opposition parties, had twice rejected. The supreme irony is that Fraser, as the leader of the opposition, had been responsible for the rejection of the bills in the Senate. Having rejected the bills on political grounds, he was able to rely on them for the double dissolution and the election that he and Kerr desired. The bills were never brought before a joint sitting of the Parliament for they had served their purpose as a trigger for a double dissolution of the Parliament.

Summary—Kerr

Kerr's account of the Governor-General's reserve powers is mistaken in its reliance on the assumptions of Forsey and Evatt of prerogative powers personal to monarch or the monarch's representatives. The analyses of Forsey and Evatt are limited by their literal construction methodologies, which begin by assuming the existence of the powers exercised without regard to the political scheme in which the examples have occurred. Kerr attempts, but is unable, to deduce his reserve powers as personal prerogative powers from the executive powers in the Constitution and assumes a literal interpretation of constitutional provisions such as sections 61 and 64 to confer a discretionary power upon himself.

Kerr's claim to have personal powers about which the Constitution is silent is reliant on the assertion of a vice-regal prerogative power and a literal interpretation of executive power provisions, especially section 64, of the Constitution. His attempt to source personal discretionary powers to the Commonwealth Constitution for use in exceptional circumstances is inconsistent with the Constitution as it was originally intended by the Founders and with its liberal democratic principles whereby the Governor-General always acts with ministerial advice.

He distinguishes the common law and the prerogative powers of the Crown from the executive power of the Commonwealth by saying that the latter was extended by them. He does this in order to argue that his reserve powers are personal prerogative powers of the monarch which he claims exist as part of the executive power under section 61 of the Constitution. He therefore reverses the wording of section 61 of the Constitution, asserting that the executive powers of the Crown are vested in the Constitution and are exercisable by the Governor-General. While Kerr admits that he relied on the power in section 64 of the Constitution to dismiss the Whitlam government and install a caretaker government, he understood this as an exercise of his discretionary power to forego ministerial advice.

His dissolution of the Parliament, which occurred under section 57 of the Constitution, was neither a prerogative nor a discretionary act of the Governor-General, since it occurred on the advice of his caretaker prime minister. His action in obtaining an undertaking from Fraser to provide that advice, according to House of Commons at the time of King George III, was to elevate himself to an equivalent absolute monarch. Kerr's actions manifested the very abuse of power implied by Evatt in his argument that there is no legal remedy for a head of state who abuses his reserve powers. What Evatt did not notice was that a legal positivist construction could not distinguish between an abuse of power and its valid exercise. Only the political scheme permits that distinction.

Kerr argued that the parliamentary conventions are subject to the Constitution and that his reason for dismissing the Whitlam government was his belief that a government that could not obtain supply must resign in accordance with the conventions of responsible government. As he believed the government was responsible to both chambers, the Whitlam government was obliged to resign or call an election when the Senate deferred consideration of the proposed appropriation laws. He did not appreciate that such an obligation was itself only a convention and that the Constitution was silent on the correct procedure when a convention was breached; and that the Governor-General's powers were circumscribed by the Constitution. Kerr refused to acknowledge that from 1901 to 1975, a convention had operated in the Senate never to deny supply to a government with the confidence of the House of Representatives. As the Senate's action was in breach of a long-standing parliamentary convention, there could be no obligation on a government to honor another convention that placed it at a disadvantage. Kerr was unable to produce either evidence or argument, other than mere assertion, that he possessed the powers he claimed to exercise, and his actions were therefore, ultra vires the Constitution.

BARWICK'S DEFENSE

Introduction

In *Sir John Did His Duty*,[165] Barwick argues that the Constitution vests a discretionary power in the Governor-General to appoint or dismiss ministers without antecedent advice. According to his argument, "All the Governor-General's powers under the Constitution are statutory in nature: none are derivative or prerogative powers."[166] These statutory powers are his reserve powers, "although the Governor-General, in withdrawing the Prime Minister's commission, exercised his own statutory power, it is convenient to refer to such a power as a 'reserve' power in the sense that it is rarely to be used but always kept in reserve."[167]

In his review of Barwick's argument, Kennon argues that it confirms Barwick's black letter law approach[168] to construction, which is another name for the legal positivist resort to literalism. Barwick's argument that the Governor-General's power is statutory rejects Kerr's basic premise that the Governor-General has a royal personal prerogative power to appoint and dismiss ministers as Forsey suggested. Barwick sums up his conclusion as follows: "It is long standing law that relevant express parliamentary provision displaces the prerogative."[169] Barwick attempts to establish that the actual government of the Commonwealth under the Constitution is the Governor-General, who has a discretion to appoint and dismiss his own advisers. Before he can argue for that conclusion, however, he must explain the fact that there is no example of a Governor-General exercising powers of that nature.

Ordinary and Out of the Ordinary Times

The assumption on which this part of his analysis depends is that the Constitution works one way in ordinary circumstances and in an entirely different way in "out of the ordinary" circumstances. The Constitution is silent on the issue but Barwick asserts that the Governor-General's discretionary powers are there to be used on occasions that are "out of the ordinary."[170] In such times, "it is essential to have regard to constitutional actuality,"[171] that is, to the actual constitution. This assertion supports a literal interpretation[172] of specific constitutional provisions that regulate the executive power of the Commonwealth and reflects Barwick's legal positivism, discussed in chapter 5. On "out of the ordinary" occasions, he explains that "the legal power to govern the country is *vested* in the Governor-General with the advice of the Executive Council."[173] While this suggests a construction of section 62 of the Constitution, which speaks of a "Federal Executive Council to advise the Governor-General in the government of the Commonwealth,"[174] his statement is at best ambiguous since no provision of the Constitution expressly "vests" any power in the Governor-General, let alone a power to govern. Barwick describes the Executive Council as "composed of Executive Councillors, *mostly* Ministers of State in charge of the Departments of State,"[175] whose primary function and obligation "is to advise the Governor-General in the running of the government of the country."[176] Constitutional actuality, however, applies only on "out of the ordinary" occasions; the rest of the time he refers to as the ordinary course:

> In the ordinary course when constitutional requirement and parliamentary practice and usage are being satisfied and observed, we are accustomed to regarding the Prime Minister and the other members of the ministry as the government of the country and the Cabinet as the source of effective decision in all matters not requiring parliamentary endorsement.[177]

Barwick misstates the effect of section 64 of the Constitution when he explains that the ministry is appointed by the Governor-General "to be Executive Councillors and Ministers of State."[178] The section merely directs that 'the Governor-General *may* appoint officers to administer departments of state.'"[179] It then mandates, however, that "they shall be members of the Federal Executive Council, and shall be the Queen's Ministers of State for the Commonwealth."[180] In other words, it is the Constitution rather than the Governor-General that commands that the officers shall be executive councillors and ministers of state. In fact, the text of the Constitution distances the Governor-General from the creation of ministers and executive councillors, and provides a conditional direction to the Governor-General that he "may appoint" officers.

He says regarding the ordinary times that the ministry is referred to as "the 'elected' government"[181] and the Governor-General allows the elected representatives to govern

> ordinarily and in not unusual circumstances we can take it for granted that the ministry is the government and the Cabinet the body to make governmental decisions, the decisions of the Executive Council endorsing the decisions of the Cabinet will be a formality.[182]

The "ordinary" reflects the way government functions: "parliamentary usage and practice allow prominence to the Cabinet and the ministry, in and by which government decisions are ordinarily made."[183] He explains that "the Cabinet" consists of a group of ministers, led by the prime minister, who decide what advice is given to the Governor-General by the Executive Council.[184]

Barwick's assertion that the Constitution embodies provisions for "out of the ordinary" situations has no High Court or common law authority. The distinction was not discussed and the provisions to which Barwick refers were not acknowledged by any delegate to the Constitutional Convention as operating any differently because the Governor-General imagined there was a crisis of some sort. The fact that Barwick's book followed Kerr's suggests that Barwick adopted the distinction after having read Kerr's work, on the assumption that it facilitated his argument of a Governor-General who may in an instant take over the reins of government from the House of Representatives. There is no evidence that Barwick had read or was aware of the works of Carl Schmitt.

Barwick summarizes the events of November 1975 under three headings: the "Failure of Supply,"[185] by which he means "the action of the Senate in deferring consideration of the two appropriation bills";[186] a "Refusal to Resign,"[187] which he describes as the refusal of Whitlam to resign or call an election when he was unable to "secure from the Parliament moneys to carry on the ordinary services of government";[188] and the "Dismissal of the Prime Minister,"[189] whereby, "The Governor-General . . . in order to secure supply and a general election, withdrew the Prime Minister's commission notwithstanding that he was supported by a majority of members of the House of Representatives."[190]

While he mentions his distinction between ordinary and "out of the ordinary" circumstances only briefly, it sets the background for the first and second headings, which provide the factual evidence of his "out of the ordinary" occasion that, he implies, enlivens the Governor-General's discretionary powers under the Constitution. That occasion was the action of the Senate in delaying consideration of the government's supply legislation. While the importance of the supply to the executive government of the Commonwealth is an accepted fact,[191] Barwick argues that the democratic process includes control "by the Parliament of the supply of money to the executive government."[192] The fact that supply is granted annually is another part of the Westminster system.[193] While Barwick insists that supply is under the control of the Parliament, the Westminster convention required supply to be rejected by the House of Commons which, as the House representing all the British people, zealously protected its privilege of controlling supply and taxation legislation.

Failure to Pass Supply

On the three occasions when they were introduced into the Senate, the appropriation bills (referred to in section 53 of the Constitution as "proposed laws") were subject to a resolution, which began "these bills be not further proceeded with until the Government agrees to submit itself to the judgement of the people."[194] Barwick describes the Senate's action as a deferral of supply more than ten times in his book:[195] "The first event was the action of the Senate in *deferring* consideration of two appropriation bills."[196] His real argument, however, is to turn a deferral of the bills by the Senate into a failure to pass the bills: "The deferral of consideration of these bills amounted to a failure to pass the bills"[197] and a failure to pass into a rejection of supply: "I further think that if the Senate refuses either by rejection or failure to pass bills appropriating money for supply, both House and Senate should be dissolved."[198] Barwick argues that a "failure to pass" is part of the Senate's legislative power under section 53 of the Constitution with respect to appropriation bills.

His argument commences by asserting that: "Section 1 gives each chamber of the Parliament, Senate and House, equal legislative power."[199] This is stated despite section 1 of the Constitution being merely declaratory of the fact that the Constitution vests legislative power "in a Federal Parliament, which shall consist of the Queen, a Senate and a House of Representatives"[200] without apportioning power between them. He repeats his assertion that "section 1 vested equal legislative power in each chamber."[201] He adds to that misstatement with a reference to section 53 of the Constitution: "The combination of sections 1 and 53 make[s] it abundantly clear that the Senate has legislative power to fail to pass bills to appropriate revenue or money for supply."[202]

While section 53 contains a number of limitations on the Senate's legislative powers, Barwick relies on the final sentence of the section for his assertion that the Senate has equal legislative power with the House. That sentence states, "Except as provided in this section, the Senate shall have equal power with the House of Representatives in respect of all proposed laws."[203]

Referring to section 53 of the Constitution, he states that the Senate has a power *not to pass* legislation: "This means precisely what it says: the Senate has the same power as the House with respect to *all* bills, power to pass them and power *not to pass* them."[204] As his "power not to pass" is not in section 53, Barwick changes his description of the power from a power "not to pass" to a "power to *reject* or to fail to pass any bill."[205] His equation of a power to reject with a fail to pass is necessary since rejection of supply is the necessary condition for his redrafting of the Westminster convention since the Senate had never rejected supply. Barwick provides a legal justification for his argument: "In legal terms, a power *to pass* a bill connotes a power *not to pass* or to *fail to pass* it."[206] This proposition, however, is incorrect.

Barwick argues that the Senate's deferral of supply is the same as the Westminster requirement for a rejection of supply when he states that "the only way that the Senate may send a government to the polls is by *rejecting* or failing to pass an appropriation bill for supply."[207] He thus extends the Westminster convention to equate the legislative power to reject supply in section 53 with "failing to pass."

Section 53 does not contain a legislative power to fail to pass because that is not the language of a legislative power. A power to pass is a legislative power that is vested in both chambers and it implies a legislative power to reject but a failure to pass is not a connotation of either power. A legislative power is one that legislates, either a yes or a no, a power to "affirm or reject"[208]—words, as shown in chapter 2, that were included by the Founders in the relevant section of the first draft Constitution but later deleted.[209]

Peter Gerangelos says of the typical exercise of legislative power that it is "the enactment of primary legislation by Parliament pursuant to proper legislative procedure—this power can be regarded as such a core and fundamental exercise of legislative power."[210] Gerangelos's reference to "legislative procedure" is the key to understanding Barwick's "fail to pass." It is the result of procedure. The deferral of supply was the result of the Senate's procedures by which motions are authorized in accordance with the standing orders of the Senate. To the motion "that the bill be now read a second time,"[211] Standing Order 114 provides that the opposition might respond with an amendment that defers consideration for a period of time. In other words, Standing Order 114 authorizes an amending motion that can defer or delay proposed legislation. The Senate's Standing Orders are not an expression of a legislative power of the chamber, but are authorized by section 50(ii) of the Constitution, which provides: "Each House of the Parliament may make rules and orders with respect to: . . . (ii) the order and conduct of its business and proceedings either separately or jointly with the other House."[212]

Standing Orders made pursuant to section 50 permitted senators who were aligned with the leader of the opposition to defer the passage of the appropriation bills. However, since the Senate's action in deferring supply was not a rejection, it did not meet the requirements of the Westminster convention.

Barwick's argument glosses over this problem because the Senate could not afford to reject the proposed appropriation laws outright. Had supply been rejected, there would not have been funds for an election[213] and an installed caretaker government would not have a majority in the House of Representatives to pass new supply bills. While there is a convention at Westminster that when supply is *rejected* a government resigns or calls an election, the convention is enlivened by a *rejection* of supply by the House of Commons, not by the Parliament. That convention is not enlivened by a *threat* of rejecting or a deferral of supply, otherwise the House of Representatives and the government would be vulnerable to every Senate that threatened to defer supply in order to trigger the Westminster convention. This would be a constitutional recipe for political chaos.

It may appear to be of only historical importance that the Founders intended senators to protect their own state interests and to make suggestions regarding supply pursuant to section 53 of the Constitution for consideration by the House of Representatives. If senators were protecting their own states' interests, however, a coalescence of senators from sufficient states to reject supply was almost unimaginable—something the delegates recognized. However, the effect of these factors on responsible government in the Commonwealth had been realized by all senators since federation, as this chapter has demonstrated, and the possible instability in government was remedied by a parliamentary convention of senators not to deny supply to a government with the confidence of the House of Representatives.

Westminster Conventions and Supply

Barwick's interpretation of the Westminster convention as it operates in Australia begins by tacitly invoking Isaacs and the *Engineers' case*, where he describes the Commonwealth Constitution as a piece of Imperial legislation.[214] He extends Dicey's rule of construction that excludes a consideration of the political scheme of the Constitution to exclude the political scheme created by parliamentary conventions when construing the Constitution: "The Constitution does not depend upon unwritten conventions and historical precedent."[215] He also rejects the notion that responsible government as practiced elsewhere can affect a construction of the Constitution:

> It is not possible, by using the description "responsible government" and treating that concept as it is operated in some other system, to vary the language of the Constitution itself or to deny its operation. The text of the Constitution is definitive.[216]

This passage has particular significance for his argument, since it precludes a resort to the practice of responsible government in the United Kingdom where a government is responsible to the House of Commons, which alone has control over supply.[217] He makes no attempt to reconcile his argument that responsible government practiced elsewhere cannot vary the Constitution's language or its operation with statements encouraging the use of the Westminster parliamentary tradition in constitutional construction: "That [Westminster] tradition still has its place in constitutional analysis"[218] or, after acknowledging that the Founders were immersed in the Westminster tradition that: "Those who worked in the production of the text of the Constitution were steeped in the tradition and practice of the Westminster style and form of government."[219] However, he proposed an extreme literalist construction of the provisions that invoked a different form of government to that intended by the Founders. He names two elements of the "Westminster system"[220] for the control of the executive. The first is the convention of responsible government: "One of those elements was that of ministerial responsibility;"[221] Another "was the annual grant of supply to the Crown."[222] "This control is exercisable by the Parliament."[223] Sections 53 and 54 of the

Constitution enable the Parliament to pass proposed laws appropriating the ordinary annual services of government.[224]

He explains that a deadlock regarding ordinary legislation can be resolved by section 57, which he claims "emphasises the extent of the democratic quality of the constitution: the people as the ultimate source of power are to resolve a Parliamentary impasse."[225] Because of the urgency with which money is required, the three-month waiting period before proposed laws can be rejected a second time means that "section 57 provides no real solution to a deadlock on a failure to pass an appropriation bill for supply."[226] While there is no provision in the Constitution to deal with a deadlock concerning supply, the Founders were so familiar with the Westminster convention that they would expect a government to resign or go to an election:

> Those who drew the Constitution, being familiar with the Westminster practice, would have seen no need to provide for a deadlock over the failure to grant supply. They would have regarded the refusal of a ministry without supply to resign or advise a dissolution as unthinkable.[227]

As shown in chapter 2, however, "those who drew the Constitution" insisted that the government was responsible only to the House of Representatives. Barwick has now redefined the contest between the Senate and the House of Representatives over supply as a "deadlock" for which the Constitution does not provide a remedy. He asserts that the only remedy available is the Westminster convention, which in Australia obliges a government to resign or call an election when it is unable to secure supply from the Parliament:

> Parliamentary practice and usage in a Westminster system reflects this constitutional situation by the adoption of a universal practice under which a Prime Minister when unable to secure supply from the Parliament immediately resigns for himself and the members of the ministry.[228]

It is clear why Barwick excluded the practice of responsible government in "some other system" when considering its practice in Australia. Under the Westminster convention as practiced in the United Kingdom, the House of Commons alone was responsible for the provision of supply. The House of Lords breached that convention in 1909 to deny supply to the Asquith government, which had the confidence of the Commons—a comparison that Barwick seeks to exclude. However, he insists, contrary to the original meaning of the Founders, that the government is responsible to both the House of Representatives and to the Senate, since he maintains that the Senate has a power over supply.

Barwick rejects any suggestion that a Commonwealth parliamentary convention similar to that which traditionally had prevented the House of Lords from rejecting supply existed even when he admits the facts from which such a convention can be inferred: "In my view not only was there no convention of the kind suggested: there could not be any such convention. The legislative power of the Senate could not be foregone."[229] The Senate's power rules out a convention:[230]

> No resolution or positive act of a Senate has been produced in any attempt to found a convention in that respect: that is not surprising. It is inescapable that the ability to reject or to fail to pass a bill for supply was deliberately given to the Senate.[231]

However, he confirms that the Senate had never rejected a government's supply prior to 1975: "It has been said that there existed a convention that the Senate would not reject or fail to pass a bill appropriating revenue or moneys for supply. *It is true.*"[232] It was an example, adopting Barwick's language, of a "regular observance of parliamentary practice and usage,"[233] of what he calls the "ordinary course," which he denies was a convention. The destabilizing effect of the Senate's equal power clause for responsible government in the Commonwealth appears to have been realized by all parties since federation, and the threat of instability in government was remedied, as explained previously, by successive Senates observing a convention not to deny supply to a government with the confidence of the House of Representatives.[234] Whatever the nature of the power that the Constitution vested in the Senate indirectly through the equal power sentence in section 53, the senators recognized the principle that control over supply and responsible government lay in the House of Representatives. As a result, the Senate had never, since 1901, rejected supply for a government with the confidence of the House of Representatives.[235] This was the convention. Barwick's assertion that there could be no convention misunderstands or misstates the nature of a parliamentary convention which Dicey described in the context of the British Constitution as a body of "political ethics."[236] That definition applies equally well to the conventions of the Commonwealth Constitution.

The existence of the convention by which the Senate had eschewed recourse to its constitutional power since federation in 1901 points to an essential defect in Barwick's conclusion. As parliamentary conventions do not arise by legal compulsion, but rather to control legal powers, they are a voluntary standard of political ethics among people, a sign of trust that mutually agreed political principles between groups with opposing political agendas will be honored by each group in the future in order to make the scheme of the Constitution work in accord with its spirit. Since it is a question of trust and propriety that parliamentary conventions are observed, that duty is negated by a party who betrays the trust and breaches convention as the Senate did in 1975 by delaying the passage of the supply bills until after Whitlam government had been dismissed. It is clear that, despite Barwick's denial, the evidence points unmistakably to a convention relating to the Senate's power regarding supply that the Senate refused to honor.

Barwick's argument, that there is a convention that the Whitlam government is obliged to honor when the Senate denies supply, is therefore not only partisan but, by the terms of the same argument that justifies the Senate's breach of the convention, any government breach is also justified.

As the Constitution contains no solution regarding a breach of a convention, Barwick asserts that the Governor-General can, on such "out of the ordinary" occasions, exercise discretionary powers in order to dismiss a prime minister and the whole ministry that has the confidence of the House of Representatives. Barwick's argument in favor of those powers required that he construe the provisions of the Constitution relating to the appointment of ministers of the Crown in order to effect a link between the power to appoint ministers and members of the Federal Executive Council and the holding of office "during the pleasure of the Governor-General."[237] He identifies two different phrases in the Constitution that authorize the Governor-General to exercise personal discretionary powers as those denoted where appointments exist during "the pleasure" of the Governor-General and where the "Governor-General," but *not* the "Governor-General in Council," is directed by the provision to perform certain acts.

During the Pleasure of the Governor-General

For the purpose of this argument, Barwick draws attention to sections 62 and 64 of the Constitution, both of which refer to an office being held during the pleasure of the Governor-General. Section 62 of the Constitution provides that "there shall be a Federal Executive Council to advise the Governor-General in the government of the Commonwealth, and the members of the Council shall be chosen and summoned by the Governor-General and sworn as Executive Councillors, and shall hold office *during his pleasure*."[238]

He provides two different constructions of the phrase "during the pleasure" of the Governor-General. His first is brief and is consistent with the conventions of responsible government: "That means that the ministry, including the Prime Minister, has no term of office: the ministry has no entitlement to hold office for any fixed or defined period of time."[239] This is consistent with the convention that ministers lose office on the advice of the prime minister or after resigning. On neither occasion does the Governor-General exercise discretion. His second construction, however, is literalist. He asserts that:

"The power to appoint to an office to be held at pleasure of necessity carries with it the power to withdraw or put an end to the appointment."[240] This is correct because the phrase "during the pleasure" means nothing more than an appointment with no specific term. But that is not the issue: it was always whether the Governor-General alone could signify the end of his "pleasure" by exercising a personal discretionary power to dismiss a government that enjoyed the confidence of the House of Representatives.[241]

Like Kerr, Barwick applies the doctrine of ex post facto responsibility, where a newly appointed minister takes responsibility for a monarch's decision taken without antecedent advice. Pursuant to that doctrine, Malcolm Fraser, as the appointed caretaker prime minister, is assumed to accept responsibility for Kerr's discretionary dismissal of Whitlam: "There are occasions when these discretionary powers of the Governor-General may have to be exercised without the antecedent or any advice of a Minister of State though responsibility for the action taken by the Governor-General must always be accepted by a Minister after the act has been done."[242]

That doctrine, however, had long fallen into desuetude. Alpheus Todd described a general rule that "new Ministers shall be held responsible to Parliament for the policy which occasioned the retirement of their predecessors in office."[243] Todd admits that this rule applied when the king had a "free choice in the appointment of the prime minister."[244] It would be inconsistent, however, with Barwick's definition of responsible government, where the Governor-General's "choice *must* be of that Leader who is supported by a majority of members of the House."[245] The reason for the abandonment of the doctrine is evident when Todd recounts the dismissal by King William IV of Lord Melbourne's ministry in 1834 and the acceptance by Sir Robert Peel of a commission to form a ministry. William was obliged to reappoint Melbourne when Peel's government was defeated at an election in 1835. Given the monarch's public reputation and legal status of being unable to err, the incident was more than embarrassing, happening at a time when democratic reform of the House of Commons had begun. But its rejection can be recognized in the successful policy of Queen Victoria, who throughout her reign never acted without the antecedent advice of her ministers.[246] This was the principle of responsible government to which Walter Bagehot referred when he remarked that "the sovereign has, under a constitutional monarchy such as ours, three rights: the right to be consulted, the right to encourage, the right to warn."[247] The doctrine of ex post facto responsibility formed no part of the Constitution approved by the Founders and did not exist in 1975.

Barwick's "out of the ordinary" or actuality constitutionalism is the justification he requires for a literal construction of sections 62 and 64 of the Constitution isolated from the political scheme represented by the Westminster conventions. In the "out of the ordinary" circumstances, he alleges that the Governor-General can avail himself of powers in the Commonwealth Constitution for which he has no power without ministerial advice. Barwick must demonstrate cogently, however, that the discretionary powers of the Governor-General can be found in the Constitution. His construction of an appointment that exists "during the pleasure" of the Governor-General, where it is found in sections 62 and 64 of the Constitution, allows him to assert that "the express power given to the Governor-General to appoint persons to hold office during his pleasure inherently authorises him to terminate the appointment at any time."[248] The immediate question, though, is whether he can do that without antecedent ministerial advice. By ignoring the need for such advice, Barwick's Governor-General can, as Thomas Erskine May reported of George III, give himself advice to appoint or dismiss as if he were an absolute monarch.[249] The Constitution itself provides the rebuttal to Barwick's construction, since it does not vest any executive power in the Governor-General as it does executive power in the Queen. Section 61 states: "The executive power of the Commonwealth is vested in the Queen and is exercisable by the Governor-General as the Queen's representative, and extends to the execution and maintenance of this Constitution, and of the laws of the Commonwealth."[250]

In regard to the Governor-General, section 2 of the Constitution states that the Governor-General is appointed by the Queen with "such powers and functions of the Queen as Her Majesty may be pleased to assign to him,"[251] but this does not and cannot include the executive power of the Commonwealth that, pursuant to section 61, is not a "power and function of the Queen" nor one that she can exercise on the advice of British ministers under the Constitution. Barwick attributes an actual executive power of appointment (in times of his constitutional actuality) to the Governor-General in sections 62 and 64 of the Constitution, even though such a power under section 61 of the Constitution is vested in the Queen, who holds it in trust for the people. Barton explained during the first session of the Convention in relation to the executive power: "If the Bill is accepted as drawn he can take this conclusion: that all executive powers must be in trust for the people."[252] This translates the exercise of the power to the advice of the people's representatives in responsible government.

Section 61 says that it is exercisable by the Governor-General, but if no power is vested in the Governor-General, something else is needed before the power can be exercised. That is the substance of the Westminster convention when the Commonwealth Constitution was drafted and which was originally intended by the Australian Founders. It assumed that the Queen acted on the advice of the Imperial ministers who were responsible to the British people. In Australia, the Governor-General acts on the advice of the Commonwealth ministers, and ministerial advice authorizes the power to be exercised. Under section 61, executive powers are held in trust by the Queen for the people, not the Governor-General. It is the people's representatives who advise the Governor-General about how the powers will be executed. Barton's statement of principle, when understood in conjunction with section 61 of the Constitution, is sufficient to negate Barwick's argument, which assumes that the Constitution vests personal powers in the Governor-General that permit him to exercise executive powers without antecedent advice. After referring to the need for "antecedent advice for all acts done by the Governor-General in Council,"[253] Barwick continues:

> But not all acts of the Governor-General are acts done in Council and by the authority of the executive council. These are statutory powers in the personal discretion of the Governor-General e.g. appointment of the Executive Council. They are not powers exercisable in Council and may be exercised without any antecedent ministerial advice.[254]

This brief passage epitomizes Barwick's argument for the Governor-General's personal discretionary powers. Acts done by the authority of the executive council are not discretionary, but acts by the Governor-General that are not done in Council are, according to Barwick, at the Governor-General's personal discretion. His assertion that the Governor-General exercised a personal discretion to appoint the Executive Council is ambiguous unless he includes in it a power to appoint the executive councillors. Section 62 of the Constitution contains no power of appointment; rather, it establishes a Federal Executive Council and the "members of the Council shall be chosen and summoned by the Governor-General and sworn as Executive Councillors."[255] A power of appointment is to be found in section 64 of the Constitution, but it is not an express power to appoint either executive councillors or the Federal Executive Council or even ministers. Rather, section 64 states:

> The Governor-General may appoint officers to administer such departments of State of the Commonwealth as the Governor-General in Council may establish.
>
> Such officers shall hold office during the pleasure of the Governor-General. They shall be members of the Federal Executive Council, and shall be the Queen's Ministers of State for the Commonwealth.[256]

Thus, while the departments of state are established by the Governor-General *in Council*, the section states only that the Governor-General "may" appoint *officers* to administer those departments of state. Section 64 mandates that the officers shall be "members" of the Federal Executive Council (*not* executive councillors) and ministers of state, but the Governor-General does not appoint them. Section 64 uses the permissive form of the verb "may" appoint; however, as there is no executive power vested in the Governor-General but only in the Queen, the Governor-General cannot act without some sort of authority or permission to appoint officers. Barwick must deny this, because he has asserted that the Governor-General holds a discretion. However, the use by the section of the permissive form "may" reflect what is consistent with responsible government as understood by the Founders, that is, the convention whereby the prime minister advises the Governor-General who will be appointed; he permits the appointment.

Barwick wrongly asserts that the prime minister and the other ministers "are advisers to the Governor-General. They are appointed by him to be Executive Councillors and Ministers of State."[257] The language of section 64, when understood in the light of responsible government, does not support this statement. In fact, his statement conflates the essentials of sections 62 and 64 while omitting those aspects of both which tell against it. By asserting that ministers and executive councillors are appointed by the Governor-General, Barwick gives a distorted description of the intention of the Constitution and hence of the Governor-General's power. The Constitution provides through section 64 that the officers so appointed become "members" of the Federal Executive Council and ministers of state. However, until such time as they are "chosen and summoned by the Governor-General and sworn" pursuant to section 62 of the Constitution, which do not constitute an exercise of executive powers, the members are not executive councillors. This interpretation is indirectly confirmed by the title of section 62, which is "Federal Executive Council," not "Federal Executive Councillors." When sections 62 and 64 of the Constitution are considered in the context of the scheme of responsible government, rather than literally and in isolation, Barwick's construction can be seen to have no other purpose than to infer discretionary powers of appointment from sections 62 and 64 to be attributed to the Governor-General, when no such discretion exists.

In terms of the Westminster convention as practiced in Australia, ministers are appointed on the advice of the prime minister and the Member of Parliament who has the support of a majority of the House of Representatives is appointed as prime minister. Barwick confirms this as parliamentary practice after an election,[258] when the Governor-General is *compelled* to appoint a prime minister: "The choice *must* be of that Leader who is supported by a majority of members of the House and is therefore most probably able to carry an appropriation bill for supply."[259] While that criterion is satisfied by the leader of the majority in the House of Representatives, Barwick implies through a series of rhetorical questions that the Governor-General gets to choose who will be his advisers: "how is the Governor-General to *choose* his advisers? Whom shall he *choose*? On what basis is the *choice* to be made?"[260] The wording of these questions suggests that the permissive verb "may appoint" in section 64 of the Constitution gives the Governor-General a personal discretion to choose from the list of prospective ministers presented to him by the newly appointed prime minister. However, in order to vest a discretionary power in the Governor-General, Barwick must reveal where the power is in the Constitution. He suggests that the power to appoint ministers in section 62 is discretionary "in a legal sense":

> In contrast no conditions are imposed by the Constitution on the exercise of the power to appoint, and by implication to dismiss, Ministers. Indeed, the language of the power to appoint in section 62 is clear enough to make the choice of appointee in a legal sense discretionary and specifies that the appointee holds office during the Governor-General's pleasure.[261]

While his use of the term "legal sense" suggests a legal positivist construction of the provision has occurred, the term has been used to give unwarranted credit to what is only his assertion when the assertion demonstrates confusion. The word "ministers" is not mentioned in section 62, so a minister cannot be the "appointee." The first sentence must therefore be a reference to section 64, except that there the Governor-General "may appoint officers to administer such departments" of state, but not ministers. His second sentence asserts the existence of a power to "appoint" in section 62, when in fact the word "appoint" is not mentioned in that section, which serves a different purpose. He has, however, managed to import the meaning of the first sentence into the second by commencing the second with "Indeed," as if the two sentences refer to the same section of the Constitution. He concludes that the Governor-General holds a power of appointment in section 62. He disguises this *non sequitur* by asserting that the Governor-General has a discretionary power under section 62 "to appoint," which he qualifies as existing "in a legal sense," even though the words are not there in any sense. It is an assertion without foundation. Nevertheless, Barwick asserts that section 62 contains the words "shall appoint" and actually places them in parentheses, in order to stress their presence:

> Whilst it may be said that section 62 imports a duty to appoint—it says "*shall* appoint"—it leaves no room for the implication of any legally enforceable conditions upon the exercise of the power whether viewed at the time of appointment or at the time of withdrawal.[262]

This is a fundamental point in his argument, yet it is a mere assertion that is easily disproved by brief reference to the Constitution and a consideration of the scheme of responsible government as it is now universally practiced.

There is no power to "appoint" in section 62 of the Constitution. The section speaks of "members" of the Federal Executive Council being chosen and summoned and sworn as executive councillors, a subtle but important distinction. Barwick further confuses the issue by asserting that section 62 places an obligation on the Governor-General to appoint a Federal Executive Council, which he interprets as an obligation "to choose and appoint executive councillors and to appoint Ministers pursuant to section 64,"[263] contrary to the actual words of the sections. He then asserts that section 62 states that the Governor-General *shall choose* and appoint while section 64 obliges him to appoint ministers of state: "Section 62 says the Governor-General '*shall* choose,' and although section 64 does not repeat the imperative there is yet, in my view, an obligation on the Governor-General to appoint Ministers."[264]

He concludes this section of his argument by stating that

> the power to appoint to an office to be held at the pleasure of necessity carries with it the power to withdraw or put an end to the appointment. Thus, the express power given to the Governor-General to appoint persons to hold office during his pleasure inherently authorises him to terminate the appointment at any time.[265]

While an office that is held during the pleasure has no fixed term, Barwick's argument merely asserts that the Governor-General holds the requisite power. Barwick's argument purports to give the Governor-General a discretionary power both to appoint and to dismiss ministers and executive councillors because they are only appointed "during the pleasure of the Governor-General."[266] The Governor-General needed an absolute discretion if he was to legally avail himself of the opportunity to terminate ministers held during his pleasure. Barwick discovers that discretion in section 62, where the "Governor-General," not the "Governor-General in Council," was directed to act: "But the Governor-General's authority (and duty) to terminate [Whitlam's] commission was not an act to be done 'in council.' It was a discretionary act for which antecedent advice was not necessary."[267] Barwick distinguishes executive acts done in council, for which he asserts ministerial advice was necessary, from the discretionary acts of the Governor-General where the words "in council" do not exist.

Governor-General, Not Governor-General in Council

As well as the implied statutory powers that he claims the Governor-General possesses from the use of the words "during the Governor-General's pleasure," Barwick argues that the Governor-General also holds personal discretionary powers in the Constitution. He rejects the notion that the Governor-General derives any powers, including prerogative powers, from the monarch. "All the Governor-General's powers under the Constitution are statutory in nature: none are derivative or prerogative powers."[268] He explains that acts done by the Governor-General *in Council* will have been done with the advice of the executive councillors. However, not all of the Governor-General's acts "are acts done in Council and by the authority of the executive council. These are statutory powers in the personal discretion of the Governor-General e.g. appointment of the Executive Council."[269] By statutory, Barwick means only that the powers are in the Constitution. Discretionary powers that are at the personal discretion of the Governor-General include "the power of appointing (and, by implication, of dispensing with) executive councillors and Ministers of State, of proroguing and dissolving the House and of dissolving both houses under section 57."[270]

As there is no term for an appointment to office held during the Governor-General's pleasure, Barwick asserts that the Governor-General has a personal discretionary power with which to dismiss such an appointment if it is made by the Governor-General, not the "Governor-General *in Council*." In that context, he says that in sections 5, 62, and 64, "the powers are given not to the Queen, but to the Governor-General. Further, they are not given to the Governor-General in Council."[271] He says of section 64: "The Governor-General appoints the Ministers but the Governor-General in Council establishes the Departments of State."[272] This difference, he argues, expresses the Governor-General's discretionary powers: where he acts with the advice of the Executive Council and where he can act without the advice of Executive Council. This, he says, is only possible because of a convention regarding such discretionary action, that "responsibility for the action taken by the Governor-General must always be accepted by a Minister after the act has been done."[273] I have explained previously why this rule was abandoned during the reign of Queen Victoria. The difficulty with Barwick's argument, however, is that if the Governor-General has clearly defined, constitutional discretionary powers, he has no need for a minister to take responsibility for his actions. The power would speak for itself. But Barwick's construction of the words "Governor-General," without the qualifying words, "in Council," is refuted by the Constitution itself.

First, sections 62 and 64 direct the Governor-General to exercise executive powers. Barwick's assertion that "the powers are given not to the Queen but to the Governor-General" is refuted by the plain words of section 61 of the Constitution, which states, where relevant, that "the executive power of the Commonwealth is vested in the Queen," as previously stated. Second, his construction is contradicted by section 58 of the Constitution, which *expressly* confers a personal discretion on the Governor-General. Section 58, where relevant, states, "When a proposed law passed by both Houses of the Parliament is presented to the Governor-General for the Queen's assent, he shall declare, *according to his discretion*, but subject to this Constitution, that he assents in the Queen's name."[274]

Section 58 is the only section in the Commonwealth Constitution that expressly vests a personal discretion in the Governor-General, and the section does not contain the words "in Council." The fact that the discretion is explicitly stated in section 58, and that it is to be exercised by the Governor-General without executive council advice, contradicts Barwick's argument that a discretion is to be inferred from provisions where the Governor-General is directed to act, not the Governor-General *in Council*. The Governor-General is expressly granted a personal discretion in section 58, but the words "in Council" are not there. Section 58 allows only one conclusion: that where the Constitution confers a discretionary power upon the Governor-General, it does so expressly and not as something to be inferred or implied. Had Barwick's argument been correct, the omission of "in Council" from section 58 would have been sufficient to confer a discretion on the Governor-General.[275] The absence from every other section of the Constitution of an explicit discretion is a clear indication that the Founders intended the Governor-General to act on ministerial advice.

A compelling criticism of Barwick's construction of the words "Governor-General" and "Governor-General in Council," by Edmund Barton during the Constitutional Convention, was provided in chapter 2.[276] A concern was expressed by convention delegate George Reid that if the words "by and with the advice of the Executive Council" were not included whenever the Governor-General was mentioned in the Constitution, it might be thought that the Governor-General exercised actual power on his own. Barton explained to the Convention that, first, the use or nonuse of the phrase "in council" was a drafting technique that would be required by the Imperial authorities at Westminster and he explained that its use related to the two classes of Executive Acts: those exercised by the prerogative and those that are ordinary Executive Acts, where it is prescribed that the Executive shall act in Council.[277] Barton explained that it was not possible in the Commonwealth Constitution for the prerogative to be exercised as a personal act of the Crown. The prerogative was never in these days exercised as a personal act of the Crown as we understand it.[278] He concluded that there was no prerogative in the Constitution that was personal to the Governor-General because those who exercised it must answer to the people.[279]

> [I]t is understood that the Crown exercises the prerogative only upon ministerial advice, and it is exercised not personally by the Crown, but only with the advice of the Ministry or a Minister. . . . But we all know that it is exercised with the advice of those who must answer to the people. The point of the matter

> is that where the expression of the Act is in the form commonly used to indicate prerogative act—that is without the addition of the words, "in Council"—that does not indicate any real personal power in the depositary of the Crown's authority.[280]

Thomas Erskine May had stated this as a principle of Queen Victoria's reign almost twenty years earlier when he said:

> Vast as is the power of the Crown, it has been exercised, throughout the present reign, by the advice of responsible ministers, in a constitutional manner, and for legitimate objects. It has been held in trust, as it were, for the benefit of the people.[281]

May's description of the prerogative as held by the Crown in a trust for the people means only that it is exercised on the advice of ministers responsible to the people's representatives. May's opinion was endorsed by the eminent jurist, Alpheus Todd nine years later when he stated: "No public act of the sovereign is valid which is not performed under the advice of some responsible minister,"[282] a view also endorsed later by the English jurist, Sir Ivor Jennings.

The danger of Barwick's argument was well recognized by other Convention delegates, even if they did not anticipate that it would be expressed by a future Chief Justice of the High Court. Joseph Carruthers, a NSW country solicitor, thought it important that George Reid's proposed amendment be agreed to, even if it attracted criticism:

> We do not want the Governor to have the power to do wrong; we want to have him limited by the terms of the Constitution Act, and kept to the straight paths by a Federal Judiciary. . . . We do not want the Federation to be plunged into a broil through the Governor taking responsibility on his own shoulders. I hope my hon. friend's suggested amendment will be carried.[283]

Barton rejected Carruthers's demand. Crucially, however, Carruthers wanted merely to ensure that no one would ever doubt that the Governor-General always, on every occasion, only acted with ministerial advice. Barton's explanation reconciles all the provisions of the Constitution in which the words are either present or absent with those where both are present. That it was an accurate statement of the law is suggested by the fact that it was unchallenged by any legal delegate other than Carruthers, and it expressed the view that sovereignty of the people was not to be handed to an unelected official. That, unfortunately, was the remedy suggested by Barwick and acted upon by Kerr.

Summary—Barwick

Barwick argues that the Senate has a constitutional power under section 53 to reject the appropriation bills and he rejected the existence of a Senatorial convention to always grant supply to a government that had the support of the House of Representatives. The evidence for that convention is incontrovertible, and it was a crucial convention supporting the federal Commonwealth's Westminster-style responsible government. The Senate's deferral of supply in 1975 was a breach of that convention. Barwick argues that the Senate's deferral of supply was a failure of supply—the equivalent of a rejection of supply, which obliged the government to resign or call an election in accordance with the Westminster convention. That argument fails for two reasons. First, a deferral of supply does not meet the requirement of the Westminster convention that supply be rejected; and, second, the deferral of supply was itself a breach of the convention and an act in bad faith, which did not necessitate the government resigning and calling an election. As chapter 2 demonstrated, responsible government in the Commonwealth Constitution, requiring responsibility only to the House of Representatives, was ratified by the people. There is another equally valid reason for denying responsibility to the Senate which is fatal to Barwick's argument. A government's accountability to the popularly elected chamber was based on the fact that the money it spent was financed by the taxes paid for by all the people. It had been argued by John Locke that no one had the right to tax another without that other's consent.[284]

Barwick argued that the deferral of supply was sufficient to oblige the government, pursuant to the Westminster convention, to resign or call an election, and when it did neither he argued that the Governor-General held a discretionary constitutional power to dismiss the government, although it still had the confidence of the House of Representatives. He derived that power from two sources. In the first, he undertook a literal consideration of sections 62 and 64 in order to attribute the power of appointment of ministers and executive councillors to the Governor-General in "out of the ordinary times," a temporal consideration previously unknown to constitutional scholarship. In such circumstances, the words "during the pleasure" of the Governor-General, found in section 62, applying to executive councillors and similar words in section 64, applying to ministers, meant that their appointment could be terminated by the Governor-General at any time. Barwick's literal construction of those two provisions identified the Governor-General's discretionary power to dismiss ministers without ministerial advice since the power was to be exercised by the Governor-General but not the Governor-General in Council. He argued that the absence of the words "in Council" implied the existence of the Governor-General's discretionary power to appoint and dismiss.

In the first place, Barwick's construction of the words "in Council" is expressly contradicted by Edmund Barton's detailed explanation to the Convention, discussed in chapter 2, that the words reflect a necessary rule of legal drafting to distinguish between prerogative powers and statutory powers to be undertaken by ministers answerable to the people. His explanation negated Barwick's argument that it signals a power for a Governor-General to act without antecedent ministerial advice.

Second, Barwick's argument that the absence of the words "in Council" indicates the presence of a discretionary power personal to the Governor-General is implicitly contradicted by section 58, the one provision in the whole Constitution that *expressly* confers a personal discretion on the Governor-General, stating "he shall declare, *according to his discretion*." The fact that a personal discretion is expressly conferred on the Governor-General by section 58 (without the qualifying phrase "in Council") contradicts Barwick's construction that the discretionary power is an inference when the words "in Council" are omitted from a section. The evidence of section 58 allows only one conclusion: that where the Constitution confers a discretionary power upon the Governor-General, it does so *expressly*.

His argument articulated a scheme of responsible government with conventions that were unknown to the Founders and to the people of Australia. His argument that a Governor-General had a constitutional discretion with which to dismiss a government that enjoyed the confidence of the House of Representatives was a proposition that was inconsistent with a written Constitution drafted by delegates of the people and subsequently ratified by those people. It defies belief that a Chief Justice of the High Court of Australia would seriously propose it.

CONCLUSION

There is an overwhelming similarity between Kerr's analysis and that of Barwick in that each resulted in a literal or legal positivist interpretation of sections 62 and 64 of the Constitution without regard to the relevant conventions of responsible government in order that the Governor-General might exercise a power implicit in those sections without antecedent ministerial advice. Kerr argued that he had a royal prerogative in the form of a discretion to exercise constitutional powers but was unable to source that discretion with a coherent argument. Barwick appears to have recognized that and has argued, following Winterton, that Kerr's power was constitutional, a statutory power in his language, which was revealed by a literal interpretation of sections 62 and 64, made in isolation from the elements of responsible government as articulated by the Founders. George Winterton's statement, that: "any attempt to ground an independent vice-regal discretion in the language of the Constitution is futile,"[285] at first sight contradicts Kerr's assertion that the Governor-General's reserve powers were a discretion to act without advice. However, Winterton's following sentence, that "nevertheless, it is possible to base such a claim on the nature of the particular power conferred, considered in the light of the conventions of responsible government"[286] provided a sufficient connection with the Constitution on which Barwick's argument was based. When one asks, what was the nature of the particular power, Winterton, like Barwick and Kerr, can only reply, a reserve or unwritten power. It has, therefore, no place in a written Constitution, especially one whose draftsmen implicitly denied the existence of either a regal or vice-regal discretion. In the arguments of both Kerr and Barwick, the power was there to be used when "out of the ordinary" occasions demanded it, the Governor-General alone determining when such an occasion arose. Until the publication of their arguments, the existence of such an important constitutional consideration in the Commonwealth Constitution was unknown, either judicially or notoriously. Further such a consideration was also unknown to the Founders and played no part in the formation of the Constitution. When considered in that light, it is nothing more than an invention.

Much was made of the necessity for the government to follow the conventions of responsible government once the Senate had blocked supply while ignoring the effect on that argument of a breach of convention by a Senate that had never, since federation, blocked supply for a government enjoying the confidence of the House. Barwick was obliged to deny that this was a constitutional convention or parliamentary practice even while acknowledging its existence, since such a convention would negate the binding nature of any reciprocal convention on the House. Nor did he provide any theoretical support for that denial.

His whole argument essentially corrects errors that he detects in Kerr's argument. Where Kerr characterized his power to dismiss a government as prerogative, Barwick characterizes it as statutory. He ignores the arguments in favor of a prerogative power of Forsey and Evatt, appealing to literal interpretations of those constitutional provisions under which ministers are appointed and their advice is given, sections 64 and 62, respectively. As these provisions invoke statutory powers, Barwick concludes that the Governor-General holds a discretion to exercise them without antecedent ministerial advice where the words "Governor-General" are used without the qualifying words "in Council." This argument, however, is contradicted by section 58 of the Constitution which expressly invests a discretion in the Governor-General who "shall declare, according to his discretion," despite the qualifying words "in Council" not being present. While Winterton (and Evatt) was reluctant to conclude that the reserve powers actually existed, his assertion of where they may be construed from the Constitution[287] appears to have been the source of Barwick's conclusion that the reserve powers were constitutional. Winterton's call for codification of these seeming powers is presented as a defense against a repeat of the events of 1975,[288] a resolution that resembles Evatt's call for codification. It is not, however, a defense of responsible government. Winterton makes no attempt to reflect on the effect on responsible government, the presence of such discretionary powers would have in the hands of a Governor-General. Doubt as to the wisdom, let alone existence, of reserve powers after the events of 1909–1911 at Westminster has meant that they have only been used once in Australia. Were they introduced into the Constitution, the risk of them being used for political advantage would be uncontrollable and the reward for their misuse would go to him who took the greatest risks with the most audacious acts. Like Evatt, Winterton did not understand the nature of the political scheme that the Constitution supported and was not, therefore, able to judge the constitutionality of the Governor-General's actions correctly. That defect was the direct result of their legal positivism for which such considerations were immaterial.

Barwick's and Kerr's arguments failed to establish that the Governor-General held any reserve power, whether a statutory power under the Constitution or a royal prerogative with which to dismiss a government that had the confidence of the House of Representatives. The analysis demonstrates that responsible government under the Commonwealth Constitution is built on the unalienable right of a government to continue to govern while it has the confidence of the House of Representatives.

NOTES

1. Sir John Kerr, *Matters for Judgment* (Sun Books, 1988). The hardback edition was first published in 1978.

2. J.H. Kennan, "Sir John Did His Duty—Book Review" (1984) 14(4) *Melbourne University Law Review* 735.

3. G. Barwick, *Sir John Did His Duty* (Griffin Press, 1983).

4. Sir John Kerr, *Matters for Judgment* (Sun Books, 1988) p. 5.

5. Kerr's opinion that he held a prerogative power is supported by George Winterton: "Accordingly, the vesting of executive power in the Crown had the effect of bringing the appropriate prerogatives to the Crown in right of the Commonwealth." G. Winterton, *Parliament, The Executive and the Governor General A Constitutional Analysis* (Melbourne University Press, 1983) p. 31.

6. A.V. Dicey, *Introduction to the Study of the Law of the Constitution*, 3rd ed. (Macmillan, 1889) p. 342.

7. Official Record of the Debates of the Australasian Federal Convention, Adelaide (1897), 22 (Edmund Barton).

8. *House of Representatives Practice*, ed. J.A. Pettifer (Department of House of Representatives, 1981).

9. Ibid., 74.

10. Ibid.

11. Ibid., 75.

12. Ibid., 84.

13. G. Barwick, *Sir John Did His Duty* (Griffin Press, 1983) p. 104.

14. Official Record of the Debates of the Australasian Federal Convention, Adelaide (1897), 22 (Edmund Barton).

15. The express power to *affirm or reject* was included in the 1891 draft Bill: Official Record of the Debates of the Australasian Federal Convention, (1891), 953–4. It was also included in clause 53 of draft Bill of April 1897: Official Record of the Debates of the Australasian Federal Convention, Adelaide (1897), 480. It was still part of clause 55 during the second session: Official Record of the Debates of the Australasian Federal Convention, Sydney (1897), 481. The phrase "affirm or reject" appears to have been removed from the Constitution by the drafting committee of the Convention without debate after the conclusion of the second session.

16. John Kerr, *Matters for Judgment* (Macmillan, 1978).

17. Sir John Kerr, *Matters for Judgment* (Sun Books, 1988). All references in this essay are to the paperback edition.

18. Ibid., xviii.

19. Ibid., xxii.

20. Ibid., xxv.

21. Ibid., 209. Kerr cites extracts from E.A. Forsey, *The Royal Power of Dissolution of Parliament in the British Commonwealth* (Oxford University Press (Canada), 1968) and relates his personal contact with Forsey during the crisis and while writing his autobiography.

22. Ibid., 52, 83.

23. Ibid., 209–11.

24. H.V. Evatt, *The King and his Dominion Governors*, 2nd ed. (Frank Cass & Co, 1967). The complete text of this edition of Evatt's work is included in facsimile copy in *Evatt and Forsey on The Reserve Powers* (Legal Books, 1990), together with a facsimile copy of E.A. Forsey, *The Royal Power of Dissolution of Parliament in the British Commonwealth* (Oxford University Press, 1968). The page numbering and the content of each page are identical with the page numbering and content of each page in each original text. E.A. Forsey, *The Royal Power of Dissolution of Parliament in the British Commonwealth* (Oxford University Press, 1968).

25. E.A. Forsey, *The Royal Power of Dissolution of Parliament in the British Commonwealth* (Oxford University Press, 1968).

26. John Kerr, *Matters for Judgment* (Sun Books, 1988) p. 53.

27. A clear example of this style of disagreement is found in E.A. Forsey, *The Royal Power of Dissolution of Parliament in the British Commonwealth* (Oxford University Press, 1968) pp. 233–9.

28. John Kerr, *Matters for Judgment* (Sun Books, 1988) p. 7.

29. Ibid., 7.

30. Ibid. The idea of a Governor-General's reserve powers formed no part of the constitutional debates of the Founders during any of Constitutional Convention debates.

31. Ibid., 8. Forsey is identified as the source at p. 210.

32. Ibid., 213.

33. E.A. Forsey, *The Royal Power of Dissolution of Parliament in the British Commonwealth* (Oxford University Press, 1968) p. 270 n 1. Repeated in John Kerr, *Matters for Judgment* (Sun Books, 1988) p. 213.

34. Ibid., 7; repeated in John Kerr, *Matters for Judgment* (Sun Books, 1988) p. 215.

35. Commonwealth of Australia Constitution, s. 28. This is acknowledged in John Kerr, *Matters for Judgment* (Sun Books, 1988) p. 215.

36. Commonwealth of Australia Constitution, s. 68.

37. John Kerr, *Matters for Judgment* (Sun Books, 1988) p. 218.

38. Ibid., 221.

39. See Leo Strauss, Notes on Carl Schmitt, *The Concept of the Political*, J. Harvey Lomax trans.

40. Carl Schmitt, *The Concept of the Political*, trans. George Schwab (Chicago University Press, 1996) p. ix.

41. Carl Schmitt, *Political Theology: Four Chapters on the Concept of Sovereignty*, ed. & trans. George Schwab (University of Chicago Press, 2006).

42. Ibid., 5.

43. Ibid., 6.

44. Carl Schmitt, *Dictatorship*, trans. Michael Hoelzl and Graham Ward (Polity Press, 2014) p. 219 [Trans of: *Dictatorship: From the Beginning of the Modern Concept of Sovereignty to the Proletarian Class-Struggle*, first published 1922].

45. Tiago Melo Cartaxo, "Commanders-in-Chief Beyond the Border: Analysing the Powers of Heads of State in Northern American Federalism" (2017) 9(1) *Perspectives on Federalism* E99.

46. E. Forsey, *Freedom and Order* (Carleton University Press, 1974) p. 30.

47. John Kerr, *Matters for Judgment* (Sun Books, 1988) p. 222.

48. Carl Schmitt, *The Concept of the Political*, trans. George Schwab (University of Chicago Press, 2007), Introduction by J Cropsey, p. x.

49. Ibid., xx.

50. Sir John Kerr, *Matters for Judgment* (Sun Books, 1988) p. 221.

51. Ibid., 222; emphasis in original.

52. H.V. Evatt, *The King and his Dominion Governors*, 2nd ed. (Frank Cass & Co., 1967) pp. 240–8.

53. Ibid., 240.

54. Ibid., 242.

55. Ibid.

56. Ibid., 243.

57. Thomas Erskine May, *Constitutional History of England Vol. 1*, 6th ed. (Longman Green, 1878) p. 16.

58. James Madison explains that such a government is actually republican: James Madison, *The Federalist Papers, No. 10*, ed. Clinton Rossiter (New American Library, 1961) p. 81: "A republic, by which I mean a government in which the scheme of representation takes place." To be a true democracy, each of the adult persons would have to participate in the deliberations and choosing.

59. H.V. Evatt, *The King and his Dominion Governors*, 2nd ed. (Frank Cass & Co., 1967) p. 3.

60. Ibid., 12.

61. Ibid., 78, point (ii).

62. Ibid., 80.

63. J.E. Parsons Jr, "Halifax: The Complete Trimmer Revisited" (1978) 7(3) *Interpretation* 80. It was originally associated with republican politics.

64. H.V. Evatt, *The King and His Dominion Governors*, 2nd ed. (Frank Cass & Co., 1967) Ch. 5.

65. HV Evatt, "The Discretionary Authority of Dominion Governors" (1940) XVIII (1) *The Canadian Bar Review* 1.

66. Ibid., 5.

67. Ibid., 5.

68. Ibid.

69. H.V. Evatt, *The King and his Dominion Governors*, 2nd ed. (Frank Cass & Co., 1967) p. 45.

70. Sir John Kerr, *Matters for Judgment* (Sun Books, 1988) pp. 135–7.

71. Ibid., 136.

72. Ibid.

73. H.V. Evatt, *The King and his Dominion Governors*, 2nd ed. (Frank Cass & Co., 1967), Introduction to 2nd edition by Zelman Cowen, p. xxv.

74. Ibid.

75. Sir John Kerr, *Matters for Judgment* (Sun Books, 1988) p. 138. Being oral, no record exists of what was advised.

76. Ibid.

77. Sir Robert G. Menzies QC., Documents Relating to the Simultaneous Dissolution of the Senate and the House of Representatives by His Excellency the Governor-General on March 19, 1951, p. 4 (4).

78. H.V. Evatt, *The King and his Dominion Governors*, 2nd ed. (Frank Cass & Co., 1967), Introduction to 2nd edition by Zelman Cowen, p. xxvi.

79. Ibid., 45.

80. Evatt has one example: that of Governor-General Ferguson.

81. H.V. Evatt, *The King and his Dominion Governors*, 2nd ed. (Frank Cass & Co., 1967) p. 286.

82. Sir John Kerr, *Matters for Judgment* (Sun Books, 1988) p. 58.

83. H.V. Evatt, *The King and his Dominion Governors*, 2nd ed. (Frank Cass & Co., 1967) p. 286; it is important to note that Evatt wholeheartedly believes that the reserve powers exist, but when he lists them he equivocates in respect of each of

them—either "not certain to what extent and under what conditions" or "not precisely ascertained" or "also undefined" or "cannot be precisely stated."

84. Ibid., 115–6 (emphasis in original). Evatt's conclusion, taken literally and in respect of personal discretions, means nothing more than that the king (or governor) can do no wrong. Evatt's legal solution would see a constitutional monarchy returned to the eighteenth century.

85. Kerr cites the above passage from Evatt with approval in *Matters for Judgment* (Sun Books, 1988) p. 59.

86. As this book includes references to the writings of jurists who have spoken ex-curial at certain times and curial at others, the inclusion of an honorific to distinguish the one and the exclusion of the honorific to reflect the other caused sections of the work to lack that clarity of style which a reliance on the context alone could have provided. Accordingly, after an initial identification of the person by his or her honorific, I have usually (but not always) chosen to dispense with the inclusion of the honorific to which the writer was entitled and have relied on context to permit the reader to correctly identify the person concerned.

87. Sir Zelman Cowen, "The Crown and Its Representative in the Commonwealth" (1985) *Australian International Law News* 584, 596.

88. Ibid., 598.

89. H.V. Evatt, *The King and His Dominion Governors*, 2nd ed. (Frank Cass, 1967) Chapters IV, XIV, XV, XIX.

90. Ibid., Chapters VII, VIII, IX,

91. Ibid., 50.

92. Ibid., 154–6.

93. R.W. Staveley, "The Conventions of the Constitution: Kerr's Folly" (1976) 11(1) *Australian Journal of Political Science* 16, 17.

94. Sir John Kerr, *Matters for Judgment* (Sun Books, 1988) pp. 215, 218.

95. H.V. Evatt, *The King and his Dominion Governors*, 2nd ed. (Frank Cass & Co., 1967) p. 286.

96. Commonwealth of Australia Constitution, s. 61.

97. Sir John Kerr, *Matters for Judgment* (Sun Books, 1988) p. 323.

98. Ibid.

99. Ibid.

100. Ibid., 330. He does not cite any authority from the Conventions—or indeed from anyone else—to this end, and this is completely contradicted by Barwick.

101. Sir John Kerr, *Matters for Judgment* (Sun Books, 1988) p. 58.

102. Ibid., 334–5.

103. Ibid., 335.

104. Ibid., 359–64.

105. Ibid., 360.

106. Ibid., 362.

107. Ibid., 361. While Kerr is correct for the House of Lords as a result of the *Parliament Act*, the constitutional crisis in 1909 was caused by the House of Lords rejecting Lloyd George's budget and King Edward VII refusing to take the advice of his ministers while siding with the House of Lords. Barton, relying on May, thought

the House of Lords had that power. The government, the British people and King George V thought it did not.

108. Ibid., 361.

109. Ibid., 362.

110. Ibid., 363.

111. There have been two significant periods of government shutdown in the United States when supply Bills were not passed by the Congress. The first was in 1995 during the Clinton Presidency and the second in 2019 during the Trump Presidency. On each occasion, federal employees received no pay and either worked without pay or remained at home.

112. R.W. Staveley, "The Conventions of the Constitution: Kerr's Folly" (1976) 11(1) *Australian Journal of Political Science* 16. Staveley's argument would tie the conventions of the Commonwealth Constitution more closely to that of Westminster. This Senatorial convention appears, I submit, to have been a practical attempt by the political parties to alter the Senate's powers in light of the chamber's parochial purpose being overborne by party loyalties.

113. Sir John Kerr, *Matters for Judgment* (Sun Books, 1988) p. 363.

114. Ibid., 363. Had Kerr read the Convention debates, he would have known that the Constitution was drafted to give effect, where necessary, to the convention of responsible government. The colonies had engaged in responsible government since Westminster had granted them the status of self-government. It was this familiarity with responsible government that was the tipping point for the delegates when considering the US presidential style.

115. Sir John Kerr, *Matters for Judgment* (Sun Books, 1988) p. 55.

116. Stanley Bach, *Platypus and Parliament: The Australian Senate in Theory and Practice* (Department of the Senate, 2003) p. 85. There is a more complete discussion of this in the section of this chapter that deals with Barwick's defense.

117. R.W. Staveley, "The Conventions of the Constitution: Kerr's Folly" (1976) 11(1) *Australian Journal of Political Science* 16, 17.

118. Ibid., 17.

119. This was thought to be the case in the United Kingdom until 1909, when the Lords breached the convention.

120. Sir John Kerr, *Matters for Judgment* (Sun Books, 1988) p. 362.

121. Official Record of the Debates of the Australasian Federal Convention, Melbourne (1898), 2146–7 (William McMillan).

122. Official Record of the Debates of the Australasian Federal Convention, Melbourne (1898), 2165 (William Trenwith).

123. Sir John Kerr, *Matters for Judgment* (Sun Books, 1988) p. 363.

124. Ibid. See Commonwealth of Australia Constitution, s. 114.

125. Sir John Kerr, *Matters for Judgment* (Sun Books, 1988) p. 363. He had previously referred to it (p. 314) as "the power to refuse or refrain from granting supply."

126. Ibid., 355.

127. Ibid., 363.

128. Ibid., 323.

129. Ibid.

130. Ibid., 332.

131. Ibid. If by the "Queen's powers" Kerr means power personal to the monarch of the United Kingdom being in possession of the Governor-General, he has actually reversed the meaning of s. 61, which vests the executive powers of the Commonwealth in the Queen.

132. Ibid. While Myers's advice is not annexed to Kerr's work, it can safely be assumed that an advice by the solicitor general to a prime minister would not reference the existence of a *power of dismissing Ministers under section 64*, which is an interpolation that Kerr adds to advantage his own argument.

133. Ibid., 322. As shown in chapter 2, Kerr's interpretation of the executive power finds no support in the Constitutional Convention. As Barton explained to George Reid, there is no prerogative in the Constitution that is personal to the Governor-General. The Governor-General acts on the advice of either the Federal Executive Council, or on the advice of a minister, and thus holds no discretionary power.

134. Ibid., 322; emphasis added.

135. Ibid., 323.

136. Ibid.

137. Ibid., 322.

138. Ibid., 332, emphasis added.

139. *Shorter Oxford English Dictionary*, 3rd ed. (Oxford University Press, 1964) p. 497 (2).

140. Sir John Kerr, *Matters for Judgment* (Sun Books, 1988) p. 332, emphasis added. Kerr implicitly agrees that he is a viceroy, which is a contraction of Vice-Royal. G.J. McCarry, citing *Bonanza Creek Goldmining Co Ltd v Rex* (1879) 5 App. Cas. 102 in "Reflections on Control of Governor-General's Powers" (1978) 13(3) *Western Australian Law Review* 327, argues that the Governor-General "was not held to be in the same position as a Viceroy."

141. Thomas Erskine, *Constitutional History of England Vol. 1*, 6th ed. (Longman Green, 1878) p. 114.

142. A. Todd, *Parliamentary Government in England Vol. 1*, 2nd ed. (Longmans, Green & Co, 1892) p. 265.

143. Ibid., 80.

144. Ibid., 158.

145. H.V. Evatt, *The King and his Dominion Governors*, 2nd ed. (Frank Cass & Co, 1967) p. 33.

146. Sir John Kerr, *Matters for Judgment* (Sun Books, 1988) p. 332. Kerr claims also to have an advice by Maurice Byers, the Crown Solicitor General, to the effect "that the Queen's powers have been handed over to the Governor-General by the Constitution." Since he does not provide access to that advice by direct quote with its context, and does not explain what powers were held by Queen Elizabeth II, little can be said except that Kerr's understanding of the advice directly contradicts the plain meaning of section 61 when that is construed as intended by the Founders as well as the notion that Queen Victoria in 1901 (the date of federation) held personal prerogative powers, a notion denied by Prime Minister Gladstone.

147. Commonwealth of Australia Constitution, s. 64 (paras 1 & 2).

148. Sir John Kerr, *Matters for Judgment* (Sun Books, 1988) p. 214.

149. Ibid., 243, emphasis added.

150. Ibid., 213, emphasis added. Forsey argues from the hypothetical existence of a monarch's personal prerogative to justify the actions of a governor in a self-governing province with a unitary Constitution.

151. Ibid., 305.

152. Ibid., 366.

153. Ibid., 367. The significance of Kerr demanding an undertaking from Fraser, which Fraser willingly gave, will be discussed later for it ignores a warning inherent in an historical precedent.

154. Ibid., 371.

155. Ibid., 372–3.

156. Thomas Erskine May, *Constitutional History of England Vol. 1* (Longman, 1861) pp. 87–8.

157. Ibid., 90.

158. Ibid.

159. House of Commons, Hansard, 9 April 1807, columns 285–6; repeated in Thomas Erskine May, *Constitutional History of England Vol. 1* (Longman, 1861) p. 96.

160. Thomas Erskine May, *Constitutional History of England Vol. 1* (Longman, 1861) pp. 90–1.

161. Sir John Kerr, *Matters for Judgment* (Sun Books, 1988) p. 337.

162. See below references to the statements by William Gladstone in respect of Britain.

163. Sir John Kerr, *Matters for Judgment* (Sun Books, 1988) pp. 326–7.

164. Kerr, however, could not be held responsible in this way. While Whitlam apparently refused to call an election for the simple reason that his government's popularity in the opinion polls had severely declined and he was likely to lose, it is also open to argument that the Opposition some eighteen months earlier used the same tactic, obstructing the government's legislation in the Senate in the hope of forcing him again to an election.

165. Garfield Barwick, *Sir John Did His Duty* (Griffin Press, 1983).

166. Ibid., 99.

167. Ibid., 107. Winterton describes the reserve powers as being constitutional in nature even if he is not sure of their existence: "The specifically conferred executive powers in respect of which the Governor-General has, *or may have*, power to act without or contrary to ministerial advice—in other words, a reserve power." He then cites specific provisions of the Constitution, ss. 64, 5, & 57. George Winterton, *Parliament, The Executive and the Governor General A Constitutional Analysis* (Melbourne University Press, 1983) p. 150; emphasis added.

168. J.H. Kennan, the Victorian Attorney-General in 1984, described this aspect of Barwick's argument as "black letter law": J.H. Kennan, "Book Review, *Sir John Did His Duty*" (1984) 14(4) *Melbourne University Law Review* 736. While he declined to argue about the Senate's power to refuse supply or the Governor-General's power to dismiss a prime minister (at 736), he thought Kerr acted prematurely and might have waited to see if the two chambers could work out their differences before he acted;

which solution accepts that Kerr did have the powers he exercised. In some respects, this solution mirrors Barton's view expressed in chapter 2.

169. Garfield Barwick, *Sir John Did His Duty* (Griffin Press, 1983) p. 107. The "parliamentary provision" to which he refers appears to be that of the Constitution as a legislative act of the Westminster Parliament.

170. Ibid., 6.

171. Ibid.

172. This supports the view of J.H. Kennan, who described this aspect of Barwick's argument as "black letter law": J.H. Kennan, "Book Review, *Sir John Did His Duty*" (1984) 14(4) *Melbourne University Law Review* 736.

173. Garfield Barwick, *Sir John Did His Duty* (Griffin Press, 1983) pp. 6–7, emphasis added.

174. Commonwealth of Australia Constitution, s. 62.

175. Garfield Barwick, *Sir John Did His Duty* (Griffin Press, 1983) p. 7, emphasis added. His emphatic "mostly" suggests that a power to appoint executive councillors exists in a section other than section 64. That constitutes a gross misreading of section 62 of the Constitution.

176. Ibid. His reference to the FEC consisting "mostly of Ministers" implies a separate power to appoint executive councillors in section 62.

177. Ibid., 6.

178. Ibid., 7.

179. Commonwealth of Australia Constitution, s. 64.

180. Ibid.

181. Garfield Barwick, *Sir John Did His Duty* (Griffin Press, 1983) p. 6.

182. Ibid., 8.

183. Ibid., 100.

184. Ibid., 7.

185. Ibid., 1.

186. Ibid., 28.

187. Ibid., 2.

188. Ibid.

189. Ibid., 2.

190. Ibid.

191. Ibid., 17.

192. Ibid., 16. He will refer to "parliamentary control" and "control by the parliament" of supply a total of ten times, at pp. 18, 21, 25, 45, 106, and 106; and at pp. 16, 24, 26, and 104, respectively.

193. Ibid., 15.

194. Ibid., 29. The reasons given by the Opposition senators for demanding that Whitlam resign or call an election also formed part of the resolution, but were partisan and immaterial to this essay.

195. Ibid., 28, 29, 33, 41, 45, 46, 57, 79.

196. Ibid., 28, emphasis added.

197. Ibid., 33.

198. Ibid., 35.

199. Ibid., 32.

200. Commonwealth of Australia Constitution, s. 1.

201. Garfield Barwick, *Sir John Did His Duty* (Griffin Press, 1983) p. 37.

202. Ibid., 38.

203. Commonwealth of Australia Constitution, s. 53. Quite obviously, the section denies the Senate equal power with the House.

204. Garfield Barwick, *Sir John Did His Duty* (Griffin Press, 1983) p. 38, emphasis added.

205. Ibid., emphasis added.

206. Ibid., 31, emphasis added.

207. Ibid., 42. The convention requires the rejection of supply, but the convention is not a legal requirement.

208. This is implicit in Barton's explanation at Official Record of the Debates of the Australasian Federal Convention, Adelaide (1897), 576 (Edmund Barton).

209. See section 53(1) of the Bill at Official Record of the Debates of the Australasian Federal Convention, Adelaide (1897), 440.

210. P.A. Gerangelos, "Interpretational Methodology in Separation of Powers Jurisprudence: The Formalist/Functionalist Debate," in Peter Gerangelos, Simon Evans, Sarah Murray, Patrick Emerton and Adrienne Stone (eds), *Winterton's Australian Federal Constitutional Law, Commentary and Materials* (Law Book Co, 2017) pp. 35, 43.

211. Australian Senate Standing Orders no. 114.

212. Commonwealth of Australia Constitution, s. 50(ii).

213. Garfield Barwick, *Sir John Did His Duty* (Griffin Press, 1983) p. 111.

214. Ibid., 14. Barwick does not acknowledge Isaacs's authority anywhere in *Sir John Does His Duty*; however, his preferred methodology, as shown in chapter 5, is Isaacs's literalism. Since it is Barwick's whole case that it was constitutionally obligatory for Whitlam to comply with a convention, to resign or go to the people once supply failed to pass, his statement shows the impossibility of excluding the scheme of the Constitution from a construction of the text.

215. Ibid., 14.

216. Ibid., 44.

217. This is not dissimilar to Isaacs's real reasons for excluding US Supreme Court decisions in the *Engineers' case* in order to prevent their unwanted implications for the political scheme he intended to craft from the Commonwealth Constitution.

218. Garfield Barwick, *Sir John Did His Duty* (Griffin Press, 1983) p. 14.

219. Ibid., 15. This implies nothing less than that the Constitution was drafted by men with the Westminster conventions in mind. The Westminster tradition, by definition, operated in "other systems," for example, the unitary colonial constitutions established by the Imperial Parliament and the Imperial Parliament itself.

220. Ibid., 15.

221. Ibid.

222. Ibid.

223. Ibid., 19.

224. Ibid., 28.

225. Ibid., 16.
226. Ibid., 35.
227. Ibid., 36.
228. Ibid., 55.
229. Ibid.
230. J.H. Kennan, "Book Review, *Sir John Did His Duty*" (1984) 14(4) *Melbourne University Law Review* 736, characterizes Barwick's statement that there could be no convention, as an assertion that wherever a power exists there cannot be a convention against its use. He describes Barwick's argument as "A novel concept . . . admirably argued."
231. Garfield Barwick, *Sir John Did His Duty* (Griffin Press, 1983) p. 41.
232. Ibid., 41, emphasis added.
233. Ibid., 19.
234. Stanley Bach, Platypus and Parliament: The Australian Senate in Theory and Practice (Department of the Senate, 2003) p. 85.
235. Ibid.
236. A.V. Dicey, *Introduction to the Study of the Law of the Constitution*, 3rd ed. (Macmillan, 1889) p. 342.
237. Commonwealth of Australia Constitution, ss. 62 and 64.
238. Commonwealth of Australia Constitution, s. 62, emphasis added.
239. Garfield Barwick, *Sir John Did His Duty* (Griffin Press, 1983) p. 106.
240. Ibid.
241. Kerr seemed to accept this principle when he accepted Whitlam's advice to sack Cameron and Cairns: John Kerr, *Matters for Judgment* (Sun Books, 1988) p. 243.
242. Garfield Barwick, *Sir John Did His Duty* (Griffin Press, 1983) p. 102. As demonstrated in chapter 2, that theory passed into history during the reign of Queen Victoria, who never acted without the antecedent advice of her ministers.
243. A. Todd, *Parliamentary Government in England Vol. 1* (Sampson Low, Marston & Co, 1887) p. 112 n 3. This is cited in H.V. Evatt, *The King and His Dominion Governors*, 2nd ed. (Frank Cass & Co, 1967) p. 33.
244. Ibid., 112.
245. Garfield Barwick, *Sir John Did His Duty* (Griffin Press, 1983) p. 104, emphasis added.
246. It is probable that Lord Melbourne was the source of this prudent change of practice. He is credited with having "imparted to her much of his wisdom on men and affairs." W.S.C. Churchill, *The History of the English Speaking Peoples Vol. 4*, 4th ed. (Cassell, 1967) p. 45.
247. *The Works of Sir Walter Bagehot Vol. IV*, ed. Forrest Morgan (Travellers Insurance Company, 1891) p. 112.
248. Barwick accepts this view in *Sir John Did His Duty* (Griffin Press, 1983) p. 107.
249. Thomas Erskine May, *Constitutional History of England Vol. 1* (Longman, 1861) pp. 90–1.
250. Commonwealth of Australia Constitution, s. 61.
251. Ibid., s. 2.

252. Official Record of the Debates of the Australasian Federal Convention, Adelaide (1897), 913 (Edmund Barton).

253. Garfield Barwick, *Sir John Did His Duty* (Griffin Press, 1983) p. 116.

254. Ibid. The powers are described as statutory because he has characterized the Constitution as an Imperial statute.

255. Commonwealth of Australia Constitution, s. 62.

256. Commonwealth of Australia Constitution, s. 64.

257. Garfield Barwick, *Sir John Did His Duty* (Griffin Press, 1983) p. 7.

258. Ibid.

259. Ibid., 104, emphasis added. However, given Barwick's theory of responsible government, there is no compulsion.

260. Ibid., 103; emphasis added.

261. Garfield Barwick, *Sir John Did His Duty* (Griffin Press, 1983) p. 83.

262. Ibid., 83.

263. Ibid., 101.

264. Ibid., 101.

265. Ibid., 106–7.

266. Garfield Barwick, *Sir John Did His Duty* (Griffin Press, 1983) p. 83.

267. Ibid., 114.

268. Ibid., 99. This view has been taken up by most if not all academic commentators, who still refer to the Governor-General's reserve powers, but now define them as constitutional powers held in reserve.

269. Ibid., 116; this is a mere assertion.

270. Ibid., 116.

271. Ibid., 101. He ignores the literal fact that no powers are vested by the Constitution in the Governor-General. To understand Barwick's truncated explanation, it must be recalled that in section 61 of the Constitution, the executive power is vested in the Queen, and is exercisable by the Governor-General, but it seems that the power to appoint ministers is not an executive power but rather one personal to the Governor-General to be exercised according to the monarch's discretion.

272. Ibid., 102.

273. Ibid. This matter has been dealt with previously in this essay. This rule was evident in the period leading up to the reign of Queen Victoria, but it is of no constitutional worth given that, during her reign, ministerial responsibility passed from the monarch to the people's representatives in the Parliament.

274. Commonwealth of Australia Constitution, s. 58, emphasis added.

275. According to James A. Thomson, Barwick's argument combined "dogmatism, errors and misleading propositions": James A. Thomson, "Book Review: *Sir John Did His Duty*" (1983) 6(2) *University of New South Wales Law Journal* 255.

276. Edmund Barton graduated from the University of Sydney with a Bachelor of Arts in classics in 1868 and a Master of Arts (by examination) in 1870. He was admitted to the New South Wales Bar in 1871 and was appointed Queen's Counsel in 1889. During the 1891 Constitutional Convention, he had assisted Sir Samuel Griffith in drafting the draft bill that resulted from that Convention.

277. Official Record of the Debates of the Australasian Federal Convention, Adelaide (1897), 910 (Edmund Barton).

278. *Official Record of the Debates of the Australasian Federal Convention*, Adelaide, (1897), 910 (Edmund Barton). Reid was not asking for the words "With the advice of the Governor in Council" to be inserted; rather, he wanted "with the advice of Executive Council." However, it is obvious from Barton's *ex tempore* reply that he was addressing Reid's request.

279. Official Record of the Debates of the Australasian Federal Convention, Adelaide (1897), 910–1 (Edmund Barton).

280. Official Record of the Debates of the Australasian Federal Convention, Adelaide (1897), 910–1 (Edmund Barton).

281. Thomas Erskine May, *Constitutional History of England Vol. 1*, 6th ed. (Longman Green, 1878) p. 163.

282. A. Todd, *Parliamentary Government in England Vol. 1* (Sampson Low, Marston & Co, 1887) p. 384.

283. Official Record of the Debates of the Australasian Federal Convention, Adelaide (1897), 914–5 (Joseph Carruthers). Almost half of the fifty delegates to the Convention were lawyers of which eleven were either Queens Counsel or Privy Councillors.

284. The demand by the American revolutionaries that they not be taxed without their consent is a declared grievance in the Declaration of Independence. However, it can be traced back to John Locke's *Two Treatises of Government* (Cambridge University Press, 1960) p. 408 §140. The chant of "no taxation without representation" was a common call demanding reform of the English Constitution.

285. George Winterton, Parliament, *The Executive and the Governor General A Constitutional Analysis* (Melbourne University Press, 1983) p. 16.

286. Ibid.

287. George Winterton, *Parliament, The Executive and the Governor General: A Constitutional Analysis* (Melbourne University Press, 1983) p. 150.

288. Ibid.

Chapter 7

Afterword

RIGHT OF REVOLUTION

One political myth that must be dispelled is the argument that Kerr's dismissal of the Whitlam government, which proved popular at the subsequent election, was an exercise of the people's right of revolution. The right of a people to use force to change a tyrannical government was described originally by John Locke in his *Second Treatise of Government.*[1] English political leaders exercised that right in 1688 when their Glorious Revolution forced King James II's abdication and, via the Bill of Rights, introduced a new British Constitution.

On July 4, 1776, the American War of Independence commenced with a declaration of the natural right of a people to alter or abolish a tyrannical government and to institute a new form according to such principles as it will best provide for their safety and happiness. With their independence, the American people consented to a Constitution that combined a federal division of powers, democratic representation,[2] and regular elections among the means that could best achieve their safety and happiness.

When the Australian people ratified their Constitution in 1899, it too included a federal division of powers, democratic representation, and regular elections. The democratic principles of the Australian Constitution are inconsistent with Kerr's dismissal of the Whitlam government as an exercise of a natural right. The safety and happiness of the Australian people were already secured by a Constitution to which they had consented, one that mandated elections be held at least every three years. Kerr's dismissal of the Whitlam government in 1975 cannot masquerade as an exercise of the people's right to change the form of government for the term of that government had not then expired and the Senate's denial of supply, while constitutional, had no power under the conventions of responsible government to achieve the removal of Whitlam. Kerr's unilateral action was a usurpation of a power entrusted to elected members of the House of Representatives. The electoral success of the opposition parties that followed altered the people in government, but did not and was never intended to alter the scheme of government.

CONCLUSION

The two constitutional crises and their causes with which this book has been concerned were the result of the adoption by Australian jurists of the English *scientific* theory of legal positivism for interpreting the Constitution. The practical face of that science as explained previously is a literal construction although though it is sometimes combined with other refinements. While there are some more recent variants, literal constructions, ones that do not seek to discover an understanding consistent with that of the Founders, have been the methodology of choice of Australia's High Court since 1920. The essential claim of legal positivism, as for all modern science, is that it provides true or scientific knowledge about the text of any law. Paradoxically, the major concern of the people who are subject to the law, a concern of which the High Court has nothing to say, is whether the law is fair or just. Where the law is a constitution, the knowledge relied on by the Court is obtained by interpreting the text without regard to the implicit political scheme or theory that the text was intended by its framers, to represent. This is important. As this book has shown, the Court's interpretation of the Constitution's text can change the political scheme and therewith change how the Constitution affects the citizen. Whether the change to the scheme effected by the Court was fair or just, contributing to the common good, the chief concern of the Australian people, is of no concern to the Court.

As the scheme of the Constitution was decided at the Convention and the text drafted to represent that scheme, we are obliged to ask: what was the purpose of the Constitutional Convention and what use the labors of delegates that resulted in the text, when the construction methodology of the Court precludes it from considering what the founding fathers intended for the section?[3] What use the knowledge of the people who ratified it, if the meaning to which the people consented can be dismissed as subjective and a new meaning interpreted from the same words by a technical belief in a science? The contrived technicality of legal positive interpretations needs to be contrasted with the knowledge of those who framed the Constitution. Prudent deliberations based on available political knowledge, over a century of American experience of their federal regime and the delegates own experience of responsible government guided the Convention to devise a practical scheme of government for the Australian nation that united a federal division of powers with executive power responsible to the democratically elected members of the House of Representatives.[4]

In order to ensure that the Constitution expressed how the Australian people desired to live together, the five colonial governments insisted that they agree with its substance. It was from their act of consenting to the Constitution that the independence of the Australian people from the Imperial Parliament can be inferred. If ratification of the Constitution was an expression of that independence, section 128 of the Constitution was an expression of their sovereignty, their sovereign control of the future terms of their Constitution. The English philosopher, Thomas Hobbes[5] thought legal sovereignty was a sign of political power and authority. The American Declaration of Independence, however, and the war that followed showed that legal sovereignty only arises after political independence has been secured.

When chapter 3 and the cases decided by the early High Court is viewed in the light of the Convention debates related in chapter 2, they show how the early Court sought a meaning of the text that was consistent with the Founders' understanding of the scheme they framed. Thus, the early Court acknowledged the people's authority to control the meaning of the Constitution that they made permanent by ratification subject to section 128 alterations. As chapter 2 relates, the Convention was particularly careful to ensure that the executive power was responsible to the House of Representatives, even going so far as to insist that the relevant constitutional provisions ensure the Governor-General held no personal discretionary power, either prerogative or statutory, let alone one with which to dismiss a government. The Convention debates provide a complete rebuttal of the arguments that sought to justify the constitutionality of the 1975 dismissal.

In one of the very first cases heard by the High Court of Australia,[6] an English rule of construction was adopted that precluded the court's reference to the Convention debates. With that decision as a precedent, the political scheme of Constitution and the wisdom of the men who framed it was quarantined from access by future courts. Had those debates and the significance of the democratic principle of the *consent of the governed* been elements of academic instruction for prospective lawyers, neither the *Engineers' case* nor the dismissal would have been possible. It seems unimaginable that a Court, unsure of the meaning of a text, would not consult its author or authors. Yet that quarantine was the effect of the jurist's acceptance of what was a speculative scientific theory that promised a predictive science of law while refusing to acknowledge the objective fact of the opinions of those who drafted the Constitution.

Theoretically, the positive science of jurisprudence is unable to differentiate between a written Constitution and an ordinary law. While an ordinary law is generally replete with all the necessary detail for comprehension, implementation, and application, the inherent difficulty of interpreting a Constitution was alluded to by Chief Justice Marshall:

> A Constitution, to contain an accurate detail of all the subdivisions of which its great powers will admit, and of all the means by which they may be carried into execution, would partake of the prolixity of a legal code, and could scarcely be embraced by the human mind. . . . Its nature, therefore, requires that only its great outlines should be marked, its important objects designated, and the minor ingredients which compose those objects be deduced from the nature of the objects themselves.[7]

By quarantining the Constitution from the Founders' deliberations, legal positivism forces a jurist to manufacture Marshall's subdivisions of powers, the means of execution, and the minor ingredients for him or herself. When speaking of the separation of powers in the US Constitution, Alexander Hamilton thought that "the judiciary, from the nature of its functions, will always be the least dangerous to the political rights of the Constitution."[8] He reckoned without the deductive (quasi-mathematical?) charm of legal positivism. As chapters 2 and 4 demonstrated, Isaacs's analysis in the *Engineers' case* was nothing more than his arguments for a unitary political scheme, either like the British or the Canadian, that he had urged upon the Constitutional Convention and which the Convention had rejected. That he was prepared to deny the effect of the ratification by the people puts a lie to his professed support for a democracy. His demand for a literal construction of the Constitution secured the basis of his judgment and is still the binding precedent for High Court interpretation. When the Founders entrusted the protection of the Constitution to an independent judicature, they did not anticipate that the guardians would be seduced by a promise of scientific jurisprudence that has corrupted the guardianship hoped for in *Marbury v Madison*.[9]

It might be argued that the Commonwealth of Australia has successfully survived its two constitutional crises—after all, it continues to be a liberal democracy. Such a view mistakes the constitutional form for its substance. Australia was never intended, either by the people or by the delegates, to be a pure democracy and the political science that opposes a pure democracy were stated clearly by James Madison. The long-term effect of the *Engineers' case*, however, has been the gradual centralization of almost all legislative authority in the federal parliament, a process only made possible by the High Court's interpretations of the Constitution. It cannot be said, however, that the events of 1975 have led to changes in the way that responsible government is practiced in Australia. The effect of the legal opinions provided by both Kerr and Barwick in relation to the law of the dismissal has been more prospective in nature, providing for a future potentiality. The opinions of both men have led to the general acceptance by jurists and others on all sides of the political divide of their mistaken interpretations that vests reserve powers in the office of Governor-General, a constitutional interpretation that is at odds with both responsible government and the idea of a constitutional monarchy.[10] The legal opinions analyzed in chapter 6 justified a negation of responsible government and established a precedent for future vice-regal interference in the Commonwealth government whenever the Governor-General identifies an out-of-the-ordinary circumstances. Neither the circumstance nor the exercise of the reserve power are capable of being reviewed by the High Court; they are nonjusticiable. It should be of some concern among those who defend responsible government that the existence of the reserve powers has cast a dim light over the link between the Commonwealth Constitution and the monarchy.

The most visible effect of that dim light has been a renewed agitation for the removal of the monarch and the Governor-General from the Constitution and their replacement by a President, a scheme that is promoted as converting Australia into a "republic."[11] As if to add insult to the injury, the same people suggest that the Governor-General's "reserve powers" be codified in the Constitution for the use of the President in "out of the ordinary" circumstances and reserving to the High Court the unenviable task of determining if circumstances are out-of-the-ordinary enough. That scheme would replace the constitutional monarchy, what is in effect a republic, with the rule by the President. These "republicans" seem unaware that the Constitution would then contain two contradictory and incompatible sources of executive power, which would render the Constitution and responsible government irrelevant.

None of that, however, would be necessary if juristic attention would focus on the Convention debates where Edmund Barton explained that the Constitution denies the Governor-General any executive powers. Barton's linking of democratic representation to responsible government as practiced before the existence of reserve powers showed clearly why the dismissal was unconstitutional. The regime proposed by republican activists would not be republican; it would be despotic.

It would be a mistake to assume that Australian constitutional crises are not relevant to the United States of America. By giving their consent to their Constitution and reserving its amendment to their elected representatives, the American people implicitly placed their Supreme Court as guardians of the Constitution under the same moral obligation to defend the meaning to which the people consented, that is, the meaning intended by the founding fathers. In that context, the rights guaranteed by the Constitution were understood by the founding fathers as natural rights that were applicable to all people at all times. As a result, a construction of as if they were only positive rights and not natural can enlarge a right beyond its natural limit or restrict it to favor the few with arbitrary qualifications at the discretion of the judge.

American constitutional law came under the influence of a novel theory of sociological realism jurisprudence, one that was modeled on August Comte's science of social physics.[12] Comte invented the word, sociology, to designate his science of social physics. Roscoe Pound's theory of sociological realism extended Comte's positivist sociology[13] in the field of jurisprudence. Although Pound repeats Ahrens's contrast between morals and law approvingly: "In the case of morals our deductions give us a subjective science while in law they give us an objective science";[14] it was, as shown previously, only after Comte's death that the sociologist Georg Simmel explained that all evaluations (values) were subjective, a discovery that rendered all science subjective. Comte had assumed morals to be a valid field of scientific knowledge[15] and the subjective nature of value judgments was a concept unknown to Pound when he originated sociological realism, for he assumes, like Comte, that the positive science of sociology can objectively know values. That assumption is fatal to his science for if values are subjective, then all knowledge of them is subjective and all values are relative to the individual. If all values are relative, no particular value is choice-worthy for its own sake.

The Australian legal crises outlined in these pages have demonstrated the ease with which the political scheme of a Constitution can be altered by jurists who interpret the words of the text without regard to its scheme; it has shown also that the theory or scheme can be manipulated to reflect the jurist's personal wishes. In two major analytical works, the late Harry Jaffa revealed, through his direct correspondence with leading American jurists, that the influence of legal positivism on their understanding of the US Constitution was largely unnoticed.[16] The analysis of this book has revealed a similar state of affairs with Australian High Court jurists for whom the promise of a determinate scientific theory and stare decisis have triumphed over any prudent reconsideration of exactly what the *Engineers' case* replaced. Like the American jurists, the Australian who followed *Engineers'* were unaware or unconcerned that the changes to the scheme that their constructions rendered breached the political scheme for which the Constitution was founded. The danger to political life where political principles can be so readily set aside as a result of a value-free dogma should be self-evident despite the attraction of the simple deductive logic that positivism promised. This was the danger to which Griffith CJ referred when he warned that interpretations by

> an "astral intelligence," unprejudiced by any historical knowledge, and interpreting a Constitution merely by the aid of a dictionary, might arrive at a very different conclusion as to its meaning from that which a person familiar with history would reach.[17]

Griffith's "history" in these days means only the records of our respective Constitutional Conventions in which the arguments for the political scheme can be found.

NOTES

1. John Locke, *Two Treatises of Civil Government* (Cambridge University Press, 1960) p. 460 §222–6.

2. As mentioned previously, James Madison defined a republic as a government by representation: (*Federalist 10*). The importance of representation in contrast with a pure democracy was explained in his speech to the Virginian Ratifying Convention, June 20, 1788: "I go on this great republican principle, that the people will have virtue and intelligence to select men of virtue and wisdom."

3. *Cole v Whitfield* (1988) 165 CLR 360 at 385.

4. Democratically elected, but not a democratic chamber; see *The Federalist Papers, No. 10*, ed. Clinton Rossiter (New American Library, 1961) p. 81.

5. Thomas Hobbes, *Leviathan*, ed. M. Oakeshott (Blackwell, 1946) chapter 18.

6. *Sydney Municipal Council v Commonwealth* (1904) 1 CLR 208 at 213. While only Barton and O'Connor were delegates to the Convention, Griffith (at the time the Queensland Chief Justice) had been in contact with the leading group of delegates and provided legal advice on drafts of the Constitution.

7. *McCulloch v. Maryland*, 17 U.S. 4 Wheat. 316 407 (1819).

8. Alexander Hamilton, *The Federalist Papers, No. 78*, ed. Clinton Rossiter (New American Library, 1961) p. 465.

9. *Marbury v. Madison*, 5 U.S. 1 Cranch 137 (1803).

10. While English statesmen referred to Great Britain after the Glorious Revolution of 1689 as a constitutional monarchy, Montesquieu in his *Spirit of the Laws* (1748) referred to Great Britain as a republic.

11. Members of that movement have demonstrated a persisting ignorance of the nature of a republic.

12. Auguste Comte, *The Positive Philosophy, Vol. 2*, trans. H. Martineau & F. Harrison (Calvin Blanchard, 1856) p. 201. It is not until well after the events of 1975 that Pound's theory can be identified in the Australian jurisdiction.

13. Auguste Comte invented the word sociology to designate his positive science of social physics (Auguste Comte, *The Positive Philosophy, Vol. 2*, trans. Harriet Martineau (Calvin Blanchard, 1856) p. 201). Roscoe Pound asserted the need for positive sociologists to discover "general laws of social phenomena . . . in the same way, as the laws of physics or of astronomy"; Roscoe Pound, *Law and Morals* (Oxford University Press, 1924) p. 6.

14. Roscoe Pound, *Law and Morals* (Oxford University Press, 1924) p. 104.

15. Auguste Comte, *The Positive Philosophy Vol. 2*, trans. H. Martineau & F. Harrison (George Bell & Sons, 1896) p. 247.

16. Harry V. Jaffa, *Original Intent & The Framers of the Constitution* (Regnery, 1994) and *Storm Over the Constitution* (Lexington Books, 1999) relate his disputations with American jurists over their positivist methodologies.

17. *Baxter v Commissioners of Taxation (NSW)* (1907) 4 CLR 1087 at 1106.

Bibliography

SECONDARY SOURCES

Allan, James, "The Three 'Rs' of Recent Australian Judicial Activism: Roach, Rowe and (No) Riginalism" (2012) *Melbourne University Law Review* 36.

Allan, James & Aroney, Nicholas, "An Uncommon Court: How the High Court of Australia Has Undermined Australian Federalism" (2008) 30(2) *Sydney Law Review* 245.

Anastaplo, George, "In re Antonin Scalia" (1999) 28(1) *Perspectives on Political Science Philadelphia* 22.

Anderson, Grant & Dawson, Daryl, "Sir Owen Dixon (1886–1972)" *Australian Dictionary of Biography Vol. 14* (Melbourne University Press, 1966), http://adb.anu.edu.au/biography/dixon-sir-owen-10024

Anstey Wynes, W., "Supremacy of Commonwealth Law under the Constitution" (1933) 7 *Australian Law Journal* 222.

The Argus (Melbourne 1848–1957) Trove, National Library of Australia, https://trove.nla.gov.au/newspaper/article/4586733?browse=ndp%3Abrowse%2Ftitle%2FA%2Ftitle%2F13%2F1920%2F09%2F01%2Fpage%2F410792%2Farticle%2F4586733

Aristotle, *Metaphysics*, Joe Sachs trans (Green Lion Press, 2002).

Aristotle, *Nicomachean Ethics*, R.C. Bartlett & S.D. Collins trans (University of Chicago Press, 2011).

Aristotle, *Politics*, Carnes Lord trans (University of Chicago Press, 1984).

Aroney, Nicholas, "An Uncommon Court: How the High Court of Australia has Undermined Australian Federalism" (2008) 30(2) *Sydney Law Review* 245.

Aroney, Nicholas, "Constitutional Choices in the WorkChoices Case, or What Exactly is Wrong with the Reserved Powers Doctrine" (2008) 32(1) *Melbourne University Law Review* 1.

Aroney, Nicholas, "The Ghost in the Machine: Exorcising Engineers" (2002) 14 Conference of the Samuel Griffith Society, http://www.samuelgriffith.org.au/papers/pdf/Vol14.pdf

Austin, John, *The Province of Jurisprudence Determined* (John Murray, 1832).

Austin, John, *The Province of Jurisprudence Determined Vol. 1* (John Murray, 1861).

Austin, John, *The Province of Jurisprudence Determined Vol. 2* (John Murray, 1863).

Austin, John, *The Province of Jurisprudence Determined Vol. 3* (John Murray, 1863).

Austin, John, *Lectures on Jurisprudence or the Philosophy of Positive Law* (Frederick Linn & Co, 1869).

Australasian Federation Conference (First Session), 22 March–5 May 1897, https://parlinfo.aph.gov.au/parlInfo/search/display/display.w3p;query=Id:%22constitution/conventions/1897-1059%22

Australasian Federation Conference (First Session), Commonwealth of Australia Bill, 22 March–23 April 1897, https://parlinfo.aph.gov.au/parlInfo/search/display/display.w3p;db=CONSTITUTION;id=constitution%2Fconventions%2F1897-1067;query=Id%3A%22constitution%2Fconventions%2F1897-1059%22

Australasian Federation Conference (Second Session), 2–24 September 1897, https://parlinfo.aph.gov.au/parlInfo/search/display/display.w3p;query=Id:constitution/conventions/1897-1087

Australasian Federation Conference (Third Session) 20 January–17 March 1898, https://parlinfo.aph.gov.au/parlInfo/search/display/display.w3p;db=CONSTITUTION;id=constitution%2Fconventions%2F1898-1127;query=Id%3A%22constitution%2Fconventions%2F1898-1104%22

Australasian Federation Conference (Third Session) Commonwealth of Australia Bill, 16 March 1898, https://parlinfo.aph.gov.au/parlInfo/search/display/display.w3p;db=CONSTITUTION;id=constitution/conventions/1898-1131;query=Id:%22constitution/conventions/1898-1104%22

Australian Electoral Commission, Federation Fact Sheet 1—the Referendums (sic) 1898–1900, https://www.aec.gov.au/about_aec/Publications/Fact_Sheets/factsheet1.htm

Australian Senate, Standing Orders, https://www.aph.gov.au/About_Parliament/Senate/Powers_practice_n_procedures/Odgers_Australian_Senate_Practice

Ayres, Philip, 'Federalism and Sir Owen Dixon' (1999) Eleventh Conference of The Sir Samuel Griffith Society, http://www.samuelgriffith.org.au/papers/pdf/Vol11.pdf

Bach, Stanley, *Platypus and Parliament: The Australian Senate in Theory and Practice* (Department of the Senate, 2003), http://www.aph.gov.au/About_Parliament/Senate/Powers_practice_n_procedures/platparl

Bagehot, W., *The Works of Walter Bagehot Vol. IV* (The Travellers Insurance Company, 1891).

Barwick, G., *Sir John Did His Duty* (Griffin Press, 1983).

Beasley, F.R., 'Appeals to the Judicial Committee: The Case for Abolition' (1955–57) 7 *Res Judicatae* 399.

Bennett, Scott, *Federation* (Cassell Australia, 1975).

Bentham, J., *A Fragment on Government* (Clarendon Press, 1891).

Bentham, J., *An Introduction to the Principles of Morals and Legislation Vol. 1* (Lincoln's-Inn Fields, 1828), http://www.econlib.org/library/Bentham/bnthPML.html

Bentham, J., *Deontology or The Science of Morality Vol. 1*, J Bowring ed. (Longman, 1834).

Bentham, J. *Deontology or The Science of Morality Vol. 2*, J Bowring ed. (Longman, 1834).

Berman, Mitchell N., "Originalism is Bunk" (2009) 84(1) *New York University Law Review* 1.

Bernays, Charles Arrowsmith, *Queensland Politics During Sixty (1859–1919) Years* (A.J. Cumming, Government Printer, 1920).

Blackshield, Tony, "*New South Wales v Commonwealth*: Corporations and Connections" (2007) 31(4) *Melbourne University Law Review* 1135.

Blackstone, Sir William, *Commentary on the Laws of England Vol. 1* (Clarendon Press, 1765).

Blackstone, Sir William, *Commentary on the Laws of England Vol. 2* (Clarendon Press, 1768).

Blackstone, Sir William, *Commentary on the Laws of England Vol. 3* (Clarendon Press, 1768).

Blackstone, Sir William, *Commentary on the Laws of England Vol. 4* (Clarendon Press, 1770).

Bogdanor, V., *The Monarchy and the Constitution* (Oxford Academic Parliamentary Affairs), https://doi.org/10.1093/pa/49.3.407

Bogdanor, V., *The Monarchy and the Constitution* (Oxford University Press, 1995).

Brest, Paul, 'The Misconceived Quest for the Original Understanding' (1980) 60 *Boston University Law Review* 204.

Bryce, J., *The American Commonwealth Vol. 1*, 3rd ed. (Macmillan, 1893).

Bryce, J., *The American Commonwealth Vol. 2*, 3rd ed. (Macmillan, 1895).

Bryce, J., *Studies in History and Jurisprudence Vol. 1* (Oxford University Press, 1901).

Burgess, John W., "Ideal of the American Commonwealth" (1895) 10 *Political Science Quarterly* 404.

Carney, G. and Corkery, J., "Sir Owen Dixon" (2006) *Owen Dixon Society eJournal*, http://epublications.bond.edu.au/odsej/4

Cartaxo, Tiago Melo, "Commanders-in-chief Beyond the Border: Analysing the Powers of Heads of State in Northern American Federalism" (2017) 9(1) *Perspectives on Federalism* E99.

Churchill, W.S.C., *The History of the English Speaking Peoples Vol. 4*, 4th ed. (Cassell, 1967).

Clement, W.H.P., *The Law of the Canadian Constitution* (Carswell, 1892).

Cohen, Morris R. & Nagel, Ernest, *Introduction to Logic and Scientific Method* (Harcourt and Brace, 1935).

Comte, Auguste, *The Positive Philosophy Vol. 1*, H. Martineau & F. Harrison trans (George Bell & Sons, 1896).

Comte, Auguste, *The Positive Philosophy Vol. 2*, H. Martineau & F. Harrison trans (George Bell & Sons, 1896).

Comte, Auguste, *The Positive Philosophy Vol. 3*, H. Martineau & F. Harrison trans (George Bell & Sons, 1896).

Connolly P.D., "*Cole v Whitfield*: The Repeal of Section 92 of the Constitution" (1991) 16(2) *University of Queensland Law Journal* 290.

Conway, M., *Autobiography, Memories and Experiences of Moncure Daniel Conway* (Houghton, Mifflin, 1904).

Conway, M.D., *Republican Superstitions as Illustrated in the Political History of America* (Henry King & Co, 1872).

Cooper, M., *Encounters with the Australian Constitution* (CCH Australia, 1987).

Coper, Michael, "Critique and Comment: Concern About Judicial Method" (2006) 30 *Melbourne University Law Review* 554.

Cowen, Z., "The Crown and Its Representative in the Commonwealth" (1985) *Australian International Law News* 584.

Cowen, Z., "Sir Isaac Isaacs and the Workings of the Australian Constitution" (2003) 29(1) *Monash University Law Review* 1.

Cowen, Zelman, *Isaac Isaacs* (University of Queensland Press, 1993).

Craven, Greg, "After Literalism, What?" (1992) 18(4) *Melbourne University Law Review* 874.

Craven, Greg, "Cracks in the Facade of Literalism: Is there an Engineer in the House?" (1992) 18 *Melbourne University Law Review* 540.

Craven, Greg, "Heresy as Orthodoxy: Were the Founders Progressivists?" (2003) 31 *Federal Law Review* 87.

Craven, Greg, "Judicial Activism in the High Court: A Response to John Toohey" (1999) 28 *University of Western Australia Law Review* 323.

Craven, Greg, "Original Intent and Australian Constitution" (1990) 1 *Public Law Review* 166.

Craven, Greg, "Reflections on Judicial Activism: More in Sorrow than in Anger," Ninth Conference, Sir Samuel Griffith Society (1997), http://www.samuelgriffith.org.au/papers/pdf/Vol9.pdf

Craven, Greg, "The Crisis of Constitutional Literalism in Australia" (1992) 30(2) *Alberta Law Review* 492.

Craven, Greg, "The High Court and the Founders: An Unfaithful Servant" (1997) 30 *Papers on Parliament*, http://www.aph.gov.au/About_Parliament/Senate/Research_and_Education/~/~/link.aspx?_id=5E06E8E0F33440EFAA4D819755DD6F28&_z=z

Crommelin, Michael, "Governor-General and the Republic Powers of the Head of State" (2015) 38(3) *Melbourne University Law Review* 1118.

Deakin, Alfred, *Federal Story: The Inner History of the Federal Cause*, Herbert Brookes ed. (Robertson & Mullens, 1944).

Diamond, M., Fisk, W.M. & Garfinkel, H., *The Democratic Republic* (Rand McNally, 1966).

Dicey, A.V., *Introduction to the Study of the Law of the Constitution* (Liberty Classics, 1915).

Dicey, A.V., *Introduction to the Study of the Law of the Constitution*, 3rd ed. (Macmillan, 1889).

Dickinson College Archive, "Moncure Daniel Conway (1832–1907)" (2005), http://archives.dickinson.edu/people/moncure-daniel-conway-1832-1907

Dixon, Rosalind & Williams, George (eds.), *The High Court, the Constitution and Australian Politics* (Cambridge University Press, 2015).

Dixon, Sir Owen, "Marshall and the Australian Constitution" (1955) 29 *Australian Law Journal* 420.

Dixon, Sir Owen, "Concerning Judicial Method" (1956) 29 *Australian Law Journal* 468.

Dixon, Sir Owen, "Address upon Taking the Oath of Office in Sydney as Chief Justice of the High Court of Australia on 21st April, 1952," in Judge Woinarski (ed.), *Jesting Pilate and Other Papers and Addresses* (Melbourne, 1965).

Donaghue, Stephen, "The Clamour of Silent Constitutional Principles" (1996) 24(1) *Federal Law Review* 133.

Durchslag, Melvyn R., "The Supreme Court and the Federalist Papers: Is There Less Here Than Meets the Eye?" (2005) 14(1/9) *William & Mary Bill of Rights Journal* 243, 252, 254–255.

Elder, D.R., *House of Representatives Practice*, 7th ed. (Department of House of Representatives, 2018).

Erler, Edward J., "Originalist Sin" (2014) XIV(3) *Claremont Review of Books,* https://www.claremont.org/crb/article/originalist-sin

Erler, Edward J., "Still Separate but Equal" (2004) IV(3) *Claremont Review of Books*, https://www.claremont.org/crb/issue/vol-iv-number-3-summer-2004

Evatt, H.V., "The Discretionary Authority of Dominion Governors" (1940) XVIII(1) *The Canadian Bar Review* 1.

Forsey, E., *Freedom and Order* (Carleton University Press, 1974).

Forsey, E., *How Canadians Govern Themselves* (Secretary of State of Canada, 1980), http://deslibris.ca/ID/10062955

Forsey, E., *The Royal Power of Dissolution of Parliament in the British Commonwealth*, 2nd ed. (Frank Cass & Co, 1967).

Gageler, S., "Foundations of Australian Federalism and the Role of Judicial Review" (1987) 17 *Federal Law Review* 162.

Gageler, Stephen, "The Federal–State Balance in Federal Systems," in Gabrielle Appleby, Nicholas Aroney & John Thomas (eds.), *The Future of Australian Federalism* (Cambridge University Press, 2012).

Garran, Robert, *The Coming Commonwealth* (Angus & Robertson, 1897).

George, Robert P., "Natural Law" (2008) 31 *Harvard Journal of Law & Public Policy* 171.

Gerangelos, P.A., "Interpretational Methodology in Separation of Powers Jurisprudence: The Formalist/Functionalist Debate," in Peter Gerangelos, Simon Evans, Sarah Murray, Patrick Emerton & Adrienne Stone (eds.), *Winterton's Australian Federal Constitutional Law, Commentary and Materials* (Law Book Co, 2017).

Gibb, S.J., "Book Review: *Sir John Did His Duty*" (1983–85) 9 *Adelaide Law Review* 426.

Gladstone, W.E., *Gleanings of Past Years* (John Murray, 1879), https://archive.org/details/a583183601gladuoft

Goldsworthy, Jeffrey, "Constitutional Implications and Freedom of Political Speech: A Reply to Stephen Donaghue" (1997) 23(2) *Monash University Law Review* 362.

Goldsworthy, Jeffrey, "Interpreting the Constitution in Its Second Century" (2000) 24(3) *Melbourne University Law Review* 677.

Goldsworthy, Jeffrey, "Justice Windeyer on the Engineers' Case" (2009) 37(3) *Federal Law Review* 363.

Goldsworthy, Jeffrey, "Originalism in Constitutional Interpretation" (1997) 25(1) *Federal Law Review* 1.

Griffith, Sir Samuel, "Former Justices of the High Court" http://www.hcourt.gov.au/justices/former-justices/former-justices

Gummow, William, "Common Law," in Cheryl Saunders & Adrienne Stone (eds.), *The Oxford Handbook of the Australian Constitution* (Oxford University Press, 2018).

Hall, Katherine, "Theory, Gender and Corporate Law" (1988) 9(1) *Legal Education Review* 31.

Hamilton, A., *The Federalist Papers, No. 62*, Clinton Rossiter ed. (New American Library, 1961).

Hamilton A., *The Federalist Papers, No. 84*, Clinton Rossiter ed. (New American Library, 1961).

Hamilton, A., Madison, J. & Jay, J., *The Federalist Papers*, Clinton Rossiter ed. (New American Library, 1961).

Hare, J. Innes Clark, *American Constitutional Law Vol. 1* (Little, Brown and Co., 1889).

Hare, J. Innes Clark, *American Constitutional Law Vol. 2* (Little, Brown and Co., 1889).

Hart, H.L.A., "Positivism and the Separation of Law and Morals" (1958) 71 *Harvard Law Review* 593.

Hart, H.L.A., *The Concept of Law*, 3rd ed. (Oxford University Press, 2012).

Heydon, J.D., "One Small Point About Originalism" (2009) 28(1) *University of Queensland Law Journal* 7.

Hobbes, Thomas, *Leviathan* (Cambridge University Press, 1946).

Hobbes, Thomas, *Behemoth or the Long Parliament* (Frank Cass, 1969).

Hocking, Jenny, Gough Whitlam, *Elements of Law Natural and Politics: His Time* (Melbourne University Press, 2012).

Holmes, O.W. "Natural Law" (1918) *Harvard Law Review*, http://teachingamericanhistory.org/library/document/natural-law

House of Commons, *Hansard*, 1803–2005, Commonwealth of Australia Constitution Bill, 14 May 1900 vol. 83 cc 46-104, https://api.parliament.uk/historic-hansard/commons/1900/may/14/commonwealth-of-australia-constitution

House of Commons, *Hansard*, 9 April 1807, https://hansard.parliament.uk/Commons/1807-04-09/debates/3d9b3e6d-b85a-4760-b2f7-9346aaedac3b/ChangeOfAdministration

Hume, David, *A Treatise of Human Nature*, L.A. Selby-Bigge ed. (Clarendon Press, 1951).

Hume, David, *A Treatise of Human Nature Vol. 1* (JM Dent & Sons, 1966).

Hume, David, *A Treatise of Human Nature Vol. 2* (JM Dent & Sons, 1966).

Hume, David, *Enquiries Concerning the Human Understanding and Concerning the Principles of Morals*, 2nd ed. (Clarendon Press, 1902).

Hutchinson, William T. et al., *The Papers of James Madison Vols. 1–10* (Chicago: University of Chicago Press, 1962).

Irvine, Helen, "Constitutional Interpretation, The High Court, and the Discipline of History" (2013) 41(1) *Federal Law Review* 95.

Jaffa, Harry V., *Equality & Liberty* (Oxford University Press, 1965).

Jaffa, Harry V., "The Logic of the Colorblind Constitution," *Claremont Review of Books*, 6 December 2004, https://www.claremont.org/crb/basicpage/the-logic-of-the-colorblind-constitution1

Jaffa, Harry V., *A New Birth of Freedom: Abraham Lincoln and the Coming of the Civil War* (Rowman & Littlefield, 2000).

Jaffa, Harry V., *Original Intent & The Framers of the Constitution* (Regnery, 1994).

Jaffa, Harry V., *Storm Over the Constitution* (Lexington Books, 1999).

Joyce, Roger B., *Samuel Walter Griffith* (University of Queensland Press, 1984).

Kelsen, Hans, *General Theory of Law and the State* (Lawbook Exchange, 2007).

Kennan, J.H. "Book Review, *Sir John Did His Duty*" (1984) 14(4) *Melbourne University Law Review* 736.

Kerr, Sir John, *Matters for Judgment* (Sun Books, 1988).

Kirby, M., "The Australian Use of International Human Rights Norms: From Bangalore to Balliol—a View from the Antipodes" (1993) 16 *University of New South Wales Law Journal* 363.

Kirby, M. "Constitutional Interpretation and Original Intent: A Form of Ancestor Worship?" (2000) 24 *Melbourne University Law Review* 1.

Kirby, M. "Deep Lying Rights: A Constitutional Conversation Continues, The Robin Cooke Lecture 2004," http://www.hcourt.gov.au/assets/publications/speeches/former-justices/kirbyj/kirbyj_25nov04.html

Kirby, M., "The Role of the Judge in Advancing Human Rights by Reference to International Human Rights Norms" (1988) *Australian Law Journal* 62.

Lane, P.H., "The Present Test for Invalidity under Section 92 of the Constitution" (1988) *Australian Law Journal* 604.

Lee, H.P. & Winterton, G., *Australian Constitutional Landmarks* (Cambridge University Press, 2003).

Lehrman, Lewis E., "On Jaffa, Lincoln, Marshall and Original Intent," in Harry V. Jaffa (ed.), *Original Intent & The Framers of the Constitution* (Regnery, 1994).

Lim, Brendan, "Legitimacy," in Cheryl Saunders & Adrienne Stone (eds.), *The Oxford Handbook of the Australian Constitution* (Oxford University Press, 2018).

Little W., Fowler, H.W. & Coulson, J., *Shorter Oxford English Dictionary*, 3rd rev. ed. (Clarendon Press, 1956).

Locke, John, *Two Treatises of Civil Government* (Cambridge University Press, 1960).

MacDonald, Vincent C., "The Privy Council and the Canadian Constitution" (1951) 29(10) *Canadian Bar Review* 1021.

Madison, James, *The Federalist Papers, No. 10*, Clinton Rossiter ed. (New American Library, 1961).

Madison, James, *The Federalist Papers, No. 14*, Clinton Rossiter ed. (New American Library, 1961).

Madison, James, *The Federalist Papers, No. 45*, Clinton Rossiter ed. (New American Library, 1961).

Madison, James, *The Federalist Papers, No. 62*, Clinton Rossiter ed. (New American Library, 1961).

Magna Carta, "English Translation" https://www.bl.uk/magna-carta/articles/magna-carta-english-translation

Marriott, Sir J.A.R., *Modern England 1885–1945*, 4th ed. (Methuen, 1948).

Martin, A.W., "Sir Henry Parkes," *Australian Dictionary of Biography*, http://adb.anu.edu.au/biography/parkes-sir-henry-4366

Martin, Marie A., "Misunderstanding and Understanding Hume's Moral Philosophy" (1991–92) 19(2) *Interpretation* 169.

Mason, Anthony, "The High Court of Australia: A Personal Impression of Its First 100 Years" (2003) 27(3) *Melbourne University Law Review* 864.

Mason, Anthony, "The Interpretation of a Constitution in a Modern Liberal Democracy," in Charles Sampford and Kim Preston (eds.), *Interpreting Constitutions Theories, Principles and Institutions* (Federation Press, 1996).

Mason, Anthony, "Constitutional Interpretation: Some Thoughts" (1998) 20(1) *Adelaide Law Review* 49.

Mason, A., "The Statement" (2012), https://whitlamdismissal.com/2012/08/27/mason-largely-confirms-kerrs-account-of-discussions.html#more-685

May, Thomas Erskine, *Constitutional History of England Vol. 1*, 6th ed. (Longman Green, 1878).

May, Thomas Erskine, *Constitutional History of England Vol. 2*, 12th ed. (Longman, 1901).

May, Thomas Erskine, *Constitutional History of England Vol. 3*, Francis Holland ed. (Longman, 1911).

May, Thomas Erskine, *A Treatise upon the Law, Privileges, Proceedings and Usage of Parliament*, 10th ed., Reginald Palgrave et al, eds. (William Clowes & Sons, 1844).

McConnell, Michael W., "Textualism and the Dead Hand of the Past" (1998) 66 *George Washington Law Review* 1127.

McHugh, M., "The Constitutional Jurisprudence of the High Court" (2008) 30(1) *The Sydney Law Review* 5.

Meier, Heinrich, *Carl Schmitt and Leo Straus: The Hidden Dialogue*, J. Harvey Lomax, trans (University of Chicago Press, 1995).

Melo Cartaxo, Tiago, "Commanders-in-chief Beyond the Border: Analysing the Powers of Heads of State in Northern American Federalism" (2017) 9(1) *Perspectives on Federalism* E94.

Menzies, Robert G., Documents Relating to the Simultaneous Dissolution of the Senate and the House of Representatives by His Excellency the Governor-General on 19th March, 1951, https://www.peo.gov.au/uploads/peo/docs/closer-look/Documents_1951_double_dissolution.pdf

Menzies, Robert G., Documents Relating to the Simultaneous Dissolution of the Senate and the House of Representatives by His Excellency the

Governor-General on 19th March, 1951, on web at https://ecm1.fxdms.net/senat_prd/ies/iv_web_client.iv_getdoc?SessionKey=LnGS4Be3T00000027DEA&docid=*88092uV6(20JWba9uBYi7qs2neuPOi59CvS1XbgdlSepsrNd1C7w7tJGsg32tOB&PageNo=1

Montesquieu, Charles Louis de Secondat, *The Spirit of the Laws Vol. 1*, David Biden trans (London, 1750).

Montesquieu, Charles Louis de Secondat, *The Spirit of the Laws Vol. 2*, David Biden trans (London, 1793).

Morris, Kathleen & Allsop, James, "The United States and the Australian Constitution: Influence of US Constitutional Model on Development and Interpretation of the Australian Constitution" 89 *Australian Law Journal* 309.

Nethercote J., "The Engineers' Case: Seventy Five Years On," Sixth Conference of The Samuel Griffith Society, Melbourne, 17–19 November 1995, https://static1.squarespace.com/static/596ef6aec534a5c54429ed9e/t/5c9d2ca3f4e1fce625dcb6e4/1553804461117/Vol6.pdf

Nietzsche, Friedrich, *Daybreak*, Maudemarie Clark and Brian Leiter eds, R.J. Hollingdale trans (Cambridge University Press, 1997).

Odgers Senate Parliamentary Parliament of Australia, https://www.aph.gov.au/About_Parliament/Senate/Powers_practice_n_procedures/Odgers_Australian_Senate_Practice

Parliament of the Commonwealth of Australia, *Journals of the Senate*, 5 November 1975, https://parlinfo.aph.gov.au/parlInfo/download/chamber/journals/1975-11-05/toc_pdf/jnl_05-11-1975_118.pdf;fileType=application/pdf

Parliament of Australia, The Crisis of 1974–75, http://www.aph.gov.au/About_Parliament/Senate/Research_and_Education/platparl/c04

Parsons, J.E. Jr., "Halifax: The Complete Trimmer Revisited" (1978) 7(3) *Interpretation* 66.

Patapan, Haig, *Judging Democracy* (Cambridge University Press, 2000).

Patapan, Haig, "Politics of Interpretation" (2000) 22 *Sydney Law Review* 247.

Plato, *Laws*, Thomas Pangle trans (University of Chicago Press, 1988).

Posner, Richard A., *The Problems of Jurisprudence* (First Harvard University Press, 1993).

Posner, Richard A., "Bork and Beethoven" (1990) 42 *Stanford Law Review* 1365.

Pound, Roscoe, *Law and Morals* (Oxford University Press, 1924).

Quick, John and Garran, Robert R., *The Annotated Constitution of the Australian Commonwealth* (Angus & Robertson, 1901).

Raz, J., *The Concept of a Legal System*, 2nd ed. (Oxford University Press, 1980).

Reid, George, National Archives of Australia: Australian Prime Ministers, http://primeministers.naa.gov.au/primeministers/reid/fast-facts.aspx

Reynolds, H., "Clark, Andrew Inglis," *Australian Dictionary of Biography*, http://adb.anu.edu.au/biography/clark-andrew-inglis-3211

Rich, William, "Approaches to Constitutional Interpretation in Australia: An American Perspective" (1993) 12(2) *University of Tasmania Law Review* 150.

Richardson, J.E., 'The Legislative Power of the Senate in Respect of Money Bills' (1976) 50 *Australian Law Journal* 273.

Riverina Development Australia, Riverina New South Wales, http://www.rdariverina.org.au

Rossiter, Clinton (ed.), *The Federalist* (New American Library, 1961).

The Samuel Griffith Society, Various papers, http://samuelgriffith.org.au/all-papers-by-date

Saunders, Cheryl, "The Concept of the Crown" (2015) 38(4) *Melbourne University Law Review* 873.

Saunders, Cheryl and Stone, Adrienne, *The Oxford Handbook of the Australian Constitution* (Oxford University Press, 2018).

Sawer, G. (1950), "Implication and the Constitution Part I" (1950) *Res Judicatae* 15.

Scalia, Antonin, "Address" in Edwin Meese (ed.), *Original Meaning Jurisprudence: A Sourcebook* (Department of Justice, 1987), https://www.ncjrs.gov/App/publications/Abstract.aspx?id=115083

Scalia, Antonin, "Originalism: The Lesser Evil" (1989) 57 *Cincinnati Law Review* 849.

Schmitt, Carl, *The Concept of the Political*, George Schwab, trans (University of Chicago Press, 2007).

Schmitt, Carl, *Dictatorship: From the Beginning of the Modern Concept of Sovereignty to the Proletarian Class-Struggle*, Michael Hoelzl and Graham Ward trans. (Polity Press, 2014).

Schmitt, Carl, *Political Theology, Four Chapters on the Concept of Sovereignty*, George Schwab ed. and trans. (University of Chicago Press, 2006).

Schwartz, B., *American Constitutional Law* (Cambridge University Press, 1955).

Simmel, Georg, *Einleitung in die Moralwissenschaft* (Verlag von Wilhelm Hertz, 1892).

Smith, Sir David, KCVO AO, "The Role of the Governor-General" (1997) Eighth Conference of The Samuel Griffith Society 88, http://www.samuelgriffith.org.au/papers/pdf/Vol8.pdf

Solum, Lawrence B., "Original Methodology" (2017) 84(1) *University of Chicago Law Review* 269.

Staveley, R.W., "The Conventions of the Constitution: Kerr's Folly" (1976) *The Australian Journal of Political Science* 11, http://dx.doi.org/10.1080/00323267608401535

Stokes, Michael, "Original Intentions: Interpretation in the Freedom of Speech Cases" (1994) 16 *Sydney Law Review* 250.

Stoljar, Natalie, "Counterfactuals in Interpretation: The Case Against Intentionalism" (1998) 20(1) *Adelaide Law Review* 29.

Story, Joseph, *Commentaries on the Constitution of the United States Vol. 1* (Hilliard Gray & Co, 1833), http://www.earstohear.net/heritage/Commentaries-On-The-Constitution-by-Joseph-Story-Abridged.pdf

Story, Joseph, *Commentaries on the Constitution of the United States Vol. 2* (Hilliard Gray & Co, 1833), http://www.earstohear.net/heritage/Commentaries-On-The-Constitution-by-Joseph-Story-Abridged.pdf

Story, Joseph, *Commentaries on the Constitution of the United States Vol. 3* (Hilliard Gray & Co, 1833), http://www.earstohear.net/heritage/Commentaries-On-The-Constitution-by-Joseph-Story-Abridged.pdf

Strauss, Leo, *Hobbes's Critique of Religion and Related Writings*, Gabriel Bartlett & Svetozar Minkov ed and trans (University of Chicago Press, 2011).

Strauss, Leo, *Leo Strauss on Political Philosophy*, Catherine H. Zuckert ed. (University of Chicago Press, 2018).

Strauss, Leo, *Natural Right and History* (University of Chicago Press, 1953).

Strauss, Leo, "Notes on Carl Schmitt," in J. Harvey Lomax (trans.), *The Concept of the Political* (University of Chicago Press, 1996).

Strauss, Leo, *Persecution and the Art of Writing* (University of Chicago Press, 1988).

Strauss, Leo, "Relativism," in Helmut Schoeck & James W. Wiggins (eds.), *Relativism and the Study of Man* (Van Nostrand, 1961).

Strauss, Leo, *Leo Strauss on Political Philosophy*, Catherine H. Zuckert ed. (University of Chicago Press, 2018).

Strauss, Leo, *Thoughts on Machiavelli* (University of Washington Press, 1969).

Supreme Court of Canada, "Creation and Beginnings of the Court," https://www.scc-csc.ca/court-cour/creation-eng.aspx

Tham, Joo-Cheong, "Political Participation," in Cheryl Saunders & Adrienne Stone (eds.), *The Oxford Handbook of the Australian Constitution* (Oxford University Press, 2018).

Thomson, James A., "Book Review: *Sir John Did His Duty*" (1983) 6(2) *University of New South Wales Law Journal* 255.

Todd, A., *Parliamentary Government in England Vol. 1* (Sampson Low, Marston & Co, 1887).

Todd, A., *Parliamentary Government in England Vol. 2* (Longmans, Green & Co, 1894).

Toohey, John, "Without Fear or Favour; Affection or Ill-will: The Role of Courts in the Community" (1999) 28(1) *Western Australian Law Review* 1.

Twomey, Anne, "Independence," in Cheryl Saunders & Adrienne Stone (eds.), *The Oxford Handbook of The Australian Constitution* (Oxford University Press, 2018).

Twomey, Anne "The Knox Court," in Rosalind Dixon and George Williams (eds.), *The High Court, the Constitution and Australian Politics* (Cambridge University Press, 2015).

Walker, G. de Q, "The Seven Pillars of Centralism: Engineers' Case and Federalism" (2002) 76 *Australian Law Journal* 678.

Ward, Alan J., "Responsible Government and Recent Constitutional Change in Australia and New Zealand" (1993) 15(2) *Adelaide Law Review* 165.

Wheeler, Fiona, "Book Review: *Owen Dixon*" (2003) 31(2) *Federal Law Review* 415.

Williams, George, "Engineers is Dead, Long Live the Engineers" (1995) 17(1) *Sydney Law Review* 62.

Williams, John M., "The Griffith Court," in Rosalind Dixon and George Williams (eds.), *The High Court, the Constitution and Australian Politics* (Cambridge University Press, 2015).

Wurman, Ilan, "Originalism's New Critics, Part 1: Fixing Fixity," *Claremont Review of Books*, 15 January 2019, https://www.claremont.org/crb/basicpage/originalisms-new-critics-part-1-fixing-fixity/?pushc

Whittington, Keith E., "Originalism: A Critical Introduction" (2013) 83 *Fordham Law Review* 375.

Winfree Smith, J., "Aristotle's Ethics" (1973) *St John's College Review* 24.

Winterton, G., *Parliament, The Executive and the Governor General: A Constitutional Analysis* (Melbourne University Press, 1983).

Zines, Leslie, "Sir Owen Dixon's Theory of Federalism" (1965) 1(2) *Federal Law Review* 220.

Zines, Leslie, "The State of Constitutional Interpretation" (1984) 14(4) *Federal Law Review* 277.

Zinman, M. Richar, "Review Essay: Thinking About the Founding" (2009) 36(2) *Interpretation* 103.

US Senate Judiciary Committee hearing (5 October 2011) Associate Justice Stephen Breyer and Associate Justice Antonin Scalia, 'Considering the Role of Judges Under the Constitution of the United States', http://www.judiciary.senate.gov/meetings/considering-the-role-of-judges-under-the-constitution-of-the-united-states

CASES

Australia

Amalgamated Society of Engineers v Adelaide Steamship Co Ltd (1920) 28 CLR 129.

Attorney-General (Cth); Ex rel McKinlay v Commonwealth (1975) 135 CLR 1.

Attorney-General of the Commonwealth v Colonial Sugar Refining Company Limited (1913) 17 CLR 644 (Privy Council).

Attorney-General Qld (ex rel Goldsbrough, Mort & Co Ltd) v Attorney-General Cth (1915) 20 CLR 148.

Australian Capital Television Pty Ltd v Commonwealth (1992) 177 CLR 106.

Baxter v The Commissioners of Taxation, New South Wales (1907) 4 CLR 1087.

Cheatle v R (1993) 177 CLR 541.

Clyde Engineering Co Ltd v Cowburn (1926) 37 CLR 466.

Cole v Whitfield (1988) 165 CLR 360.

Colonial Sugar Refining Co Ltd v *Attorney-General for the Commonwealth* (1912) 15 CLR 182.

Commonwealth v New South Wales (1923) 32 CLR 200.

Cunningham & Ors v Commonwealth of Australia & Anor (2016) 259 CLR 536.

D'Emden v Pedder (1904) 1 CLR 91.

Davis v Commonwealth (1988) 166 CLR 79.

Deakin v Webb (1904) 1 CLR 585.

Federated Amalgamated Government Railway & Tramway Service Association v NSW Railway Traffic Employees Association (1906) 4 CLR 488 (*Railway Servants Case*).

Fox v Robbins (1909) 8 CLR 115.

Grain Pool of Western Australia v Commonwealth (2000) 170 ALR 111.

King v Jones (1972) 128 CLR 221.

Langer v Commonwealth (1996) 186 CLR 302.
Leeth v Commonwealth (1992) 174 CLR 455.
The Lord Mayor, Councillors and Citizens of the City of Melbourne v Commonwealth (1947) 74 CLR 31 (*State Banking case*).
McGinty v Western Australia (1996) 186 CLR 140.
Momcilovic v The Queen (2011) 245 CLR 1.
Nationwide News v Wills (1992) 177 CLR 1.
New South Wales v Commonwealth (2006) 229 CLR 1 (*WorkChoices case*).
Pedder v D'Emden (1903) TLR 146.
R v Barger (1908) 6 CLR 4.
R v Kirby; Ex parte Boilermakers' Society of Australia (1956) 94 CLR 254 *(Boilermakers' case).*
R v Smithers: Ex parte Benson (1912) 16 CLR 99.
Re Wakim (1999) 198 CLR 511.
Re Webster (1975) 132 CLR 270.
Roach v Electoral Commissioner (2007) 233 CLR 162.
Rowe v Electoral Commissioner (2010) 243 CLR 1.
Stock Motor Ploughs Ltd v Forsyth (1932) 48 CLR 128.
Sydney Municipal Council v Commonwealth (1904) 1 CLR 208.
Tasmania v Commonwealth (1904) 1 CLR 329.
Theophanous v Herald & Weekly Times Ltd (1994) 182 CLR 104.
Victoria v Commonwealth (1971) 122 CLR 353 *(Payroll Tax case).*
Victorian Stevedoring & General Contracting Company Pty Ltd v Dignan Informant (1931) 46 CLR 73.
Webb v Outtrim (1906) 4 CLR 356.
West v Commissioner of Taxation (NSW) (1937) 56 CLR 657.
Worthing v Rowell & Muston Pty Ltd (1970) 123 CLR 89.

United States

The Collector v Day 78 U.S. 11 Wall. 113 113 (1870).
Dred Scott v Sandford 60 U.S. 393.
Gray v Sanders (1963) 372 US.
Grutter v Bollinger, 539 U.S. 306 (2003).
Keller v The United States 213 U.S. 138.
Marbury v Madison 5 U.S. 1 Cranch 137 137 (1803).
Martin v Hunter's Lessee 14 U.S. (1 Wheat.) 304.
McCray v United States 195 US 27.
McCulloch v Maryland, 17 U.S. 4 Wheat. 316 (1819).
New York v United States 326 U.S. 572.
Ogden v Saunders, 25 U.S. 12 Wheat. 213.
Wesberry v Sanders (1964) 376 US 1.
White v Register (1973) 412 US 755.

United Kingdom

Attorney-General for Ontario v Attorney-General for Canada (1912) AC 571.
Grey v Pearson (1857) 6 HLC 61.
Heydon's Case (1584) 3 Rep., 7a.
R v Burah (1878) 3 AC 889.
The Sussex Peerage 11 Cl. & Fin., 85.
Webb v Outtrim (1906) 4 CLR 356 (PC).
Vacher & Sons Ltd v London Society of Compositors (1912) UKHL 3.
Taylor v New Zealand Poultry Board (1984) 1 NZLR 394.

LEGISLATION

Constitutional documents

Australasian Federation Enabling Act 1895 (NSW) No. XXIV.
Australasian Federation Enabling Act 1895 (SA) No. 632.
Australasian Federation Enabling Act 1896 (Tas) No. 57.
Australasian Federation Enabling Act 1896 (Vic) No. 1143.
Australasian Federation Enabling Act 1896 (WA) No. XXXII.
Australasian Federation Enabling Act 1897 (NSW) No. 35.
Australasian Federation Enabling Act 1897 (NSW) No. 35.
Australasian Federation Enabling Act 1897 (SA) No. 689.
Australasian Federation Enabling Act 1897 (WA) No. XLVI.
Australasian Federation Enabling Act 1899 (NSW) No. 2.
Australasian Federation Enabling Act 1899 (Qld) No. 1.
Australasian Federation Enabling Act 1900 (WA) No. LV.
Bill of Rights 1688 (UK) 1 William & Mary Sess 2 c 2.
British North America Act 1867 (UK) 30&31 Vict. c3.
Commonwealth Electoral Act 1918–1975 (Cth).
Commonwealth of Australia Constitution Act (63 & 64 Victoria, Chapter 12) 1900.
Constitution of the United States of America.
Judiciary Act 1903 (Cth).
Judiciary Act 1903–1912 (Cth).
Judiciary Act 1907 (Cth).
Judiciary Act Amendment Act 1907 (Cth).
New Zealand Constitution Act 1852 (15 & 16 Vict. c. 72).
Representation Act 1905–1974 (Cth).

Index

About the Author

David Long commenced his academic studies in the faculty of Science at the University of Queensland in the 1960s before transferring to the faculty of Arts in order to study the political philosophy and economics of ancient Greeks and the lovers of wisdom who followed. This study of political science continues.

After completion of a thesis that examined the economic theory of John Kenneth Galbraith which determined its repetitive character, he graduated with Honors in 1974 and tutored economic theory in the Economics Department in 1975.

David worked as an economist with the Queensland State government for twelve years and tutored in the Business School at the University of Queensland.

He studied law in the 1980s, was employed as an associate (or clerk) for a Queensland Supreme Court Justice and was admitted to practice by the Queensland Supreme Court and the High Court of Australia in 1992. He was employed in litigation for almost twenty-five years and retired in 2016.

His examination of the legal arguments relating to the constitutional crisis of the 1975 dismissal of Australia's Prime Minister commenced in 2010 at the Griffith University, Queensland where he tutored in constitutional law during 2017. He was awarded his Doctor of Philosophy in 2019.

The arguments on which the analysis of his book relies would not have been possible without the insight into the political nature of the human condition and the place of law in the political solutions for that condition first addressed in ancient Greece. The insights of those lovers of wisdom provided the framework for his understanding of the fundamental relationship between the Australian constitutional law crisis of 1975 and the concerted attacks on its federal scheme in 1920.

David and Jennifer Long were married in 1974. They have three children and five grandchildren.

www.ingramcontent.com/pod-product-compliance
Lightning Source LLC
LaVergne TN
LVHW091533200926
848483LV00002B/383